SCIENCE EXPERIENCES FOR THE EARLY CHILDHOOD YEARS
An Integrated Affective Approach

Tenth Edition

Jean D. Harlan

Mary S. Rivkin
University of Maryland–Baltimore County

PEARSON

Boston   Columbus   Indianapolis   New York   San Francisco   Upper Saddle River
Amsterdam   Cape Town   Dubai   London   Madrid   Milan   Munich   Paris   Montreal   Toronto
Delhi   Mexico City   São Paulo   Sydney   Hong Kong   Seoul   Singapore   Taipei   Tokyo

KH

Vice President and Editor in Chief: Jeffery W. Johnston
Senior Acquisitions Editor: Julie Peters
Editorial Assistant: Andrea Hall
Vice President, Director of Marketing: Margaret Waples
Senior Marketing Manager: Chris Barry
Senior Managing Editor: Pamela Bennett
Senior Project Manager: Mary M. Irvin
Senior Operations Supervisor: Matt Ottenweller
Photo Coordinator: Carol Sykes
Cover Designer: Candace Rowley
Cover Art: Olivia Williams Ridge
Composition: Aptara®, Inc.
Full Service Project Management: Jogender Taneja/Aptara®, Inc.
Printer/Binder: Courier
Cover Printer: Courier
Text Font: Palatino

Photo Credits: Sheila Williams Ridge/Dodge Nature Center Preschool, pp. 5, 11; Jenny Leeper-Miller, pp. 19, 38, 77, 88; Susan Humphries, pp. 23, 244; Bob Bailie/Schlitz Audubon Nature Center Preschool, pp. 47, 48, 171, 255; Nancy Pennington Alexander, pp. 66, 141, 265, 275, 293; © BmPorter/Don Franklin, pp. 86, 131, 179; Heather Erickson/Dodge Nature Center Preschool, pp. 92, 246; Ellen B. Senisi, pp. 109, 151, 158; Jean Harlan, p. 112; John Harlan, pp. 114, 165; Meg Menkedick, pp. 181, 281; Priscilla Woyke, p. 195; Sybil Shelton/PH College, p. 215; Janet Brown, pp. 225, 264; Kathy Sible, p. 236; Gary Goodman, p. 262; Mary Rivkin, p. 270 (both); Elizabeth Nichols, p. 277; Julia Torquati, pp. 296, 307.

Every effort has been made to provide accurate and current Internet information in this book. However, the Internet and information posted on it are constantly changing, so it is inevitable that some of the Internet addresses listed in this textbook will change.

Library of Congress Cataloging-in-Publication Data
Harlan, Jean Durgin.
  Science experiences for the early childhood years : an integrated affective approach / Jean D. Harlan, Mary S. Rivkin.
    p. cm.
  ISBN-13: 978-0-13-237336-4
  ISBN-10: 0-13-237336-X
  1. Science—Study and teaching (Early childhood)   I. Rivkin, Mary S.   II. Title.
  LB1139.5.S35H37 2012
  372.3'5—dc22   2011000451

10 9 8 7 6 5 4 3 2 1

www.pearsonhighered.com

ISBN 10:   0-13-237336-X
ISBN 13: 978-0-13-237336-4

10/4/11

We dedicate this edition to the memory of
Stanley Greenspan, friend, advisor.

*Emotion is the orchestra conductor, getting
the whole brain and mind working together.*

Stanley I. Greenspan, MD
1932–2010

Preface

This is the tenth revised edition of the first textbook published in the then new field of early childhood science teacher education. Its rationale continues to emphasize that meaningful science for young children builds on the emotional underpinnings of their innate curiosity, their concerns about their everyday world, and their pleasure in exploring it. Its aim is to help new teachers inspire children to live appreciatively and thoughtfully on this amazing planet: to lead children toward eventual science literacy and willing stewardship of Earth.

We are gratified to observe current national trends that are consonant with themes in this edition. The movement to return children's right to play and learn in natural outdoor settings actually has been emphasized in the past five editions. School grounds improvements, including gardening, continue to be suggested to promote children's science learning as well as children's creativity and healthy exercise.

The trend toward reducing toxins in the environment as a childhood health concern again is expressed as advocacy for forbidding the use of harmful pesticides in schools and school yards through the use of Integrated Pest Management.

The new standards for K-12 science education being developed by the National Academies of Science focus on teaching a few core ideas from each science discipline, along with cross-cutting ideas such as causality. Making fundamental science concepts accessible in ways that allow young children to learn best has been intrinsic to this textbook from its inception.

As the global economy brings science and technology to ever greater prominence, today's children need a strong foundation in these disciplines. May they and their teachers learn the disciplines and retain their sense of curiosity and feeling of joy at the wonder of the world.

NEW TO THIS EDITION

- Embedded math skills are identified for concept-related science activities.
- Appropriate assessments are reviewed in response to the current emphasis on STEM (Science, Technology, Engineering, Math) education.
- Updated neuroscience research findings strengthen understanding of the biological inseparability of cognitive and emotional functioning in learning.
- Three cognitive development theories are described, and their consequent inferences for teaching are identified.
- The revised Chapter 16 promotes bonding with nature and an appropriate stewardship role for young children.
- Updated selections of related children's literature have been annotated to extend the pleasure of learning science and to foster literacy.

- New references and online resources for teachers have been added to increase their confidence in doing science with children.
- Chapter openers encourage new teachers to draw from the inspiration of personal experiences to enrich their science teaching.

ACKNOWLEDGMENTS

We are grateful for the generous contributions of new photographs from Bob Bailie taken at the Schlitz Audubon Nature Center Preschool, from Sheila Williams Ridge and colleagues at the Dodge Nature Center Preschool, and from Julia Torquati and Jennie Leeper-Miller at the University of Nebraska, Lincoln. We also wish to thank Julia for other contributions to the revision process, especially in discussions of assessments, Web sites, and school gardens.

Helpful comments for planning this revision were made by the following reviewers: Karen Bauer, Edinboro University of Pennsylvania; Frank D'Angelo, Bloomsburg University; Deirdre Englehart, University of Central Florida; Martha Nabors, College of Charleston; Karen Ray, Wake Technical Community College; Latisha Shipley, Northwestern Oklahoma State University; and Julia Torquati, University of Nebraska, Lincoln.

Finally, we are grateful for the thoughtful and responsive guidance in the publication process of our editor, Julie Peters, our production manager, Mary Irvin, and our photo editor, Carol Sykes.

Mary especially thanks her UMBC students and colleagues for insights, and her children and their families for anecdotes, wisdom, and play. Husband Steve made many meals and always was there, keeping the household going during revisions. Son Jesse has shared enthusiasm for being outdoors, which has been fun. As always, Jean has been the best colleague!—MR

Jean is grateful to the Columbus Metropolitan Library, the designated 2010 Library of the Year, for the use of its wonderful resources. Its excellent staff, and the fine staff of the State of Ohio Library, eased my research for this edition. I also thank Susan Borghese for her word sensibilities and Betsy Harlan for untangling Word problems.

For expecting me to keep learning and growing, I thank my children: Betsy Harlan, Anne Strohm, John Harlan, Susan Borghese, and Julie Harlan-Schneider; and their children Christopher, Rachel, Lauren, Kate, Liz, Laura, Nina, Sophia, Elinor, Simone, and Josie. Mary's deep commitment to a healthy planet and thriving children inspires our work together and keeps our friendship strong.—JH

Brief Contents

Contents

8   # Water   **154**

11   Magnetism   210

12   The Effects of Gravity   223

13   Simple Machines   238

APPENDIX B
Exploring at-Home Activities   314

Part One

THE RATIONALE

An Integrated Affective Approach to Science Learning

THE INGREDIENTS OF LEARNING

"Look, Teacher, my hand!" Jimmy spoke! At last, Jimmy had broken through the stoic silence of his first anxious month in Head Start. Crouched on the carpeted floor to blot up his juice spill, Jimmy was transfixed with wonder at the imprint of his hand on a paper towel. Until that moment, the novelty of every aspect of the preschool day had overwhelmed him into unfocused muteness. But the unexpected sight of his handprint was just different enough from his familiar hand experiences to capture his attention both cognitively and emotionally. As he questioned his teacher and experimented with fresh towels, he happily chattered about his discovery with other children. His own irrepressible curiosity had finally drawn him into the circle of learners at our center.

How can a four-year-old like Jimmy focus with such intensity on a mundane experience with capillary action? Why, for that matter, do children want to know *why?* Because learning the causes of things happening around them is the natural work of young children. Infants are born with billions of brain cells (neurons) in place, ready to start making sense of the world. Remarkable brain mechanisms are present to promote learning and exploring as the infant experiences the world. The neurons begin to connect into networks for communicating with other neurons in direct response to stimulation from the environment, steadily shaping the infant brain into a thinking/feeling mind.

Attention

Infants can focus attention on sensory information coming from the environment because of two tangible brain responses. Information picked up by the senses activates neurons in memory regions of the brain. At the same time, neurochemicals from the emotional functioning regions of the brain are sent to the memory regions. The neurochemicals enhance focusing and attention-giving, actually causing changes in the memory neurons. Those changes result in learning. Without attention, the information that the senses constantly take in does not register in the brain. So, attention is the critical first step in learning (Carter, 2009).

Early on, infants are able to recognize faces and objects. They begin to pay greater attention to the new and to unexpected changes in the familiar. As increasing mobility makes small-scale discoveries of cause and effect possible, babies begin to pay attention to the results of their own actions. This allows young babies to reason, make predictions, solve problems, and then reach out for new experiences (Gopnik, 2009). The new sensations, emotional responses, memories, and actions stimulate more neural branching and connections. Each new learning changes the brain in a way that allows for more learning, a capacity—plasticity—that has lifetime potential. If infants' exploring is encouraged, their probing for meaning broadens further as language and locomotion develop. With appropriate stimulation and support, this inherent urge to know continues to deepen and motivates increasingly complex causal investigations such as Jimmy's.

When this innate human desire to understand the world is organized into careful ways of collecting, analyzing, and sharing the resulting information, it is called *science*. Indeed, the word *science* is derived from the Latin root word *scire*, meaning "to know." When we offer intriguing science experiences to young children, we nourish their compelling need to know. Early childhood science explorations continue the natural reaching out for knowledge that began with attention in infancy.

Curiosity

Jimmy's urgent wish to know why a shadowy imprint of his hand appeared on the towel has a familiar name: *curiosity*. There is debate about whether curiosity is an innate exploratory drive or a basic need for knowledge. Perhaps it is just an adaptive legacy of our foraging ancestors from the ancient past. Their ability to find and distinguish the nourishing from the noxious was critical for their very survival.

Today's neuroscientists have been able to identify the dynamic brain activities set in motion by curiosity behavior. When something new is encountered by our senses, the *attention system* releases certain neurochemicals to enhance focusing. This activates a specific brain region that appears to be involved in *anticipating* reward (Kang et al., 2009). Exploratory behavior is then triggered, leading to the discovery of new information. When new information is found, the *reward system* releases specific neurochemicals, resulting in positive emotion, and the *memory region* is engaged. In this way, *curiosity enhances recall* of new information (Knutson & Cooper, 2006). Finally, if the outcome is positive, the reward system promotes the emotional desire to repeat this satisfying process (Wittman, Branzeck, Dolan, & Dunzel, 2007).

Curiosity, energized as it is by emotion, is a significant part of spontaneous learning. It adds to the rapid trajectory of learning in our earliest months and years, when we have so much to learn. Scientists and those in other creative occupations often refer to curiosity as a driving energy in their work. For all of us, well-maintained curiosity and openness to wonder can result in a deeply experienced

Bridge technology practiced on the preschool creek.

life. Whether curiosity ultimately leads us to groundbreaking discoveries or simply enriches our lives by stimulating learning and personal growth, it is a mechanism to respect and encourage in our work with children.

Emotions

Emotions can be thought of as brain processes triggering physical and cognitive responses that prompt us to act. We often use the terms *emotions* and *feelings* interchangeably, but emotions are largely unconscious and feelings are the way our emotions are expressed consciously.

Traditionally, emotion was misunderstood and dismissed as having no bearing on rational thinking or as being its opposite. For instance, a reviewer of the first edition of this book in 1976 was startled by its then radical affective-cognitive orientation. He scribbled across one page with exaggerated pen strokes (perhaps revealing his own strong feelings), "What have feelings got to do with anything? This is a book about science!"

Since then, significant advances in the neurosciences have provided a more complete understanding of the complex interactions between emotions, thought processes, and memory. The word *emotion* comes from two Latin root words meaning "to stir up" and "to move." Emotion is now seen as an amazing orchestration of mental functions. In a simplified way, we can think of these processes as a continuous sensory relay system. As we experience our environment with our senses, the information passes to the brain through structures in the midbrain. A reaction to the information registers in this emotion-processing area, where it is assessed as to how the environment is affecting us. This reaction simultaneously integrates with specific reasoning and planning areas of the brain. It also sets in motion a cascade of neuronal and biochemical activities that stimulates both the brain and the rest of the body.

The areas and systems of the brain involved with emotional responses are connected by neurons to the rest of the brain. They form networks as part of the central nervous system, communicating with the rest of the body as *electrical information carriers*.

Numerous biochemicals in the brain also contribute to emotional states. They are exquisitely sensitive to behavioral and environmental stimuli. These *biochemical information carriers* allow the brain to communicate rapidly with the body by way of the bloodstream. They also affect the neurons associated with learning, shaping our memories as we are forming them (Storbeck & Close, 2008). This explains why emotionally charged information lasts much longer in memory and is recalled with greater accuracy than emotionally neutral input (Medina, 2008).

According to Dai and Sternberg (2004), emotions are necessary for evaluating the significance of events and for planning. They point out that human thinking begins in an intimate association with emotions and feelings that is never entirely lost. In sum, emotions are fundamental to our ability to focus attention, and they are critical to how we process, use, and store information. Emotion shapes all cognitive development (Lewis, 2010).

Affect and Learning

Psychologists use the term *affect*, referring to emotion, feelings, or mood, as a way to view the part of our experience that differs from thought and behavior. In reality, of course, thinking and behavior are intimately connected with affect. Intellectual functioning is now widely understood as an integrated mix of cognition, emotion, and motivation (Dai & Sternberg, 2004).

The interplay between affect and thinking is of particular importance to teaching and learning, because two of the functions of emotions are to arouse interest and prioritize what we pay attention to. Our emotional state when we receive information determines whether, and how well, we remember it (McGaugh, 2006). Emotion also plays a part in children's willingness to engage in a task and to persist in it (Linnenbrink & Pentrich, 2004).

Classroom atmosphere has an affective impact. A positive classroom environment can raise the level of children's endorphins, biochemicals that induce pleasurable feelings and facilitate memory. The opposite is true of a negative environment. Children in stressful child-care situations have shown elevated levels of cortisol, the stress hormone that inhibits memory processes (Greenspan, 2002).

Positive Affect and Learning

Pleasure in learning awesome, intriguing, or comforting features of the world furthers affective and cognitive growth. This was true for six-year-old Amanda during her class visit to a tropical butterfly display. Her face registered delight when she coaxed a spectacular blue morpho butterfly to step onto the back of her hand. As she studied the beautiful creature, her expression suddenly changed to open-mouthed surprise. She whispered to a staff member, "Do butterflies pee?" The staff member queried back, "What do you notice?" Amanda thoughtfully examined the tiny orange droplet on her hand. A succession of expressions crossed her face: astonishment, a flicker of dismay, then recognition. "So that's what this is. He's just like us!" She sat transfixed, quietly observing the placid blue morpho until it was time to leave. She then gently transferred the butterfly to a convenient leaf and slowly backed away. It's safe to surmise that Amanda's memories of this event will maintain her curiosity about butterflies and etch lasting feelings of connectedness to a fellow creature not entirely unlike herself. Judging from the intensity of her engagement, she responded with deeply evoked emotions of *awe* and *wonder*.

Negative Affect and Learning

We know from our own experience that negative affect of boredom, dislike, or frustration can diminish learning. Ample research confirms that overwhelming sadness or anxiety can paralyze curiosity and disrupt attention, memory, and problem solving (Blair, 2002). However, it is also true that a mild level of anxiety can motivate learning. Persistent worry about unexplained, imagined, or frightening events can sharpen focus and spur young children into finding answers.

Negative feelings like anger can also fuel the need to know. This seemed to be true of Jake's ready anticipation of trouble. One of the smallest children in our class, Jake endured regular pummeling by his older brother at home. The boys' parents did not intervene, because their "boys-will-be-boys" policy required no action from them. But Jake brought his resentment to school, moving warily among his male classmates with clenched fists at the ready. Then Jake became fascinated by our gravity experiences. As often as he could coax a partner to join him, Jake claimed the playground teeter-totter, where he could be in control. He could keep a bigger boy dangling above the ground or be in charge of creating a balance between them. In the classroom, he focused long, solitary attention on using the balance scale and on finding ways to balance pennies on a ruler placed on a half-circle block fulcrum. Each time he mastered his self-created balance challenges, he exulted, "Now they're even!" Gradually, Jake began to let down his guard and cautiously make friendly overtures to a boy about his size. We like to think that his perseverance with the balancing activities helped him grow emotionally and socially.

Anxiety about misunderstood or frightening events also may lure children into finding answers. Occasionally, the connection between a child's anxious concern and his or her eagerness to find answers is clearly apparent. For example, the mother of four-year-old Matthew asked for advice on how to help her son get to sleep at night. He was unable to shut his eyes until he had counted all the stars he could see from his window. He needed to count them over and over to make sure they were still all in place. That provided reassurance for him that a star wouldn't fall on him while he was sleeping.

In response to his concern, a series of experiences was provided to build understanding about why things fall to Earth or, in this case, why they don't fall. Matthew enjoyed some tangible explorations of the effects of magnetism, an invisible force that could, nonetheless, be felt in the hands of a fascinated boy. After many experiences with magnets, Matthew experimented with some simple effects of the greater invisible force of gravity. He found that the hardest toss by a strong boy couldn't send a ball beyond the pull of Earth's gravity. Even he himself always came back to Earth after his highest leaps. Matthew helped build a carton spaceship to play at being an astronaut, floating so far from Earth that its gravity could not pull him down. He frequently asked to be read a story about astronauts who traveled three days to reach the moon because it was so far away. He always chimed in at the part that told how stars were even farther away from Earth than the moon.

The day finally came when Matthew's mother reported that it was now easier for him to get to sleep. He only had to do one quick scan of the stars before climbing into bed. He explained confidently to his parents that Earth's gravity isn't strong enough to pull down a star. In the years since then, Matthew's fascination with astronomy has continued. He and his family made many visits to observatories and planetariums, and he has since become a meteorologist.

MULTIPLE LEARNING PATHWAYS

Two Ways of Thinking

Cognitive neuroscientists assure us that we have two valid but different ways of thinking that work simultaneously: *conscious thinking*, which we are aware of doing, because we use language to process it, and *nonconscious thinking*, which goes on continuously beyond our conscious awareness without involving language. We use both conscious and nonconscious thought in all of our mental activities. This is somewhat like the computer's unseen digital operating system (DOS), which is constantly running under the software we are aware of using.

Pattern-seeking is one of the key nonconscious thought processes. It is the way young children pick up the complex patterns and unspoken rules of social behavior and of learning to talk. It explains three-year-old Caroline's use of her nonconscious knowledge of past-tense formation: "I teached him how to throw." *Imaging* is another nonconscious thought process. For example, we regularly call up mental images when we think nostalgically about a special event. *Metaphor use* is a third well-studied nonconscious thought process. Young Jake seemed to use his fascination with balancing things as a metaphor for making his social relationships come out even.

We all have had unexpected "Aha, now I've got it!" breakthroughs when our nonconscious processes continued to work out a solution that had stumped our conscious thinking. In the realm of scientific thinking, such intuitive insights, as well as imagination, can be essential both for identifying problems to be solved and for having hunches about how to pursue a solution. Nonconscious processing takes in vastly more details about what is going on around us than we perceive consciously. Solving a problem through insight even involves different brain mechanisms than analytical problem solving uses (Kounios & Beeman, 2009). Creative thinking is largely produced this way, outside of our conscious thought processes.

When Eli offered a surprisingly sophisticated insight to a class discussion, he considered his words briefly, then said, "Wow! I didn't know I knew that!" Eli couldn't explain verbally how he came up with his sudden burst of understanding, but it was the result of valid, though nonconscious, mental activity. His teacher didn't dismiss it as a lucky guess. She respected it, commenting, "That was good thinking, Eli." Conscious thinking is important, but so are the nonconscious cognitive, emotional, and motivational processes (Kounios & Beeman, 2009). Some familiar teaching tools draw on both forms of thought. For instance, time awareness, such as remembering rhythm patterns, is developed and encoded in memory nonconsciously. When we embed science concepts in well-remembered rhythmic songs and fingerplays, such as pegging the evaporation concept into "The Eency Weency Spider," the consolidation makes for stronger encoding and retrieval of the concept (Cook, Mitchell, & Goldin-Meadow, 2008). We strengthen learning when we encourage children to express imaginatively what they are learning with the creative qualities of nonconscious thinking.

Multiple Intelligences Theory

We have long known that there are many ways for our incredible brains to take in and process information into working knowledge. Yet, in 1983, when Harvard educator Howard Gardner described his theory of multiple intelligences (MI) in his book *Frames of Mind*, it stirred controversy among psychologists. But Gardner's theory has steadily gained acceptance among educators, because it explains their commonsense observations. It also offers theoretical support for providing a wide variety of media to teach concepts.

Gardner recognizes that intelligence is more than the single logical-mathematical processing of stored facts that intelligence tests assess. He sees intelligence as problem-solving, problem-creating, and problem-finding across a range of situations. He originally identified seven distinct interlocking *kinds* of intelligence possessed by all of us to some degree. They are *logical-mathematical:* the ability to understand and use mathematical, logical, and scientific concepts; *linguistic:* the capacity to use language to express ideas; *musical:* the ability to "think in music" and to hear, recognize, and remember patterns; *spatial:* the ability to mentally represent the spatial world; *bodily-kinesthetic:* the capacity to use the body to solve a problem or make something; *interpersonal:* the ability to understand other people; and *intrapersonal:* the capacity to think about one's feelings and to understand oneself (1993). Later, Gardner (2006) added an eighth intelligence—*naturalist:* the ability to recognize and classify living things and see patterns in other aspects of the natural world. Identifying the naturalist form of intelligence happily coincided with the urgent grassroots movement to reconnect children with nature (Louv, 2008). Gardner proposes that each of us uses different combinations and degrees of these eight intelligences as we learn about and respond to our environment.

The multiple intelligences theory has been supported by recent neurological evidence (Gardner, 2006). Identifying these capacities has provided early childhood educators with a stronger rationale for using integrated curricula. Other research verifies the value of teaching subjects in multiple contexts (Brandsford, Brown, & Cocking, 2003). Note that Gardner does not claim that *all* topics must be taught in multiple ways, but rather that using several formats flexibly and imaginatively will reach more children. Those multiple approaches help children to effectively construct and use socially valued knowledge such as science.

AN INTEGRATED LEARNING FRAMEWORK

When we integrate meaningful science experiences with other curricular areas, we help children enhance their mental performance. Different features of an experience are encoded in different parts of the brain. These features are then linked together to form more enduring memory systems deeper in the brain. The more fully information is revisited and processed over time, the more connections we make. The more consolidation takes place, the better the memory will be (McGinnis & Roberts-Harris, 2009). Our teaching needs to provide a range of connections among different ways of absorbing, associating, and applying information. We need to help children reflect on the information they are gathering, relate it to something they already know, and form meaningful associations. We need to help children see that otherwise abstract concepts actually function in their familiar world. We need to spread a wide net of opportunities to capture the interest of diverse learners. Then children with varying intellectual talents can find emotionally satisfying, meaningful paths to learning.

For these reasons, a variety of enriching extensions are suggested for each of the major science topics found in Part Two of this book. Each of the learning opportunities described in the following paragraphs draws on one or more of the multiple forms of intelligence identified by Gardner. The effect is diagrammed in Figure 1–1.

Math activities are embedded as an integral part of all science because they provide ways to quantify and record observations and recognize patterns. These will be identified within activity plans as necessary parts of a science experience. Other suggested activities use science themes to provide a new context for using math skills. Both quantifying and numerical reasoning rely on the *logical-mathematical* intelligence identified by Gardner.

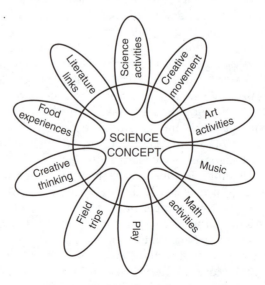

FIGURE 1–1 Multiple Pathways to Science Learning

Music in the form of songs or ballads was used to educate for centuries before books and schools existed. Singing about science concepts can strengthen understanding in many ways. Melody can evoke positive feelings about these concepts. Lyrics can use literal or metaphorical ideas to strengthen recall. Rhythm reinforces song ideas through repetitive patterns. Hearing, in itself, is a sensory system that evokes strong memories. When tunes run through children's minds, they are reminded of the ideas expressed in the lyrics.

Music can trigger both memory and emotion systems simultaneously, like a key unlocking all the experiences associated with the memory of a song (Levitin, 2006). Also, there appear to be separate pathways in the brain for music and for speech processing. They integrate as memory traces when tune and text consolidate in singing (Perretz & Fox, 2004). So, we humans seem to be predisposed to remember and respond emotionally, physically, and cognitively to music. It's no wonder that singing commercials are such powerful advertising tools! Tapping into *musical* intelligence makes learning easier, more durable, and fun.

Literature links extend science concepts by associating them with fresh language and images, both metaphorically and as narrative. Whether incidentally embedded in fiction or introduced as focal themes of science-based stories and poems, science ideas register emotionally in children's minds as they encounter familiar knowledge in new situations. Reading or listening to science-related stories can inspire children to explore and experiment. Encouraging children to write or tell their own stories promotes creative thinking: synthesizing fact, fantasy, and feelings using *linguistic* intelligence.

Poems are easier to recall than is text describing the same idea, because three encoding pathways are engaged: rhythm, language, and rhyming sounds. When children create poetry, they build on what a concept reminds them of. They use analogy to think flexibly about what they are learning, connecting more brain circuits (Crown & Cipriani, 2009), another aspect of *linguistic intelligence.*

Xavier integrates his observations of plants and shadows at the easel.

Art activities are suggested in Part Two to stimulate intuitive creative expressions of children's own ideas. They are deliberately open-ended to encourage personal interpretations of science events (Posner & Patoine, 2009). As children enjoy drawing, painting, and modeling to represent what they have learned, they engage both *spatial* and *bodily-kinesthetic* intelligence. Some of the art suggestions incorporate materials used in the science experiences. This encourages divergent thinking, because children invent new ways to use the materials. Craft projects that require children to follow specific directions to achieve a certain end-result product devalue creativity and are *not* suggested as art activities.

Play: Spontaneous play is so important to healthy development that it has been recognized as a right for every child by the United Nations Human Rights Commission.* Authentic play gives children chances to freely pursue their own interests. It also allows them to try out and apply science ideas imaginatively at their own pace. Outdoor play in school grounds with natural features allows children to enjoy and, with modest guidance, to observe nature (Rivkin, 1995). Researchers studying young children as they casually played with an interesting new toy found that the children were also exploring cause and effect. But once the children figured out how the toy worked, it lost its play appeal (Schulz & Bonawitz, 2007).

Dramatic play has been considered a valid form of integrating knowledge since the pioneering days of nursery school nearly 80 years ago. We offer suggestions about two forms of play: creative drama ideas for impromptu guided dramatization of known stories and spontaneous play themes for which a few props are supplied to stimulate children's own play ideas. Memory is enhanced when concepts can be acted out by the learner (Glenberg, et al 2004). Note, however, that any play loses its value as relaxed, pleasurable activity if adults hover closely, ever ready to capitalize on "teachable moments." Play can draw on *linguistic, spatial, bodily-kinesthetic,* and *interpersonal* forms of intelligence.

Creative movement is a joyful, relaxing way to increase conceptual understanding and strengthen retention of information. Motor memory encoding happens when abstract ideas are intuitively translated into concrete physical movements of the body (Grafton, 2009). Attention must be focused to accomplish a physical task well. Spontaneous expression through movement calls forth both *spatial* and *bodily-kinesthetic* forms of intelligence, and sometimes *musical* and *interpersonal* intelligences.

Creative thinking is encouraged by using open-ended strategies that reframe concepts with new associations. Using visualization and imagination, science concepts can be tested and clarified by reversing events, taking ideas apart to create fantasy solutions, and looking at ideas from new perspectives. Such activities encourage flexibility in shifting between rational and intuitive styles of thinking and can stimulate new interest in a science topic. Creative thinking activities draw on *intrapersonal* intelligence.

Food experiences use the sensory input of taste and smell to strengthen the recall of concepts. The pleasure of being involved in preparing or sampling good things to eat provides a heightened emotional state for creating lasting memories. All of us have made vivid connections between particular foods and the memories of the feelings we associated with those foods. Edible science experiences can strengthen concept retention by using *bodily-kinesthetic* intelligence.

Field trips add relevance and validate the science information learned in school. Children are proud to recognize that what they learned in the classroom

---

*United Nations Commission for Human Rights Convention on the Rights of the Child, November 1989.

has significance in the wider world. We usually think of field trips as organized events happening off-site, but shrinking school budgets call for a more thoughtful approach. The "field" can sometimes be brought to the classroom. Children long remember visiting critters brought to them through nature center outreach programs. When school policies and locations permit them, walking trips to nearby sites have potential for extending classroom learning. Reduced field trip funding can also lead to more creative use of the school grounds as the "biggest classroom."

Improving school grounds can be the best way to connect classroom learning to the wider world. There is a strong need to make the school grounds as enriching as classrooms, particularly in child-care settings where so many children spend a majority of their waking hours. Just getting outdoors to exercise influences learning directly, at the neuron level, improving the potential to process new information (Ratey, 2008). Other research corroborates the long advocacy of the outdoors by early childhood educators and environmental educators. It reveals even more benefits from connecting children with nature this way (Frost, Keyburn, & Sutterby, 2010). Children whose education emphasized the outdoor environment as a context for learning have shown higher academic achievement and were less stressed than children in traditional classrooms (Cornell University, 2005). Each chapter in Part Two includes goals for improving and enriching school grounds to provide these benefits.

This integrated approach to science education weaves physical, sensory, and emotional activities into the total learning process. It encourages the use of both conscious and nonconscious thinking. It builds on children's powers of imagination and creativity. This approach has been affirmed by the National Association for the Education of Young Children (2009) in its *Standards for Early Childhood Professional Preparation Programs*. It is also consistent with the recommendations of the *National Science Education Standards* (1996), which were established by a consensus of hundreds of teachers, scientists, and policymakers. These standards call for a developmentally appropriate curriculum that is connected to other school subjects, coordinated with mathematics programs, and interesting and relevant to children.

PROMOTING CONCEPT CONNECTIONS

Promoting concept connections ensures that concepts don't fade simply because a particular curriculum unit has been completed. Children need to reflect on new information and make meaningful associations, relating it to things already known. Two important ways of doing this are less direct than the integrating activities, as they depend on a teacher's ability to plan ahead to apply them. The methods are (a) *maintaining concepts* by applying them and (b) *linking concepts* to previously acquired concepts, putting the new information into the context of the larger picture. If the topics to be linked are presented sequentially whenever possible, children can be greatly helped to pull together relationships by themselves. The understandings gleaned from one set of activities can then lead directly or transfer indirectly to those that follow. Each chapter in Part Two offers general suggestions for

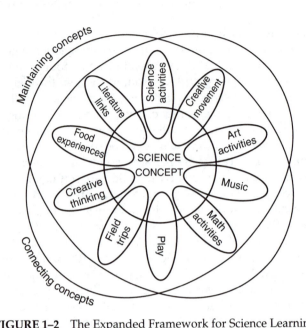

FIGURE 1–2   The Expanded Framework for Science Learning

maintaining concepts and linking *new concepts* to already established concepts. These concept connections surround the integrating activities model, as depicted in Figure 1–2. When we integrate a science topic into other aspects of the curriculum, we mirror the way that all of us make new information our own. We confirm it often, even unexpectedly, in other contexts. When we gladly invite children to use their curiosity, to focus their attention, and to enjoy finding amazing details in the commonplace, we hand them a master key to learning about the world.

REFERENCES

BLAIR, C. (2002). Integrating cognition and emotion in a neurobiological conceptualization of children's functioning at school entry. *American Psychologist, 57,* 111–125.

BRANSFORD, J., BROWN, A., & COCKING, R. (eds.). (2003). *How people learn: Brain, mind, experience and school* (p. 54). Washington, DC: National Academy Press.

CARTER, R. (2009). *The human brain book.* New York: Dorling Kindersley.

COOK, S., MITCHELL, Z., & GOLDIN-MEADOW, S. (2008). Gesturing makes learning last. *Cognition, 106,* 1047–1058.

CORNELL UNIVERSITY. (2005). *Garden-based learning: Research that supports our work.* Retrieved July 16, 2010, from http://blogs.cornell.edu/garden.

CROWN, K. W., & CIPRIANI, S. (2009). Developing inquiry through analogy. *Young Children, 64*(6), 62–63.

DAI, D., & STERNBERG, R. (2004). *Motivation, emotion and cognition: Integrative perspectives on intellectual functioning and development.* Mahwah, NJ: Erlbaum.

FROST, J., KEYBURN, D., & SUTTERBY, J. (2010). Transforming a sterile urban schoolyard into a nature wonderland. In J. Hoot & J. Szente (Eds.), *The earth is our home: Children caring for the environment* (pp. 131–147). Olney, MD: Association for Childhood Education International.

GARDNER, H. (1993). *Frames of mind.* New York: Basic Books. (Original work published 1983).

GARDNER, H. (2006). *Multiple intelligences: New horizons*. New York: Basic Books.

GLENBERG, A., GUTIERREZ, T., LEVIN, J., JAPUNTICH, S., & KASCHAK, M. (2004). Activity and imagined activity can enhance young children's reading comprehension. *Journal of Educational Psychology, 96*(3), 424–436.

GOPNNIK, A. (2009). *The philosophical baby: What children's minds tell us about truth, love, and the meaning of life*. New York: Farrar, Strous & Girow.

GRAFTON, S. (2009). *What can dance teach us about learning?* Retrieved April 18, 2010, from http://dana.org/news/cerebrum/detail.aspx?id=23500.

GREENSPAN, S. (2002). *The four-thirds solution: Solving the day care crisis in America*. Cambridge, MA: Perseus Books.

KANG, M., HSU, M., KRAJBICH, I., LOEWENSTEIN, G., MCCLURE, A., WANG, J., & CAMERER, C. (2009). The wick in the candle of learning: Epistemic curiosity activates reward circuitry and enhances memory. *Psychological Science, 20*(8), 963–973.

KNUTSON, B., & COOPER, J. (2006). The lure of the unknown: *Neuron, Vol. 51*, 280–282.

KOUNIOS, J., & BEEMAN, M. (2009). The "aha!" moment: The cognitive neuroscience of insight. *Current Directions in Psychological Science, 18*(4), 210–215.

LEVITIN, D. (2006). *This is your brain on music! The science of a human obsession*. New York: Dutton.

LEWIS, M. (2010). Desire, dopamine and conceptual development. In S. Calkins & M. Bell (Eds.), *Child development at the intersection of emotion and cognition*. Washington, DC: American Psychological Association.

LINNENBRINK, E., & PENTRICH, P. (2004). Role of affect in cognitive processing in academic contexts. In D. Dai & R. Sternberg (Eds.), *Motivation, emotion and cognition* (pp. 57–87). Mahwah, NJ: Erlbaum.

LOUV, R. (2008). *Last child in the woods*. Chapel Hill, NC: Algonquin Books.

MCGAUGH, J. (2006). Make mild moments memorable: Add a little arousal. *Trends in Cognitive Sciences, 10*(8), 345–347.

MCGINNIS, R., & ROBERTS-HARRIS, D. (2009). A new vision for teaching science. *Scientific American: Mind, 20*(5), 62–67.

MEDINA, J. (2008). *Brain rules*. Seattle: Pear Press.

NATIONAL ASSOCIATION FOR THE EDUCATION OF YOUNG CHILDREN. (2009). *NAEYC Standards for Early Childhood Professional Preparation Programs: Early Learning Standard 5. Using Content Knowledge to Build Meaningful Curriculum*. Washington, DC: Author.

NATIONAL COMMITTEE ON SCIENCE EDUCATION STANDARDS AND ASSESSMENT. (1996). *National Science Education Standards*. Washington, DC: National Research Council.

PERRETZ, P., & FOX, J. (2004). *A well tempered mind*. New York: Dana Press.

POSNER, M., & PATOINE, B. (2009). How arts training improves attention and cognition. In D. Gordon (Ed.), *Cerebrum, 2010: Emerging ideas in brain science* (pp. 12–22). New York: Dana Press.

RATEY, J. (2008). *Spark: The revolutionary new science of exercise and the brain*. New York: Little, Brown.

RIVKIN, M. (1995). *The great outdoors: Restoring children's right to play outside*. Washington, DC: National Association for the Education of Young Children.

SCHULTZ, L., & BONAWITZ, E. (2007). Serious fun: Preschoolers engage in more exploratory play when evidence is confounded. *Developmental Psychology, 43*(4), 1045–1050.

STORBECK, J., & CLOSE, G. (2008). On the interdependence of cognition and emotion. *Cognition and Emotion, 21*(6), 1212–1237.

WITTMAN, B., BRANZECK, N., DOLAN, R., & DUNZEL, E. (2007). Anticipation of novelty recruits reward system and hippocampus while promoting recollection. *Neuroimaging, 38*(1), 194–202.

Science Participants: Children, Teachers, Families, and Communities

YOUNG CHILDREN AS THINKERS

It is tempting to think of young children's minds as fresh pages to be written on or clay to be molded by skillful, caring teachers. It is so tempting, in fact, that many inexperienced teachers and parents equate "telling" with teaching. Unfortunately, much writing about education characterizes teaching as "delivery of instruction," as if children's minds were loading docks upon which teachers can deposit boxes of information and skills.

A more realistic view of how children's minds work comes from an ever-widening stream of cognitive psychology research. This view is reinforced by the once-again-appreciated observations of parents and teachers who work daily with children. Both sources see children's minds constantly engaging in sense-making. Consider this story a mother reported to her son's teacher:

> Three-year-old Christopher was baking gingerbread with his mother when he asked, "Where is the cinnamon god?" His surprised mother probed gently to puzzle out the meaning of his question. She learned that the rabbi from a neighboring synagogue had recently visited the children at Christopher's preschool. God, synagogue, cinnamon, cinnamon god: Christopher had put all the pieces together. He had constructed his own knowledge.

Most likely, Christopher had used previous experiences with cinnamon—something he could touch, smell, taste, and see—as a base of understanding on which to hook the new information. His mother then helped him refashion the connection to conform to more commonly held definitions and pronunciations of *cinnamon* and *synagogue.* Because his mother offered more information, Christopher could form new, more sophisticated knowledge. He could do this without being aware of how marvelously his mind was working. Because at his age he is learning effortlessly about nine new words a day, every experience Christopher has is a source of developing knowledge for him.

Cognitive Development Theories

Since the time of Socrates and Plato, philosophers and scholars have theorized about how humans begin to think and develop knowledge. Education throughout the ages has reflected their theories. The importance of active experience in learning was both theorized about and demonstrated by John Dewey and Maria Montessori early in the 20th century.

But only since Jean Piaget began his systematic research 80 years ago has attention turned to actual investigations of the thinking of infants and children. Piaget's intriguing cognitive development theories made a strong impact on education policy in this country, contributing immeasurably to the formation of early childhood education as a separate focus of elementary schools.

In recent decades, more sophisticated research methods and techniques used by developmental psychologists have revealed that young children are far more capable of abstract thinking than Piaget had proposed. Interestingly, two of today's most influential cognitive development theories echo two competing philosophies that have prevailed for 2,500 years: *rationalism* and *empiricism* (Kail, 2004).

Domain Specific Cognition Theory reflects rationalist philosophy, which proposed that we have innate ability to think from the beginning of life, and that we acquire knowledge by reasoning alone. Rationalists claimed that the most important things to know are ready to mature without having to be learned from experience. Domain specific theory shares these elements. Cognition researchers like Elizabeth Spelke and Susan Carey have carried out extensive laboratory studies of responses by infants and young children to testing events. Those studies, together with brain scan evidence, suggest to them that innate, core systems of thinking and knowing begin during infancy, and continue to develop independently and non-consciously throughout the lifetime, with modest input from experience. Domain specific theory proposes that these abilities are innate, but in Spelke's view, their presence at birth can only be inferred (Spelke & Kinzler, 2009).

Supportive neuroimaging scans have found brain structures in young babies that seem to serve as organizers of specific core domains (areas) of knowledge: the motions and interactions of objects, number, and the geometry of relating oneself to space. These are seen as foundational for reasoning and learning (Carey, 2009). Other research suggests that language, intuitive biology, and understanding the minds of others are also core domains that begin to develop spontaneously and independently during the months of infancy.

The belief that concepts within those abstract core domains are learned more easily and rapidly than others has led to *constructivist* learning and teaching theory. It encourages children to build conceptual knowledge independently, through repeated information-seeking activities relevant to the core domains. Knowledge *construction*, rather than knowledge *reproduction*, is promoted (Eshach, 2006). The core "big ideas" underlying the activities in the constructivist program, *Preschool Pathways to Science* (Gelman, Brenneman, MacDonald, & Roman, 2010), are "change and transformation, form and function, and locomotion."

Domain General Cognition Theory reflects empirical philosophy which proposed that all knowledge starts with experience and evidence from the senses, rather than building on innate ideas alone. Piaget theorized that young children independently constructed knowledge from experience alone. But he also believed that thinking progressed through separate stages as new, general systems of thinking emerged. These systems of thinking applied broadly to all domains of knowledge: a domain general view.

Domain General Cognition Theory identifies cognitive strategies and mechanisms that even infants begin to use, like doing cause/effect thinking about their physical world and testing the effect of their actions on the actions of others (Gopnik, Meltzoff, & Kuhl, 1999). Domain general theory recognizes a more active role for adults in promoting children's cognitive development.

Researchers propose that very young children begin to use something like the scientific method: making inferences from cause/effect thinking, making predictions and testing them, and imagining alternatives (Gopnik, 2009). The teaching programs stemming from domain general theory are based on the skills and processes of science. Inquiry-based programs, such as the Lawrence Hall of Science Foss curriculum, exemplify the domain-general approach.

Situated Cognition Theory departs from domain specific and domain general theories of cognitive development. It states that all knowledge is part of the wider social and physical environment, which strongly shapes an individual's thinking, knowledge, attitudes, motives, and skills (Duschl, Sweingruber, & Shouse, 2007).

Stanley Greenspan, a researcher, pediatrician, and psychiatrist, studied the development of cognition in the context of individual differences stemming from physical, emotional, and social/cultural influences. Greenspan's perspective situated the origins of thinking and learning in the intimate emotional-social relationship between infants and primary caregivers, from birth onward, as part of the total developmental processes. He recognized that cognition is incapable of operating independently; rather, it is totally dependent on emotional motivation for development. He identified evolving positive social-emotional interactions that are essential foundations for the emergence of reasoning and language (Greenspan & Lewis, 1999), and he believed that unless they achieve healthy affective development, children are vulnerable to serious cognitive, communicative, and social delays.

Greenspan's strongest research collected data from parent questionnaires and clinical assessments of the emotional and cognitive functioning of 1,640 infants and young children drawn from a countrywide representative population. This method contrasts with the behavioral observation and neuroimaging research of far smaller numbers of babies and children whose parents voluntarily bring them to university laboratories for study by researchers (Greenspan & Shanker, 2004).

Thus far, Greenspan's research has found an association between children's affective development and the foundational cognitive abilities of pattern recognition, mutual attention with caregivers, and the capacity to read the intentions of others. Its focus on the vital link between positive adult-child emotional relationships and cognitive growth supports our integrated affective approach to teaching young children. Situated cognition–oriented teaching promotes acquainting young children broadly with the wonders of the natural and physical worlds, as we do in our integrated affective approach. Reggio Emilio education is an excellent example of this holistic viewpoint (Lewin-Benham, 2008).

All three cognitive development theories, and consequent teaching strategies, respect the amazing, rapid growth of thinking in the earliest years. Examining them helps us reflect on our expectations of young children and of ourselves in relation to them as learners.

YOUNG CHILDREN AS PERSONS

Earlier, we looked at the influence that children's feelings about themselves and their physical world have on their ability to think and learn. Learning, or failing to learn, is also strongly influenced by children's feelings about their place in the social world. The characteristic ways children feel about themselves and relate to others are central parts of their personalities. The classic work of Erik Erikson (1977) identified general developmental trends in personality growth that both contribute to and are enhanced by successful learning. These trends are significant affective components of cognitive development.

Sense of Initiative

If children's earliest experiences have promoted trust in others, and if children have then developed a good sense of autonomy, the next positive personality trend, a *sense of initiative,* unfolds. Three- and four-year-olds who are developing a sense of initiative have great energy to invest in activity. They want to know what they can do. They are eager for new experiences and new information about their world. Emerging reasoning powers blend with a developing imagination, leading the child to ask searching questions. Children's delightful curiosity during this phase is endlessly expressed as "Why?" A budding behavior control system allows children to slow their activity long enough to become immersed in events that capture their attention.

Preschoolers seek the acceptance of children who are like themselves in some way and who have mutual interests. This sociability means that preschool children rarely work alone at the science table, although sharing equipment and materials with others may still be somewhat difficult for them. In general, personality developments at this stage make it an ideal time to explore with children the regularities, relationships, and wonders of the world close at hand.

"He's looking at me!" Live observation connects children to other living things.

Sense of Industry

Young school-age children who have succeeded in developing a sense of initiative move toward the next positive personality trend, described by Erikson as the *sense of industry*. Eagerness to do meaningful tasks and to become good at them is evident. Children may persist in working at a task until it is completed, just for the sake of satisfaction in accomplishment. During this phase, mastering challenges enhances children's sense of competence. These children are able to work cooperatively with others because they have good inner control over their behavior. The desire to follow the classroom rules is especially visible in kindergartners. If all goes reasonably well in children's lives, this positive personality trend continues throughout the remaining early childhood years.

Respecting Personal Development Traits

Unfortunately, not every child comes to school having had the positive interactions with supportive environments needed to move smoothly through these personal growth stages. They need to find emotional security in our classrooms to enjoy learning.

The natural tendencies to learn where one belongs and what one can do in the social and physical worlds, to create and imagine, to seek answers, to become increasingly effective as an active doer and thinker, and to take pride in independent accomplishment and growing competence all support the interest and persistence needed to learn throughout life. These tendencies and abilities, however, can be misdirected and even diminished to the point of eventual failure in first grade when they are channeled too early into formal training in academic skills and fact memorization (Marcon, 2002). These tendencies are respected and nurtured when preschools and kindergartens allow children to choose whether or not to participate in science explorations.

THE TEACHERS

Who Can Teach Science?

Any teacher who is capable of maintaining a classroom atmosphere of warmth, acceptance, and nurturance meets the basic qualifications for guiding young children in discovery science. Children are more engaged in learning activities when teachers are emotionally warm and involved. In addition, a positive attitude toward science and the ability to carry out the catalyst, consultant, and facilitator roles are needed for good teaching. However, little can be taught when close rapport between child and teacher is missing. Children learn most from people with whom they feel the bond of personal interest and caring.

Attitude Contagion

Children's long-term attitudes toward science as subject matter begin with the attitudes of teachers whom children encounter in their earliest exposures to science.

A teacher's positive attitudes toward science may have a long history. For some teachers, these good feelings accumulated during their own satisfying exposures to science in elementary and secondary school situations. Other teachers may have retained strong science interests in spite of inadequate school experiences. They may have had an "answer person" in their lives: a parent, a grandparent, or perhaps a camp naturalist who had interesting information to share and the patience to help a child find answers. People with such fortunate backgrounds feel comfortable teaching science. They can teach with conviction and even a sparkle of fun. Teachers who have memories of positive emotional engagement with nature or with other science-linked experiences bring that personal significance with them into the classroom. Sharing their own sense of awe and wonder with children creates the positive contagion that spreads appreciation of nature and makes science meaningful in children's lives (Stolberg, 2008).

On the other hand, children's negative attitudes toward science may have been "caught" from unenthusiastic teachers who relied on textbooks as the only source of information. Those teachers may have been too unsure of themselves to allow children to consider alternatives to the textbook explanations or to discover science concepts through experimentation. Some female students lose interest in science when they encounter lingering, outdated gender bias in the classroom—"science is a boy thing." Still others are discouraged by science courses that emphasize memorizing facts rather than understanding the concepts that affect our daily lives.

Negative attitudes toward teaching science can be turned around by providing opportunities to observe and participate in hands-on science experiences with eager young children. Teachers' participation as knowledge seekers themselves in activity-based science workshops can restore lost confidence and revitalize faded interest. Classroom follow-up studies of teachers who have participated in activity-based science workshops reflect clear shifts toward more positive attitudes.

Authentic Interest

The teacher's authentic interest in finding out more about something is a vital part of the positive teaching attitude. This interest implies teachers' willingness to learn along with the children as co-learners when they lack answers. The ability to admit to not knowing everything is one of the traits of a good teacher.

The teacher's own interest in finding out sustains the children's ready curiosity. It can revive curiosity in children who have been belittled for asking questions, and it can rebuild curiosity that has atrophied in an unstimulating environment. When the teacher's own interest in an outcome is alive and active, curiosity behavior is modeled for the children. This important attitude has a fundamental place in the science-teaching framework, as indicated in Figure 2–1. If the teacher is indifferent about how things work, why should the children care?

In this text, we try to guide teachers in helping children construct powerful science understandings. By appealing to children's emotional and intellectual interest, by providing multidisciplinary approaches to concepts, and by modeling how teachers can spark and maintain children's engagement with science, we

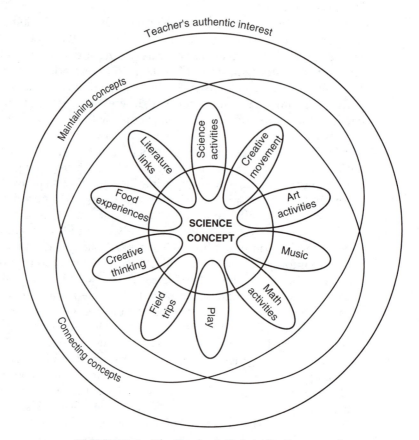

FIGURE 2–1   The Teacher's Role in the Framework

hope to encourage a community of learners. In this community, children and teachers work together to build understanding from their daily efforts.

Teaching Roles

Effective guidance of discovery science calls for four teaching roles:

1. The *facilitator* creates a learning environment in which each child has a chance to grow. Planning, gathering needed cast-off materials, and actually trying experiments are science facilitator tasks. In this role, there is a tolerance for messiness as children work, a willingness to risk new ventures, and an ability to profit from mistakes.

2. The *catalyst* turns on children's intellectual power by helping them become aware of themselves as thinkers and problem solvers. This role contrasts with the "teacher" image so many of us carry from our own school days, in which the teacher seemed to be the ultimate source of all knowledge. A teacher like this can dim children's intellectual power by somehow magnifying the distance between the teacher's knowledge and that of the child. Catalysts, on the other

hand, set a positive, encouraging tone by staying in touch with their own excitement in discovery and by making their own thinking and wondering visible to children (Dorl, 2007).

3. The *consultant/collaborator* observes carefully, listens closely, and answers questions simply while children engage in their explorations. In this role, small bits of information can be offered as learning cues, and questions can be asked of a child to help him or her focus on the relevant parts of a problem. The consultant allows each child time to reflect on the new idea and tackle the solution independently. This role often intimidates beginning teachers until they can accept themselves as learners, too. The consultant role is a supportive coaching role rather than a directive one.

4. The *model* deliberately demonstrates to children the important traits of successful learners, such as curiosity, appreciation, persistence, and creativity. Lillian Katz defined these characteristics as *dispositions:* habits of mind or tendencies to respond to situations in particular ways. She pointed out that although these qualities are essential, adults rarely identify and demonstrate these dispositions toward learning, yet these dispositions are best learned through example (Helm & Katz, 2001). We model these positive learning dispositions when we share our personal experiences and thought processes with children. We model persistence by describing our own efforts; for example: "At first I couldn't make it work, but I just kept on trying until it did work." We model creativity when we reveal a problem we solved in a new way; for example: "I needed a better way to let you see both sides of the moth. Then I had an idea that worked. I taped these two plastic lids together to make this neat display case for the moth."

The teacher as consultant observes carefully, listens closely, and answers questions simply.

Teachers who hold positive attitudes and understand their necessary roles are well rewarded by personal growth and by the pleasure of sharing the sense of mastery that children find through their science discoveries.

THE FAMILIES

All parents have information about the world that can be passed on to their children—to their mutual benefit. Daniella's grandmother contributed the cecropia cocoon that, months later, provided us an hour of breathless wonder as the moth struggled free in full view of 20 children. Four-year-old Maya was able to share solid information about many kinds of boats and their uses because she and her parents watched all the boats in the bay in front of their house. These family members enriched the learning of a whole class. They also intensified the interest of their own children in knowing the world because they endorsed the value of that knowledge.

The teaching role of family members is unique and vital. They, not classroom teachers, have the only continuous opportunity to guide a child's intellectual growth. The earliest imprinting of attitudes of appreciation or disregard for the natural or built world takes place within that primary relationship. This teaching by example occurs as part of the child's socialization, whether consciously or not.

The power of parents' supportive interest as motivation for children's immediate learning achievement is well documented. Bloom's (1985) classic study of the early development of successful, talented adults (including scientists) consistently revealed parental support for the child's special interests, as well as encouragement to persevere and pursue those interests wholeheartedly. Our own science teaching can help generate parental interest where it might be lacking. When children take home evidence of practical problem-solving ability or share science information that has meaning in the adult world, parents rarely fail to respond positively.

Since its inception, early childhood education has striven for a teaching partnership with families. The National Association for the Education of Young Children standards for for early childhood professionals emphasizes building family and community relationships (2009). The National Science Teachers Association position statement on parental involvement in science education (1994) gives priority to encouraging parents to help their children by seeing science everywhere, doing science activities together, and taking advantage of community resources of many kinds—efforts this textbook has been advocating since its first edition in 1976.

Unfortunately, many parents do not recognize that their own knowledge of how everyday things work can be shared with their ever-curious children. They may hesitate to point out simple wonders of nature for lack of the correct name for a bird or flower. Misunderstanding the importance of their own teaching role can deny them the easy pleasure of watching an impressive caterpillar with their child. Suggestions from teachers, such as the Family and Community Support ideas listed in each activity chapter in this text, can draw parents into contributing to classroom inquiries. They can support their children's interest in science by helping with the Exploring at Home projects for each of the major science topics presented in Part Two of this book. These projects are found in Appendix B.

The projects are intentionally presented in a lighthearted way to avoid inappropriate performance demands by parents that discourage rather than encourage their children's efforts. Each of these related activities may be duplicated by classroom teachers and sent home with the clear intent of offering family fun rather than required homework. To emphasize the special part the family plays in children's education, most of these activities are those that are best done at home at night, that directly relate to the home, or that are long-term and encompass beginning-to-end cycles that can have special value for families.

COMMUNITIES

Wonderful resources to enhance science education informally outside the classroom are flourishing in communities throughout the country. Grassroots initiatives, such as *Leave No Child Inside,* are bringing together nonprofit groups and regional agencies to promote nature activities for families to enjoy. Exciting partnerships have been developing between nature centers and early childhood programs to increase children's access to outdoor learning, and a few have evolved into nature-based preschools (Baillie, 2010). The American Community Gardens Association encourages the development of school gardens and estimates that 15,000 were flourishing across the country in 2010 (interview, August 11, 2010).

Interactive children's science museums, nature centers, zoos, aquariums, and planetariums offer informal science programs for children and families in pleasurable, noncompetitive settings. Those with professional educators on staff can plan class field trip programs with teachers to comply with their state's teaching standards. They recognize that simply bringing classes on site without appropriate goals and guidance misses a valuable learning opportunity (Tenenbaum, Rappolt-Schlichtman, & Zanger, 2004).

Youth groups, religious organizations, libraries, universities, and other municipal organizations are sponsoring recreational science activities to stimulate children's interest in science. These agencies are creating science linkages with schools through hands-on science as leisure activities, summer camps, family science festivals, traveling museum units, and outreach classes for teachers. Many programs are designed to reach underserved populations where families are less able to encourage their children's curiosity about the world. Through such projects, these youngsters can come to formal school science activities better prepared to enjoy and benefit from them.

Much of this growth has resulted from initiatives and partial funding by the National Science Foundation over the past four decades to improve the quality of science education and to raise the general level of science literacy in this country. Excellent television science programs such as *Nova* and *Dragonfly* are underwritten by collaborating funding sources.

The Internet has become a powerful resource for families seeking science information and activities for their children. We especially recommend using it for plant and animal identification ("We can look it up together!"). The Internet, especially

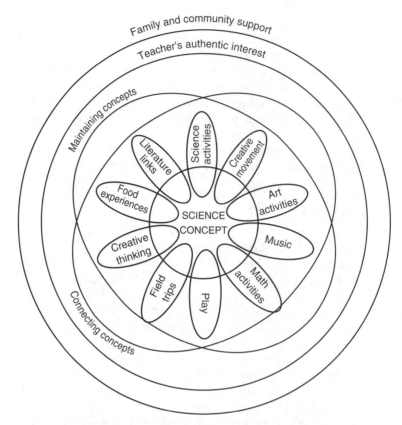

FIGURE 2–2   Family and Community Support Science Learning

when accessed with a personal digital assistant (PDA), can provide instant satisfaction to the curiosity of both children and adults.

We caution against taking science activities randomly off Web sites because many of them are trivial and have no lead-on power. They don't develop or connect to any lasting science knowledge. When teachers' e-mails to families include exciting new Web sites, the recommendations enhance home science activities. Families that follow the sources can offer useful feedback.

The influence of family and community support completes the science learning framework, as shown in Figure 2–2.

REFERENCES

BAILLIE, P. (2010). From the one-hour field-trip to a nature preschool: Partnering with environmental organizations. *Young Children, 65*(4), 76–82.

BLOOM, B. W. S. (ed.). (1985). *Developing talent in young people.* New York: Ballantine Books.

CAREY, S. (2009). *The origin of concepts.* New York: Oxford University Press.

DORL, J. (2007). Think aloud! Increase your teaching power. *Young Children, 62*(4), 101–105.

DUSCHL, R., SWEINGRUBER, H., & SHOUSE, A. (2007). *Taking science to school: Learning and teaching science in grades K-8* (p. 203). Washington, DC: National Academies Press.

ERIKSON, E. (1977). *Childhood and society.* New York: Norton.

ESHACH, H. (2006). *Science literacy in primary schools and pre-schools.* Dordrecht, the Netherlands: Springer.

GELMAN, R., BRENNEMAN, K., MACDONALD, G., & ROMAN, M. (2010). *Preschool pathways to science: Facilitating scientific ways of thinking, talking, doing, and understanding.* Baltimore: Brookes.

GOPNIK, A. (2009). *The philosophical baby: What children's minds tell us about truth, love, and the meaning of life.* New York: Farrar, Straus, & Giroux.

GOPNIK, A., MELTZOFF, A., & KUHL, P. (1999). *The scientist in the crib: What early learning tells us about the mind.* New York: Morrow.

GREENSPAN, S., & LEWIS, N. (1999). *Building healthy minds: The six experiences that create intelligence and emotional growth in babies and young children.* New York: Perseus.

GREENSPAN, S., & SHANKER, S. (2004). The developmental pathways leading to pattern recognition, joint attention, language, and cognition. *New Ideas in Psychology, 25*(2), 173–187.

HELM, J., & KATZ, L. (2001). *Young investigators: The project approach in the early years.* New York: Teacher's College Press.

KAIL, R. (2004). Cognitive development includes global and domain-specific processes. *Merrill-Palmer Quarterly, 50*(4), 445–455.

LAWRENCE HALL OF SCIENCE. *Foss Project.* University of California, Berkeley: Author. http://www.lawrencehallofscience.com

LEWIN-BENHAM, A. (2008). *Powerful children: Understanding how to think and learn using the Reggio approach.* New York: Teacher's College Press.

MARCON, R. (2002). Moving up the grades: Relationship between preschool model and later school success. *Early Childhood Research and Practice.* Retrieved March 12, 2006, from http://ecrp.uiuc.edu/v4n1/marcon.html

NATIONAL ASSOCIATION FOR THE EDUCATION OF YOUNG CHILDREN. (2009). *2009 Standards for Early Childhood Prefessional Preparation Programs. Standard 2.* Washington, DC: Author.

NATIONAL SCIENCE TEACHERS ASSOCIATION. (1994, August). *NSTA position statement: Parent involvement in science education.* Washington, DC: Author.

SPELKE, E., & KINZLER, K. (2009). Innateness, learning and rationality. *Child Development Pespectives, 3*(2), 96–98.

STOLBERG, T. (2008). Whither the sense of wonder of pre-service primary teachers when teaching science?: A preliminary study of their personal experiences. *Teaching and Teacher Education, 24*(8), 1958–1964.

TENENBAUM, H., RAPPOLT-SCHLICHTMAN, G., & ZANGER, V. (2004). Children's learning about water in a museum and in the classroom. *Early Childhood Research Quarterly, 19*(1), 1–20.

3

Guiding Science Learning and Assessments in the Early Years

GUIDED SCIENCE

Minstrel Tom Hunter was wondering aloud with first and second graders about clouds. He had learned that asking about action leads to fruitful thinking, so he asked, "What do clouds do?" A flurry of answers emerged: They make rain, they move fast, they move slow, they cover the sun, they disappear. One child seemed distant from the conversation but finally put up her hand. "I know what clouds do—they pretend." "Really?" "Yes, they pretend to be an old man. Or a horse, or a castle, or a tree."

This story illustrates the joy and difficulty of guiding young children to develop core scientific concepts. Children observe, listen, reflect, and then invent their own understandings of the world in "personally and culturally familiar ways" (NAEYC, 2009, p. 16). Some of these understandings are what we can call *science*, and others are poetry, ethics, or fantasy, for example. As teachers, one of our goals is to give children access to the widely shared understandings of the natural world that constitute science, and another is to help them experience the processes that create those understandings: observation, experimentation, careful recording of information, and willingness to think creatively.

In this text, we guide teachers in helping children meet national and state standards for science education in content, disposition, and processes. We focus on "the big ideas, methods of investigation and expression" of science (NAEYC, 2009, p. 16). The experiences offered here will encourage children to enjoy science as a school subject and to think of themselves as competent in science. The processes used in these experiences, as summarized by the National Association for the Education of Young Children (NAEYC), are as follows.

Raise questions about objects and events around them.
Explore materials, objects, and events by acting upon them and noticing what happens.

Make careful observations of objects, organisms, and events, using all their senses.

Describe, compare, sort, classify, and order in terms of observable characteristics and properties.

Use a variety of simple tools to extend their observations (e.g., hand lens, measuring tools, eye droppers).

Engage in simple investigations, including making predictions, gathering and interpreting data, recognizing simple patterns, and drawing conclusions.

Record observations, explanations, and ideas through multiple forms of representation.

Work collaboratively with others, share and discuss ideas, and listen to new perspectives. (NAEYC, 2001, p. 24)

These skills have widespread use in the preschool and primary years; competence in them provides a strong basis for ongoing academic success in science as well as other disciplines. It is regrettable, therefore, that science is typically neglected in early childhood classrooms. The national emphasis on reading and mathematics scores is a major cause of the relegation of science education to the sidelines. Yet science education can help children in learning both math and reading, so we urge teachers, both new and experienced, to reflect on the powerful reasons to include guided science in their curriculum.

Reasons for Guided Discovery Science

One of the best means of helping children know the world at hand is to organize materials so that children can explore, question, reason, and discover answers through their own physical and mental activity. This guided discovery approach to science learning emphasizes *how* to find answers, as well as *what* can be learned. When discovery science experiences are seen as part of the child's continuous search for knowledge, it makes good sense to support and enable that search in the classroom in these basic ways:

- Discovery science values and rewards curiosity as a valid learning tool.
- Discovery science encourages individuality and creativity in children's problem solving. This leads to better retention of the concepts attained.
- Discovery science validates the fundamental learning style of direct involvement with materials. It builds on spontaneous experiencing, touching, and trying by the very young. Active participation remains so important to knowing throughout life that our language uses the term *firsthand* to mean something that is known from the original source.
- Discovery science experiences in early schooling help to gradually replace the young child's intuitive explanations of the unknown. Such experiences demystify bewildering events but respectfully retain the profound and beautiful aspects of natural occurrences.
- Discovery science provides a means of focusing the attention of the restless child, the anxious child who is preoccupied with personal concerns, and

the bored child who is understimulated by less challenging aspects of the curriculum.

- Discovery science has appeal for resistant learners who have come to protect themselves from inappropriate pressure to perform formal learning tasks. The playlike quality of exploring real materials reduces the stress that more precise paperwork tasks produce. Discovery science allows more physical and social involvement than do the more structured forms of schoolwork. Pressured children can put aside their resistance and restore their sense of themselves as learners when they engage in science activities.
- Discovery science, by its very nature, provides an intriguing path to the goal of developing children's intellectual potential. Any form of learning that includes the manipulation of interesting materials is highly motivating to children. The discovery science activities and cross-curricular extensions in this book lend themselves to programs in which language learning and content are integrated, such as the language experience approach and the project approach to curriculum development. The sensory and psychomotor extensions work well for English language learners (ELLs), as they help clarify and extend the language component of learning.
- Guided discovery investigations are foundation-building experiences, shaped toward particular learning outcomes. Both factual and conceptual knowledge are needed to support learning with understanding.
- Guided discovery science recognizes and builds on the central importance of emotional engagement to thinking, doing, and understanding.

GUIDING LEARNERS

Teaching Styles

During a half century of constructivism theory and practice, some attentive teachers learned to "scaffold" children's thinking with their own insights, while other, more behavioristic teachers continued to consider children to be empty vessels needing to be filled with teachers' ideas. We try to recognize the value of both positions, depending on who and what is to be taught. For example, four- and five-year-olds can and do directly observe evaporation as rainy streets become dry. A teacher can supply the term *evaporation* and direct children to further examples, experimentation, and record keeping. Other natural phenomena, such as those described in Part Two of this book, may not be readily observed by children. Then it is essential for teachers to bring them into children's awareness.

A teacher who can empathize with a child's efforts and share a child's feelings of excitement and satisfaction in solving problems is better able to guide and encourage children's intellectual development. Children learn by imitating and interacting with others, as well as through their own exploration and problem solving. The teacher serves as the social facilitator of children's problem-solving abilities.

Guided discovery learning calls for this social facilitation as direct and indirect guidance. The teacher supplements the child's active exploration of problems by helping the child draw meaning from the experience and by extending conceptual learning. The crucial affective element here is the teacher's belief in the importance of this effort. Without commitment to a central purpose for teaching science, our lesson plans fail to inspire children and our hands-on activities lose vitality. When we are committed to the spirit of sharing with children the powerful constants that make their world more predictable, science comes alive in the classroom. When our focus shifts from teaching *facts* to teaching *children,* the process of helping to uncover enlightening knowledge remains fresh and dynamic.

If you would like to see guided discovery learning in action, we recommend viewing the video *All Sorts of Leaves,* which shows a first-grade teacher guiding her children through inquiry into properties of leaves. Search using the title at http://www.learner.org/about/aboutus.html. A companion video shows teachers discussing the video.

Organizing Approaches

There are two distinctive approaches to organizing socially facilitated science activities: child-instigated experiences (the incidental approach) and teacher-instigated experiences. The child-instigated approach is ideal for very small classes of preschool children, for nurturing the individual interests of gifted older children, and for creating an atmosphere of inquiry in the classroom.

Incidental science can occur at any time or place, whenever a child's curiosity is aroused by something significant: a sparkling bit of quartz embedded in the sidewalk, the iridescent sheen of a beetle's back, or an evaporating playground puddle. The teacher capitalizes on the child's discovery by asking questions that lead to further discovery, by relating the find to something the child already knows, by extending the experience to other classroom activities, and by offering to help the child locate other resources for expanding his or her information. We urge teachers of young children to make time for these spontaneous investigations. They add freshness to the classroom and create a partnership in the knowledge business between the children and the teacher. Learning something when you want to learn it—on a need-to-know basis—is both memorable and emotionally satisfying.

The teacher-instigated approach, however, is more practical in this era of standards, both state and national. Although the 1996 National Science Education Standards (NSES) continue to offer a useful and comprehensive array of concepts, skills, and dispositions to the states and districts, revisions are currently underway, led by two groups. State governors and chief state school officers are crafting "Common Core State Standards" to cover all K-12 mathematics and English language arts curricula; this is the underpinning of the long-avoided national curriculum. Most states have signed on. The National Research Council of the National Academies of Science continues its decades of science education leadership with a "Conceptual Framework for Science Education" that incorporates technology and engineering education as well. Both efforts are in process as we write. The teacher-instigated approach of this text serves teachers' need to help children meet these evolving state and national standards.

Inquiry. The inquiry approach provides children with a rich experience of "doing science": having questions, thinking about how to answer them, applying observational and experimental investigations, and drawing conclusions. Our basic discovery approach to exploring everyday events and interests of young children describes activities in detail to provide beginning teachers with a usable, tested model. Specific inquiry experiences in each activity chapter, denoted with a **?**, are less prescriptive, allowing teachers and children to investigate further with greater openness. Children can gain confidence in their own thinking through such experiences, which is vital in the increasingly complex, information-laden society in which they are growing up.

Inquiry can be used as the major approach to science teaching integrated across the curriculum, as described by Lewin-Benham (2008) and Chaille (2008) in discussing their Reggio-inspired school experiences. Lewin-Benham observed that while the Reggio teachers seemed effortless in their teaching, it is based on years of ongoing intense study and collaboration. Typically, American teachers do not have the opportunity for such ongoing and extensive collaboration.

American teachers are told by the science education establishment to teach using *the* inquiry method. Our reading of the literature shows that there are many kinds of inquiry teaching (Duschl, Schweingruber, & Shouse, 2006). We believe that the term *inquiry* contains diverse possibilities for young children, such as "messing about," gathering data, setting up experiments, or seeking causes. Furthermore, in keeping with our affective approach to science education, we note that the emotional crucible of inquiry is curiosity. Teachers successfully encourage inquiry science by responding sensitively to children's curiosity.

The Outdoors as Context for Learning. For children as well as adults, lasting learning takes place through many encounters with the same ideas in a variety of contexts. A particularly important context is the outdoors, especially because today's children are indoors so much of the time. For this reason, every activity chapter (Chapters 4–16) has outdoor activities noted with the clover ♣ symbol. In addition, each chapter contains suggestions for improving the school grounds in ways that support the concepts of the chapter. All such suggestions are more easily made than implemented, but in working with others, including parents, all are possible and increasingly seen at schools (Mullin, 2010).

Science learnings can be referred to and renewed throughout the school year when they relate to other learnings and classroom occurrences. Material reviewed and built onto over a period of time can be retained remarkably longer than isolated fragments of material that have been presented only once. Science knowledge further takes hold when it has utility and when it becomes part of a continuous chain of learning that develops throughout life.

Preparation for Teaching Science to Young Children

There is no question among educators and researchers about the superiority of active discovery over the textbook and lecture method of learning science. Yet it appears that most kindergarten and primary grade teachers continue to use the less effective methods. Reasons include teachers feeling undereducated in science, the pressure of math and reading tests, and the fact that it is easier to read aloud a book about plants than to provide soil, seeds, space, and time for actually growing plants. Teachers should know about current research, however, showing that the *combination* of reading and activity is powerful (Brenneman, 2009; Patrick, Mantzicopoulos, & Amarapungayan, 2009).

Most of us have much more practical science information than we may recognize. We can fill in knowledge gaps as we prepare to teach. A beginning teacher can supplement basic knowledge by carefully reading the *concepts* and *activity directions* in this book. We strongly suggest trying out the experiments and recording the results, problems, and personal reactions to the experience before presenting them to children. This will increase one's confidence and also reveal any technical difficulties. Reading some of the reference books written at the young child's level of understanding will add appropriately to one's knowledge base. Reference books suggested for teachers will provide depth of information to enlarge the teacher's developing interests and to provide answers prompted by a child's urgent curiosity. In addition, we have found Wikipedia and other Internet resources valuable, especially because they are so accessible. Our most useful sites are listed at the end of each chapter.

The recommended literature links include children's reference books and stories that connect real-world experiences of children to science topics. We have selected authors who know both the science concepts and the young learner's capacity to absorb core ideas, often with humor and excitement. Other resources were chosen primarily to supplement material in this book with additional activities that children can accomplish easily. Some, such as basal reader–style books, were included as sources of hard-to-find illustrations of science principles at work and because the controlled vocabulary can be particularly useful for ELLs. Others provide additional challenges for children who are fascinated by a particular topic. The most recent books at our publication time predominate for availability reasons, but good out-of-print books may still show up in secondhand bookstores and yard sales. Buy them!

Renewing and strengthening our science information, using some of the suggested teacher references, just before we teach a unit helps us to be well prepared, confident, and enthusiastic when implementing the science activities. Then the satisfaction gained in becoming reacquainted with the concepts will be fresh and available to spark the interests of children.

Indirect and Direct Teaching

Discovery learning is guided *indirectly* through thoughtful questioning and listening and by sensitive discussion leading. It is guided *directly* by offering conceptual cues and by encouraging effort and suggesting more effective strategies when things aren't working out. Because many of us were not exposed to these kinds of guidelines in our own schooling, it will be helpful to analyze these techniques.

Thoughtful listening to children's ideas is an indirect way to guide and sustain their interest in discovery learning. We do this when we avoid passing judgment on a child's erroneous ideas or private logic that differs from a scientific explanation. A belief developed from everyday experiences can be difficult to give up if the theory seems to be working well enough. When there are gaps in the information they can assemble, children typically fill in those gaps imaginatively to form their personal theories, as did Matthew, whom we met in Chapter 1. Conflicting information can even be adapted a bit to fit into the private theory (Gardner, 2004, p. 56).

What's more, there is research evidence that hands-on learning alone may not be enough to shift children away from their naive beliefs. Unless they have opportunities in many contexts to challenge their comfortable misconceptions and feel a sense of disequilibrium, children tend to interpret new experiences in terms of their old convictions. They tend to reject conflicting explanations (Donovan & Bransford, 2005, p. 425).

This process is not unique to children, however. As revealed in a fascinating series of videotapes, *Minds of Our Own* (Schneps, c. 1997), adolescent and adult thinking is both idiosyncratic and limited regarding everyday phenomena such as seasons, electrical currents, and mirrors. (These videos can be viewed at http://www.learner.org.) Teachers of young children thus tend to have a double task: clarify their own understanding of science concepts and help children achieve better understanding. As we struggle with our own misconceptions, it is important to remember that children gain confidence when we respect their naive attempts to figure things out instead of devaluing them as amusing or quaint, or as serious misconceptions that must be eradicated immediately. Intuitive theories can be gradually clarified and reorganized when discovery experiences reveal the more systematic and complete way of looking at things that we call *science.*

We indirectly guide children's thinking when we show them our own reasoning processes by "thinking out loud." That can occur when we say something like this: "When I found this tiny leaf on the sidewalk, I thought to myself, 'This isn't like any other tiny leaf I've seen before—hmmm. But it has five points, like a star. A big sweet gum tree leaf has that shape, too. I wonder if a new sweet gum leaf starts out as tiny as this?' So, what do you think I did to find out for sure?" Modeling and labeling thought, we offer children conscious knowledge of nonconscious thinking processes.

Learning to Question

Just as the quality of scientific research depends on asking worthwhile questions, the quality of discovery science learning is indirectly guided by helpful questioning. Open-ended questions are useful for generating several appropriate answers (divergence). *Divergent questions* can serve many purposes.

- *Instigating discovery:* A science activity becomes a discovery challenge when it is initiated as a question to answer. Most activities suggested in the following chapters are headed in bold type by the question the activity can answer. These questions can be used both to introduce the activity and to elicit children's conclusions about their activity. The questions can be printed on index cards and posted in the science area to help reading children stay focused in their work.

- *Eliciting predictions:* Before children experiment, elicit their predictions: "What do you think will happen if . . .?" Record the responses of preschool and kindergarten children. Older children can write their own predictions and then record their results.
- *Probing for understanding:* "Why do you think that side of the balance went down?"
- *Promoting reasoning:* "Why do you think this arm feels dry and this arm feels wet?"
- *Serving as a catalyst:* Sometimes a question can be a catalyst that sparks renewed interest in a problem, whereas a specific direction from the teacher could make finding out unnecessary. "What could you change to try to make your lever work?" encourages new effort. "If you move the block closer to Robert, you'll be able to lift him with your lever" discourages independent effort.
- *Encouraging creative thinking and reflection:* "What does this remind you of?" "What else works this way?"
- *Reflecting on feelings:* In a group discussion, ask questions such as "What was the best part of the dark box experiment?"

There is ample research demonstrating that teachers tend to overuse *convergent questions,* that is, those with a single correct answer. Convergent questions are less effective in stimulating creative thinking or synthesizing; however, it is useful and suitable to ask certain convergent questions to promote learning. Convergent questions are beneficial for:

- *Directing attention:* By asking a question like "Does the red cup hold as much water as the blue cup?" we can direct a child's attention to a key part of the activity she has overlooked. The child can then correct her own course of action without feeling criticized.
- *Recalling the temporal order:* "What did you do first? What did you do next?" "When did this happen? What happened afterward?"
- *Recalling prior conditions:* "Does the jar of beans look just the same today as it did yesterday?"

Follow-up questions to convergent questions can be divergent. They can lead to further reflection or to fresh investigation: "How can you find out?"

It is helpful for beginning questioners to role-play with other beginners to improve and feel at ease with new techniques. To overcome habitual closed questioning, it can take concerted effort to change the way we shape our questions. Many of us use the pattern of stating in the form of a question the answers we wish to hear from children. We may say, "So, the cup of snow melted into a smaller amount of water, right? Isn't that what you found?" This style of questioning reduces children's need to discover answers for themselves or tells them that the main discovery is to find out what the teacher wants them to say.

Leading Discussions

Discussions serve different purposes at different points in learning new concepts.

- *Introductory discussions* whet interest in a new topic when children are encouraged to recall events they have encountered personally and to contribute what they already know about the subject. At this time, children's private theories are noted without any challenge to evident flaws. Children are encouraged to raise their own questions about what they would like to find out in the activities.
- *Small-group discussions* follow children's individual activity to process what took place in their investigations and to help clarify their thinking. These discussions can reveal that more than one conclusion can be reached from an activity. They can lead to shifts in naive theories.
- *Summary discussions* with the whole class pull together the concepts that have been explored in the activities and extensions. They help children get comfortable with new concepts and consolidate associated information. Each of the following chapters offers suggestions appropriate to summary discussions under the heading "Connecting Concepts."

Group discussions are the time to introduce new, accurate vocabulary to children. Knowing science words is both satisfying and enriching. When the teacher reflects on what are the most useful new words in a unit and uses them often and in context, children absorb them easily. ELLs acquire new, interesting words along with the native speakers. None of the four-year-olds knew *evaporation* before the water unit but afterward, everyone could use the term; the cause of educational equity was served.

Group discussions also allow children to learn from one another if the teacher models respect for the ideas and experiences that children express. To encourage interactive responses among children, quiet children may have to be drawn out in low-risk ways. Recognize a nod of agreement or a responsive smile from such a child as involvement: "It looks as if Carrie agrees with your idea." If some children have trouble staying involved in large-group discussions, this concrete illustration can be helpful.

> Ask two children to each get a crayon and then exchange the crayons with each other. Have them verify that each had one crayon *before* sharing with the other, and each still has only one crayon *after* sharing with the other. Next, ask each child to share an idea with the other on a topic such as the day's weather. After each has shared an idea, point out that now each child has two ideas about the day's weather. Add "We grow in ideas when we share and listen to each other."

It is important not to close off the exchange of ideas as soon as a child offers key information. Keep the discussion open until each willing child has had a chance to be heard, even if the ideas begin to echo one another.

Adults often overlook the fact that it takes a little time for children to produce thoughtful answers to questions. Many people feel that they are unsuccessful at teaching if their questions are not answered immediately. The results of Mary Budd Rowe's (1996) seminal research indicate that just the opposite is true.

Teachers who waited 3 seconds or more for answers received longer answers, answers that built on other children's comments, and often from typically silent children. Younger children as well as ELLs may need even longer "wait time" to formulate and express ideas.

A good discussion puts the teacher in the catalyst role by empowering children to think and express their ideas. This seems to be a difficult shift for some teachers to make, especially if they are accustomed to having their own voices dominate the classroom. With practice, it becomes easier to support and elicit children's comments by using bridging remarks such as "That was an interesting idea, and others may have different thoughts about it."

The catalyst teacher underscores what children accurately contribute, adds bits of information to expand those ideas, and clarifies misconceptions that might still linger. The teacher summarizes the various points children make in the discussion. If the contributed ideas do not include certain salient points, the teacher can add, "Scientists also tell us . . ." Group discussions are most successful when they are guided with the goal of stimulating children's thinking and reasoning powers.

Organizing Time and Space for Science

The logistics of making exploration time available to small work groups will vary for each classroom. Problems of managing science activities can be eased with the help of an assistant in the room. It is best to delegate overseeing ongoing activities to the assistant. If a child has a full-time special needs assistant, that person can often help with small-group work. In some instances, simple directions printed on index cards or a computer screen allow children to handle science projects fairly independently.

A good location for science activities facilitates thinking by inviting children to participate and by controlling distractions. Proximity to storage and cleanup aids is important. Varying the setting for activities can build interest. Anticipation is heightened on days when light experiments take place under a blanket-covered table! An easy way to keep science pertinent to ongoing activities is to display indestructible materials being used in the discovery activities.

Computers capable of accessing the Internet and displaying large graphics are an increasingly rich resource for extending science teaching. Without question, there is no substitute for a live gerbil in an aquarium for learning about its size, shape, smell, habits, bright eyes, and sharp teeth. But it is also valuable to see images of the distant deserts where gerbils are native and wild. If, because of limited resources, one has to choose between the real and the image, clearly the multisensory real has more power than the merely visual image.

Preschoolers can use drawing programs to represent their ideas; when teachers help with the written language, digital stories are created. ELL children can especially benefit from this kind of expressiveness; the child's home language can be used as well, a powerful tool for connecting to families (Blagojevic, Chevalier, MacIsaac, Hitchcock, & Frechette, 2010). Second and third graders can learn to record and chart data using computer programs. Beginning and more advanced writers can use the simpler word processing programs. But the ready-made icons

Emma captures the essence of the iris with her own eye and hand.

that computers provide abundantly should be avoided. Not only are they stereotypical but, more seriously, they discourage children's own efforts to create informative drawings. Children can produce text on the computer and hand-illustrate their own observations of the phenomenon. The Reggio Emilio centers have demonstrated how well children can draw from life if systematically encouraged.

The role of information and communication technology (ICT) in early childhood classrooms is complex. Used as assistive technology for children with some disabilities, used as language encourager for ELLs and other children, and used to expand horizons, ICTs have much to contribute. Children are experiencing technology through digital cameras, cell phones, games, and remote controls, as well as computers and television. They are truly "digital natives" (Lloyd, 2010). However, with the statistics on the rising rates of obesity and other health issues, the value of additional "screen time" for young children has been powerfully challenged (see Alliance for Childhood, 2004; American Academy of Pediatrics, 2006; and White House Task Force on Childhood Obesity, 2010). It may be that children are lacking experience with simpler technologies, such as juice-can telephones and stick houses, the making of which would illuminate science and technology concepts as importantly as ICT.

Introducing Science Activities

There are many creative ways to focus children's attention on a new science activity. A physical science activity might be presented as a child-size problem that needs to be solved. "A box of paper clips spilled at the sand table and got mixed into the sand. Perhaps some of you can find a way to get them out." A spur-of-the-moment thinking game could build interest: "There's something that we see in our room every day that we will use in science today. It has a handle on the outside and rollers on the inside." One relaxed teacher intrigues his students as he patiently searches through his pockets for the "something I thought you would like to know about." Opening a brown bag to reveal an unexplained object of science interest can provide enticement to find out more. With attention focused, then ask the question, "What do you know about this?"

A topic can be introduced by reading a related story or poem and then following it with an open-ended question to be answered by the discovery activity. A simple description of an occurrence could start the explorations. "Today, when I stood on my porch, a heavy, noisy repair truck rumbled by and I felt the porch shake. Have you ever felt shaking near something noisy? Today you can find out more about shaking and sounds happening together." Although it is not advisable to oversell science as fun and games, placing activities in the context of the child's world sparks interest and adds importance to "doing" science.

Guiding Explorations

Hands-on for children should imply, as much as possible, *hands-off* for teachers. There will be occasions when a tactful offer to steady a screwdriver or to knot a parachute string can help a discouraged child achieve success, but unsolicited help should not be given in the interest of saving time. We need to listen carefully to how children are describing and interpreting their explorations. It is the conversation with children that occurs during and after a hands-on activity that makes a difference in their thinking.

The consultant role is a delicate one: quietly offering a reasoning cue to highlight the important part of an experiment or asking a question and allowing the child time to reflect on the answer. (Reasoning cues can be taken from the concept statement headings for activities in this book: "You pushed *down* to lift him *up* with the lever.") Wise consultants resist the temptation to hurry a child along to discover what they, the consultants, already know. They are careful not to smother a child's tender spark of inquiry with a heavy blanket of directions and facts. Experiential learning is weakened when a child is rushed to a premature conclusion or "helped" out of arriving at the child's own solution.

NURTURING LEARNERS

In the decades since self-esteem came to be recognized as a crucial element in what we are able to accomplish in life, a corollary effort spread through classrooms: "building" self-esteem by making it easy for children to win praise. This was expected to motivate learning achievement. Children would stay on task, perform well, feel smart, and enjoy learning. However, pouring on praise didn't necessarily have those outcomes.

Instead, researchers found that automatic, excessive praise for intelligence and correct performance could weaken children's intrinsic learning motivation. It distracted them from focusing on the activity that prompted the praise. They lost interest in the activity for its own sake and kept working only as long as the teacher did the motivating for them by giving approval. The motivation shifted toward getting more praise rather than getting the satisfaction from learning that actually strengthens self-worth.

Carol Dweck's studies (2006) uncovered another significant aspect of learning motivation, one that applies to adults as well as children. It is whether an individual believes that intelligence is a permanent, unchanging quality, or that intelligence is a *potential* that can develop and grow. A child who believes in fixed intelligence, and who is praised for intelligence and good performance, associates being smart with being worthy. A lot is at stake if this child's performance slips and some part of learning doesn't come easily. Doubts about being smart and worthy creep in. It

Table 3–1   Limiting Praise Versus Encouraging Feedback

Situation	Limiting Praise	Encouraging Feedback
Amelia checks her seed-sprouting jar. She exclaims, "My sprouts have leaves!"	"Aren't you smart?"	"It's exciting to see that happen."
Jake beams with joy when he gets two loads balanced on the scale.	"Good job!"	"It feels great to finally get both sides even!"
Nina reports doing yesterday's light-bending experience a new way at home. It worked!	"Superscientist!"	"You kept exploring and figured out something new!"

seems safer, then, to avoid a challenging activity, because in this view, "only people who aren't smart have to work hard to learn." The challenging problems aren't seen as opportunities to learn more, and the child's performance suffers.

In contrast, the child who believes intelligence can grow, and who is helped to work more effectively, is likely to tackle challenges and grow smarter. When these children's efforts are encouraged after a setback, they are helped to focus on the process of their work. They stay with the activity because they are trying to understand something new and become more competent. *They are empowered to learn.* Watch some of the numerous YouTube videos illuminating Dweck's "growth mindset" research.

Alfie Kohn (2006) helps us resist the chorus of excessive praise. He points out that even though praise is positive, it *is* a judgment. It isn't necessary to constantly judge children in order to encourage them. Instead, he suggests joining with them to celebrate their accomplishments by giving nonjudgmental feedback on what they are doing (p. 155).

Differences between encouraging feedback and limiting praise are illustrated in Table 3–1.

When children invest their attention deeply in an activity and achieve a meaningful result, or when they go beyond what is expected of them and uncover something new, they grow. They feel the joy of meeting a challenge. This rewarding feeling of increased personal competence is the genuine source of intrinsic learning motivation.

Dispelling Stereotypes

Gender and minority stereotypes about intellectual capabilities perpetuate self-doubt and create needless limitations to the development of this nation's problem solvers. Teachers' actions and beliefs contribute heavily to the self-attitudes being formed by their students. In two kindergarten classrooms where children experienced 5 or 10 weeks of sustained, conceptually coherent science study, both boys and girls said that they liked science and felt competent to do science more frequently than children in classrooms where science was not a focus (typical of American schools). In the latter classrooms, boys liked science more (Patrick et al., 2009). At the beginning of the year, children reflected the overall culture, in which many more men than women are scientists, but by the end of the year, the teachers' work engaging all children in science achieved equity. Girls and boys achieve about equally in both science and math through the fourth grade (NAEP, 1996–2009). Teachers seem to be the key for equal achievement by boys and girls—70% of minority and female chemists and chemical engineers surveyed in 2010 said that K-8 teachers were the most important persons for encouraging science (Bayerus, 2010).

Although we may voice our desire to help each child develop her or his intellectual potential, our actions may belie our words. Our actions are based on our values, some of which we hold unconsciously. We may be acting on buried, leftover prejudices about the thinking capacities and "natural" interests of women and minorities that were passed on to us as schoolchildren. Many people in our society seem to believe that scientists are older white males, although this is increasingly less true. To encourage all children to think of themselves as connected to science, we can take several actions when we teach (National Science Teachers Association, 2000, 2003, 2004; Sparks & Edwards, 2010):

- We give girls and minority children as much verbal and social encouragement as Caucasian boys to answer science questions, contribute to science discussions, and persist at experimenting.
- We offer activities that appeal to all children.
- We give the first chance to try new activities to all children equally.
- We are aware that science professionals who visit our classes, or whose pictures are posted on our bulletin boards, need to include females and non-Caucasians as well as Caucasian males.

When we communicate in these ways our belief that each child can participate effectively in some form of science experiences, we are making a valid effort to combat crippling stereotypes.

Adapting Experiences for Younger Children

Although the activities in this text's framework were planned for children four through eight years of age, many of the experiences can be adapted for younger preschool children. Two-year-olds can enjoy simple sensory explorations such as feeling air as they move it with paper fans, spinning pinwheels, or swinging streamers on a breezy day; feeling rock textures and weights; touching ice, then touching the water it melts into; watching, then moving like a goldfish; tasting raw fruits and vegetables that have grown from plants; listening to loud and soft sounds; or gazing through transparent color paddles to see surroundings in a new light.

Three-year-olds might be expected to engage in similar activities, taking in greater detail. They will be able to direct deeper attention to activities such as exploring new dimensions with a magnifying glass. This group can enjoy some of the classifying experiences on a beginning level: sorting rocks from objects that are not rocks; things that float from those that do not float; and objects that are attracted by a magnet from objects that are not attracted.

Adapting Experiences for Children with Special Needs

Science is an approach to thinking and behaving that has value for children at any level of motor, behavioral, sensory, communication, or mental functioning. Because discovery science calls for collaboration among children, it fosters the personal interactions that children with special needs often miss. It can help classmates recognize the child with limitations as an individual with ideas and talents to contribute. Nobody laughed at Lori once her worm-scouting skills came to light. Her problems with pencils and numbers and letters didn't interfere with her passion for capturing insects. Her generosity in sharing them improved her social relationships. Scott's "slow" right leg and droopy right arm didn't limit his deep involvement in science. Frequently left behind on the playground, Scott was in his social and intellectual element at the science table. With good-humored inventiveness, Scott found his own way to water our plants. He soaked a clean sponge in the pitcher of water that was too heavy for him to manage. Then he squeezed the sponge for each plant, giving them a simultaneous drink and sponge bath!

Adapting materials to make them more manageable can enable success for a child with special needs. A plastic basting syringe is easier to use than a small medicine dropper for a child who finds it difficult to grasp objects. Bamboo toast tongs may help children with fine motor control problems to pick up small objects. Assistive technologies may be appropriate (Bouck & Okolo, 2007).

Changes in approach are important for children with vision and hearing impairments. Advance information about what is going to take place helps the child who has a vision impairment deal with new experiences comfortably. Face-to-face communication is necessary with the child who has a hearing impairment. Because a hearing loss is invisible to others, it is easy to forget that communications are cut off when that child's back is turned.

A child who uses a wheelchair will need to have materials brought into close range. A highlight event might be connecting a child with attention to invest and a grasshopper with a new cage to explore. If obstacles to full participation are too great for a child, assign a record-keeping job or lab assistant role, such as keeping track of materials that might be misplaced.

Potentially disruptive children are often judged by teachers to be risks in science activities, but researchers in Anchorage, Alaska, disproved this when they offered carefully planned hands-on science to a class of children with a variety of significant behavioral problems. Videotape analysis showed that these children remained focused on their science activities 90% of the time. They also expressed positive feelings about learning science. These same children were on task only 25% of the time in a less inviting classroom where other subject matter was presented with heavy emphasis on behavior control (Welton, Smith, Owens, & Adrian, 2000).

An easily distracted child benefits from a simplified, clear arrangement of materials to focus on. Tangible boundaries, such as individual trays of equipment, can help the child with poor control feel assured of a fair share of things with which to work. The teacher's close presence can help ensure an island of calm around these children to help them pursue their work. Tiny pebbles or seeds that could be inserted into ears or nostrils should not be available without supervision to children who lack safety awareness. Time given to planning for successful activities minimizes the time and attention such vulnerable children demand when frustrating tasks lead to disruptive behavior.

Make use of available professional consultants for specific ways to maximize the potential of a child who has a handicapping condition. Until such help arrives, put yourself imaginatively in the child's situation to think of ways to work around the child's limitations and through the child's strengths. Whatever accommodations you make to provide satisfying science experiences can help children with special needs grow in ability to cope with the challenges that they face. Information about science activities designed for youngsters with visual impairment or a physical disability is available from the Center for Multisensory Learning, Lawrence Hall of Science, University of California, Berkeley, California, 94720. NSTA's position statement, *Students with Disabilities* (2004), provides additional ideas.

Children who face difficulties in mastering developmental tasks deserve every chance to develop confidence and initiative that teachers can provide through science activities (Prestwich, Sumrall, & Chassin, 2010). A young teacher, Jane Perkins, did this for her class of children with learning disabilities. She was deeply moved by their responsiveness to the science activities. She said, "It was the first time any of these children ever expressed curiosity. I'll never again deny them the chance to wonder why."

Learning in the Context of Cooperation

Current research on children's thinking and learning regards them as results of both individual development and social interaction. An overemphasis on individual accomplishment in our society ignores much current research about our innate disposition to cooperate with one another (Keltner, 2009). We have an impetus to return to cooperative learning methods. The discovery experiences in this book have always been presented primarily as activities to be shared by small groups, with the introductions, supplements, and follow-ups provided as whole-group experiences. They are readily usable in the cooperative learning context.

Management of discovery activities as cooperative learning tasks will vary according to the nature of the project, the availability of materials in quantity, and the experience of the youngsters in handling independent activities. It makes more sense to have only one group of four children working on a particular gravity experience that requires using the one available commercial balance and weights, with other groups working on problems suitable for homemade balance scales. Still other groups could be using that time to make entries in their topic record booklets or to record their earlier findings on a class bar graph. Other children could be working on sections of the class mural of a gravity-free fantasy or creating a skit about being astronauts.

Precisely how cooperative activities are implemented is a matter for the individual teacher to decide. It is wise to make a slow transition to cooperative learning groups from a lockstep approach where each child works independently at the same learning task. Further, the social skills of four- and five-year-olds are better suited to learning groups of two. Seven- and eight-year-olds can, with training, work comfortably in groups of four.

Typically, it is realistic to plan a science period where discovery activities are paired with less structured activities that require little supervision. Teachers can then devote maximum attention to facilitating the discovery activities. There is no particular merit in attempting to simultaneously juggle a number of different discovery activities.

Time must be allowed before the science period ends for cleanup and for processing with the whole class what has occurred in the cooperative groups. To ensure that all children in the class are given a regular opportunity to report what their group has accomplished, a number-rotation system can be used. Each child in a small group is assigned a number from 1 to 4. Then, instead of asking for a volunteer or choosing a high-visibility child to report for the group, the teacher indicates which number will identify the day's reporters.

Integrated Curriculum Themes

The science themes in Part Two of this book were developed in response to the persistent interests, questions, and concerns of a generation of children in the classroom, at play, and at home. Jean Harlan explains:

> Many of the themes evolved in response to Michael, the knowledge-hungry child in my first kindergarten class in a university laboratory school 38 years ago. The retentiveness of his mind was impressive. The range of his curiosity was boundless.
>
> Keeping Michael's curiosity satisfied became a major preoccupation for me, searching for resources that weren't to be found, so had to be improvised. Initially, I fretted about devoting too much preparation energy to meet one child's needs. But something quite unexpected was happening in the classroom. Michael was never alone at the science table; the activities always drew a crowd. Soon, during our group conversations, Michael wasn't the only child sharing interesting information about how things work. Michael wasn't the only one applying those learnings in spontaneous play or in solving practical schoolground problems. Others were chiming in to point out connections between story plots and current science projects. Others were bringing from home various artifacts that related to ongoing science learnings.
>
> By midyear, my weekly planning centered on a single new or continuing science theme. We sang science, we nibbled science, we quantified science activities, we danced science, we took science to the easels and workbench, and we trudged around the school's neighborhood to see science happening. We had a good time, the children and I, learning together.
>
> Happily, Michael and his classmates had inspired a science-oriented kindergarten program that continued to evolve over the years. It continued to fascinate children of early childhood ages who represented a wide range of intellectual abilities and family backgrounds. Eventually the pages of weekly plans and observational notes resulted in the thematic format of this book.

Themes were developed around basic science concepts that have functional value in the world of young children because they explain how and why familiar events occur. Some topics were developed to modify or replace the naive, magical explanations that children had formulated for themselves. Topics were selected according to the following criteria:

- Relevance to the child's immediate experience
- Potential for being understood through simple, hands-on activities
- Potential applicability to practical, child-level problem solving
- Significance in promoting safety and physical or emotional well-being
- Availability of low- or no-cost materials for experimentation and observation

Two topics that interest many youngsters—prehistoric animals and astronomy—do not meet these criteria for most early childhood settings. They can be more suitably explored by families who can provide for children the resources of a natural history museum, a planetarium or observatory, and the night skies.

Early childhood classes may have opportunities to participate in community environmental projects. Every class can incorporate reusing, recycling, and conserving resources into its daily routines. Such involvement allows children to have a valued role in significant matters, but it does not take the place of foundation science experiences. Basic understandings of how matter behaves in the natural and physical worlds give meaning to the more complex interrelationships of environmental issues. In the chapters that follow, many hands-on experiences are suggested that lead to broader understandings. The activities are sequenced to provide foundation concepts for subsequent activities.

Other worthwhile science topics with child appeal can be developed by creative teachers, as long as their conceptual purpose and scientific accuracy are clear. Hands-on activities must lead children to a general truth or law about how matter and living things behave. Related extensions in other curricular areas should be just as enjoyable as the active science experiences, but they, too, must have a conceptual purpose (French, 2004). Shifting children's attention from what has relevance to the attention-catching irrelevant has been shown to interfere with the recall of significant information (Mayer, Heiser, & Lonn, 2001). Gathering the newest literature resources to extend a topic should be thoughtfully done, as trade books sometimes contain misinformation. The National Science Teachers Association Web site (http://www.nsta.org), which includes "NSTA Recommends" for the newest science trade books, can be helpful.

Extensions must not be vaguely connected, aimless "things to do" that trivialize the science learning and make the concept of integrated instruction artificial and superficial. Math extensions are intended to do double duty. They provide children practice with basic math skills such as sorting, counting, weighing, and measuring, and they increase familiarity with the materials of science at hand. Responding to a frequent criticism of the U.S. math curriculum that it is too broad and shallow, the National Council of Teachers of Mathematics (2006) has set out *Curriculum Focal Points for Prekindergarten through Grade 8 Mathematics* to help teachers prioritize math instruction topics. In kindergarten, for example, the Focal Points include number and operations, geometry, and measurement. The activities suggested here typically fit the proposed categories.

A teacher's own fascination with an area of knowledge can be the emotional spark for developing a science topic; that interest and enthusiasm communicate a positive disposition toward science. The adult's range of knowledge must then be stepped down to the children's level of thinking development and to the context of the child's immediate world. Activities can then be designed around the "up close and personal" tangible aspects of that topic. A teacher's strong commitment to protecting the environment can translate into beginning, hands-on explorations with reused plastic bottle terrariums and then expand onto the playground and into the broader community.

The activities for the science topics in this book are described as one way of supplying accurate guidance for children's explorations. The concepts are in accord with those stated in the National Science Education Standards, available at http://www.nsta.org.

Activities illustrating more complex concepts could be made available as options for children who are eager to pursue more challenging ideas. Each teacher is in the best position to make this decision. Children are best served and core concepts are more durably retained when teachers offer only a few topics in depth and with cross-curricular reinforcement each school year than when many topics are touched on lightly.

Objectives and Assessment

Objectives and assessment go hand in hand when planning meaningful experiences for young children. Well-planned assessment can provide valuable information about children's learning that can help to guide teaching (Snow & Van Hemel, 2008). Gathering a variety of assessment data over time as children engage in meaningful activity can provide a comprehensive picture of children's development. The broad objectives underlying the learning experiences in this book focus as much on children's feelings and approaches to learning as they do on the acquisition of information. Children build feelings of security and confidence as they observe the basic harmony in the physical and natural worlds. Reducing fear of the unknown leads to feelings of mastery and strength. Support for curiosity promotes problem-solving ability and offers an avenue for learning how to learn. It is important to assess children's affective and cognitive development in the context of science experiences to ensure that children are building positive dispositions toward science learning and making progress in constructing accurate knowledge. Furthermore, it is helpful to involve the child in assessing his or her work. The origin of *assessment* is the Latin word *assidere*, meaning "sit by." This implies a mutual effort on the part of the child and the teacher, sitting together and seeing what has been learned and what remains. Stiggins (2005) terms this kind of assessment "for learning," rather than "formative," and notes how it is positive and hopeful for the child. The early childhood field has moved toward *curriculum-embedded assessments* that are completed by teachers while children are engaged in familiar everyday activities. This approach offers the advantages of observing children in the context of activities that are meaningful to them and that have been prepared for children with specific objectives in mind (Grisham-Brown, Hallam, & Pretti-Frontczak, 2008). Assessing children engaged in purposeful activity in a familiar context and with familiar adults provides valid and useful data for understanding individual children's development.

Science journals keep track of learning in all seasons.

Some of the most widely used curriculum-embedded assessments include Creative Curriculum (Trister-Dodge, Colker, & Heroman, 2003), High/Scope Child Observation Record (COR; High/ Scope, 2003), and the Assessment, Evaluation, and Programming System (AEPS; Briker, 2002).

Teachers can embed their own assessments of children's progress toward objectives within their lesson plans. Children's responses can be recorded most conveniently on a simple checklist designed to accompany a specific set of lesson plans. Ideally, the checklist items should center on the grasp of basic concepts, activities completed, and evidence of interest and satisfaction expressed by the child. Think about how children might "show what they know" in a variety of ways. For example, is the child engaged and interested? Does the child use science vocabulary? Does the child express observations verbally or using actions? A journal entry, drawing, painting, model, sculpture, story, or dance may result, as well as a verbal explanation. A work folder or a portfolio would include that child's representation or a description of it. "What else do you wonder about . . . ?" is a question that further assesses the distance the child has traveled. One nonverbal child demonstrated his knowledge of what happened to a seed by bending his knees and slowly standing up, reaching high with both arms. Such data also serve as self-evaluation for the teacher about the success and value of the learning experiences.

Standards, whether state, national, or local, can be the goals of teaching and learning. Teachers can keep track of progress toward standards by incorporating them into lesson plans and activity centers. Continuously observing children is the most solid way of assessing. Listening to children's comments and asking questions as they work with science materials can reveal a great deal. Such questions include "What did you find out about . . . ?" and "Can you show me what happens when . . .?" For longer plant, animal, or weather observations, the question "What did you find out about . . . ?" asked at a natural closure point provides a gauge for conceptual learning.

We should not think that individual assessments are the only way of seeing what children have learned. Just as children work in small groups to develop knowledge, they can present their work jointly. Older children may paint a mural, create a sculpture or model, or dramatize a concept. Younger children may engage in creative movement together. Teachers can jot down notes on such activities, as well as photograph or sketch them.

A collaborative effort can be a successful assessment.

In addition, group conversations about a science topic can both reveal and help develop children's understanding. Many early childhood programs in the United States are emulating the Reggio Emilia approach to blending planning and assessment within cycles of inquiry. The process begins with a "verbal outpouring" of children's knowledge and ideas about a topic, followed by initial drawings by children representing their knowledge. Next, teachers provide children with a variety of opportunities to directly experience the phenomenon of interest (such as rain or snow), and children revisit and rerepresent their knowledge. This type of documentation serves both as an assessment of children's increasingly complex understanding and as a catalyst for further learning (Edwards, Gandini, & Foreman, 1998). It also helps the teacher decide what to teach next, tightly linking curriculum and assessment.

Another group representation is the Know, Wonder, Learn (KWL) chart, with which teachers begin a unit asking and recording without comment what children say they know about a topic and then asking and recording again without comment what children wonder about a topic. Discussion ensues about what wonderments are pursuable, activities are planned to investigate, and as ideas or concepts are learned, they too are recorded, usually with comment, especially if the children can link what they are learning to the original lists of ideas. The KWL chart has an additional function of publicly recording the focus and thinking of the children and what they have learned for parents and other adults.

Teachers make assessments of the whole group in other ways too. How engaged are the children? How well do they keep track of the science materials? How often do children visit the science center, and how are materials used? How much investigation of the library books occurs? What is brought in from home or elsewhere outside the classroom? Judgments of these kinds help teachers evaluate their own effectiveness and monitor their own work.

Keep in mind that what a child really learns from an activity might not immediately be evident in the classroom. Instead, that feedback may spill out to a parent at home during a sleepy bedtime conversation. The learnings may be fragmentary until they are consolidated through participation in the integrating activities. Or perhaps the learning is applied nonverbally weeks after the classroom experience has taken place. The real nature of the teaching/learning process is obscured if we assume that children learn only and precisely what a narrow behavioral objective decrees. We encourage teachers to take a broad view of children's learning and not be railroaded into thin, constrictive curriculum outcomes.

The assessment method most appreciated by parents at conference time, however, does not involve convenient check marks on a rating scale. Rather, it consists of sharing your casual, on-the-spot jottings on Post-its filed in the child's work folder. Use a digital camera to record the constructions, projects, and drawings to create electronic folders on individual children or the class, or print photos to store in traditional paper folders. One of us has several years of digital science class photos in her computer. Viewed as a whole, they document the themes of her work with students. Such documentations are tangible evidence of having passed along life-enriching awareness of the world we know and appreciate through science knowledge.

However, formal evaluation of children's accomplishments in science is increasingly required as science is recognized as important to society. Programs mandated by the No Child Left Behind Act (NCLB), the National Assessment of Educational Progress (NAEP), and Trends in International Mathematics and Science Study (TIMSS) each have formal standardized tests. Although these tests are not administered to young children, they impact curriculum and instruction as schools seek to prepare all children for being tested.

Because so much inappropriate assessment of young children occurs in this "era of accountability," we refer you to the joint position statement of the National Association for the Education of Young Children and the National Association of Early Childhood Specialists in State Departments of Education (2003): Early Childhood Curriculum, Assessment, and Program Evaluation. This calls for "ethical, appropriate, valid, and reliable" methods that are "developmentally appropriate, culturally and linguistically responsive, tied to children's daily activities, supported by professional development, inclusive of families, and connected to specific, beneficial purposes," for example, decisions about teaching, and identifying concerns. *It is not ethical to have kindergartners crying as they try to decipher a page of bubbles to be penciled.*

Gaining from Our Mistakes

Many of the materials and activities in this text have been revised as a result of trial-and-error encounters with the logic of young minds. Jean writes:

> On one occasion, the children in my class were given matching plastic vials—some capped, some uncapped—to use in a buoyancy experiment. Then five-year-old Greg explained why his capped, empty vial floated on the water while his uncapped vial sank. According to Greg, the cap held up the first vial! To my dismay, he verified his conclusion by removing the plastic cap and floating it on the water. How confusing! According to my plan, he should have noticed that the capped vial was filled with air;

hence, it was lightweight; the uncapped vial filled with water, hence, it became heavy. It took a while for my supposedly flexible, adult thinking to find a way back to the objective of the experiment. "Greg, you had a good idea about the cap. It does float by itself. Let's see what happens if we put the cap on the container full of water. Now let's put the same kind of cap on the empty-looking container and watch them again." Tuning in to a child's logic makes teaching an exciting learning process for the teacher.

If children have difficulties with an activity, further modifications may be needed. It is important not to give up on science activities because of an occasional unexpected outcome. Keep in mind Thomas Edison's observation that a mistake is not a failure if we learn how not to do it next time.

Professional Growth

Teaching can be an endlessly challenging profession when we consider ourselves learners along with the children. On our own, taking time to investigate questions we are interested in, talking with other teachers about common concerns in science teaching, and refreshing ourselves by attending lectures, visiting museums, and reading can all help to keep us open to new ideas. Schools must provide for worthwhile professional development. The *National Science Education Standards* (NRC, 1996) state:

> Teachers should have opportunities for structured reflection on their teaching practice with colleagues, for collaborative curriculum planning, and for active participation in professional teaching and scientific networks. The challenge of professional development for teachers of science is to create optimal collaborative learning situations in which the best sources of expertise are linked with the experiences and current needs of the teachers.

Study groups seem a particularly effective way of helping teachers develop and change.

As authors, we have been enlivened by discovering resources for teachers and children. We recommend the following for your consideration.

Web Sites

- *Science & Children.* A journal of the National Science Teachers Association. The lively and informative Web site for NSTA is http://www.nsta.org/journals
- SciLinks. This free NSTA online service identifies grade-specific Web sites and resources to help teachers expand their lessons at http://www.SciLinks.org
- *Your Big Backyard,* for preschool children; *Ranger Rick,* for primary/ elementary-grade children; *Ranger Rick's NatureScope,* for teachers (includes nature activities and extensions). These publications of the National Wildlife Federation are available at http://www.nwf.org

To nurture your own interest in science discoveries, not necessarily to teach them to young children, use these Internet resources. You might be surprised how interesting they are!

The American Association for the Advancement of Science (AAAS) has a Web site for children who can read well: http://www.eurekalert.org/ scienceforkids/

The *New York Times* science section is published on Tuesdays: http://www. nytimes.com

The Nature Publishing Group has a lively Web site: http://www.nature.com/scitable

"Science Fridays" with Ira Flatow on NPR Radio on Friday afternoons is a great way to wind down a work week. Check little videos at http://www.sciencefriday.com/videos/watch/10177

Scientific American, published monthly, maintains an active Web site: http://www.sciam.com

Newton, Office of Science, U.S. Department of Energy, answers all kinds of science-related questions. http://www.newton.dep.ani.gov/askasci/week.htm

The teaching framework will achieve its greatest effectiveness when it stimulates teachers to continue growing and generating their own ideas for presenting science experiences to the children they know best.

REFERENCES

ALLIANCE FOR CHILDHOOD. (2004). *Tech tonic: Toward a new literacy of technology.* College Park, MD: Author. Retrieved July 25, 2006, from http://www.allianceforchildhood.org/projects/computers/pdf_files/tech_tonic.pdf.

AMERICAN ACADEMY OF PEDIATRICS. (2006, May). Policy statement: Active healthy living: Prevention of childhood obesity through increased physical activity. *Pediatrics, 17*(5), 1839–1840.

BAYERUS. (2010). *Bayer facts of science education survey XIV.* Retrieved August 20, 2010, from http://www.bayerus.com/MSMS/MSMS_Home.aspx.

BLAGOJEVIC, B., CHEVALIER, S., MACISAAC, A., HITCHCOCK, L., & FRECHETTE, B. (2010). Young children and computers: Storytelling and learning in a digital age. *Teaching Young Children, 3*(5), 1–5. Retrieved August 14, 2010, at http://www.naeyc.org/files/tyc/file/TYC_V3N4_Blagojevicexpanded.pdf.

BOUCK, E., & OKOLO, C. (2007). Research about assistive technology: 2000–2006. What have we learned? *Journal of Special Education Technology, 22*(3), 19–33.

BRICKER, D. (Series Ed.). (2002). *Assessment, evaluation and programming system for infants and children* (2nd ed., Vols. 1–4). Baltimore: Brookes.

BRENNEMAN, K. (2009). Preschoolers as scientific explorers. *Young Children, 64*(6), 54–60.

CHAILLE, C. (2008). *Big ideas: A framework for constructivist curriculum.* Boston: Allyn & Bacon/Pearson.

DONOVAN, M. S., & BRANSFORD, J. (2005). *How students learn: History, mathematics, and science in the classroom.* Washington, DC: National Academies Press.

DUSCHL, R. A., SCHWEINGRUBER, H. A., & SHOUSE, A. W. (2006). *Taking science to school: Learning and teaching science in grades 4–8.* Washington, DC: National Academies Press.

DWECK, C. (2006). *Mindset: The new psychology of success.* New York: Random House.

EDWARDS, C., GANDINI, L., & FORMAN, G. (1998). *The hundred languages of children: The Reggio Emilia approach—advanced reflections.* Greenwich, CT: Ablex.

FRENCH, L. (2004). Science as the center of a coherent, integrated early childhood curriculum. *Early Childhood Research Quarterly, 19*(1), 138–149.

GARDNER, H. (2004). *Changing minds: The art and science of changing our own and other people's minds.* Boston: Harvard Business School Press.

GRISHAM-BROWN, J., HALLAM, R. A., & PRETTI-FRONTCZAK, K. (2008). Preparing Head Start personnel to use a curriculum-based assessment: An innovative practice in the "age of accountability." *Journal of Early Intervention, 30*(4), 271–281.

HIGH/SCOPE. (2003). *Preschool child observation record (COR)* (2nd ed.). Ypsilanti, MI: High/Scope Research Foundation.

KELTNER, D. (2009). *Born to be good.* New York: Norton.

KOHN, A. (2006). *Unconditional parenting: Moving from rewards and punishment to love and reasoning.* New York: Atria.

LEWIN-BENHAM, A. (2008). *Powerful children: Understanding how to teach and learn using the Reggio approach.* New York: Teachers College Press.

LLOYD, M. (2010). The world is flat: ICT and education for sustainability in the early years. In J. Davis (Ed.), *Young children and the environment: Early education for sustainability* (pp. 212–241). Cambridge: Cambridge University Press.

MAYER, R., HEISER, J., & LONN, S. (2001). Cognitive constraints on multimedia learning: When presenting more material results in less understanding. *Journal of Educational Psychology, 93*(1), 187–198.

MULLIN, K. (2010). *Toolkit for schoolyard habitat program development.* Annapolis: Maryland Association for Environmental and Outdoor Education, U.S. NOAA, U.S. Fish and Wildlife Service. Retrieved August 25, 2010, from http://www.fws.gov/chesapeakebay/school/PDF/SchoolyardProgramToolkit.pdf.

NATIONAL ASSESSMENT OF EDUCATIONAL PROGRESS (NAEP). (1996–2010). *The nation's report card. Science 2005, Mathematics 2009.* Washington, DC: National Center for Educational Statistics. Retrieved December 4, 2010, from http://nationsreportcard.gov.

NATIONAL ASSOCIATION FOR THE EDUCATION OF YOUNG CHILDREN (NAEYC). (2001). *2001 standards for the baccalaureate or initial level.* Washington, DC: Author.

NATIONAL ASSOCIATION FOR THE EDUCATION OF YOUNG CHILDREN (NAEYC). (2009). *Professional preparation standards.* Retrieved August 20, 2010, from http://www.naeyc.org/files/naeyc/file/positions/ProfPrepStandards09.pdf.

NATIONAL ASSOCIATION FOR THE EDUCATION OF YOUNG CHILDREN & NATIONAL ASSOCIATION OF EARLY CHILDHOOD SPECIALISTS IN STATE DEPARTMENTS OF EDUCATION. (2003). *Position statement: Early childhood curriculum, assessment, and program evaluation—Building an effective, accountable system in programs for children birth through age 8.* Retrieved December 5, 2010, from http://www.naeyc.org/position statements/cape.

NATIONAL COMMITTEE ON SCIENCE EDUCATION STANDARDS AND ASSESSMENT. (1996). *National science education standards.* Washington, DC: National Research Council.

NATIONAL COUNCIL FOR TEACHERS OF MATHEMATICS. (2006). *Curriculum focal points for prekindergarten through grade 8 mathematics.* Reston, VA: Author.

NATIONAL SCIENCE TEACHERS ASSOCIATION. (2000, 2003, 2004). *Position statement: Gender equity in science education. Position statement: Multicultural science education. Position statement: Students with disabilities.* Arlington, VA: Author.

PATRICK, H., MANTZICOPOULOS, P., & AMARAPUNGAYAN, A. (2009). Motivation for learning science in kindergarten: Is there a gender gap and does integrated inquiry and literacy instruction make a difference? *Journal of Research in Science Teaching, 46*(2), 166–191. Retrieved August 20, 2010, from http://onlinelibrary.wiley.com/doi/10.1002/tea.20276/pdf.

PRESTWICH, D., SUMRALL, J., & CHASSIN, D. (2010). Science rocks! *Science and Children, 47*(7), 86–88.

ROWE, M. B. (1996). Reprint: Science, silence and sanctions. *Science and Children, 34*(1), 35–37.

SCHNEPS, M. H. (c. 1997). *Minds of our own.* Videotape series. Cambridge, MA: The Private Universe Project at Harvard–Smithsonian Center for Astrophysics. Retrieved December 4, 2010, from http://www.learner.org/resources/series28.html/

SNOW, C. E., & VAN HEMEL, S. B. (Eds.). (2008). *Early childhood assessment: Why, what, and how.* Washington, DC: National Academy of Sciences.

SPARKS, L., & EDWARDS, J. (2010). *Anti-bias education for young children and ourselves.* Washington, DC: NAEYC.

STIGGINS, R. (2005). From formative assessment to assessment for learning. *The Kappan, 87,* 324–328.

TRISTER-DODGE, D., COLKER, H., & HEROMAN, C. (2003). *The creative curriculum for preschool* (4th ed.). Washington, DC: Teaching Strategies.

WELTON, N., SMITH, W., OWENS, K., & ADRIAN, M. (2000). Hands-on science as a motivator for children with emotional/behavioral disabilities. *Journal of Elementary Science Education, 12*(2), 33–37.

WHITE HOUSE TASK FORCE ON CHILDHOOD OBESITY. (2010, May). *Report to the president.* Washington, DC: Executive Office of the President of the United States.

Part Two

CONCEPTS, EXPERIENCES, AND INTEGRATING ACTIVITIES

Plants

Bursts of brilliant fall color, first daffodils announcing spring, orchards in full bloom: bring your own vivid memories of nature's glory into the classroom with you. Your pleasure in the wonders of plant life inspires children as you build their innate interest in growing things. We couldn't live on Earth without plants!

They feed us, clothe us, shelter us, purify the air we breathe, and fill our visual world with beauty: the living things called *plants*. Children may be captivated by towering giant plants or the tiniest weed blossoms underfoot. When we share their delight, we renew our own appreciation of nature's exquisite order. The following concepts will be explored in this chapter:

- There are many kinds of plants; each has its own form.
- Most plants make seeds for new plants.
- Seeds grow into plants with roots, stems, leaves, and flowers.
- Most plants need water, light, minerals, warmth, and air.
- Some plants grow new plants from their roots.
- Many foods we eat are seeds.
- Some plantlike forms grow from spores.

The first suggested experience will be limited by climate to areas where deciduous trees grow. The next group of activities calls for gathering natural materials. This may require the ingenuity of teachers in urban schools. The concluding experiences with seeds and plant growing should be possible anywhere. Suggestions for seedling care and for transplanting are included.

CONCEPT: **There are many kinds of plants; each has its own form.**

1. ☘ *How do the parts of different plants look?*

LEARNING OBJECTIVE: To enjoy finding similarities and differences in plants and trees.

MATERIALS:

Large collecting bag full of found items such as

    leaves (2 or 3 of each kind)

    tall grasses (include seeds or blossoms)

    flowers

    twigs

    bark

    seed pods,* nuts

    mosses, lichens

Paper lunch bags

GETTING READY:

Sort the found materials.

Fill a teacher's bag with one of each kind of item.

Distribute an assortment of materials into small bags for the children.

Place a closed bag at each place at the science table.

SMALL-GROUP ACTIVITY:

(Complete this activity after taking a walk to collect nature materials.)

1. Take one object from your bag. "Look into your bags to see if you can find a leaf that matches this one."
2. As children find similar items to compare, encourage them to notice details: "Is it just like mine? Are the tips of your leaf rounded like this one? It almost matches. Who found one with rounded tips?" (Children may have a lot of information about plants already. Listen.)
3. Point out that all leaves from the same kind of tree have the same general shape. (Size and fall coloration may vary.) For example, "When they have finished growing, all sweet gum tree leaves have five points. That's one way to know that the tree is a sweet gum tree."

Math Skill: Comparing shapes.

Note: Specimens can survive close inspection by enclosing them in a no-cost display cover. Use a drop of glue to attach a well-dried specimen to the inside of a clear plastic deli carton lid. Cover it with a matching lid. Join the rim edges to form a case and seal it with tape (Figure 4–1). (Remove any dating ink by warming the lid over a cup of steaming liquid, then wiping with nail polish remover.)

Read: Fall Leaf Project by Margaret McNamarara.

---

*Do not bring the following poisonous berries into your classroom: castor beans, berries from pokeweed, nightshade, bittersweet, yew, holly, privet, or mistletoe. Do not allow experimental eating of buckeyes, daffodil bulbs, iris or lily tubers, or poinsettia leaves.

FIGURE 4–1

2. ♣ *How do some plants rest for winter?*

LEARNING OBJECTIVE: To make a satisfying connection with nature's seasonal changes.

MATERIALS:

Shopping bag

Old, thick phone book

Newspaper

Waxed paper

Electric iron or bricks

GETTING READY:

Try to do this a week in advance. Save waxed leaves for another year.

Get a good specimen leaf from each tree you plan to visit with the class.

Press leaves for several days between pages of newspaper inserted into the phone book. Weight with the iron or bricks.

Fold waxed paper over each dried leaf. Press warm iron on paper to coat leaves with wax.

Tape the leaves to a low bulletin board and label them.*

SMALL-GROUP ACTIVITY:

1. When deciduous trees start to change color, take a tree trip. Have children circle a tree, holding hands. "What can you see above you? Below?" Repeat with an evergreen tree. (Old needles on the ground have been replaced by new ones, but not all at once.) Visit shrubs if trees are not within walking distance.
2. Supply these ideas, as needed: Leaves make food for trees to grow; chlorophyll (green color in leaves) uses the energy from sunlight to help turn water, minerals, and air into food; this work is finished for leaves on some trees when summer ends.
3. Gather leaves from the ground.
4. Let children put like kinds of leaves together when you get back. Ask them to try to match their finds with the mounted specimens. Encourage them to bring leaves from home to try to match them.
5. Save the surplus leaves for art activities or for compost.

*Other methods of preserving leaves are detailed in *Science and Children,* September 1994, 32.

Math Skill: Matching shapes.

Group Discussion: Recall the fun of collecting leaves. Ask what happens to the leaves from deciduous trees and shrubs that rest for winter. Introduce the idea that leaves need green stuff called *chlorophyll* to help make food for trees. When food making stops for winter, the green chlorophyll goes out of these leaves. Then the other colors that are in the leaves show instead. (You might be able to find mottled leaves that fell before all the chlorophyll left.) Talk about how the leaves can still be valuable after they fall. If possible, start a compost bag or heap (see p. 77).

Read: Leaves Fall Down by Lisa Bullard or *Leaf Jumpers* by Carole Gerber.

CONCEPT: Most plants make seeds for new plants.

1. What can we find out about fruit seeds?

LEARNING OBJECTIVE: To be reassured that most plants form seeds to create more plants of the same kind.

Introduction: Show a large seed pod (e.g., daylily, iris, milkweed), preferably still attached to its stalk. Ask for children's ideas about it. Summarize that each kind of plant has a job to do: make seeds for new plants just like it. Each plant forms seeds when its flowers stop blooming. "Some seeds are protected by covers we like to eat. Let's explore some fruits and vegetables to see if they are seed covers."

MATERIALS:

Any seed pods, like flower, tree, shrub, or tall grass seed head

As many of these as can be brought in: apple, tomato,* pomegranate, peach, ear of corn in husk, orange, nuts in shells, melon, squash,* green beans, apricot, cucumber*

Foam produce trays

Paring knife *(adult use only)*

Smocks

Newspapers

SMALL-GROUP ACTIVITY:

1. Let children predict if seeds will be inside each item. Find out. Carefully cut the fruits open. Share tastes and sniffs with everyone.
2. Save melon and squash seeds. Later, let children wash them and dry them on trays. Save seeds for bird feeders. If corn is fresh, pull back the husks and hang it to dry. Let children shell dried corn for the birds. Tack one dried husk and ear of corn to a tree for the birds, if possible.
3. Ask older children to figure out a way, such as grouping, to count the large number of seeds in a pumpkin.

---

*The edible part of a plant that develops from a flower is a fruit, but some are commonly called vegetables. Children can make the botanical distinction in more advanced science classes.

GETTING READY:

Wash fruits and vegetables.

Cover table with papers.

Have all children wash their hands.

Put out plants with seed pods to examine first.

Math Skills: Counting and grouping to count.

Group Discussion: When discussing this experience, consider how many seeds each fruit or vegetable has, and that a new plant could grow from each one. Comment on the abundance of nature: a welcome thought for children who hear frequently and worry about endangered species.

Read: How Many Seeds in a Pumpkin by Margaret McNamara and Brian Karas.

2. How are seeds scattered?

LEARNING OBJECTIVE: To be intrigued by the ways different seeds are scattered.

MATERIALS:

Locally available seeds from garden plants; weeds (teasel, milkweed, burdock); grasses (wheat, oats); and trees (ailanthus, locust, oak, pine,* chestnut)

Magnifying glasses

Old fuzzy mittens and socks

Trays

GETTING READY:

Gather ripe seed stalks in advance.

Store in open containers or hang in tied bunches to dry.

Preserve husks and pods intact.

Find weeds in vacant lots or in roadside ditches.

SMALL-GROUP ACTIVITY:

1. Arrange materials on trays. Let children shake seeds from pods, brush hairy seeds against the mitten, and beat grass seed spikes against trays to release grains.
2. Examine burrs and hairy seeds with magnifiers to see the tiny hooks on the tips.
3. Take winged seeds and a few heavier nuts to the playground. Let children launch them from a high place. Compare what happens to each kind of seed.

---

*Seeds lie beneath separate cone scales. Old cones on trees may no longer contain seeds. Tightly closed new cones can be dried in a warm oven with the heat turned off. Seeds can then be found in the open cones.

Group Discussion: Ask if children have seen plants growing in places where people couldn't plant them—in sidewalk cracks or rock crevices. How could seeds get there? How many ways can children think of?

Read: What Seeds Are These? By Heidi Roemer.

CONCEPT: **Seeds grow into plants with roots, stems, leaves, and flowers.**

1. What is inside a seed?

LEARNING OBJECTIVE: To delight in finding a beginning plant in seeds.

Introduction: "There is a surprise inside a seed. Let's find it."

MATERIALS:

Dried beans, several for each child

Desirable if available: maple tree seeds, avocados, fresh green beans or peas

Magnifying glasses

GETTING READY:

Soak beans overnight in enough water to cover.

Keep a few beans dry for comparison.

SMALL-GROUP ACTIVITY:

1. Demonstrate by carefully slipping off a seed coat. Pull apart the two parts (cotyledons, the food source for starting a new plant). Find the "surprise": the tiny new plant (embryo) ready to start growing.
2. Let children continue to open seeds to find new plants, and examine them with magnifying glasses.
3. If a very ripe avocado is available, slice the fleshy part in half. Twist slightly to pull apart. Examine the seed. Peel the seed coat at the base. A ripe fruit seed may already be splitting, revealing a root tip. Do not split it open if you want to plant it.

To Start an Avocado Tree: Slice away about ¼ in. (1 cm) from the base of the avocado seed. Insert three round toothpicks midway through the seed to suspend the seed in a jar of water. Keep the jar in a warm place away from direct sunlight. Change the water weekly. (If a seed fits in a water-filled carafe, toothpicks aren't needed; see Figure 4–3 on page 67.) After the root appears, move the jar to a sunny location. When leaves appear on the stem, gently plant the seed in a pot at a depth of about 5 in. (13 cm). Leave the top quarter of the seed exposed above the soil. Water it at least every other day. Spray or wash leaves frequently.

2. How do seeds start to grow?

LEARNING OBJECTIVE: To focus on the wonder of new plant life beginning.

MATERIALS:

Method 1

Matching disposable plastic
tumblers

Transparent tape

Cotton balls or sand

Dried legumes: navy or lima
beans, lentils (fresh stock)*

Water

Plastic prescription vial

Desirable: mung beans (natural
food store)

SMALL-GROUP ACTIVITY:

Method 1

1. Make a sprouting dome: Wet four or five
   cotton balls, press out excess water, and
   flatten (or dampen sand). Line the bottom
   and sides of one tumbler with wet cotton
   or sand.
2. Let children see and feel the beans. As the
   children help place 4 beans between the
   cotton and the tumbler side, recall the surprise inside the seeds. (Try to use more
   than one kind of legume to see which
   sprouts first, which gets tallest, and which
   grows for the longest time.)
3. Upend the matching tumbler on the rim of
   the prepared tumbler. Tape the rims to
   make a dome enclosure (Figure 4–2).

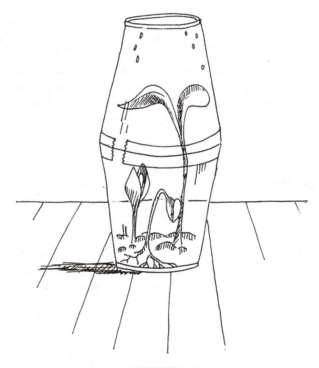

FIGURE 4–2

---

*Two common causes of germination failure are old seeds and an overheated, dry room.
Don't expect good results with seeds of unknown vintage or with uncovered sprouting
containers.

4. Place it away from direct sunlight where temperature will be even.
5. Put one of each kind of seed in the vial for later comparison. Start a calendar record of the starting date, first root, first stem, and first leaf appearance. Crayon-mark the daily growth level on the tumbler.

Method 2

Plastic sandwich bags
White paper toweling
Stapler
Masking tape

Method 2

1. Each child makes a sprouting bag. Fold toweling to fit bag and dampen the toweling. Place five lentils on damp toweling; seal bag with tape. Label with child's name on a piece of tape. Staple bags to a bulletin board.
2. Children keep daily sprout growth logs by sketching or writing descriptions and by measuring root and stem length.

Math Skills: Measuring plant growth and keeping a calendar record.

Read: Seeds Sprout! by Mary Wade or *A Seed Is Sleepy* by Deanna Aston.

Note: It's a good idea to start two germinating domes. Keep one available for children to pick up for a close look. If sprouts don't survive the inspection, the other dome will be available. It's hard to only look and not touch when leaves are showing beneath a rakish seed cover cap.

3. How do roots and stems grow?

LEARNING OBJECTIVE: To verify the surprising tendency of roots to grow downward toward water and of stems to grow upward toward light.

MATERIALS:

Same as for the seed-sprouting experience

SMALL-GROUP ACTIVITY:

1. "Notice which direction the seedling roots and stems take. Is it the same for each seedling?"
2. Gently turn one seedling so that the stem points down and the root reaches up. Mark an X on the glass beneath it.
3. Children draw picture records; you take pictures of daily growth changes. Check the cotton behind the seeds. Roots may poke down into it toward water.

Math Skills: Measuring root and stem growth; recording with pictures.

Group Discussion: Ask children if trees grow with their branches and leaves in the soil and their roots in the air, if flowers bloom underground, or if plants send roots into the ground and other parts into the air. Why is this so? Help the children recall that leaves need light and air to perform their food-making job. Roots have the job of getting water and minerals from the soil so that the plant can live and grow. The upended seedling root and stem twisted and turned to grow in the directions where each could get what it needed.

Read: What Do Roots Do? by Kathleen Kudlinski.

CONCEPT: **Most plants need water, light, minerals, warmth, and air.**

1. What do seeds need to start growing?

LEARNING OBJECTIVE: To experience the joy of nurturing plant growth.

Part l.

Note: To be sure that seeds are viable, try planting a few of the seeds you purchase at least three weeks in advance before starting Part 1 in class. Also, plant at least two seeds in each of three medium-sized flower pots in order to have three more fully developed plants ready for Part 2. Make arrangements for seedling watering if observations extend over weekends.

MATERIALS:

Zinnea or marigold seeds, package-dated for the current year

Commercial potting soil (sterilized)

Teaspoons

Empty yogurt cups, enough for each child, plus a few extras

Masking tape

Water

Trays

Water spray bottle

Plastic wrap

For part 2: 3 medium-sized flower pots, 2 paper grocery bags

SMALL-GROUP ACTIVITY:

Let the children

1. Fill cups almost to the top with soil.
2. Use a spray bottle to dampen soil well.
3. Place one seed on soil, then cover lightly with soil, press firmly, and water again. Plant some seeds in extra cups to replace possible failures.
4. Place trays of cups in a spot away from drafts, radiators, and direct sunlight. Cover loosely with plastic wrap.
5. As soon as tiny shoots appear, remove plastic cover. Move trays to a sunny spot. Keep soil damp with sprayer.
6. Have children draw records of seedling growth stages. Take pictures as well.

GETTING READY:

Collect empty yogurt cups well in advance, more than enough for each child.

Cover table with newspapers.

Make masking tape name labels for each child's cup.

7. Set aside a seedling dampening time about every other day (check soil daily to determine need for water). Ask, "If you were a tiny new plant, how would you want to be cared for?"

Group Discussion: After the first sprouts appear, compare the calendar records of the germination dome and the plant-raising experiences. (Different seeds have different germinating times.) Were seeds treated alike in both experiences? What was missing from the germination dome? Which seedlings stopped growing and withered? Which ones kept growing? (The seedlings in *soil*.) Moist seeds can grow only until their built-in food supply is used up. Plants rooted in soil can soak up minerals and moisture from the soil to help the leaves make food for their growth. Would the seeds grow in a refrigerator? Find out.

Seedling Care: After leaves appear, provide moderate light, such as a northern exposure. Cover only at night to retain moisture. Allow children to water their own plants with the sprayer. It's hard to overwater this way, but if it happens, blot up standing water with absorbent materials. Check each cup before covering trays at night in case someone forgets to water a plant.

Transplanting: For several days after the second pair of leaves appears, give seedlings a few hours of direct sunlight, preferably outdoors in a sheltered spot. Send thriving plants home with the children. (Try to have a few extra plants on hand to compensate for any failed plants.) Tell parents that if the bottoms are cut off, the cups can be planted directly in the ground when the soil is warm.

Read: Plants Grow by Mary Wade.

Part 2.

? *Inquiry Activity: Whole-group discussion:* (Have the three pots of larger plants in view.) Recall what children provided for their seeds to grow into tiny plants. Recall that seeds could sprout without being in soil but didn't continue to grow without it. "Do you think our new plants also will still need to have water and daylight to keep growing?" "Here are some bigger plants. Do you think they need water and sunlight to keep growing? Any ideas about how we could find out for ourselves?" (Consider all ideas, guiding or modifying them toward useful test methods.)

"Shall we stop watering all three plants?" . . . "Shall we put paper bags over all three plants? . . . Would that tell us just about needing water and just about needing light?" . . . (Guide the discussion to the point of devising a fair test of giving one plant light, but no water; one plant water, but no light; and one control plant both water and light for comparison.) Mark the pots accordingly. Take a pretest digital picture of the three plants. Work out plans to carefully water the two plants getting water, to check all three plants daily, and to keep records with drawings for about a week. When the results are very obvious, end the study with a discussion of the results. Post the written records and drawings as proud research evidence that *the leaves of plants need to soak up sunlight and have water to make food for the plants so they will grow.* Find a way to keep these pet plants growing for the rest of the school year, either transplanting them to larger pots to grow in the classroom or, if permitted and if the ground is warm enough, plant them outside in a sunny location.

2. How do plants take up water?

LEARNING OBJECTIVE: To watch the fascinating way water moves up a stem.

MATERIALS:

2 stalks of celery, with leaves

2 jars

Food coloring, blue or red
  (enough to make a dark color)

Water

SMALL-GROUP ACTIVITY:

1. "How does water get into the leaves of a plant?"
2. "Let's see if we can figure out how water moves up these stalks of celery." Let children stir food coloring into one jar of water.
3. Check within an hour for signs of color in leaf tips. Separate a dyed tube from the stalk so the dye can be seen throughout the whole length. Slice a cross section from the bottom of the stalk to examine.
4. "What do you think would happen to a stalk of celery if it had no water for a while? Let's find out." Leave the other stalk in the empty jar overnight. Check its condition the next day.
5. "Do you think water will change this stalk? Let's try it." Trim ¼ in. (1 cm) from the stem bottom and add water to the jar. Check it the next day. Has it revived? Clarify that celery plants have roots in the ground when they are growing. Roots soak up water from the soil, and the water travels up through the stalk tubes.

Tanisha studies the sweet potato roots, leaves, and stems.

Read: Plant by Penelope Arlon.

CONCEPT: **Some plants grow new plants from their roots.**

1. What can we find out about growing potatoes?

LEARNING OBJECTIVE: To observe the satisfying ways tubers and bulbs produce new plants.

Whole-Group Observation: Ask the class for predictions about whether
or not new plants can start from parts of plants other than seeds. "Let's find
out."

You'll need an old potato that has been in a cool, dark storage place (or
forgotten) long enough to have developed some sturdy sprouts. For comparison,
also have an organic* unsprouted potato, which will just have tiny "eyes" showing.
Help the children experiment by planting the potatoes in two medium-sized
flower pots, cutting the potatoes to fit the pots, if necessary. Be sure to have the
sprouts facing up, and at least two of the fresh potato "eyes" facing up as the
potatoes are covered with potting soil.

Tape a label to each pot, "sprouted" or "not sprouted." Place the pots in a
sunny spot and water when dry. Compare times for the appearance of new green
plants. Keep a written calendar or a series of observational drawings and measurements to record the plants' growth. If there is a suitable place, plant them
outdoors, where they could grow a small crop of potatoes!

Math Skills: Measuring plant growth; keeping a calendar record.

---

*Organic potatoes are not commercially treated to retard sprouting.

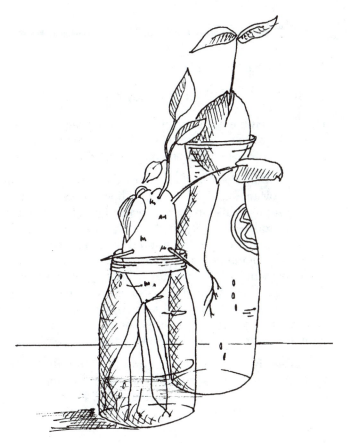

FIGURE 4–3

Read: Two Old Potatoes and Me by John Coy.

Follow-Up Observation: Suspend an organic* sweet potato in a glass jar of water (see Figure 4–3). Ask for predictions about what will happen to it. Keep it out of direct sunlight until the first sprouts appear. Check its growth frequently. Add to or change water weekly. A successful sweet potato vine will flourish for months before its food supply is depleted. It may be planted in the ground when the old potato starts to cave in. It can still produce a new crop of potatoes if planted.

Plant some daffodil bulbs outdoors in the fall. If you find a sprouting onion in your kitchen, slice it open vertically so that children can see the new plant tucked inside its food supply bulb. Talk about the bulbs outdoors waiting for the spring sunshine to warm the earth and for the rain to start them growing.

---

*Organic potatoes are not commercially treated to retard sprouting.

CONCEPT: **Many foods we eat are seeds.**

1. Which seeds do we eat?

LEARNING OBJECTIVE: To enjoy discovering that seeds can be healthy foods.

The list of edible seeds is long, including legumes, nuts, and grains. Grains are staples for diets in almost every culture in the world. As a basic food plant in this country, corn can be eaten as a nutritious, gluten-free whole grain, and it's fun to eat!

Sprouting Popcorn: Open a discussion by reaching into your pocket for "a very important small thing that millions of people eat every day. Perhaps you ate something like this (show a popcorn kernel) changed into a different shape for breakfast today." (Family food preferences can be sensitive subjects, so avoid asking children direct questions about what has been served at home.) Identify popcorn as one of many kinds of corn seed, part of a group of seeds called *grain*, that make very important food for healthy, growing bodies. Encourage children to share their knowledge of ways to eat corn and other food grains. Pass a sealed plastic bag of popcorn seeds (kernels) around for children to feel *but not bite.* "Do you think a hard grain like this could grow into a plant? Let's find out." Keep some seeds for comparison at the end of the experience.

Note: Be sure to try this sprouting project at home, at least 10 days in advance, to gauge the time for starting the classroom experience. Different varieties of popcorn may vary in sprouting times. Plain, natural popcorn is widely available in grocery stores.

MATERIALS:

Natural popcorn, red, white, or yellow (not dried sweet corn seeds). *Do not use microwave packet popcorn. It won't sprout.*
¼ cup measure

Small-mouthed quart jar

6-oz (½ mL) foam cup

Thick needle

Saucer

Safety scissors

GETTING READY:

Look over the seeds. Remove any with blemishes.

Use a needle to pierce the bottom and sides of the cup all over to form drainage holes. (Figure 4–4.)

WHOLE-GROUP ACTIVITY:

1. Explain sprouting as a way to learn if the popcorn seeds will grow and a way to grow sprouts to eat. "We'll soon know if the seeds will grow, but big sprouts may take about a week longer. We can all help that happen."
2. Let children measure ¼ cup of popcorn into the jar. Half fill the jar with water. Allow seeds to soak for 24 hours at room temperature, away from bright light.
3. Firmly insert the drain cup into the mouth of the jar as far as it will go. Tip the jar upside down over the sink to drain away the soaking water through the holes in the cup.
4. Refill the jar with cool water. Allow children to help at the sink with rinsing, swirling seeds in the water, and draining carefully over the sink.

FIGURE 4–4

For a large class, prepare two sprouting jars and drain cups to allow more child participation and to provide more sprouts.

5. Invert the jar so that the cup rim serves as a stand, as shown in Figure 4–4. Place it on the saucer. Keep the jar away from direct sunlight and at room temperature.

6. Set up a careful rinsing and draining schedule two or three times each day so that each child has a chance to help the seeds sprout. Plan to take sprouting jar home with you over the weekend to continue the rinsing/draining.

Math Skill: Measuring with a standard kitchen unit.

When the first pale sprout tips push through the seeds, remind children of the question: "Can popcorn seeds grow into plants?" "Yes! They're starting to grow!" Interest mounts when green shoots and tiny leaves form. Then it's time to put the jar in sunlight to allow sprouts to develop chlorophyll, but don't stop the regular rinsing and draining. Those sprouts need water to grow.

When green shoots are about 1 in. (2.5 cm) long, set aside a few seeds and shoots in a separate cup of water. At last, the crop of shoots is ready to be sampled!*

*Improper rinsing and draining can promote spoilage. Do not eat moldy-smelling shoots.

(Popcorn hulls won't soften during the sprouting, so *they can't be eaten*.) Let each child snip a few shoots with scissors, taste them, and be delighted by the fresh, sweet corn flavor of the crop children have helped to raise. Keep the crop growing, and continue snipping fresh shoots until the seeds stop sprouting.

Find the rest of the answer to the seed-to-plant growing question by planting a few of the reserved sprouts in a large flower pot filled with good potting soil or, if permissible, planting several sprouts in a sunny location in good soil in a protected part of the school grounds. Keep the sprouts watered regularly, and the answer should be clear in a few weeks. The plant will grow as tall as the pot size allows, but it won't form ears.

Read selectively: Corn by Gail Gibbons.

CONCEPT: **Some plantlike forms grow from spores.**

1. What is mold?

LEARNING OBJECTIVE: To notice the amazing ways simple plantlike forms
                    grow and develop.

Group Discussion: Bring a piece of bread,* two screw-top jars, and a drop-top bottle (like a soy sauce bottle) of water to a group gathering. Recall with the children that most plants make new plants from seeds or from root and stem parts. Ask what they know about mold. Say that we are going to grow mold plants that use *spores* instead of seeds. Spores are very tiny bits, too tiny to see, but the air is full of them. When spores land on a warm, moist food source, they grow into plants that we can see.

"Perhaps we can make some spores grow on bread." Put half of the bread in each jar. Cover one jar. Let the children sprinkle water on the piece of bread in the second jar. Leave this jar uncovered for an hour. Then cover it and store it in a warm, dark place for a few days. Compare the two pieces of bread. Do they look the same? Leave the moldy bread in the jar to develop a luxuriant fur coat. (Perhaps the black spore clumps will be visible as specks on the mold.) *Always keep the jar closed so that spores won't be inhaled by the children or* you.

Mushroom caps are another source of spores. It is possible to make them visible. Remove the stem from a store-bought mushroom just below the cap. Place the cap, gills down, on a piece of white paper, cover it with an overturned jar, and put it where it will not be disturbed for a day. The next day, remove the jar and the mushroom (carefully). Hopefully, the mushroom left a collection of spores on the paper. They appear as black specks, hopefully in an identifiable pattern. Preserve the pattern with hairspray so the spores won't blow away. These spores would become mushrooms, not mold, of course.

---

*Use bakery bread, which is not treated with preservatives. Prepackaged bread is treated with preservatives to prevent mold growth.

Safety Precaution: Caution children that some growing things are poisonous. Eating or tasting such things could make them extremely sick. They should never pick or eat wild mushrooms. Find out what the children already know about this subject.

INTEGRATING ACTIVITIES

Math Experiences

Keeping Records. Take a shopping bag on nature walks to hold things found along the way. Use these things in the classroom for sorting, classifying, and counting experiences. Record the results on a bulletin board or an experience chart. (*We found:* 12 leaves, 10 acorns, 8 bits of bark, 1 piece of moss.) For younger children, use numerals and samples of the material; for older children, create a bar graph to compare the quantities.

Accumulate Collections. Chestnuts, acorns, pinecones, sweet gum "balls," buttonwood "buttons," and sticks can be collected. Use them as materials to sort, match, count, and weigh. Use them as markers in bingo games. Group them on produce trays to make sets to match with numeral cutouts or numerals marked on cardboard squares. Arrange sticks in order according to their length.

Recording Growth. Use narrow strips of colored paper to record plant growth. Hold a strip beside the plant stem. Cut the strip at the level of the stem height. Tape the strips each day to a posterboard chart, and label each strip with the date to keep a visual record of the plant's growth.

Classifying Seeds. Give children a jar of varied dried beans and legumes to sort into ice cube trays. Have them describe the differences and similarities among the seeds.

Estimating Large Numbers. For older children, give small groups pint jars of beans. Ask for estimates of the number of beans. "How could we find out?" Actual counting is an acceptable way. Children may want to count out a row of beans, then count the number of rows, or devise other shortcut ways to avoid laborious piece-by-piece counting. For large numbers, encourage the use of calculators to simplify the repeated adding or multiplying involved.

Music (Resources in Appendix A)

Sing these children's songs about plants.

1. Sing with Rick Charette "Popcorn" and "Plant a Seed" from his CD, *Popcorn and Other Songs to Munch On.*
2. Sing from *The 2nd Raffi Songbook* "In My Garden" (the digging, planting, and picking could be pantomimed as well), "Popcorn," "All I Really Need" (the rain and the sun to give life to the seeds), and "Apples and Bananas."

3. Sing with Raffi "Everything Grows." Diversity and growth are themes in his song found in the book and CD by this name.

4. Sing "Inch By Inch, the Garden Song."

5. The Spanish/English songbook *La Tierra el Mar,* by the Banana Slug String Band, includes "I'm a Tree" and "Roots, Stems, Leaves."

Plants as Music Makers. Dried gourd maracas are well-known plant instruments. Drums or resonant rhythm instruments can be made from hollow logs and coconut shells. Don't forget willow whistles, dandelion or grass stem whistles, wooden flutes, and recorders. Try to show a set of wooden tone blocks. Chilean rain sticks are made from dried cactus plants.

Literature Links

ALIKI. (2009). *Quiet in the garden.* New York: Harper/Collins. Charming illustrations by the author share the power of observation with listeners.

ARLON, PENELOPE. (2006). *Plant.* New York: DK. Major plant concepts are presented in simple terms for emergent readers. A vibrant layout with clever foldouts adds excitement.

ASTON, DEANNA. (2007). *A seed is sleepy.* San Franscisco: Chronicle. A gentle, informative text and gorgeous illustrations invoke the awesomeness of plant diversity.

BANG, MOLLY. (2009). *Living sunlight: How plants bring the earth to life.* New York: Blue Sky. This strikingly illustrated, remarkable poetic text told in the voice of the sun, describes photosynthesis and its broad significance for life on earth.

BULLARD, LISA. (2011). *Leaves fall down.* Mankato, MN: Picture Window. A mother shares simple leaf processes with her son as they enjoy a fall day outdoors.

COOPER, SHARON. (2007). *Using plants.* Chicago: Heinemann. Plant concepts are presented in simple terms, but the photographs are rich and abundant.

COY, JOHN. (2003). *Two old potatoes and me.* New York: Knopf. This is a patient portrayal of the work, the wait, and the wonder of producing a whole crop from two old potatoes.

EHLERT, LOIS. (2004). *Pie in the sky.* New York: Harcourt. Spectacular collages and a simple story follow a cherry tree from spring blossoms until summer harvest and pie baking, recipe included.

EHLERT, LOIS. (2005). *Leaf man.* New York: Harcourt. Look carefully to match the narrative with brilliant leaf collage forms in this award-winning book. It's sure to inspire leaf collecting and creativity.

GERBER, CAROLE. (2006). *Leaf jumpers.* Watertown, MA: Charlesbridge. Leaves of eight common deciduous trees are identified in the cheerful rhyming text. End page notes explain fall leaf color changes.

GERBER, CAROLE. (2008). *Winter trees.* Watertown, MA: Charlesbridge. In a simple poetic text, the rarely described winter aspects of trees are presented.

GIBBONS, GAIL. (2008). *Corn.* New York: Holiday House. This picture book for independent readers links corn to other times and cultures, considers the many fine ways to eat corn, reveals the unique details of corn pollination, and will surely answer any questions a child could ask.

KUDLINSKI, KATHLEEN. (2005). *What do roots do?* Mankato, MN: Northward. This question is fully answered with a rhyming text in this striking picture book.

LANDAU, ELAIINE. (2003). *Popcorn.* Watertown, MA: Charlesbridge. A mischievous raccoon cavorts through the pages of this compendium of popcorn science, history, and anthropology.

MATTERN, JOANNE. (2006). *How pine trees grow.* Milwaukee, WI: Weekly Reader. This book for beginning readers combines simple concepts with striking, relevant photographs.

McNAMARA, MARGARET. (2006). *Fall leaf project.* New York: Aladdin. Beginning readers will take in simple leaf information in this satisfying story of a first-grade undertaking.

McNamara, Margaret, & Kane, Brian. (2007). *How many seeds in a pumpkin?* New York: Schwartz & Wade. An excited class tackles the messy task of verifying their estimates of seeds in three pumpkin sizes. They work out grouping methods. NSTA* recommended.

Morrison, Gordon. (2004). *Nature in the neighborhood.* Boston: Houghton Mifflin. The author's richly detailed sketches and lovely prose open our eyes to the seasonal unfolding of the natural world at our doorsteps. NSTA* Outstanding Trade Book.

Muldrow, Diane. (2010). *We planted a tree.* New York: Golden Book. An appealing story effectively introduces the very young to the key role trees play in the environment.

Peterson, Christine. (2008). *Trees.* Ann Arbor, MI: Cherry Lake. Basic concepts are given in a text that inspires questioning, observing, and connecting emotionally with trees.

Pfeffer, Wendy. (2004). *From seed to pumpkin.* New York: HarperCollins. Observations of pumpkin growth from seed to Thanksgiving pie includes a seed-roasting recipe.

René, Ellen. (2009). *Why leaves change their color.* New York: Power Kids. A comfortable narrative explains complex leaf processes for advanced young researchers and you.

Ribke, Simone. (2004). *A garden full of sizes.* New York: Children's Press. Plants are the subjects of comparison for height, width, length, and weight in this simple concept book. NSTA recommended.

Roemer, Heidi. (2006). *What seeds are these?* Minnetonka, MN: Northword. Seed dispersal riddles are answered in appealing illustrations. Interesting seed activities are included.

Silverstein, Shel. (1986). *The giving tree.* New York: Harper & Row. In this classic book, a boy grows up with a tree that gives him shade, apples, shelter, and finally, a resting stump.

Star, Fleur. (2005). *Plant.* New York: Dorling Kindersley. This attractive reference book will be useful to fluently reading young researchers. It's a good botany refresher for teachers, too.

Swanson, Susan. (2008). *To be like the sun.* San Diego, CA: Harcourt. A young child reflects on the important work of a sunflower seed in this lyrical story with its uplifting art.

Wade, Mary. (2009). *People need plants.* Berkeley Heights, NJ: Enslow. Impressive, detailed, informative photographs and a relevant text make this book stand out. Also in this fine series: *Seeds—big and small, Plants grow,* and *Seeds sprout.*

Weiss, Ellen. (2008). *From kernel to corncob.* New York: Childrens' Press. The unique life cycle of corn is clearly explained to independent readers. Fine photographs add interest.

Zweibel, Alan. (2005). *Our tree named Steve.* New York: Putnam. A homely but welcoming backyard tree becomes a significant part of a family's life in this true account.

Poems (Resources in Appendix A)

The collection *Poems to Grow On,* compiled by Jean McKee Thompson, has four poems about seeds appropriate to read during the seed investigations:

> "The Little Plant" by Kate Louise Brown
> "The Seed" and "Carrot Seeds" by Aileen Fisher
> "Seeds" by Walter de la Mare

J. Kennedy's poem, "Art Class," in *I Thought I'd Take My Rat to School* by Dorothy Kennedy (Ed.), describes a child's speculations about drawing a tree.

Nancy Turner's poem, "A Popcorn Song," is in the collection *Sing a Song of Popcorn,* compiled by B. DeRegniers.

---

*National Science Teachers Association.

Fingerplays

This traditional fingerplay fits well with the concept that living things reproduce in their own special form.

The Apple Tree	
Way up high in the apple tree	(Stretch arms up.)
Two red apples, I did see.	(Make circles with hands.)
I shook that tree as hard as I could.	(Shake "trunk.")
Mmmmm, those apples tasted good!	(Pat tummy.)

—AUTHOR UNKNOWN

Substitute "orange carrots, green pears, two bananas," and so on for "two red apples, I did see." The children will enjoy catching and correcting your mistake. Ask them why it must be apples growing on the apple tree. "Really? Don't carrots grow on apple trees? Then, where do they grow? Do they grow in the ground from apple seeds?"

My Garden	
This is my garden	(Hold one hand palm up.)
I'll rake it with care.	("Rake" with curled fingers of other hand.)
Here are the seeds	(Pantomime planting, seed by seed.)
I'll plant in there	
The sun will shine	(With arms, make circle above head.)
The rain will fall	(Fingers flutter down.)
The seeds will sprout	(Spread fingers of one hand. Push up other fingers between them.)
And grow up tall.	(Bring hands and forearms together. Move up, spreading palms outward as arms move up.)

—AUTHOR UNKNOWN

Art Activities

Collage. Dried grasses, leaves, pressed flowers, flat seeds, and small twigs make lovely collage materials. Tape may be needed when younger children include twigs and long grasses in their work. Read *Leaf Man* by Lois Ehlert, for inspiration.

Rubbings. Tape a single fresh leaf or a pattern of small leaves to the table in front of each child. Cover with a sheet of heavy paper. Let the children rub a crayon over the paper to bring out the relief design of the leaf veins.

Translucents. Fresh leaves, flower petals, and grasses can be sealed between two sheets of waxed paper to make translucent window hangings. Do not use an electric iron in the classroom to seal the paper. For safety, and for maximum child participation, use a newspaper-covered electric food-warming tray as a heat source. Give children a pizza roller or a child-size rolling pin to apply light strokes of pressure to the waxed paper.

Leaf Mobile. Let the children cut out freehand leaf shapes (or whatever satisfies them as appearing leaflike). In spring, use green paper; in fall, use orange, brown, and red. Use 5-in. (13-cm) squares of paper. Suggest making the job easier by folding the paper in half. Let the children punch a hole in each leaf and thread it with a small bit of yarn. Help them tie or tape their leaves to an interestingly shaped branch. Hang the branch from a ceiling beam or staple it to a bulletin board, with some of the twigs extending into the room.

Play

Farming. Playgrounds that offer a bit of shady ground for digging are natural settings for spontaneous farm play. Provide children with small, sturdy rakes, hoes, shovels, buckets, and a wheelbarrow. They will find rocks or cones to plant and leaves, grasses, or pine needles to harvest without further suggestion. Children will need to know the boundaries of the permissible digging area. Listen to their planting ideas.

Sand Table Indoor Gardens. A collection of twigs, pinecones of several sizes, dried grasses and pods, or perhaps blossoms can be arranged by the children to create small temporary gardens and fairy houses in the sand table. (Dampened sand will hold better than dry sand.).

Blossom Fun. If you can find an abundance of grassflowers for children to gather, use the small blossoms to make beautiful (though short-lived) decorations. Show children how to make a split midway in a dandelion stem in which to insert another dandelion stem, and so on. The resulting rope can be looped into necklaces or crowns or be allowed to get as long as possible. Leaves and sturdy blossoms can be threaded on soft, covered wires from a telephone cable to make bracelets. Large leaves strung together can become headdresses. Two hollyhock blossoms can be stacked and joined through the center with a toothpick to make dolls with hollyhock-bud heads and daisy hats.

CREATIVE MOVEMENT

Curl up on the floor with the children, pretending to be seeds that have been planted in spring (or bulbs planted in fall if this is a class project). Move with the children to enact the growing story as you softly tell it. "Here we are, waiting under the ground. The sunshine makes the soil warm; rain falls, and we begin to expand. The tiny plant inside grows bigger and pokes out of the seed cover. We send a root down to get water. Now our stem starts to push its way up . . . up . . . up to find the sunlight." Slowly describe the growth of the plant above the ground: leafing, budding, blooming, swaying in the breeze, feeling the sun and rain, losing petals, forming seeds, then slowly withering and scattering seeds for next year's plants.

Creative Thinking

What If? What if you were as tiny as your thumb? Which plants would you want to live near? To sleep in? To use for food? To hide under when it rains? To climb for fun? Would you enjoy curling up inside a tulip blossom for a nap? For inspiration, read "The Little Land" by Robert Louis Stevenson in *A Child's Garden of Verses* or "Oak Leaf Plate" by Mary Ann Hoberman in *The Llama Who Had No Pajama* (Appendix A).

Food Experiences

Make popcorn, of course! Use a hot-air popper and natural popcorn.

If grapes are abundant in your area, try drying raisins using purple grapes. In water to cover, boil grapes until their skins pop. Spread them on sprayed baking sheets and bake at 200 degrees Fahrenheit for about three hours until grapes are shriveled, yet supple.

Discuss the parts of plants that are being served for lunch. "Are we eating the leaf, the root, or the stem of the celery plant (the potato, the carrot)?"

Field Trips

We usually think of pleasant woods and meadows as ideal sites for plant life field trips, but the closest grocery store also has important plant learnings for children. Go there to see how much we depend on plants for food. Visit the produce section, the shelves of dry staple foods (flour, pasta, cereals, beans), and the canned and frozen fruits and vegetables. A natural foods store is a fine place to see what whole grains look like and perhaps to watch a nut-grinding mill in operation. Make sure that children are welcomed by the owners.

PROMOTING CONCEPT CONNECTIONS

Maintaining Concepts

A row of potted plants on the classroom windowsill guarantees year-round attention to plant growth needs. Plant tending can occupy an honored position on the children's daily job chart. Younger children may need some help carrying the pitcher and deciding how much water to use. Older children can handle the task independently if pots are labeled with suitable watering advice. Comment on changes taking place, such as new buds, fading leaves, and unwanted insect tenants.

Classes in session during the regional growing season might be able to keep plant life concepts in focus by planting and maintaining a garden. Other classes could try portable gardens: plants started at school in the spring, moved to the home of a child or teacher for summer care, and returned to school for a fall harvest—with luck. Start pumpkin and sunflower seeds in good soil, using 2-gallon plastic buckets with drainage holes cut in the bottom. Thin out all but one vigorous seedling. Give it full sunshine and plenty of water. The plants won't attain full growth, but the pumpkin can produce a vine with leaves, tendrils, blossoms, and

"Look what those seeds did!" Life cycle studies are essential.

possibly a fledgling pumpkin. The sunflower will develop a seed head and may grow taller than a five- or six-year-old. Slip a section of old hosiery or netting over the fading blossom to keep the birds from feasting on the seeds too soon.

If long-term growing projects cannot be worked out, perhaps you can duplicate the efforts of one very fine teacher of three-year-olds. Each fall she scouts the countryside to find a whole, dried cornstalk complete with ears of corn. It creates a fall harvest mood in her room and provides an awesome lesson for the children, who seem dwarfed by the giant that grew from a single kernel of corn. Later, shelling the corn becomes an absorbing task for the children. They feed kernels to the birds.

Improving School Grounds

In a protected place, begin a small orchard (apples, pears, plums) and berry patch (blueberry, raspberry, gooseberry). Children delight in growing real food (see Gardening, p. 306). Add a few trees each year.

Connecting Concepts

Soil Composition Relationships. The natural cycle of renewing limited materials in the ecosystem is well illustrated in the creation of fertile soil. Pulverize shale to form powdery clay (see Chapter 10), or use sand or clay if shale isn't available. Try growing an extra seedling in it. Compare its growth with that of seedlings growing in true soil that also contains bits of decayed plant and animal matter. This idea could lead to starting a compost bag in the fall. Let the children rake available leaves and grass clippings into a large plastic trash bag. When it is approximately half full, add a soup can full of fertilizer or powdered lime, a can of water, and a few shovels of dirt. Close the bag and leave it outdoors, where it won't be forgotten during the winter. It will need to be turned, shaken, and opened several times for airing. Although the completeness of the change that will occur by spring is not predictable, bacterial growth within the bag environment will have interacted with the materials to promote decay into compost to enrich the soil.

Discuss how completely rotted natural materials improve the soil and make it possible for strong, new plants to grow and produce food. Talk about renewing the soil this way as one of the wonderful cycles of nature: from living plants to decomposition, from enriched soil to healthy living plants, again and again. It is comforting to understand the concept that once-living things continue to have a function after they die.

Plants That Help Crumble Rocks. Look in shady areas for greenish-gray patches of lichen growing on rocks. Lichen are fungi and algae that live together as a single unit. Together they make acids that slowly dissolve the rock surface.

Other plants sometimes grow in rock crevices, and their roots may break off pieces of rock. Perhaps there is a section of concrete sidewalk near your school that has been cracked or pushed up by strong tree roots. Watch for them as you take walks with the children. Stop to look at them. Recall with the children that slowly crumbling rocks become part of the soil that plants grow in.

Air. The wind helps ripe dandelion and milkweed seeds float long distances under silky parachutes, and it helps maple and ash tree seeds spin down and away to germinate. Try germinating a ripe winged seed if you have a maple tree nearby. A ripe seed splits in half. Plant the seed deep in a plastic tumbler. Leave the wing part out as a reminder of how it spun down on a breeze from the tree. It can produce a sturdy sprout and a tiny leaf in about a month.

Air/Water Cycle. Use the term *evaporation* when plants are being watered. Some of the water will be taken up by the roots of the plants; the rest will evaporate.

Family and Community Support

Children may keep their parents well informed about the progress of their seedling experiences. Family help will be needed to provide a good growing location and to oversee the care of the seedling that is sent home. Printed plant care tips could be fastened to the container. Include a few lines about other aspects of the projects that can help parents become informed listeners to their children. Encourage gardening families to set aside a small space for their child to plant and tend.

Share information with parents about nearby nature center or natural history museum programs for children. Inquire about naturalist-led walks through the nature center for families. A community gardening program sponsors family gardening activities.

RESOURCES

GRAY, SUSAN. (2010). *Seeds: Super cool science experiments.* Ann Arbor, MI: Cherry Lake.

LACOCK, JANICE. (2005). *Tree.* New York: Dorling Kindersley. Reach for this compendium of tree facts when children need information or when you need to be inspired by diversity in nature.

LOVEJOY, SHARON. (2009). *Toad cottages and shooting stars.* New York: Workman.

MATT, MEGAN. (2008). Plant parts snack—a way to family involvement. *Young Children, 36*(6), 98–99.

PETERSON, DEBORAH (2008). *Don't throw it: Grow it! 68 windowsill plants from kitchen scraps.* North Adams, MA: Storey. A reliable way to start an avocado plant is offered.

PICA, RAE. (2009). *Jump into science: Active learning for preschool children* Beltsville, MD: Gryphon House.

RUSSELL, HELEN. (2001). *Ten-minute field trips: Using the school grounds for environmental studies* (2nd ed.). Washington, DC: National Science Teachers Association. Every city-bound teacher should know this book. Nature's ability to triumph over asphalt and concrete permeates the text.

 *ONLINE RESOURCES*

Annenberg Media: Science K-6: Learning through inquiry.

- *All Sorts of Leaves*: A first-grade class in Boynton Beach, Florida, studies biodiversity by taking a close look at leaves. (50 min).

- *All Sorts of Leaves*: A conversation about teaching; reflecting on the issues raised in *All Sorts of Leaves*. (55 min)

Available at *http://www.learner.org/resources/series116.html*

BELLOUS, KAREN. (2004). Looking at the trees around us. *Early Childhood Research and Practice, 6*(1) (a tree study with 5- to 7-year-olds). A University of Illinois online resource. Retrieved July 22, 2010, from *http://ecrp.uiuc.edu/v6n1/bellous.html*

U. S. Department of Agriculture

Sci4Kids."Plants."

Available at *http://www.ars.usda.gov/is/kids/plants/plantsintro.htm*

5

Animals

The unexpected sight of a grazing fawn, dolphins at play, or a heron taking flight: memories of breathtaking glimpses of wildlife can help you inspire children to care about the animals they meet through activities in this chapter.

Animals of all sizes and conditions fascinate many children, who are eager to watch, touch, and care for creatures. Other children have limited tolerance for anything that creeps, crawls, or nips. The experiences suggested in this chapter can both expand the knowledge of the creature lovers and soften the feelings of anxious children into moderate respect for the useful and beautiful small animals around us. These concepts will be explored:

- There are many kinds of animals.
- Animals move in different ways.
- Each animal needs its own kind of food.
- Many animals make shelters to rear their young.
- Humans and animals often live together.

The feasibility of this chapter's experiences will depend on having specimens for observation. Flexible planning is necessary. It would be sheer luck for a spider and a teacher to meet precisely on the day set aside for spider study.

Buying, housing, and maintaining classroom pets can be expensive. However, earthworms, spiders, and insects exist everywhere and can easily be obtained. The experiences that follow use insects, worms, fish, wild birds, and pictures to illustrate concepts. Suggestions for acquiring and understanding insects, as well as ideas pertaining to borrowed pets, are included.

CONCEPT: **There are many kinds of animals.**

Introduce this topic with a question for children to think about: "What is an animal?" Responses about specific animals will flow easily. Then suggest that there are so many kinds of animals in the world that it would take days just to say their names. "Here is a shorter way to say what an animal is: An animal is a living thing, but it is not a plant." How many animals can the children think of now? Their list can include people, spiders, earthworms, and insects. There are more than a million species of insects alone! All insects—indeed, all animals—have some features in common.

1. What is an insect?
LEARNING OBJECTIVE: To develop interest in insect features.

MATERIALS:
Temporary cages (see page 82)
Live insects
Leafy plant sprigs
Water spray bottle
Magnifying glasses
Drawing materials

GETTING READY:
Use the capture techniques that follow.
Keep live insect cages out of direct sunlight.

SMALL-GROUP ACTIVITY:
1. Ground rules for observation should be set: (a) Insects or other small animals stay in the cages and (b) cages must be handled gently.
2. Suggest looking for things that identify members of the insect family: three body parts (head, thorax, abdomen); six legs; two feelers (antennae). Spiders are *not* insects (they have eight legs); caterpillars *are* (only six legs are true, jointed legs).
3. Have children draw pictures of the insects they are watching.
4. Mention: (a) These are adult insects. First they were eggs, then larvae (wingless, wormlike) before changing to adult form. (b) Insects have no bones. They have stiff coverings protecting their soft bodies.
5. Release insects outdoors at the end of the day.

Read: I Love Bugs! by Philemon Sturges.

Capture Techniques

Locating Creatures. Start looking for specimens near your own doorstep. On warm nights, check screen doors for insects that are attracted by light. Hunt for web-building spiders on window frames and shrubs. Turn over rocks and logs on the ground to find crickets, beetles, and such. Look in flower borders for lady-bugs, bumblebees, grasshoppers, ants, and wandering spiders that chase their prey instead of catching them on webs. Examine weed clumps like Queen Anne's lace and milkweed for caterpillars.

Catching Creatures. Cold-blooded animals do not move rapidly in cool parts of the day. A bumblebee is groggy and easy to catch early on a crisp fall morning. Scoop it up with an open jar, then quickly clap on the lid. Slip in a dewy sprig of the plant that the bee rested on and re-cover the jar with a piece of nylon hosiery or netting held with a rubber band. Bees may be easier to locate during warmer parts of the day *but are quicker to defend themselves.* Try using bamboo toast tongs to catch an alert bee. Use tongs to pick up very spiky-looking caterpillars. Some cause skin rashes if touched.

Wandering ground spiders and grasshoppers may be caught by clapping an open jar over them. Both species seem to hop straight up inside the jar, making it easy to slip the lid under it. Nets are preferred for the safe capture of butterflies and moths. Sweep the net over the insect; flip the bag to fold it over the catch. Remove the butterfly by gently holding two wings folded back together. Slip it into a sandwich bag. Keep the insect out of the sun until it can be transferred to an observation terrarium or box.

Only two small spiders have a dangerous bite. **Avoid:**

- *The black widow:* Has a shiny black body with a bright red hourglass mark beneath the abdomen (back section). Young ones may have three red dots on top of the abdomen.
- *The brown recluse:* Rare. Lives indoors in attics, closets, or other dark corners. Yellow to brownish color. The fiddle-shaped mark on top of the front section (cephalothorax) is dark brown. The base of the fiddle is between the feelers; the neck of the fiddle runs toward the spider's abdomen.

Temporary Housing

There are several ways to make inexpensive cages for small creatures; however, releasing a specimen after a day in the classroom teaches responsible stewardship. Comment that the insect is needed outside for cleanup work or pest control or to help flowers make seeds (Table 5–1). This also skirts the problem of providing live food for some small animals.

A simple temporary cage for small insects can be made by covering a clean plastic tumbler with a piece of nylon hosiery, stretched and held in place with a strip of tape. For larger insects, cut large windows in the sides of a plastic deli container, as shown in Figure 5–1. Add a dampened piece of sponge and a sprig of a plant from near the insect-catching location. Pull the foot half of an old nylon stocking over the container, gathering the top tightly with a rubber band. Snap the carton lid over the gathering.

If a small terrarium is available, use it to house active grasshoppers. Put a layer of sand on the bottom along with small branches or plant sprigs for the grasshopper to climb.

FIGURE 5–1

Keep cages on hand to use whenever children bring small creatures to share. (It can be difficult to sell some children on the cage idea. Joey, for one, was in favor of keeping his caterpillar on a leash of "gotch tape.")

One fascinating exception to the same-day-release rule is a mother spider. She does not feed during the period of egg sac construction or during the weeks before the spiderlings emerge from the sac. The spiderlings also have a stored food supply for use after their birth.

Wolf spiders fasten egg sacs to their undersides. The babies migrate to the mother's back after emerging. There, they cling as passengers to knob-tipped hairs. A wolf spider and her young can survive for a week of observation in a plastic playing-card box if moisture is provided.

A potential disappointment with spider watching is that the mother spider spins an egg sac whether the eggs have been fertilized by a male spider or not. If the eggs are infertile, the mother does not tear the sac open.

Insect Pests

Some insects do more harm than good to humans and plants. Among them are flies, mosquitoes, cockroaches, black widow and brown recluse spiders, miller moths, and clothes moths. Many insects that sting to defend themselves will not bother people if they are not disturbed. Among them are wasps, hornets, bees, and spiders (Table 5–1).

2. How do insects' bodies change as they grow?

LEARNING OBJECTIVE: To observe the fascinating process of insect metamorphosis.

Introduction: Elicit children's information about the special way that most insects grow. Clarify that insects' bodies change in surprising ways as they grow

Table 5–1   Facts About Common Insects

Insect	Function	Interesting Features
Ants	Scavengers who clean their surroundings. Pollinators of flowers.	Social insects that live in colonies with separate jobs to perform: Some nurse young, some gather food.
Bees	Highly valued pollinators of plants. Producers of honey and beeswax.	Social insects that live in colonies with specialized jobs to perform.
Butterflies	Pollinators of plants. (Explain to children that they help plants make seeds.)	Slender bodies. Antennae have ball tips. Fly by day. Fold wings straight up when resting. Usually form a chrysalis.
Moths	Some are pollinators. Silk moths spin strong, lustrous fibers that are made into fabric.	Fat, furry bodies. Feather antennae. Wings spread flat when resting. Usually spin cocoons. Fly at night.
Beetles	Some kinds are scavengers that tidy up. Ladybug beetles are valued by gardeners for pest control. Some beetles destroy crops.	Many handsome varieties: striped, spotted, iridescent.
Crickets	Serve as food for other animals. Destructive to some crops.	Only male crickets chirp. They raise and rub their hard wing covers to make vibrations.
Fireflies (soft-bodied beetles)	Appreciated for adding charm to summer nights.	Fireflies signal to one another with flashes of light.
Grasshoppers and Locusts	Destroy some crops but serve as food for other animals.	Wings barely visible when flying. Use hind pair of legs to jump. Hearing area is in the abdomen.
Praying Mantis	So valuable for pest control that egg cases are sold to gardeners.	Almost 4 in. (10 cm) long, so body parts are easily seen. Frightening to see them tearing other insects apart.
Wasps and Hornets	Some wasps pollinate fruit trees. Some eat destructive larvae.	Hornets and some wasps chew dead wood into paper to make nests for their young. Some wasps make nests from mud. Beautiful engineering.

from tiny eggs to adults. The change process is called *metamorphosis* (the transforming stages of the life cycle). "We can see how some of the changes happen with one kind of insect here in our classroom. For many weeks, we will watch mealworms change forms and also discover what they can do and like." Explain that mealworms and the adult beetles they become are harmless. They can't crawl out of their containers. Because the eggs are too small to be seen without a microscope, these observations will begin with the *larva*, mealworm, stage.

MATERIALS:

Mealworms, two for each child (buy at pet store)

Pint freezer storage boxes, for each group of four or five children*

Produce trays

Marking pen

Hammer, nail

Pound of bran meal (not breakfast cereal; buy at health food store)

Apple or potato

Paring knife

Magnifiers

GETTING READY:

Mark a group number/name on each box.

Punch a few air holes in box tops with the hammer and nail.

Pour 3 in. (7.5 cm) of bran into each box.

Add a slice of apple or potato.

Gently place mealworms on the bran.

Cover with box tops after observations.

SMALL-GROUP ACTIVITY:

1. Hold a mealworm in your hand. "How would you feel if you were being held softly in a big person's hand?" Establish ground rules for studying mealworms: (a) They should be held softly; (b) they should be looked at with magnifiers; (c) they should be put on different places on the tray; (d) children wash their hands after handling mealworms.

2. Gently lift a mealworm onto each tray for children to observe with magnifiers. Watch reassuringly slow movements. Look for eyes, mouth, legs, antennae, and body segments. Have children draw their observations. Return mealworms to boxes in the science center. Add fresh apple/potato slices if mold appears, or when food is withered and dry. Mealworms also enjoy citrus peel.

3. Encourage independent daily observations for signs of activity or change such as collecting on apple/potato to suck moisture; shedding skins as worms (larva) grow; changing to inert pupa, changing to adult beetles (eggs are too small to be seen without a microscope).

4. Experiment each week with a different environmental condition to learn how mealworms prefer to live: (a) put wet paper toweling on half the tray; (b) cover half the box with dark paper to create half shade, half light; (c) put mealworms on a tray with small piles of bran, grass, or shredded

---

*Mealworms can be kept in a terrarium, but children can feel more connected to those "owned" by their small group. Each small study group is given a number.

The practice of close observation can provide lasting satisfaction.

paper; (d) put mealworms on a tray with a cotton ball dipped in vinegar. Allow an hour for mealworms to make choices. Chart children's observations.

5. You can keep a mealworm colony going indefinitely. Or you can put worms outside in the grass to become bird food or to help decompose waste products.

Group Discussion: As transformations occur, point out the persistence of characteristic body parts such as six legs, head, and antennae, in all three stages. Note that the larva sheds its skin when it outgrows the old one. The larval stage can take up to 10 weeks. The pupa rarely moves for 2 or 3 weeks, but it's changing inside. Record the children's observations and insights into this basic life process. This activity challenges children's expectations, but if the mealworms can be kept for 2 or more months, the repeated transformations will be persuasive. The process is good for measuring time, giving children a sense of how long several months are.

Math skills: Counting body parts and legs; charting observations of mealworm behaviors.

Read: Mealworms by Martha Rustad.

CONCEPT: Animals move in different ways.

1. How does an earthworm move?

LEARNING OBJECTIVE: To be intrigued by legless animal movement.

♣ *Introduction:* Ask children, "Do you need six legs to walk? If your body were bent over and close to the ground, would more legs help keep you balanced? What helps some insects and birds move through the air? Can you think of a very small animal that has no legs—one that only has muscles and tiny bristles to help it move? Perhaps we'll find some worms to watch when we go outdoors."

MATERIALS:

Shovels, if a digging place is available

Bucket

Scoop

Produce trays

Magnifiers

Light-colored sand

Potting soil

Clear plastic shoe box

Nylon stocking

Rubber band

Crumbled dry leaves (not oak leaves)

Black paper

Tape

GETTING READY:

Before taking children to the digging spot, check for presence of earthworms.

If digging isn't possible, buy worms locally or from a science supply catalog.

SMALL-GROUP ACTIVITY:

1. ♣ Let children help dig earthworms, if permitted, in light soil.
2. Let children help make a worm farm. Spread a layer of sand on the bottom of the box. Add a 2-in. (5-cm) layer of soil. Top with 2 in. (5 cm) of sand. Add a final layer of soil. Moisten with a small amount of water.
3. Cover with bits of crushed leaves. Put *all but two* earthworms *on* the leaves. Do not cover with soil. Stretch stocking over the top. Secure with a rubber band.
4. Put two worms on trays to observe movement with magnifiers. (Bristles are retractable and hard to see.) A wide, light band at the midsection is the egg case. The tail end is tapered; the head end is rounded. "Do they have eyes?" Have children record their observations as drawings, written descriptions, or creative movement.

Read: Winnie Finn, Worm Farmer by Carol Brendler.

Care of Earthworms

Earthworm Farm Care. Wrap black paper around the worm farm to encourage tunneling where it can easily be seen. It will take about a week for the earthworms to get used to the new soil before they start tunneling. Remove the paper for short periods of time to check for signs of activity.

Earthworms will not survive long in dry soil. Keep the farm away from a heat source. Sprinkle the soil frequently to keep it damp.

Maddie's gentle attention exhibits her developing care for living things.

Dark soil streaks in the light sand show how earthworms mix soils as they make tunnels. Bits of leaf will be pulled into the tunnels. Let children investigate what worms will eat, putting out a different small bit of food each day, such as celery leaves or dry oatmeal. Observe and record what disappears into the worm tunnels.

Tiny balls surrounding tunnel holes on the surface of the soil are the castings of soil digested by the earthworms. This is one way that worms enrich the soil. They also help water and air reach plant roots as they make their tunnels.

How to Hold an Earthworm. Youngsters credit adults with unlimited ability and courage. Measuring up to this idealism can be hard for some of us when it means holding a child's cherished earthworm. Bolster your courage for this eventuality by understanding your tactile senses: Compare the sensation of holding a slippery object in the palm of your hand with that of holding the same object between your thumb and forefinger. The palm of the hand has fewer nerve endings to convey tactile sensations. Therefore, a placid worm that is loosely cupped in the palm of your hand will scarcely be felt. Hand washing is required after holding earthworms.

2. How does a fish move?

LEARNING OBJECTIVE: To enjoy noticing the working parts of fish movement.

MATERIALS:

Small aquarium or wide-mouth
  gallon jar

Aquarium gravel or lake sand

Rocks

Water plant—purchased or from
  lake or stream

1 small goldfish

Black paper

Newspaper

Water

GETTING READY:

Involve children in
  preparations.

SMALL-GROUP ACTIVITY:

1. Look at the body of the fish. Discuss how it is different from the earthworm's body.
2. Recall the looping, sliding movements of worms. Compare with varied movements of the fish as it darts up, down, forward, or backward or rests.
3. Find seven fins: two pairs approximately where our arms and legs grow, topside, underside, and tail fins. (Arm and leg position fins work fast to move fish forward and back; top and bottom fins give balance; tail fins steer fish as it swings from side to side. Some fins look like fancy decorations; although they have delicate bones, they work hard.)

Let a gallon of water stand overnight in open containers so chlorine can escape.

Wash local water plants carefully. Wash lake sand in a deep pan by letting a slow stream of *hot* water fill, pan. (Plants and gravel from a good pet store need not be washed.)

Put an inch of sand or gravel in jar. Put plant roots in sand and anchor with a rock.

Cover sand with folded newspaper while pouring in water.

Remove paper.

Put fish in water.

4. Tap the tank lightly. Does the fish go faster? Does it move differently to speed up? Watch closely.

5. To keep the fish as a class pet, put fish feeding on a rotating routine chart. Each day, a different child can feed it a *pinch* of tropical fish food.* No weekend feeding is needed. Keep the aquarium away from direct sunlight. Tape dark-colored paper around the side closest to the window to reduce algae growth. Some light is needed, however. Siphon or dip out one third of the water and replace it with aerated water as needed.

Math skills: Counting fish fins, informally measuring fish swimming speed, charting feeding schedule.

Read: Out and About at the Aquarium by Amy Rechner.

CONCEPT: **Each animal needs its own kind of food.**

Introduction: Ask children, "Did you have a nice bowl of acorns and a plateful of grass with ladybugs for breakfast today? Why not? What did you have?" Help children recognize that each kind of animal needs its own kind of food in order to live. Discuss making a feeder to help winter birds get the kind of food they need. Plan to maintain the feeder until spring. Some birds may come to depend on that food supply and starve without it.

1. How can we feed winter birds?
LEARNING OBJECTIVE: To enjoy nurturing wild animals with food.

MATERIALS:
Half-gallon (2 L) milk carton
12-in. (30-cm) stick
Scissors

SMALL-GROUP ACTIVITY:
Let children help make and supply feeders.

1. *For chickadees, cardinals, and others:* Cut out long windows on two sides of the carton,

---

*Try training the fish by always dropping the pinch of food in the same corner of the tank. Children will be interested to find that fish can learn, just as they can.

Twine or monofilament fishing line*

Commercial wild birdseed plus seeds saved from plant experiences

Dried pinecones

String

Peanut butter

Plastic pint berry baskets

Suet

2 in. (5 cm) above the bottom. Push the stick through the feeder near the bottom to form two outside perches. Pierce holes through the carton top. Thread with twine or fishing line. Tie to a tree branch low enough to reach easily for refilling with wild birdseed.

2. *For nuthatches, woodpeckers, others:* Wind string around the top scales of cones to form a hanging loop. Let children use spoon handles to stuff peanut butter between the scales. Roll filled cones in birdseed. Hang them on branches.

3. *For flickers, jays, mockingbirds, others:* Let children lace two baskets together with twine to form a closed container. Add chunks of suet before the last side is lashed together. Fasten to tree.

Math skills: Counting birds at the feeder, recording data.

Read: Two Blue Jays by Anne Rockwell.

CONCEPT: **Many animals make shelters to rear their young.**

1. How can we help nest-building birds?

LEARNING OBJECTIVE: To enjoy helping nesting wild birds.

Introduction: Ask children, "Do you think that a mother bird lays eggs on tree branches and leaves them to hatch by themselves? Of course not! She works hard, sometimes with the father bird, to build a nest where she can keep the eggs warm and keep the hatched babies safe and fed. When the babies are big enough to take care of themselves, usually the whole family leaves the nest. Some kinds of birds return to old nests each year; others do not. We can help birds build new nests."

MATERIALS:

Plastic berry baskets or mesh onion bags

6-in. (15-cm) pieces of yarn

SMALL-GROUP ACTIVITY:

1. If a nest can be brought in or visited, let children examine the structure. "Is it lined with special material? Why?"

---

*Monofilament fishing line is too smooth for squirrels to grip, so they won't gobble all the bird food. Position feeders out of reach of squirrels or cats. Sprinkle seeds on the ground beneath feeders for a few days to attract birds.

Spanish moss, if available

Dried tall grass

Dryer lint

Desirable: Bird nest, legitimately salvaged* or loaned by a nature center, or existing nest to visit on-site near your school

Magnifiers

2. Let children prepare nest materials for birds that come to school feeders. Pull apart clumps of Spanish moss. Place them loosely in berry baskets. Work strands of yarn, dryer lint, short twigs, and long grass through mesh bags.

3. Hang baskets outdoors near feeders.

Read: *Even an Ostrich Needs a Nest* by Irene Kelly.

CONCEPT: Humans and animals often live together.

1. Why do people have pets?

LEARNING OBJECTIVE: To enjoy collecting personal information about pets.

? *Inquiry Activity:* Ask children, "Do you know people who have pets in their homes? Why do you think people have pets? How do they take care of their pets? Would you like to find out about pets belonging to children in our class or in our school?" Discuss how the group could conduct an inquiry about pets. Consider questions to ask and ways to keep track of and organize information. Decide how the information could be shared with others. Children could vote on the questions and survey methods suggested. This could be a collaborative inquiry for the whole class, depending on the children's interests.

Read: *Finding Susie* by Sandra Day O'Connor.

Animals in the Classroom

The Borrowed Pet. Much can be learned by children who help provide for the daily life requirements of a classroom pet. Many of those learnings can also be sampled during a short visit by a borrowed pet.

Before the pet arrives, discuss with the children safe ways to watch and care for it. For small pets accustomed to pens, make an observation box from a large carton. Cut windows in the sides and cover them with plastic wrap, if needed. Some pets are better off being held by their owners during the visit. Try to let children see the animals eating and drinking water. Help children find answers to questions about how the animal moves, gets its food, and protects itself. Does the

---

*The Migratory Bird Treaty Act of 1918 forbids the collection of most *migratory* bird nests, eggs, or feathers without a Federal Migratory Bird Permit. For information about applying for a salvage permit for educational purposes, contact your State Fish and Wildlife Service. **Health precaution:** Children should not be allowed to touch a nest, since it may harbor mites or other allergens.

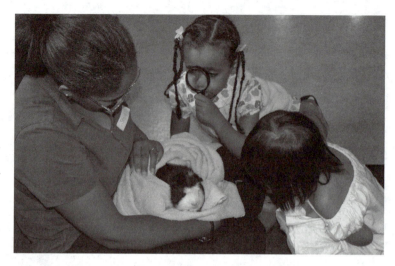

Love of Biscuit is combined with studying him with simple science tools.

pet have bones inside or a hard outside covering? Does it have hair or fur, smooth skin or feather-covered skin? Does it nurse its young? Does it build a shelter for its young?

Animal visitors to our school included a pet boa constrictor, which laced itself through the rungs of a chair, and a small pony that was unexpectedly led into the building by a mischievous owner.

Animal Rearing. Rearing butterflies or moths from the caterpillar, chrysalis, or cocoon stage can be enthralling or disappointing. Strong interest and luck are required for success. Using commercial butterfly kits may have the unfortunate effect of introducing nonnative species to your area and may release butterflies into an environment lacking appropriate food. If you can find caterpillars or cocoons in your local environment, rearing them is environmentally more sensible. Follow the procedures described in *The Family Butterfly Book* by Rick Mikula.

The same mixture of dedication and luck also contributes to a good outcome with an egg-incubating project. A commercial incubator is probably a better choice than improvised equipment for classroom use. Follow the instructions included with the incubator. Be sure that the fertile eggs have not been allowed to cool after being laid. Plan to find a home for the chick or duckling after it has hatched.

Are Classroom Pets Necessary? Good teachers allow for individual differences in children's responses to animals. They do not assume that all children adore animals. They do not insist that a fearful child make physical contact with animals. Although they should avoid expressing negative attitudes about animals to children, teachers should extend the same consideration to their own feelings about animals.

Teachers need not feel obligated to undertake year-long care of an animal if they cannot manage the responsibility. The teacher's primary affective focus and primary responsibility are caring about children. Feeling similar warmth toward animals is an asset but not a requirement. It should be a consideration, however, that many urban children have no other opportunity than classroom pets to interact positively with animals.

INTEGRATING ACTIVITIES

Math Experiences

Animal Math Materials. Many commercial math materials incorporate animals. These include:

1. Animal match-up puzzle cards that link numerals with sets of animals
2. Magnet and flannel board counting sets
3. Sequence puzzles showing the development from egg to butterfly, from egg to frog, and from nest building to robin egg hatching
4. Animal rummy puts set-making into a game context; the cards can also be used for playing Memory (Concentration)

Record Keeping. Take digital pictures of all animals seen in class. Laminated photographs can be sorted by the children by type, size, or color.

If your class tries a chick-incubating project, make a chain of 21 large paper clips to represent the days of the incubation period. Remove a clip each day and count the days left in the waiting period.

Measuring. Read *Measuring Penny* by Loreen Leedy to introduce standard and nonstandard measuring activities.

Graphing. Read *Tiger Math* by Ann Magda and *The Great Graphing Contest* by Penny Leedy.

Fractions. Read *Inchworm and a Half* by Eleanor Pinczes for beginning ideas about fractions.

Music (Resources in Appendix A)

1. Try to find and listen to the electronic birdsong "Identiflyer," recorded in the field by For the Birds at http://www.identiflyer.com. Look for sounds of nature tapes at yard sales or on E-Bay with birdcalls in the background. Play a tape when a peaceful ambience is helpful.
2. Sing along with "You Can't Make a Turtle Come Out" on Mary Miche's cassette, *Earthy Tunes.* It reminds children that, to observe animals, "you'll have to patiently wait."
3. Listen to songs about raccoons, ants, otters, fish, moose, and more on *Penguin Parade,* a CD by the Banana Slug String Band.
4. Sing along with Rick Charette "Frogs in the Road" and "If I Had One Wish (I'd Wish I was an Animal)" from his CD, *Bubble Gum.*

5. Listen to *Birds, Beasts, Bugs, and Little Fishes,* sung by Pete Seeger. The songs were written by Ruth Seeger in *Animal Folk Songs for Children.*

6. Younger children enjoy "I Like the Animals in the Zoo," sung by Ella Jenkins on *Seasons for Singing.* The song provides a good pattern for improvising about the animals that visit your room:

> *I like the grasshopper, in the jar.*
> *I like the grasshopper, it jumps far.*

Also note that animal horns were among the earliest forms of musical instruments. Conch shells are still used as horns in some parts of the world. A ram's horn, the *shofer,* is blown through in Jewish High Holiday ceremonies. One of the percussion instruments on our classroom music shelf was an unoccupied box turtle shell. The children enjoyed tapping rhythms on it.

Literature Links: Animal Characteristics

BALLINGER, EMILY. (2004). *Bird beaks.* Washington, DC: National Geographic. In this book for beginning readers, excellent photographs illustrate how a single adaptation in beak shape allows different birds to find appropriate food.

BATTEN, MARY. (2008). *Please don't wake the animals: A book about sleep.* Atlanta: Peachtree. Here are fascinating facts about diverse animal sleep patterns.

COLLARD, SNEED. (2008). *Wings.* Watertown, MA: Charlesbridge. Follow a single feature, wings, to discover astonishing diversity among animals. NSTA* Outstanding Trade Book.

GRAHAM-BARBER, LYNDA. (2004). *Spy hops and belly flops: Curious behavior of woodland animals.* Boston: Houghton Mifflin. In rhyming fun, large type inspires children to imitate animal movements, while small-type asides explain the purpose of the animal behavior.

JENKINS, STEVE. (2008). *How many ways can you catch a fly?* Boston: Houghton Mifflin. Capturing prey and finding shelter are explored. NSTA* Outstanding Trade Book.

KANER, ETTA. (2005). *Animals migrating: How, why, when, and where animals migrate.* Toronto: Kids Can Press. Migratory patterns of 28 animals will awe advanced readers.

SCHWARTZ, DAVID. (2007). *Where in the wild? Camouflaged creatures concealed . . . and revealed.* Berkeley, CA: Tricycle Press. Witty poem hints at hidden animals; fold-out pages reveal them. Listeners will love this book. NSTA* Outstanding Trade Book.

STEWART, MELISSA. (2009). *Under the snow.* Atlanta: Peachtree. This beautiful book offers respect for creatures surviving on their own. NSTA* Outstanding Trade Book.

STOCKLAND, PATRICIA. (2004). *Red eyes or blue feathers: A book about animal colors.* Minneapolis: Picture Window. Focused graphics and an inviting text identify three ways that color helps animals survive in the wild. Intriguing sidebar and end page facts add usefulness. NSTA* Outstanding Tradebook.

Literature Links: Insects, Spiders, and Earthworms

BARNER, BOB. (2004). *Bug safari.* New York: Holiday House. Equipped with a hand lens, a youngster crawls along with a line of ants, sharing their adventures and learning their characteristics as he goes. Bold art and a charming story will spark preschoolers' imagination. NSTA* recommended.

BISHOP, NIC. (2009). *Nic Bishop's butterflies and moths.* New York: Scholastic. Intimate photographs and a comfortable, meticulous text make this a treasure to share.

BREDESON, CARMEN. (2006). *Monarch butterflies up close.* Berkeley Heights, NJ: Enslow. Learn how adaptations shaped monarch behavior. NSTA* recommended.

*National Science Teachers Association.

Brendler, Carol. (2009). *Winnie Finn, worm farmer.* New York: Farrar, Straus, Giroux. Enterprising Winnie's gifts of worms solve her neighbor's problems and teach us the value of earthworms. Worm farm construction directions are given.

Cronin, Doreen. (2005). *Diary of a spider.* New York: HarperCollins. What does our world look like to a busy young spider? Humorous illustrations from intriguing perspectives start imaginations flowing! Also by this author: (2003). *Diary of a worm.*

Frost, Helen. (2008). *Monarch and milkweed.* New York: Atheneum. Parallel life cycle narratives of a host plant and a monarch come together when the butterfly lays an egg under one leaf. Endnotes include migration. NSTA* Outstanding Trade Book.

Glaser, Linda. (2008). *Dazzling dragonflies: A life cycle story.* Minneapolis: Millbrook. This gentle description and pleasant art will clear up misconceptions about dragonflies.

Gran, Julia. (2007). *Big bug surprise.* New York: Scholastic. A girl's passion for insects prevents a classroom disaster in this lighthearted picture book.

Haskins, Lori. (2004). *Butterfly fever.* New York: Kane. Ellie's class tracks and celebrates the annual migration of monarchs to California. Sidebars add information on butterflies.

Hodge, Deborah. (2004). *Ants.* Tonawanda, NY: Kid's Can Press. This lively book informs and intrigues with accurate, clear illustrations and photos. It should win respect for these useful creatures. Ant experiments are offered.

Koontz, Robin. (2010). *What's the difference between a butterfly and a moth?* Minneapolis: Picture Window. Here are complete, intriguing, and satisfying answers to childrens' frequently asked questions.

Loewen, Nancy. (2004). *Living lights: Fireflies in your backyard.* Minneapolis: Picture Window. Firefly characteristics and life cycle stages are cheerfully described and illustrated from interesting perspectives. Other titles in this Backyard Bug series are *Night fliers: Moths; Tiny workers: Ants; Buzy buzzers: Bees;* and *Hungry hoppers: Grasshoppers.* Both independent readers and listeners will enjoy them. NSTA* recommended.

Markle, Sandra. (2004). *Spiders. Biggest! Littlest!* Honesdale, PA: Boyds Mills Press. Size helps various spiders adapt well to their special habitats. Fascinating photos explain how.

Mortensen, Lori. (2009). *In the trees, honey bees.* Nevada City, CA: Dawn. Incredible art gives an inside-the-hive perspective on a wild bee colony! NSTA* Outstanding Trade Book.

Pfeffer, Wendy. (2004). *Wiggling worms at work.* New York: HarperCollins. A pleasant narrative style helps children respect the interesting characteristics of worms and the important work they do. NSTA* recommended.

Rinehart, Susie. (2004). *Eliza and the dragonfly.* Nevada City, CA. Dawn Publications. In this charming story, Eiza watches the metamorphosis from nymph to dragonfly. Directions for making a simple waterscope and accurate information are woven seamlessly into the narrative. NSTA* Outstanding Trade Book.

Rockwell, Anne. (2005). *Honey in a hive.* New York: Harper. Charming illustrations and a relaxed narrative style add warmth to information about the complex social life of honeybees. NSTA* Outstanding Trade Book.

Rustad, Martha. (2009). *Mealworms.* Mandato, MN: Capstone. The metamorphosis of mealworms from eggs to adult beetles is clearly presented to emergent readers.

Smith, Molly. (2008) *Helpful ladybugs.* New York: Bearport. Young readers will be pleased that such an appealing beetle can be so important for organic gardeners.

Stewart, Melissa. (2009). *How do spiders make webs?* New York: Marshall Cavendish. Share amazing information about web materials and types selectively with children.

Sturges, Philemon. (2005). *I love bugs!* New York: HarperCollins. Bold graphics and a simple rhyming text are easy for preschoolers and beginning readers to enjoy. Endnotes provide information about insect species. Available in a Spanish edition.

Wadsworth, Ginger. (2009). *Up, up, and away.* Watertown, MA: Charlesbridge. This empathically told story of the lives of new-hatched spiderlings.might ease spider phobia!

*National Science Teachers Association.

Classics

FACKLAM, MARGERY. (2002). *Bugs for lunch.* Watertown, MA: Charlesbridge. Charming, detailed animal world illustrations enhance this food chain poem. It's perfect for bilingual classes, with Spanish and English verses appearing on each page spread. NSTA* recommended.

GLASER, LINDA. (2003). *Brilliant bees.* Brookfield, CT: Millbrook Press. Follow a honeybee as she guides her hive, and build respect for honeybees as "brilliant dancers, builders, honey makers, and important pollinators." NSTA* Outstanding Trade Book.

LLEWELLYN, CLAIRE. (2003). *Starting life: Butterfly.* Chanhassen, MN: Northwinds Press. Stages of the butterfly life cycle are emphasized in detailed illustrations on progressively larger page sizes to reflect growth step dimensions. NSTA* Outstanding Trade Book.

PATENT, DOROTHY. (2003). *Fabulous, fluttering tropical butterflies.* New York: Walker. Here, at last, is a great book about the exotic tropical butterflies found in live butterfly exhibits. Great preparation for a butterfly garden field trip. NSTA* Outstanding Trade Book.

POSADA, MIA. (2002). *Ladybugs: Red, fiery and bright.* Minneapolis: Carolrhoda. The author's illustrations add charm and close-up views of this favorite beetle to the rhyming text. NSTA* Outstanding Trade Book.

WALKER, SALLY. (2001). *Fireflies.* Minneapolis: Lerner. This is a fine resource for independent readers who want detailed information about the characteristics of this fascinating insect. NSTA* recommended.

Literature Links: Fish, Mollusks, Amphibians, and Reptiles

BERKES, MARIANNE. (2004). *Over in the ocean in a coral reef.* Nevada City, CA: Dawn. The characteristic movements of 10 fish found in coral reef communities are featured in this rich book, combining music, math, inspiring art, and factual information about the fish and the threatened coral reefs. Creative movement and art ideas are offered.

CHRUSTOWSKI, RICK. (2006). *Turtle crossing.* New York: Henry Holt. This engaging story seamlessly introduces listeners to the slow pace of turtle maturation from egg to reproducing adult.

COWLEY, JAY. (2005). *Chameleon, chameleon.* New York: Scholastic. Readers follow a cautious chameleon's slow search for food and shelter. But wait! Surprises are in store. The author's close-up photographs are amazing. NSTA* recommended.

DAVIES, NICOLA. (2005). *One tiny turtle.* Cambridge, MA: Candlewick. Shimmering art draws readers into a shoreline setting as this tender saga follows the amazing 30-year life span of a sea turtle. NSTA* Outstanding Trade Book.

DAVIES, NICOLA. (2005). *Surprising sharks.* Cambridge, MA: Candlewick. In this award-winning book, unexpected information about the many species of sharks is fascinating and reassuring for older children.

FIRESTONE, MARY. (2010). *What's the difference between a frog and a toad?* Minneapolis: Picture Window. Clear illustrations make the distinctions between these two amphibians easy to notice. A friendly text makes them interesting.

MARKLE, SANDRA. (2007). *Octopuses.* Minneapolis: Lerner. An engaging narrative style and awesome action photos lend immediacy to intriguing octopus forms and their strategies for eluding predators. NSTA* Outstanding Trade Book.

PRINGLE, LAWRENCE. (2004). *Snakes! Strange and wonderful.* Honesdale, PA: Boyd's Mill. Children who are fascinated by snakes will soak up the range of information and detailed illustrations in this book. NSTA* Outstanding Trade Book.

RECHNER, AMY. (2004). *Out and about at the aquarium.* Minneapolis: Picture Window. A class takes a field trip to see animals from around the world that live in, or next to, the water.

RYDER, JOANNE. (2007). *Toad by the road: A year in the life of these amazing amphibians.* New York: Henry Holt. Charming poems highlight the features of these surprising creatures, following their life-cycles and their lifestyles.

---

*National Science Teachers Association.

SAN SOUCI, DANIEL. (2004). *The dangerous snake and reptile club*. Berkeley, CA: Triangle Press. Rollicking illustrations will invite readers to this story about the trials of young collectors of slithery creatures.

SILLS, CATHERINE. (2004). *About crustaceans*. Atlanta: Peachtree. The easy-to-read, fascinating story combined with a beautifully detailed illustration format introduces children to diverse shelled animals.

SMITH, MOLLY. (2009). *Roly-poly pillbugs*. New York: Bearport. These familiar garden dwellers have surprising crustacean relatives in the sea: lobsters, crabs, and shrimp!

Classics

CYRUS, KURT. (2001). *Oddhoppers opera: A bug's garden of verses*. San Diego, CA: Harcourt. The hilarious odyssey of seven snails trekking through their vegetable garden habitat, passing other small creatures struggling to grow and survive. NSTA* Outstanding Trade Book.

HOROWITZ, RUTH. (2000). *Crab moon*. Cambridge, MA: Candlewick. Daniel's moonlit observation of masses of horseshoe crabs crawling ashore to lay their eggs is described and illustrated with warmth and awe. NSTA* Outstanding Trade Book.

SAYRE, APRIL. (2001). *Dig, wait, listen: A desert toad's tale*. New York: Greenwillow. Other desert dwellers pass overhead as a patient spadefoot toad listens underground. She's waiting to hear the rainfall she needs to lay her eggs. NSTA* OutstandingTrade Book.

SILLS, CATHERINE. (2002). *About fish*. Atlanta: Peachtree. Specific fish characteristics and outstanding illustrations will hold the attention of young children.

Literature Links: Birds

BATEMAN, ROBERT. (2005). *Bateman's backyard birds*. Hauppauge, NY: Barron's. The warm narrative style of the author, a fine artist and naturalist, introduces a dozen or so birds common to the Eastern United States.

BECKER, JOHN. (2004). *Owls*. Elizabethtown, PA: Continental Press. Here is a small, reassuring story for young readers, beautifully illustrated, including endnotes, owl facts and a Web site to hear owl calls.

HENKES, KEVIN. (2009). *Birds*. New York: Greenwillow. Bold illustrations swooping off the pages of this simple story will lead listeners to creative responses.

JOHNSON, SYLVIA. (2005). *Crows*. Minneapolis: Carolrohda Books. Why do crows thrive in cities? Do crows have families? Build respect for this common bird as you share this intriguing book with children. NSTA* recommended.

KELLY, IRENE. (2009). *Even an ostrich needs a nest*. New York: Holiday House. A charming author-illustrated text presents the nest-building habits of 40 fascinating birds. NSTA* Outstanding Trade Book.

KIRBY, PAMELA. (2009). *What bluebirds do*. Honesdale, PA: Boyds Mill. The courtship, nest building, and family rearing of two bluebirds living in the author's backyard. NSTA* Outstanding Trade Book.

MARKLE, SANDRA. (2005). *A mother's journey*. Watertown, MA: Charlesbridge. Precise firsthand knowledge, flowing prose, and striking illustrations make this epic tale of penguin motherhood unforgettable. NSTA* Outstanding Trade Book.

Rockwell, Anne. (2003). *Two blue jays*. New York: Walker. A pair of blue jays nest and raise a brood of young just outside a classroom window. The children chart their observations of the awe-inspiring event.

SAYRE, APRIL. (2009). *Honk, honk goose! Canada geese start a family. New York:* Holt. There is drama in the art, alliteration in the text, and great information in this story.

STEWART, MELISSA. (2009). *A place for birds*. Atlanta: Peachtree. Lush illustrations and a modest text tell this story at one level; the subtext gives the environmental message.

---

*National Science Teachers Association.

TAGLIAFERRO, LINDA. (2004). *Birds and their nests.* Mankato, MN: Capstone Press. Beautiful close-up photos and simple text make this book appealing for beginning readers. Safe Internet sites are listed for more information. NSTA* Outstanding Trade Book.

Classics

COLLARD, SNEED. (2002). *Beaks!* Watertown, MA: Charlesbridge. Gorgeous cut paper collages add fascination to the amazing adaptations of bird beaks to the available food sources. NSTA* recommended.

GIBBONS, GAIL. (2001). *Gulls . . . gulls . . . gulls.* New York: Holiday. Colorful, informative drawings enliven the basic facts about the herring gull, familiar to many children.

GRAY, SAMANTHA. (2002). *DK eyewonder: Birds.* New York: DK Publishing. Amazing photos emphasize the diversity of birds with shared characteristics.

Literature Links: Mammals

ANDERSON, JILL. (2005). *Giraffes.* Minnetonka, MN: Northword. Fine photographs from the field make this simple book exciting.

BIDNER, JENNI. (2006). *Is my cat a tiger? How your cat compares to its wild cousins.* Ashville, NC: Lark. Competent readers will enjoy this intriguing perspective on cats. NSTA* recommended.

CROSSINGHAM, J., & KALMAN, B. (2004). *The life cycle of a raccoon.* New York: Crabtree. Here you'll find encyclopedic information and safety tips for observing these familiar mammals.

DAVIES, NICOLA. (2005). *Ice bear: In the steps of the polar bear.* Cambridge, MA: Candlewick. Penetrating cold lifts off the illustrations of this fine book. Science facts are tucked into crevices in the layout, allowing the lovely prose to flow uninterrupted. All elements combine to bring new respect and concern for polar bear. NSTA* Outstanding Trade Book.

DAVIES, NICOLE. (2005). *Bears.* New York: HarperCollins. Handsome photographs make this beginning reader book with its very simple concepts good for browsing.

LIES, BRIAN. (2008). *Bats at the library.* New York: Houghton Mifflin. A library becomes a delightful playground when a flock of book-loving bats find its window left open one night!

MARKLE, SANDRA. (2006). *Little lost bat.* Watertown, MA: Charlesbridge. This exciting, informative story has a satisfying ending. Listeners and readers will give it rapt attention.

MARKLE, SANDRA. (2008). *Finding home.* Watertown, MA: Charlesbridge. This tense story, based on a real event, tells of an Australian koala bear's venturesome search for food and shelter for her baby after a forest fire. NSTA* Outstanding Trade Book.

PATENT, DOROTHY. (2005). *Big cats.* New York: Walker. Great illustrations add excitement to this introduction to lions, tigers, and smaller big cats.

RYDER, JOAN. (2009). *Panda kindergarten.* New York: Harper Collins. Follow 16 endearing panda cubs growing up in a nature preserve until they are able to thrive in the wild.

SOBOL, RICHARD. (2004). *An elephant in the backyard.* New York: Dutton. Here is an appealing portrayal of a particular Thai village where young elephants are trained for work.

STEWART, MELISSA. (2008). *Rabbits.* New York: Marshall Cavendish. Competent readers will learn much about these familiar animals with which we share the planet.

WHITEHOUSE, PATRICIA. (2004). *Moles.* Chicago: Heinemann. Simple text and good color photographs provide basic information about this mammal's habits. Also in this series of *Animals under my feet: Chipmunks* and *rabbits.*

Classics

BUNTING, EVE. (2003). *Whales passing.* New York: Scholastic. In this lovely, simple story, a boy questions his dad about a passing pod of whales they watch from shore. The boy imagines how a baby whale would wonder about the humans he observes from the ocean.

---

*National Science Teachers Association.

CARLE, ERIC. (2002). *"Slowly, slowly, slowly," said the sloth.* New York: Philomel. The strange behavior patterns of the super-relaxed three-toed sloth are revealed in this color-splashed book for young children.

DAVIES, NICOLA. (1997). *Big blue whale.* Cambridge, MA: Candlewick. Playful graphics and comfortable language make this a broadly appealing book. Factual information is separated from the flow of the larger-type text. NSTA* Outstanding Trade Book.

DAVIES, NICOLA. (2001). *Wild about dolphins.* Cambridge, MA: Candlewick. The zoologist author recalls the excitement of an expedition in Newfoundland waters. NSTA* recommended.

Literature Links: Habitats

BAUER, MARION. (2005). *If frogs made the weather.* New York: Holiday. Young children will enjoy the lyrical text that invites reading aloud.

BRENNER, BARBARA. (2004). *One small place in a tree.* New York: HarperCollins. This gentle story follows the evolving ecosystem in a single tree as a succession of animals find shelter there. NSTA* Outstanding Trade Book.

CARLE, ERIC. (2004). *Mister seahorse.* This factual story appeals to youngsters on two levels: Fascinating acetate pages form the habitat for fish hiding on the next page, and the comforting news that certain father fish care for eggs and hatchlings.

COLE, HENRY. (2003). *On the way to the beach.* New York: Greenwillow. We join a child walking through four habitats from home to the beach, observing animal life along the way. Foldout pages reveal hidden creatures in each habitat. NSTA* Outstanding Trade Book.

GEORGE, LINDSAY. (2006). *In the garden: Who's been here?* New York: Greenwillow. Lifelike illustrations by the author invite close attention to the signs of animals that, uninvited, share the vegetable garden.

JENKINS, STEVE, & PAGE, ROBIN. (2005). *I see a kookaburra.* New York: Houghton Mifflin. Clever collage illustrations of animals hidden in their habitats will fascinate children. NSTA* Outstanding Trade Book.

Literature Links: Baby Animals, Hatching, and Pets

ASTON, DIANNA. (2006). *An egg is quiet.* San Francisco: Chronicle. Exquisite illustrations and charming descriptions of 60 eggs reveal the awesomeness of diversity. Zolotow Award.

BERENZY, ALIX. (2005). *Sammy: The classroom guinea pig.* New York: Henry Holt. Children will campaign for a classroom pet after reading this charming story.

DODDS, DAYLE. (2006). *Teacher's pets.* Cambridge, MA: Candlewick. The very patient Miss Fry accommodates a burgeoning menagerie of pets that make long-term "visits" to her classroom.

FRENCH, VIVIAN. (2000). *Growing frogs.* Cambridge, MA: Candlewick. A mother helps her daughter collect frog eggs to observe their metamorphosis at home.

GEORGE, KRISTINE. (2004). *Hummingbird nest.* San Diego, CA: Harcourt. A real family's patio was claimed by a hummingbird as she built a tiny nest and raised two babies. Their fascinated observations are told here as charming journal-entry poems.

GRAHAM, BOB. (2008). *How to heal a broken wing.* Cambridge, MA. Candlewick. A caring boy finds a hurt bird on a city sidewalk and cares for it. Sure to be a favorite. Zolotow Award.

LANDAU, ELAINE. (2007). *Your pet gerbil.* New York: Scholastic. Gerbils are ideal classroom pets: easy to maintain, fun to watch, and easy to tuck into a small shelf. Excellent instructions prepare readers for responsible care.

McDONALD, MEGAN. (2005). *Stink, the incredible shrinking kid.* Cambridge, MA: Candlewick. Readers will enjoy tracking the fate of Newton, the class newt, when Stink "pet sits" for a weekend.

---

*National Science Teachers Association.

O'CONNOR, SANDRA DAY. *Finding Susie*. New York: Random House. This childhood memory of longing for a pet was written by the former Supreme Court justice.

SIMON, SEYMOUR. (2004). *Dogs*. New York: HarperCollins. Elegant and appealing portraits accompany each page of descriptive text shaped toward choosing a pet. A companion book by this author: *Cats*.

SKLANSKY, AMY. (2005). *Where do chicks come from?* New York: HarperCollins. This simple description of the development from egg to chick and the mother hen's protection of them.

SPILSBRY, LOUISE, & SPILSBRY, RICHARD. (2006). *Hamsters*. Chicago: Heinemann. Nothing is left out of this book! Hamster characteristics, care tips, health problems, and even managing the loss of a loved pet are covered. Other books in this *Keeping pets* series are *Cats*, *Dogs*, *Mice*, *Guinea Pigs*, and *Rabbits*.

STOCKDALE, SUSAN. (2005). *Carry me! Animal babies on the move*. Atlanta: Peachtree. Preschoolers will delight in this striking book on how animal mothers carry their young.

Classics

COHEN, MIRIAM. (1989). *Best friends*. New York: Aladdin. The friendship of Jim and Paul is cemented by their mutual rescue of the classroom incubation project in this classic story.

MCCLOSKEY, ROBERT. (1976). *Blueberries for Sal*. New York: Puffin. Four sets of mothers and their offspring are part of this story: Sal and her mother, plus bear, quail, and crow families.

MCCLOSKEY, ROBERT. (1979). *Make way for ducklings*. New York: Viking Press. Finding a suitable home and raising a brood of ducklings occupy Mrs. Mallard's time in this timeless book.

POSADA, MIA. (2007). *Guess what is growing inside this egg*. Minneapolis: Millbrook. Intriguing clues in verse and vivid art lead to warm descriptions of the hatchlings.

Literature Links: Animal Math

ELLIOTT, RACHEL. (2004). *From egg to butterfly*. Washington, DC: National Geographic. Math adds meaning to the monarch life cycle. Photographs shown in actual scale facilitate measuring the size of the butterfly at each stage.

HULME, JOY. (2005). *Wild Fibonacci: Nature's secret code revealed*. Berkeley, CA: Tricycle Press. The fascination of the Fibonacci Sequence, plus great animal art and a clever layout, make this book a treasure.

LEEDY, LOREEN. (2001). *Measuring Penny*. New York: Henry Holt. Lisa chooses her pet terrier, Penny, as her homework assignment to measure something. Lisa quantifies Penny's anatomy, as well as the time requirements and cost of her upkeep. NSTA* recommended.

LEEDY, LOREN. (2005). *The great graph contest*. New York: Holiday House. Two animals, collectors of rocks and nature finds, compete to see whose data are organized into the best graphs. Quantity graphs, circle graphs, bar graphs, and Venn diagrams are explained in endnotes.

MAGDA, ANN. (2000). *Tiger math*. New York: Holt. The engaging story of raising an orphaned tiger cub occupies one side of this clever book. Learning to graph his growth in various ways occupies the other side. NSTA* Outstanding Trade Book.

PINCZES, ELINOR. (2001). *Inchworm and a half*. Boston: Houghton Mifflin. A sprightly inchworm nibbles as she measures vegetables in the garden. Smaller worms introduce the concept of fractions.

SCHWARTZ, DAVID. (1999). *If you hopped like a frog*. New York: Scholastic. This book introduces the concepts of ratio and proportion by imagining comparisons of what kids could do if they shared different animals' physical capabilities. It provides inspiration for creative thinking and movement.

SCHWARTZ, DAVID. (2006). *If dogs were dinosaurs*. New York: Scholastic. Math combined with imagination, humor, and delightful art introduces relative sizes.

---

*National Science Teachers Association.

STEWART, MELISSA. (2007). *Giraffe graphs*. New York: Scholastic. A zoo field trip is a fun way to put bar graphs into real life and life into math! NSTA* recommended.

Poems (Resources in Appendix A)

There is an abundance of evocative and amusing poems about animals for children. Some are found in these collections.

> Paul Fleischman, *Joyful noise: Poems for two voices*. Newbery Medal–award-winning poems evoke the delicate sounds of insects as they move.
>
> Douglas Florian has written many books of amusing animal poems, including *Omnibeasts, Insectlopedia, Mammalabilia*, and *Lizards, Frogs, and Polliwogs*. He has collected several notable awards along the way. His childlike illustrations will inspire young painters.
>
> Dorothy Kennedy (Ed.). *I Thought I'd Take My Rat to School*. In X. J. Kennedy's poem, "Science Lesson," children tickle tadpoles.
>
> Margery Facklam's charming food chain poem, *Bugs for Lunch,* is offered in both Spanish and English.

Fingerplays

Add to this fingerplay to include the movement of small animals observed by children in your classroom. (Also encourage children to act out the movements physically.)

Small Animal Parade	
A slow, slow snail	
Drags down the trail	(Stretch and contract the right hand, dragging along the left arm.)
A looping earthworm	
Moves along with a squirm	(Loop and wiggle one finger.)
A spider runs past	
With eight legs so fast	(Place hands one on top of the other, tuck thumbs under, wiggle eight fingers.)
The grasshopper springs	
With six legs and wings	(Cross one hand on top of the other, hold thumbs and little fingers under, leap up and down.)
The green and white frog	
Leaps over a log	(Right fist leaps over left arm.)
A seven-fin fish	
Swims by with a swish	(Palms together, hands twist and turn, moving forward.)

J.H.

---

*National Science Teachers Association.

Art Activities

Easel Painting. One of the early shapes many children paint spontaneously is a loop with many strokes radiating from it. Often these are called "spiders" or "bugs" by the painter. Provide green and brown paint on insect-watching day and casually suggest that some children could have fun making paintings of the spider, grasshopper, caterpillar, or whatever creature is of current interest. Newsprint sheets may also be cut into large butterflies or bird shapes for children to paint at the easel.

Crayon and Picture Collage. Provide pictures of animals (for children to cut out, or have some precut for those new at cutting), paste, construction paper, and crayons for crayon-enhanced collages. Animal pictures are not easy to locate in typical household magazines. Old children's magazines, free nature publications from your state natural resources department, or animal stamps from the National Wildlife Federation are good sources.

Leather and Feather Collage. Scraps of leather from a crafts shop and domestic bird feathers make interesting collage material. Use durable paper and white glue for best adhesion. Before using untreated feathers, seal them in plastic zip closure bags and microwave for a few minutes, watching closely, to kill any mites or other allergens they may carry.

Eggshell Mosaics. Broken, dyed eggshells can be glued to paper for egg-hatching project extensions. The younger the children, the larger the shell bits should be for best management of materials.

Play

Animal Puppet Play. Put out animal hand puppets for children to animate. A small table turned on its side makes a good improvised stage.

Dramatize Animal Stories. When a group of children is familiar with an animal story that involves "a cast of thousands," they enjoy acting out the story in an informal, simplified way. Assign roles to all of the children so that no one is left out, even if someone has to play the part of a tree in the forest. Good animal stories that meet the casting requirements include *Make Way for Ducklings* and *The Tortoise and the Hare.* Help move the story along informally as needed. Assign areas in the room for different scenes: "Here's the island on the river where the mallards build their nest, and the block area is the public garden where they swim." Use simple props if they help carry out the story.

Creative Movement

It's easy to draw children into the fun of acting out animal characteristics. Creative movement suggestions may also strengthen children's recall of the life cycles of animals that undergo metamorphosis. Slowly and dramatically, read animal poems aloud for children to interpret with you.

Poems about inchworms, treehoppers, and whirligig beetles, found in *Insectlopedia* by Douglas Florian (see Appendix A), irresistibly inspire children to action.

Lynda Graham-Barber's book, *Spy Hops and Belly Flops,* invites children to imitate animal movements.

Children can be invited, one by one, to travel across the floor like the animal of their choice. (Groups of young children wait their turn more patiently if they are sitting on the floor before and after their turn to travel.) One quick-thinking pair of five-year-olds brightened our day when they piggybacked to crawl together as an eight-legged spider.

Creative Thinking

What If? Read aloud Mary Anne Hoberman's poem, "Cricket," from *The Llama Who Had No Pajama.* Ask, "Imagine what it would be like if your leg could hear and your ear could walk. Imagine how the world would seem to you." Offer this as a group discussion, or let older children draw and write their responses.

Ask, "What if we had six legs to travel on? How would our lives be different? What could we do that we can't do with two legs? What couldn't we do? What if we had to spend most of our day gathering food for ourselves? What if we had working wings? How would our lives be different? What if we had to build places to live without using tools?" Encourage as many imaginative responses as possible. Let children generate their own "what if" questions to explore.

Food Experiences

Children accept the idea that people eat fish and chicken, as the terms are customarily used at mealtimes. There seems little to be gained, however, from pressing the point that the hamburgers being served for lunch were once a steer or that the ham in the sandwich was once a pig. Concentrate instead on ideas that foster positive emotions: cows giving milk, hens giving eggs, or bees making honey for people to enjoy. If simple cooking experiences using dairy products are possible in the classroom, read aloud "The Friendly Cow," by Robert Louis Stevenson, in *A Child's Garden of Verses.*

Field Trips

The list of potential problems and hazards that might be part of an outdoor animal observation hike could rule out this kind of field trip for a large group of young children. It can also be very disappointing when the objects of the trip do not display themselves. Try instead to pause for watching time whenever you encounter small animals while in the schoolyard with your children: ants at work in a sidewalk crack nest, limp worms washed out of their tunnels after a hard rain, or squirrels and birds gathering food.

Nature centers in your locality may have outreach programs to bring the field to your classroom to introduce children to a small animal in the center's care. A good resource for walking-distance field trips is Rhoda Redleaf's *Hey Kids! Out the Door, Let's Explore.*

PROMOTING CONCEPT CONNECTIONS

Maintaining Concepts

A teacher vividly reinforces concepts about the usefulness of insects by reacting calmly to an intruding bee or wasp. Remind children that insects of this sort sting only when disturbed. Open the windows from the top so that the insect can eventually fly out. Offer an observation jar to a shrieking child who is about to squash an uninvited spider. Do not undo what you have previously taught about the creature's place in the web of life by joining the chase with a can of insecticide. Do not use insecticides in school or in the yard, because the chemicals can accumulate in the environment or in the children. Kill roaches, flies, and mosquitoes directly, explaining that they are pests for people but good for birds and toads. Prevent most pests by denying them access to food and water. Investigate integrated pest management (IPM). Learn about it on the Environmental Protection Agency Web site: http://www.epa.gov/pesticides/ipm

Another reinforcement of respect for living creatures may occur if a classroom pet dies or if a dead bird is found on the playground. Let the children be aware of the death and take part in a gentle burial. Say that the animal's useful life has ended.

Improving School Grounds

Consider a "minibeast" pit like those found in many British schools, which can supply numerous insects and other crawlies as needed. In a corner of the asphalt ground or field, dig a hole about 18 in. (45 cm) deep and about 3 ft (1 m) wide and long. Fill it with logs laid on their sides. A range of bugs can congregate and breed there. A simpler method is to lay down pieces of old carpet in a low-traffic setting; bugs appreciate the dark, wet environment.

A butterfly garden stocked with native perennials will last for many years without heavy maintenance. Numerous resources exist to help, including the Schoolyard Habitat Program at the National Wildlife Federation, state departments of natural resources, and cooperative extension agencies.

Connecting Concepts

The broad ecological relationships between plants, animals, soil, water, air, and temperature are awesome and complex. Preschool and early elementary-age children can take beginning steps toward understanding ecological relationships through small, concrete instances. For example, a child may observe a bird pecking at tree bark and wonder aloud if the bird is hurting the tree. An adult can clarify the bird's immediate purpose and expand the idea of mutual dependency. "Yes, it does look a bit as if the bird is hurting the tree. Really, it is getting its food and helping the tree at the same time. The bird is catching tiny insects that are eating the tree. Can you think of a way that the tree helps the bird?" Emphasize that plants and animals need each other.

A child may question the fitness of animals eating other animals, plants, and seeds for sustenance. One can appreciate the child's concern. Then suggest that each living thing can make many more seeds or eggs than are needed to make a young plant or animal like itself. If all the seeds grew into plants and all the eggs became animals, there would not be enough room in the world for all the living things. Some of the plants and animals need to be used in this way to keep the proper amount of each kind growing well to maintain the balance of nature. Young children can be upset by the recognition of the human role in the food chain. The fact that humans are animals that eat other animals may be better tolerated after the primary-grade years.

Sound concepts can be linked to the study of animal life. Compare the high pitch of the wren's song with the low pitch of the dove's coo. Feel the vibrations of a purring cat. Think of the swelling air pockets that make a frog's loud croak possible. Recall the vibrating wing covers that can be seen when the male cricket sings. Relate air concepts to the life requirements of animals. (See Chapter 7, Air.)

Family and Community Support

Inform families early in the school year that children are encouraged to bring in captured insects. After the first few planned experiences, you may never have to track down a specimen by yourself.

Knowledgeable parents might be willing to set up a classroom aquarium, make a pet cage, set up a simple bird feeder, or arrange to bring in and show a family pet. Their children's social standing with the group usually blossoms as a secondary benefit.

Alert families to special programs being offered by the children's library or by a nearby nature center, zoo, or aquarium. Find out about interactive exhibits and events for children in the nearest natural history museum. Watch for announcements of bird-watching hikes or moonlight animal hikes offered to families by state park naturalists or national forest rangers.

RESOURCES

BENBOW, ANN, & MABLY, COLLIN. (2009). *Awesome animal science projects.* Berkeley Heights, NJ: Enslow. Here are projects to offer the fascinated child who is ready to explore independently.

BLOBAUM, CINDY. (2005). *Insectigations: 40 hands-on activities to explore the insect world.* Chicago: Chicago Review Press. This wonderful resource has intriguing experiments, projects like mealworm raising, art activities, and more. NSTA* outstanding trade book.

BURNIE, DAVID. (1998). *Mammals.* New York: Dorling Kindersley. A broad spectrum of mammals' characteristics are considered in this well-organized resource, such as newborns, growth, movements, feeding, play, defenses, and group living.

KNEIDEL, SALLY. (1999). *More pet bugs: A kid's guide to catching and keeping insects and other small creatures.* New York: Wiley. From ants to wooly bears to crayfish, 23 creatures are considered in Kneidel's comfortable approach to gathering, housing, and observing these interesting animals.

MIKULA, RICK. (2001). *The family butterfly book.* Pownel, VT: Storey Books. All aspects of butterfly raising are covered, from how to lift a caterpillar to housing and hatching conditions. NSTA* recommended.

---

*National Science Teachers Association.

MORGAN, BEN. (2004). *DK guide to birds.* New York: Dorling Kinderseley. This spectacular reference is arranged by bird characteristics and behavior patterns and crammed with information.

PYLE, ROBERT. (1994). *National Audubon Society field guide to North American butterflies.* New York: Knopf. Color photographs identify common eggs, caterpillars, and chrysalises. This is good information for those who wish to offer a butterfly-hatching experience in the classroom.

REDLEAF, RHODA. (2010). *Hey kids! Out the door, let's explore!* St. Paul, MN: Redleaf Press. This book will help you organize great field trips.

RICHARDSON, ADELE. (2003). *Mammals.* Mankato, MN: Capstone. Handsome animal photographs and clear, simple text define the mammals in the animal kingdom. Age-appropriate Internet site references are supplied.

SIBLEY, DAVID. (2000). *The Sibley guide to birds.* New York: Knopf. This book is still the most complete guide to identifying birds in North America.

STEWART, MELISSA. (2007). *Butterflies.* Minnetonka, MN: Northword. Excellent information and precise photographs of butterflies of North America.

WAGNER, DAVID. (2005). *Caterpillars of Eastern North America.* Princeton, NJ: Princeton University Press. This is the first comprehensive field guide to identifying hundreds of caterpillars. It includes photographs of the butterflies and the moths they become.

 ONLINE RESOURCES

Annenberg Media Web Site (Part of the Annenberg Foundation). Free profesional development programming for K-12 teachers. Videos and other materials for inquiry science include a *Journey North* Internet-based program on monarch migration at *http://www.learner.org/resources/series127.html*

Monarch Watch: *http://www.MonarchWatch.org/*

University of Michigan Museum of Zoology. Information on and pictures of many species of animals make this searchable encyclopedia a good teacher resource. Available at *http://animaldiversity.ummz.umich.edu/site/index.html*

The Human Body

The joy of dancing, the pleasure of feeling strong and healthy and capable, all depend on complex systems working under the guidance of your incredible brain. A heightened awareness of their own wonderful bodies can help inspire children to respect and care for them.

Young children yearn to grow and become strong. They are eager to know what is inside their bodies. The experiences suggested in this chapter contribute to clarifying misconceptions and overcoming worries that children may have about their bodies. They help children take the beginning steps toward a lifelong responsibility for their own physical well-being. The following concepts are explored:

- Each person is unique.
- Bones support us.
- Muscles move our bones.
- The heart and lungs keep us alive.
- Senses inform us.
- Our bodies need our care.

The goal of this chapter is to help children learn to value themselves as unique individuals, begin to recognize body structures and systems, and care for their own bodies. Abstract information about these subjects has limited impact on shaping long-term wellness habits. Family resources, cultural values, and media exposure all have strong influences on forming self-care attitudes. But when engaging, foundation-building experiences evoke pride in new self-awareness, the emotional responses increase the likelihood of developing good health care behaviors. The activities in this chapter will help children respect their amazing bodies and appreciate what they themselves can do to promote their own well-being.

CONCEPT: Each person is unique.

1. Am I the only one exactly like me?

LEARNING OBJECTIVE: To celebrate our individuality.

MATERIALS:

Science folders

Large mirror

Yardstick/meter stick

Scale

Ink pad

Magnifiers or jeweler's loupes*

GETTING READY:

Label the folder page:

"I am: (*name*)"

"I am _____tall. I

  weigh _____.

"I look like this."

Label other page:

"Mine alone"

SMALL-GROUP ACTIVITY:

1. Weigh and measure each child.

2. Encourage children to write or dictate what they see in the mirror, then draw pictures of themselves. Add their weight, their height, and the day's date.

3. Have children trace one hand outline on the "Mine Alone" page with the fingers outspread. Have them press each fingertip of the traced hand on the inkpad and stamp firmly onto the traced fingertips. Examine the prints with a hand lens or jeweler's loupe.

Math skills: Weighing/measuring height of each child; recording.

Group Discussion: Consider what the fingerprints look like. Have children in the group ever seen their hand- and footprints that were made when they were newborn babies? Even though their hands are bigger now, and will grow bigger still, the fingertip pattern of curvy lines will be the same but stretched bigger. "Even if we looked at them under a powerful microscope, probably no other child's fingerprint patterns will exactly match yours. Scientists tell us that it would be *very* hard to find another person with fingerprints *exactly* like yours."

Read: Sensational Human Body Science Projects by Ann Benbow and Colin Mably for helpful fingerprinting instructions.

CONCEPT: Bones support us.

1. What keeps bones strong?

LEARNING OBJECTIVE: To be intrigued by new self-knowledge.

---

*An inexpensive jeweler's loupe keeps the lens at the best distance from the eye and improves both focus and concentration by blocking out peripheral light. See Resources for ordering. Clean the open end with germicidal wipes before each use to prevent possible spreading of eye infections.

How tall am I, anyway?

Introduction: Dangling an unoccupied hand puppet, ask children why the puppet isn't able to sit up, or hold up its head or arms. We might look just as limp if we didn't have more than 200 bones to hold us up. What do you know about the bones in our bodies? Let's take some time to feel the hard bones in your arms and legs, your hands and fingers. Are the bones long or short? Feel for the bones in your shoulders and chest. Are they long and straight? Reach behind you to feel the middle of your back. Do you feel one long bone? Bend down to touch your toes. Could you do that if you had just one long bone in your back? As you are curved over, feel the middle of your back. Those bumpy places are the line of small bones called the *spine*. Bones do more than hold us up. Specially shaped bones also protect our soft inside parts. Feel the bones in your chest. How many bones can you feel? Now trace the rib bones around to your back. The ribs curve into a cage to protect your heart and lungs. They get pulled into a large shape and back into a smaller shape as we breathe. That makes more room for the lungs to fill with air. Another big curving bone protects your important brain—your skull! Elicit children's ideas and explore slowly.

"Your bones are growing every day, and they need two things to be strong and hard: exercise and special growing materials: *minerals*, especially *calcium*. Calcium comes from food we eat, like milk and cheese, tofu, and yogurt. We can find out together what bones might be like be if they didn't have much calcium."

MATERIALS:

2 chicken thigh bones (mealtime leftovers)

2 screw-top plastic jars

5% acidity plain white or cider vinegar

Water

WHOLE-GROUP EXPERIENCE:

1. Let everyone check the hardness of the two bones.
2. Put a bone in each jar. Add water to cover the bone in one jar; add vinegar* to cover the bone in the other jar.

---

*This much strong vinegar dissolves calcium, but vinegar in small amounts in our food does not.

GETTING READY:

Scrape and wash the bones.

Let them dry overnight.

3. Cover the jars. Leave them undisturbed for four or more days. Remove and dry the bones. Compare the results. (It may require a few more days to obtain a rubbery result.)

Math skills: counting own bones

Group Discussion: Share the information about vinegar in this strength, quantity, and length of exposure as a solvent for calcium. How do children feel about the change in the chicken bones? Our bones need calcium every day from food sources to stay strong all our lives. How will children use what they have learned from this dramatic example? Suggest adding a folder drawing or story about this experience.

2. What do joints do?

LEARNING OBJECTIVE: To enjoy discovering the function of joints.

Introduction: "Let's take a walk around the room in special ways. Please follow me and listen for instructions along the way. Stop now, and take time to lock on imaginary leg braces that keep your knees from moving. Let's walk again. Are you moving as easily now? How does it feel? . . . Stop again! This time, add a brace to your ankles so they can't move. Is the walking easier now or harder than ever? . . . Keep stumping along with me. Stop again! This time, lock up your toes so they can't bend. How is it going for you now? . . . Raise your arms in front of you and lock your elbows. On your way back to your places, pat the top of your head if you can. Now unlock those braces so we can talk about what happened."

Invite children's ideas about joints (places where two or more bones meet). "We have different kinds of joints in our bodies. Stand on one foot and move your other leg as many ways as you can. (The ball-and-socket hip joint swivels.) Can you move just your lower leg exactly the same way? (Knee joints are like hinges. They don't swivel). Find out how your elbow joints work. (They are both hinges and pivots.)"

MATERIALS:

Popsicle sticks

Tape

Box of assorted objects

WHOLE-GROUP ACTIVITY: ·

1. "Curl the fingers of one hand into a fist. Use your other fingers to feel the bones in your hands and fingers. How many can you count?"
2. "Now carefully feel all sides of the hard knobs you see as you open and close your fist. What do you feel happening?"
3. Help volunteers tape popsicle sticks under the index and middle fingers of one hand. "Now try to pick up something from the basket. Is that working well? Could you draw or write this way? What would make it easier?"

4. Switch splints from fingers to thumbs. "Do thumbs have a special job to do and a different way to move?"

Math skills: Counting joints/bones in hands.

Discuss the explorations and consider the value of joints. Do any children know older people who have trouble using their hands or other joints? Have children record their observations as drawings or written notes.

Read: The Busy Body Book by Lizzie Rockwell for child-size skeletal illustrations.

CONCEPT: **Muscles move our bones.**

---

1. Are all muscles alike?

LEARNING OBJECTIVE: To enjoy discovering varied muscle strengths.

Introduction: "Let's do some stretching. Lift your shoulders up to your ears. Drop your chin to your chest. Move your head from side to side. Wave your arms in circles. Wiggle your toes. Lots of bones are moving here! Did your bones move by themselves, or did you feel something pulling them? . . . Let's try those movements again. This time, pay close attention to what you are feeling as you move. What is it that you are feeling? . . . (Muscles pull the bones to move them.) What else do you know about our muscles? We have more than 600 muscles in our bodies! Do you think all of our muscles are alike? Let's do some investigating."

MATERIALS:

2-lb workout weights or an unopened 1-L water bottle weighing about 2 lb (1 kg).

GETTING READY:

Prepare three-column summary sheets (words or icons)

Easiest Lifting

Hands	Arms	Legs

SMALL-GROUP ACTVITY:

1. Demonstrate lifting weight in one hand from three positions:
   a. *Hand Lift:* stiff arm extended at shoulder height: the wrist and hand lift the weight up and down.
   b. *Forearm Lift:* upper arm "glued" to the side: forearm bends at the elbow to lift the weight up and down.
   c. *Leg Lift:* Place weight on the floor. With one arm "glued" to the side, back straight, squat to pick up the weight from the floor. Stand up, bringing the weight to mid-thigh level.
2. In small groups, each child lifts a weight in each position, repeating as needed to compare the effects, and then records on the chart which muscles lifted the weights most easily.

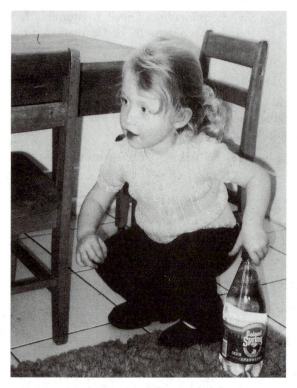

Can my leg muscles help me lift things?

Math skills: Observing/recording muscle strength: comparing, charting data.

Group discussion: Compile the charted data and share experiences. Let children grasp their hand, arm, and thigh to compare sizes of muscles lying under the skin. "Leg muscles are the largest and strongest of the three. They do the hardest work of lifting and moving the rest of the body all day long. It was easy work for leg muscles to lift the weight. Muscles grow stronger when we exercise them.

"Let's stretch lots of muscles. Good stretches move slowly. Move one leg at a time to discover how many ways you can stretch those muscles. How many ways can you stretch your arms? . . . Shoulders? . . . Neck? . . . Back? . . . Hands and fingers? Now stretch the muscles in your face to make a smile and finish by stretching the tiny eyelid muscles to make a wink!"

Read: The Monster Health Book by Edward Miller or *Bend and Stretch* by Pamela Nettleton.

2. How do muscles work in pairs?

LEARNING OBJECTIVE: To be intrigued by new self-knowledge.

Whole-Group Experience: Recall the weight-lifting experience. "Did your muscles seem to *pull* or to *push* to lift the weight? Feel your biceps with your other hand as you raise your forearm. What happens? . . . Does something get bigger? Feel the back of your shoulder with your hand as you lift your arm out straight. Did you feel a pull?

"Mucles are hooked up to our bones. They pull our bones by getting shorter and fatter or tighter. That's all that muscles can do: pull one way by getting shorter or tighter. Try feeling those muscles pulling again. . . . If muscles can only pull, let's see if we can find out how our arms got pulled back down again."

Ask pairs of children to face each other, holding hands so they can work as partners. Standing in place, one child slowly pulls the other child forward; then the other child does the pulling.

"Try it again, thinking carefully as you move slowly back and forth. Ask yourselves if either you or your partner is pushing the other person. Keep trying until you decide if that happens."

Summarize the children's findings. Our muscles work with partners, too. Each kind of muscle can pull only one way. Its partner can pull only the opposite way. That's how they work together to keep things moving, as you and your partner did just now.

"Let's see if we can feel that happening in our upper arms. The front muscle (the biceps) gets tighter as we lift our forearms; its partner muscle in back (the triceps) gets tighter as we put our forearms down. Each one pulls its own way."

"Our muscles grow stronger when we exercise them. Our bones do, too. So let's take an exercise break to stretch a bit. Afterward, draw or write about exercise you enjoy."

Read: Bodyscope: Movers and Shapers by Patricia Macnair for muscle facts and dynamic drawings of muscles.

CONCEPT: The heart and lungs keep us alive.

Introduction: Ask the class to try for a moment to be perfectly still without moving a single muscle. Is it possible? No, fortunately! Can the children feel some muscles continuously moving, even when their arms and legs are still? "Some muscles must continuously move to keep us breathing. We couldn't live if the mightiest muscle of all stopped moving; it is our blood-pumping muscle, the heart. The heart pushes blood through thin tubes to send energy and oxygen to all parts of the body. We can't see our heart working because it is safe inside our rib cage, but we can feel it working (demonstrate the location). Your heart is about the size of your hands clasped together."

Show the children how to fold their hands together, then squeeze and release the grasp rhythmically. "Your heart works something like this, pumping and pushing day and night. Let's see how long we can do this with our hands. . . . We can stop pushing our hands together when we get tired, but our hearts can never stop pumping."

LEARNING OBJECTIVE: To appreciate our heart as a powerful muscle.

1. How does our heart help us?

MATERIALS:

Paper towel tubes or 16-in.
  (40-cm) lengths of garden hose
Watch with a second hand
Stethoscope

SMALL-GROUP ACTIVITY:

1. Ask children to fold their clasped hands next to their ears to listen as they squeeze their hands together. "Your heart makes a soft thumping sound like that each time it pumps and relaxes."
2. Children can listen through paper towel tubes to hear one another's heartbeats. One ear rests on the tube end; the other is covered with a hand. Children can curve the hose to listen to their own beating hearts.

(Use disinfectant wipes on stethoscope earpieces after each child's use.)

3. Try counting heartbeats for half a minute when children are quiet. ♣ Move outdoors, if possible, to let children run freely for a few minutes. Count heartbeats immediately afterward. Compare them with resting heartbeats. What happens during exercise?

Math skills: observing and counting heartbeats.

Read: Allan Wolfe and Greg Clarke's reassuring poem "You Can't Beat Your Heart" from their book *The Blood-Hungry Spleen and Other Poems about Our Parts.*

Note: If a child seems worried about the increase in heart rate during exercise, reassure the child with more information: "Heart muscles grow stronger and work even better when they are well exercised." Children may have much to contribute to a discussion about muscle-building exercises.

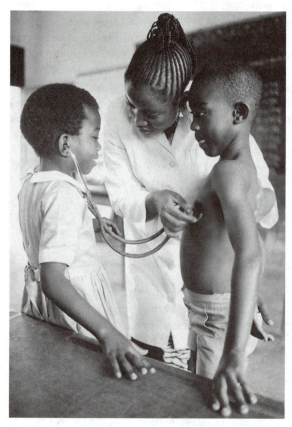
Robert's heart pumps, the visiting nurse facilitates, and Regina listens to life.

2. How is air pulled into our bodies?
LEARNING OBJECTIVE: To feel and appreciate lung functioning.

Group Experience: Ask children to recall the change they experienced in their heart-pumping rate after they exercised hard. Have they noticed another change in their bodies when they run hard?" Our breathing gets faster because our bodies need to take in more air when we run. What do you know about breathing?

"Here's a way to find out more. Everyone take a very deep breath, shut your lips tightly, and pinch your nostrils shut for as long as you can. What's happening? . . . Why have you let go of your noses or opened your mouths? . . . What did your body seem to need so much? Let's try again.

"Every part of our body needs the part of air called *oxygen.* We need to breathe new air into our bodies about every 6 seconds because the oxygen is used up so quickly inside of us. Let's count our own breathing for a minute. I'll tell you when to start and stop counting."

Guide the discussion to bring out the idea that *all living things must have air to stay alive.* Include the danger of climbing into containers with heavy lids that can't be opened from the inside. Offer the following ideas slowly:

Give each child an unfolded tissue to hold near the nose and mouth. "Let's see what happens to the tissue when you bring air into your body and when the air comes out. Try it with your lips closed; . . . now with your lips open a bit and your nostrils closed. . . . Are there two ways for the air to come in and out? . . . Blow air into your hand. How does it feel? . . . The used air we breathe out has been warmed inside our bodies. Allow children time to respond.

"Let's sit quietly, look down, and breathe deeply, just to feel and see and think about what happens to our bodies when we breathe air in and out. Lungs are the parts that get bigger when we pull in air and smaller when the air goes out. How do you think that happens? . . . Our lungs aren't like two balloons. They are more like sponges. They don't have muscles to make them get bigger and smaller. But there is a special muscle under our lungs that does the job. It's called the *diaphragm.*

"Press the sides of your hands in the middle of your chest, (like a shelf) just below the bottom of your rib cage. Notice what you feel there as you breathe deeply and easily. That is your big, flat diaphragm muscle pulling on your lungs. We can get an idea about how that muscle works. Keep your arms at the bottom of your ribs and put one hand on top of the other, palms up. Now, each time you breathe in, roll your hands down. When you breathe out, let your hands come back up. We're pretending that your hands are that big flat muscle attached to the lungs. When that muscle pulls down, it stretches the lungs bigger, so more air can come into them. When that muscle relaxes, it comes back up and the lungs get smaller. That's how the used air gets pushed out. A soft part called *cartilage* lets our rib cage expand as our lungs get bigger. The wonderful thing is that our brains take care of all of this, even while we sleep. Our brains also let us choose how we breathe when we're awake. Let's choose to take some deep breaths right now!" Awareness of muscles takes time.

Math skills: counting breaths.

Read: Breathe In, Breathe Out by Pamela Nettleton or *Outside-In* by Clare Smallman.

3. How much air can our lungs take in?
LEARNING OBJECTIVE: To be awed by our lung capacity.

(Note: The success of this activity depends upon having both a calm class and good humidity. It is unsuitable for children who might inadvertently suck on the straw.)

MATERIALS:

4 cups (1 L) water

½ cup (125 mL) Joy or Dawn dishwashing detergent

SMALL-GROUP ACTIVITY:

"We can take careful turns to see how much air our lungs can hold." Demonstrate taking a deep breath, dipping the bent ends of a straw

2 tablespoons (30 mL) sugar
Mixing bowl and spoon
Cookie baking pan
  (11 × 17 × 1 in.)
Plastic straw for each child
Scissors

GETTING READY:

1. Flatten ½ in. (1 cm) at the bottom of each straw. Make ½-in. (1-cm) cuts at each edge and in the middle to make four small flaps. Bend flaps back at right angles at the ends of the straws (see Figure 6–1).
2. Dissolve sugar completely into the water, stirring well. Add detergent, *stirring very gently* to prevent foaming.
3. Ease the mixture into the pan. Moisten the edges of the pan with solution. (Dry surfaces break bubbles.)

into the mixture, then gently exhaling into the straw as long as you can. Ease the straw upward as you exhale to gently lift the single bubble into a dome shape. When you are out of breath, pinch the straw shut. Quietly watch the life-giving air that left your lungs until the bubble dries out and bursts. Point out that success in making the biggest bubble requires careful exhaling through the straw, not hard puffing like blowing up a balloon. (Be sure to practice this fascinating technique at home before working with children.)

Math skills: observing amount of air exhaled, comparing bubble sizes.

Follow-up discussion: Let children share their reactions to seeing their lung capacity. Point out that when we are exercising vigorously, we pull even more air

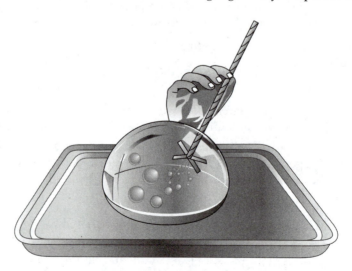

FIGURE 6–1   Dome Bubble

into our lungs. Our bodies need extra oxygen when we are using so much energy. Emphasize that exercising and breathing deeply keep our lungs strong and healthy!

Note: Build deep breathing into your classroom routines to help reduce stress and calm the class.

Read: Lungs by Veronica Ross.

CONCEPT: Senses inform us.

Begin these sensory explorations with a question for the class to consider: "How do you know what's going on around you?" Draw from the responses that we can see, hear, feel, smell, and taste. "These are the ways our brains get information about what is happening around us. We call them our *senses*. They help us stay safe and enjoy our lives. Let's investigate some ways our senses tell us what's going on around us."

Read: You Can't Taste a Pickle with Your Ear! by Harriet Ziefert.

1. What can we learn by hearing?

LEARNING OBJECTIVE: To appreciate hearing and develop empathy for the hearing impaired.

Group Experience: "What are some important sounds that we hear everyday? . . . I'll make a list of your ideas. . . . Now sit *very* quietly, cover your eyes with your hands, and try to figure out, without looking, what it is I'm doing that makes the sound." Move behind the class and create a simple sound like opening a drawer, moving a wastebasket, or dropping a pencil. When the sound is identified, choose one child at a time to be the ordinary sound maker. Make a second list of these familiar sounds. Compare the two lists. Use the list of ordinary background sounds to show that our ears are working for us to pick up sounds all day and night. Our brains decide which ones we need to pay attention to.

♣ Take this experience outdoors, sitting together in a circle in an undisturbed place, listening quietly with eyes closed for one minute. Let children share what they learned in that minute. Then listen again for another minute, most likely with increased awareness of what others have heard.

Read: Moses Goes to School by Isaac Millman for insights into hearing impairments.

Another time, continue this experience by considering what children know about hearing loss. Discuss how our ears function. Talk about ear safety hazards. Demonstrate what it would be like for a child who could not hear by silently mouthing the words in the book while holding it up to share the illustrations. Would a hearing loss make it hard to learn and play with friends at school? (Without specific guidance, children find it hard to empathize with the limitations of a classmate with a hearing loss.) Do any children in the group already know how to sign some words? The class will enjoy learning simple signing. *Isaac Sees a Play*, by Millman, offers a start.

2. What can we learn by seeing?

LEARNING OBJECTIVE: To appreciate vision and build empathy for the visually impaired.

Introduction: Invite children to find out what it is like to know what's happening around them without information from their eyes.

MATERIALS:

Lengths of soft paper toweling, long enough to fold into thick blindfolds for each child. (To avoid spreading eye infections, do not share blindfolds.)

Paperclips to secure blindfolds

Objects to identify by touch: some easy to identify: legos brush and the like; some harder: penny, nickel, book

Small mirrors

SMALL-GROUP ACTIVITY:

1. Fasten blindfolds and pass items to identify. (It's hard for young children to stay blindfolded very long, so pass only a few items.)
2. Cover the items. Remove blindfolds. What did the children find out? Could they learn the Lego color or the title of the book?
3. Let children study their eyes in a mirror and draw what they see. Do the eyes move up, down, or to the side as they look in the mirror? What are the eyelids doing?
4. Let partners take turns leading one another on blindfold tours of the room. Can they tell where they are? Is it easy to walk around without seeing possible hazards?

Discuss what was missing when the blindfolds were on and when eyelids are closed: light! Our eyes need enough light to see what's going on around us.

Read: I See Myself by Vicki Cobb.

3. What can we learn by smelling?

LEARNING OBJECTIVE: To appreciate the information smelling brings us.

Introduction: Ask the class to recall what they smelled first when they awoke today. "What did that tell you?" . . . Discuss favorite fragrances. "Can our sense of smell keep us safe?" . . . Our memories of smell are very important from the beginning of our lives. "Scientists tell us that newborn babies can tell their mothers from other people by using their sense of smell!" What can children share about animals' sense of smell? . . . Add that many animals have a better sense of smell than humans usually do. "Baby animals depend on their sense of smell to find their families. Let's see if we can use our noses to find our pretend animal pack members."

MATERIALS:

Cotton balls

Tape

Two distinctively different spray
scents

Fresh mint leaves, if available
(rub lightly to release scent)

GETTING READY:

Spray one scent on enough balls
for half of the class. Spray the
second scent on balls for the
rest of the class.

WHOLE-GROUP ACTIVITY:

Tape a ball on each child's shoulder. Using
only their scent-tracking memory, ask children to silently find and join their other pack
members.

Math skills: observing and grouping scents.

Read: Wow! The Most Interesting Book You'll Ever Read About the Five Senses by
Trudee Romanek.

4. What can we learn by tasting?

LEARNING OBJECTIVE: To be surprised by help from our senses.

Introduction: "We've been thinking about what we can learn by looking, listening, touching, and smelling. Would those senses help you find out much about
these two things from the kitchen shelf? Let's investigate."

MATERIALS:

Sugar

Table salt

Sticky note squares

Two Q-tips for each child

SMALL-GROUP ACTIVITY:

1. Place tiny amounts of salt and sugar on each
   child's square of paper. "Can you tell what
   they are by looking, touching, or smelling?
   Could another sense help you find out?"
2. Give each child two Q-tips. Demonstrate
   rolling clean, dry tips in the granules and
   touching them on the tongue so that
   another sense could help find the answer.

5. What can we learn by smelling and tasting?

LEARNING OBJECTIVE: To be surprised by the way some senses work together.

Introduction: Let children tell you what they already know about how food
tastes when a head cold dulls the sense of smell. "Let's find out more about tasting
and smelling."

MATERIALS:

Apple

Potato

Two bowls

Water

Lemon juice

Paring knife

Salt

Sugar

Fruit gelatin granules

Paper towel for each child

GETTING READY:

Peel the apple and potato.

Slice thinly and drop them into separate bowls of water.

Add a few drops of lemon juice to prevent darkening of the slices.

SMALL-GROUP ACTIVITY:

1. Ask children to hold their noses closed. "Let's use our tongues to find out what we are eating. Taste these slices and decide what they are." (If the two foods look very different, have children take turns to help each other taste with eyes and nostrils closed.)
2. "Now taste your slices without holding your nose. How do they taste now?" Encourage more experimentation with tiny amounts of salt, sugar, and gelatin granules to find out if tongues alone tell us how food tastes.

6. What does our skin tell us?

LEARNING OBJECTIVE: To admire how the sense of touch informs us.

Introduction: Ask the children to find out one thing about the contents of two containers that are on the science table without lifting or opening the containers.

MATERIALS:

Ice cubes or very cold water

Hot water

2 small containers with tight lids

Feathers

Chalk

GETTING READY:

Fill one container with ice water and the other with hot water.

Cover with layers of paper toweling to retain temperature differences until children can use them.

SMALL-GROUP ACTIVITY:

1. "What can you learn about what is inside the containers without opening them? How can you find out?" Which part of their bodies did children use? Could they find out the same thing by using their elbows? Foreheads? Backs of their hands? What covers each of these body parts?
2. Suggest finding out if it is easy for our skin to inform us about what it touches. "Try stroking your skin so gently with a feather that you can't feel it. Is it possible?"
3. Ask whether skin on some parts of the body gives better information about how things feel. "Does chalk feel the same when

stroked across an arm? When rubbed by the fingertips?"

4. Encourage children to bring in an object with a special texture to put on a "Please Touch" tray.

Read from: *Your Skin Holds You In* by Rebecca Baines.

CONCEPT: **Our bodies need our care.**

1. How can we see germs?

LEARNING OBJECTIVE: To be astonished by evidence of microbe growth.

Introduction: Read aloud *I Know How We Fight Germs* by Kate Rowan. Ask children to share what they know about germs. . . . Expand the discussion, if needed, with basic information: Microbes are everywhere, but invisible. Some kinds do important work, but others can make us sick when they get into our bodies. Recall examining fingerprints. "What did they look like when you examined them through the magnifier? . . . Germs are tiny enough to hide in all those fingertip grooves. It's hard to imagine that, but there is a way to find evidence that they do. That's because microbes can grow large enough for us to see them. Let's see if we can make that happen in a safe way."

MATERIALS:

3 small (4-in. [10-cm] square) clear plastic deli boxes with attached lids (clamshell style)

Small package of lemon gelatin (*not* sugar-free)

Water

Small saucepan

Hand lenses

Jeweler's loupes*

GETTING READY:

(Prepare this microbe culture medium away from children)

Dissolve lemon gelatin in ½ cup boiling water. Stir until *completely* dissolved.

Pour into three deli boxes.

Solution should be no more than ⅛ in. deep to stay a pale shade of yellow. Chill to solidify.

---

*Order inexpensive jeweler's loupes from The Private Eye. See Resources.

Whole-Group Experience: Explain that scientists study invisible microbes (germs) by first providing them nutrients and a warm, dark place to grow. After a few days, the microbes grow big enough to be seen under a microscope. Some kinds of microbes (molds, fungi) can even be seen with a hand lens. "We're going to do the same thing, so we can see some of the germs that stick to those fingertip grooves."

Ask three volunteers to press not-recently-washed, spread-out fingertips on the prepared growth media (one child per container). Snap the cover shut and tape it securely to make the box airtight. Label it with the day's date.

Place the box in a warm (80° to 90° F), dark place to incubate undisturbed for at least 3 days. Examine the culture with magnifiers to study the resulting spots of fungi or mold. (If jeweler's loupes are used, wipe the open end with sanitizing tissues between uses.) Continue to observe the microbe development for several days. Encourage children to draw what they observe for their science folders. *Do not allow sealed containers to be opened after mold has developed.* Carefully dispose of the sealed containers at the end of the investigation.

Math skills: Observing the time—3 days—for germs to grow.

Read from: Human Body by Caroline Bingham for good photo enlargements of bacteria and viruses.

In follow-up discussions, point out that harmful microbes on unwashed hands and fingers can be carried onto food as we eat. They can make us sick, or start infections when we touch our faces or eyes. Find out what children know about ways to get rid of those germs. Mention that doctors tell us that the *very best way* to protect ourselves is by *always* washing our hands carefully with soap and water after using the bathroom and *always* washing them carefully before we eat. Mention that liquid germicide hand cleaners and hand wipes can help if we can't get to soap and water.

Demonstrate careful handwashing: Wet hands. Turn off water. Work up enough soapsuds to scrub hands, nails, fingers, and between fingers for at least 20 seconds, then turn on water. Rinse under running water and dry with a clean towel. "Here's a timing song to sing while you scrub, so you'll know when you've washed your hands long enough."

Math skills: experiencing time—20 seconds—as a song activity.

THE SINK SONG

(To the tune of "Head, Shoulders, Knees and Toes)

Hands, thumbs and fingers, too,

Fingers, too.

Hands, thumbs and fingers, too,

Fingers too-oo-oo-oo,

Soap them, scrub them, wash the germs away.

Hands, thumbs and fingers, too,

Now I'm through!

2. *How shall we wash our hands?*

LEARNING OBJECTIVE: To enjoy investigating a personal care challenge.

MATERIALS:

Plain copier paper

Baby oil

Liquid hand soap

Bar hand soap

Waterless hand sanitizer
   (at least 60% alcohol)

Sanitizing hand wipes

Paper towels

GETTING READY:

For each child, label pages:
   (child's name) Control: Result:
Arrange bulletin board space, or string a cord in the room to hang up sticky pages.

? *Inquiry Activity:* In a whole-group discussion, ask the children to think about possible ways to clean dirty hands. Record their suggestions. Ask for predictions about the ways that would work best. Suggest exploring some of those ways. Decide which ways groups of investigators will try: just cold water, just warm water; bar soap and water, liquid hand soap and water; sanitizing wipes or waterless hand sanitizer.

Raise the important question of how to show their results. How will we know if everyone started the investigation with a hand that needed washing? "We all need to have the same way to show a soiled hand to begin our investigation. That will give us a way to compare our results and decide which methods work best. Scientists call this step having a *control.*"

Smooth a light coating of baby oil on the palm and fingers of one of each child's hands. Demonstrate pressing your own oily hand on the paper. Hold the paper up to a light so that the translucent oily print can be seen. "This is our control." Fasten control sheets to the bulletin board or clip them to a cord strung across a corner of the room.

"After you have tried your cleaning method *and dried your hand*, press it on your *result* paper. Compare your two papers. Do they look the same or different?"

Write your cleaning method on result sheets.

Discuss and tally the final results for each group of investigators. "Which results pages still have some oily smudges? Which do not? Which cleaning methods were successful in removing the oil? Which were less successful?" Compare the results with the predictions. "What else might have made a difference in results? . . . How long did you scrub? . . . How hard did you scrub?" . . .

Later, print out a copy of the investigation findings for each child to include in his or her science folder, together with the child's own experiment papers.

(Separate the experiment pages with paper toweling to prevent smudging.) Conclude the experience with a question for the class: "What will you do with what you learned about handwashing?"

Math skills: Observing, comparing, and recording data.

3. How do sneeze germs spread?

LEARNING OBJECTIVE: To be surprised that germs can travel in air, and take pride in sneezing responsibly.

MATERIALS:

Facial tissues

Clean trigger-style spray bottle

Water

Thread

Tape

GETTING READY:

Fill spray bottle with water.

Tie a tissue corner to a length of thread. Tape thread to the ceiling so the tissue dangles about 3 ft. (1 m) from the floor.

(Avoid areas with strong air currents.)

Measure standing lines 5, 4, and 3 ft. from the tissue.

Whole-Group Experience: Give each child a facial tissue. "Take a moment to get relaxed. Now hold the tissue in front of your face and quietly say, 'Ah-choo.' What happened? . . . What did that feel like? . . . Was it different from a real sneeze? . . . Now hold the tissue the same way, take a very deep breath, and pretend to sneeze with all your might. What changed? . . . Which parts of your body moved? Let's carefully watch some good, strong volunteer sneezers to see how much energy they put into a forceful, pretend sneeze. What did you observe?"

"Something else happens with a real sneeze." Move through the group with the spray bottle. Aim for the ceiling with a few strong sprays to see how far the moisture spreads out. "Is this more like a real sneeze? . . . Real sneezes rush out with much more speed and force than these small sprays. Invisible germs can travel on the tiny drops of real sneeze moisture. That's how a sick person's sneeze can make other people sick. Take turns investigating how far your blast of breath can travel."

Small-Group Activity: One child at a time stands facing the tissue, at the closest mark, takes a very deep breath, and blows forcefully toward the tissue to see it stir in the wake of that breath. The child moves back to succeeding marks to see how far away a forceful breath can move the tissue, then records the greatest distance at which the tissue was moved.

Discussion: Children report their results. Point out that children's sneeze germs can travel just as far and forcefully as their hardest blasts. "Doctors want us to help each other by covering our sneezes in a tissue or by sneezing into the crook of our elbow. Then we won't give sneeze germs a chance to spread to others, and we won't catch theirs!"

Math skills: Measuring roughly how far a sneeze travels.

4. How can we take care of our teeth?

LEARNING OBJECTIVE: To inspire pride in caring for our teeth.

Introduction: Read aloud Paul Showers's vintage humorous book *How Many Teeth?* Give children the opportunity to share their ideas about loosening and erupting teeth.

Invite a dental hygienist to present introductory dental health care information to the children. Some professionals are prepared to demonstrate good toothbrushing techniques with sets of plastic teeth and giant toothbrushes. If this is not possible, ask children to share what they already know and do to take good care of their teeth. Supplement their comments, as needed, to include regular dental checkups and eating the foods that produce strong teeth and healthy gums, especially milk and other calcium-rich foods. Talk about smart snacks for healthy teeth.

5. What do our teeth do?

LEARNING OBJECTIVE: To appreciate the functions of our teeth.

MATERIALS:

Small mirors

Tissues

Graham crackers

Slices of apple

GETTING READY:

Obtain samples of floride toothpaste well in advance (check manufacturer's Web site).

Fold a tissue into a small pad for each child.

SMALL-GROUP ACTIVITY:

1. Encourage children to smile at themselves in the mirror. What does the smile look like? Are teeth useful for more than smiles? Are teeth all alike?
2. Let children carefully bite down on the tissue pads with all their teeth. "Look at the marks on the pads. Are they all alike? Which teeth would be best for biting? Which teeth would be best for chewing and grinding food fine enough to swallow?"
3. Encourage children to use mirrors to examine the grinding teeth. Give children bits of cracker to chew. Use the mirrors to view the grinding surfaces again. Can the tongue clean away some cracker crumbs?
4. Offer apple slices to the children to chew thoroughly. Check with mirrors again. Has the apple, "nature's toothbrush," changed the way the grinding teeth look?
5. Join the children at the sink to practice swishing water around in the mouth to rinse away food bits after a snack. "We do this when we can't brush."

INTEGRATING ACTIVITIES

Math Experiences

1. Translate into concrete experience the evidence of growth from a child's birth weight to his or her present weight. Do this for each child by stacking enough hardwood blocks on a bathroom scale to equal the two weights.

2. Establish a relative measure of muscle strength by weighing the number of blocks a child can lift. (Avoid competitive emphasis by using questions like "How much weight are your muscles ready to lift now?")

3. Have children count their heartbeats for 10 seconds before and after vigorous exercise. Compare the results.

4. Have children use their hands and feet to measure distances or dimensions: "This table is as wide as 11 of my hands."

5. Allow time for children to compare measuring spoons and cup sizes when they are used in cooking experiences. Try to have enough measuring equipment on hand so that all the children can participate in measuring ingredients. "We need one cup of flour for the pancakes. Will we have enough if two children each put in one-half cup of flour? Let's find out." Use sets of plastic measuring cups at the sand and water tables so that children can practice using these utensils and develop a practical sense of their relative volumes.

6. Compare inhaling and exhaling effects using a a tape measure to check the expanding and contracting rib cage.

Music (Resources in Appendix A)

1. *Raffi's Singable Songbook* offers "I Wonder if I'm Growing?" and "Brush Your Teeth" to extend human body study.

2. Listen to how our bodies work in "What a Miracle" from Hap Palmer's cassette, *Walter the Waltzing Worm.*

Literature Links: Individuality

GLEN, SHARLEE. (2004). *Keeping up with Roo.* New York: Putnam. Gracie outgrows her former playmate, Aunt Ruth, whose childlike spirit and mind remain the same. Gracie learns that her aunt has given her much, in spite of her limitations.

HOOKS, GWENDOLYN. (2005). *Nice wheels.* New York: Scholastic. A simple story reassures young readers that a wheelchair-confined child has much to offer as a friend.

LEARS, LAURIE. (2005). *Nathan's wish: A story about cerebral palsy.* Morton Grove, IL: Whitman. A damaged owl in a raptor rehabilitation center begins to nurture orphaned baby owls. It inspires a boy to reach beyond his own physical limitations to also become a helper at the center.

MCDONALD, MEGAN. (2005). *Stink, the incredible shrinking kid.* Cambridge, MA: Candlewick. Stink copes with being the next to shortest kid in the second grade. Confident chapter book readers will relish it.

MILLMAN, ISAAC. (2001). *Moses goes to school.* New York: Farrar, Strauss. Visit Moses's cheerful classroom in a school for the deaf. The children learn to sign a new song, following the rhythms of boom box vibrations. The text is paralleled with ASL signing illustrations for hearing children to learn.

MILLMAN, ISAAC. (2004). *Isaac sees a play.* New York: Farrar, Strauss. A hearing boy, new to this country, is beginning to learn English. His class visits Moses's deaf school class to see a play. Moses teaches him (and readers) simple signing.

SHIRLEY, DEBRA. (2008). *Best friend on wheels..* Morton Grove, IL: Whitman. Sarah's wheelchair limitations don't get in the way of shared fun with her friend.

Literature Links: The Body

ALDA, ARLENE. (2008). *Iris has a virus.* Plattsburg, NY: Tundra. This simple story will spark conversation among preschoolers about handwashing and communicable illnesses.

BAINES, REBECCA. (2008). *Your skin holds you in.* Washington, DC: National Geographic.

BAINES, REBECCA. (2009). *The bones you own.* Washington, DC: National Geographic. Eye-catching illustrations, mind-catching information, and intriguing questions to pursue.

BINGHAM, CAROLINE. (2003). *Human body.* New York: Dorling Kindersley. An attractive layout and good text level provide accurate information without overwhelming young researchers.

COBB, VICKI. (2002). *I see myself.* New York: HarperCollins. Reflections and the need for light to see are described well for young children.

ELYA, SUSAN. (2008). *Tooth on the loose.* New York: Penguin Putnam. The solution to a child's loose tooth dilemma involves her whole Spanish/English-speaking family.

JOHNSON, JINNY. (2004). *Senses.* Boston: Kingfisher. This look at the senses starts from their control center: the brain. Each topic is enriched with related animal senses.

MACNAIR, PATRICIA. (2004). *Bodyscope: Movers and shapers.* Boston: Houghton Mifflin. Written for upper grades, but dynamic illustrations and intriguing facts make this a great pictorial reference for younger children. NSTA* Outstanding Trade Book.

MILLER, EDWARD. (2008). *The tooth book.* New York: Holiday House. Yes, there is an appealing book about children's teeth! This one also has weird historical information about tooth care.

NETTLETON, PAMELA. (2004). *Bend and stretch: Learning about your bones and muscles.* Minneapolis: Picture Window. Cheerful illustrations, clear concepts, and easy experiments will interest young readers.

NETTLETON, PAMELA. (2004). *Breathe in, breathe out.* Minneapolis Picture Window. This book can be read aloud selectively to give personalized information about how lungs work. Also in this series: *Look, listen, taste, touch and smell* and *Bend and stretch: Learning about your bones and muscles.*

O'SULLIVAN, ROBYN. (2004). *Numbers and you.* Washington, DC: National Geographic. Here's a way to use numbers to describe a child's body, combining intriguing facts and personal data.

PRYOR, KIMBERLEY. (2004). *Touching.* Broomall, PA: Chelsea House. Here is a careful look at what's under our skin and how touch receptors function to inform us. Other books in this series include *Tasting* and *Hearing.*

ROMANEK, TRUDEE. (2004). *Wow! The most interesting book you'll ever read about the five senses.* Toronto, Canada: Kids Can Press. The lively text and busy pages are meant to hold older readers' attention. The information is accurate and can be shared selectively with younger children. NSTA* recommended.

ROSS, VERONICA. (2005). *Lungs.* North Mankato, MN: Smart Apple. The level of information about lungs is appropriate for primary children. The photographs and illustrations are helpful.

SCHWARTZ, DAVID. (1999). *If you hopped like a frog.* New York: Scholastic. This book introduces the concepts of ratio and proportion by imagining comparisons of what kids could do if they shared different animals' physical capabilities.

---

*National Science Teachers Association.

SHOWERS, PAUL. (1999). *How many teeth?* New York: HarperCollins. The amusing text and illustrations enliven the subject of deciduous teeth.

SHOWERS, PAUL. (2004). *A drop of blood.* New York: HarperCollins. Humorous Dracula depictions remove the shiver from this detailing of the composition and functions of blood and the heart that circulates it. NSTA* recommended.

SMALLMAN, CLARE. (2010). *Outside in.* Hauppauge, NY: Barrons. Children romp through the pages of these introductory explanations of body systems and structures. Check the factual "inside" illustrations beneath flaps to be sure that your class will be comfortable with them.

TATE, LINDSEY. (2008). *Kate Larkin, bone expert.* New York: Henry Holt. In this chapter book, Kate explains what she learned about bones after she broke her arm.

TOURVILLE, AMANDA. (2009). *Go wash up.* Minneapolis: Picture Window. Cheerfully illustrated, frank and simple hygiene rules for those under age 6. Also in this series: *Get up and go: Being active* and *Brush, floss and rinse.*

ZIEFERT, HARRIET. (2002). *You can't taste a pickle with your ear.* Brooklyn, NY: Blue Apple Book. An engaging style and rollicking illustrations draw on children's experiences to lead to meaningful learning about the senses.

Literature Links: Health Care

MCDONALD, MEGAN. (2004). *Judy Moody, MD: The doctor is in!* Cambridge, MA: Candlewick. Judy's third-grade class study of the human body includes a hospital field trip, a look at petri dishes full of growing stuff, and some hilarious events.

MILLER, EDWARD. (2006). *The monster health book: A guide to eating healthy, being active, and feeling great for monsters and kids.* New York: Holiday House. A friendly monster is introduced to the concepts of physical fitness. While the text is aimed at proficient readers, the graphics carry the message effectively.

NELSON, ROBIN. (2006). *Staying clean.* Minneapolis: Lerner. Connecting with young listeners through cheery photographs, the subjects of handwashing, toothbrushing, and avoiding lice are tackled.

ROCKWELL, LIZZIE. (2005). *The busy body book: A kid's guide to fitness.* New York: Crown. Here is a clear, lively description of the human body at an appropriate level for young children. Even the illustrations are drawn to child scale! It invites children to have fun as they incidentally stay fit.

ROWAN, KATE. (1999). *I know how we fight germs.* Cambridge, MA: Candlewick. In a casual chat with his mom, Sam learns how germs spread and how white blood cells work against them.

SCHAEFER, CAROLE. (2004). *The biggest soap.* New York: Farrar, Straus, Giroux. Brilliant, splashy art, Gauguin style, enriches this heartwarming story of a South Pacific island child on a soap-buying mission.

SHOWERS, PAUL. (2001). *Sleep is for everyone.* New York: HarperCollins. Color-drenched illustrations will keep listeners and readers awake and focused on sleep facts as we currently know them.

SPILSBARY, LOUISE. (2003). *Why should I wash my body?* Chicago: Heinemann. Candid answers cover all aspects of hygiene except toothbrushing. Good photo magnifications of microbes reinforce the mandates.

Poems (Resources in Appendix A)

From *Now We Are Six* by A. A. Milne, read "Sneezles."

From *I Thought I'd Take My Rat to School* by Dorothy Kennedy, read "Lunch."

Bones, muscles, heart, lungs, senses, and more are celebrated in *The Blood-Hungry Spleen, and Other Poems about Our Parts* by Allan Wolfe and Grey Clarke.

---

*National Science Teachers Association.

Fingerplays

For a good stretching break, do *Moving Parts!* with vigor:

Clap your hands, one, two three,	*Touch your ankles, tap your toes*
Stomp your feet, just like me;	*Bend your knees and wiggle your nose;*
Turn your head from side to side	*Stand up straight, then scrunch way down,*
Reach your arms out really wide!	*Spring up fast like a pop-up clown!*
Twist and stretch, shake and swing,	*Twist and stretch, shake and swing,*
Muscles help move everything!	*Muscles help move everything!*

—SUSAN BORGHESE

Art Activities

Fingerprint Art. Children's fingerprints can create all-over designs and patterns. Use a simple paint-stamping pad for prints. Suggest using crayons to add stems to print-petaled flowers, strings on fingerprint balloons, and so forth.

Collage. Make touch collages with interesting materials you and the children gather, such as corrugated cardboard, silky fabric, corduroy, velvet, sandpaper, cotton balls, tree bark, and steel wool.

Outdoor Art. Trace children's silhouettes on sidewalks or blacktop. Let children add jointed bones and the rib cage.

Play

Hospital Play. Provide props for hospital play such as bandages and a cot; add paper towel tubes so that children can listen to heartbeats. Add discarded plastic syringes (sterilized, needles removed) to allow children to play the role of shot giver. Try to find a discarded X-ray film to add to the equipment.

Creative Thinking

Alike and Different Game. Ask one child to look around at the other children to find someone who is like her or him in one way. If Elena chooses Jenny because they are both girls, ask Jenny to stand next to Elena and find one way that she and Elena are different. Then Jenny has a turn to find someone who is like her in one way, and so on. End the game with a comment about no two people being just alike in every way. Mention the good thinking and choosing the children did.

Sense Memories. Ask the children to close their eyes and take some moments to think of their favorite fruit. "Can you see it? What color is it? Imagine that you are eating it now. Feel it in your mouth. Is it juicy? Soft? Crisp? Can you hear yourself chewing or slurping the fruit? What does it taste like? Enjoy tasting it. What does it smell like? What else does that special smell remind you of? What picture pops into your mind? Take some moments to remember as much as you want to about that memory. Then open your eyes and draw a picture of your favorite fruit and the memory its smell brought back to you." Later, add that the place in our brain where we use smell information is very close to the place where we store memories, so that smells easily bring back memories.

Creative Movement

Take plenty of time to lead a movement story,* circling the room with the children, using drum beats or hand claps to start, maintain, and stop the traveling rhythms and tempos you suggest. "In a town near ours, there is a bunch of strong kids who know how to exercise and eat smart to stay healthy. This is how they looked as they walked around the town on their strong legs, taking big steps, swinging their arms, taking deep breaths, laughing, and feeling fine! (Brief stop.) Which healthy snacks do you think they carried in their backpacks? (Child suggestions.) Show me how they chomped and slurped their snacks when they started to walk again, how they chewed with their strong, healthy teeth.

"Because they had such strong bones and muscles, they were great runners. This is how fast they could run because they were so healthy. (Keep the circle moving with other action suggestions: hopping, jumping, sliding, stomping, skipping.) This is how they stopped and reached for the sky, touched their toes, made a silly shape, and froze it still for as long as they could, until they had to collapse on the floor. And then they met a bunch of tired kids sitting on the ground. These kids didn't know how to eat smart to stay healthy, so they were limp and saggy from sitting indoors too much. They were too tired to have much fun. What do you think they ate all day?"

(Start a slow drumbeat.) "They had a hard time getting up from the ground. When they walked around the town, this is how slowly their tired muscles moved and dragged. This is how they looked when they tried to touch their toes. This is how they groaned and moaned when they stumbled along. (Repeat the movement suggestions used for the smart eaters.) How do you think this story ends? Good ending ideas! Now it's time for us to get ready for. . . ."

Food Experiences

If classroom cooking is permissible and an electric griddle is available, enjoy promoting healthy, smart, whole-grain eating by making delicious oatmeal pancakes. (See the recipe on page 316, Exploring at Home.) A single recipe will make about 30 sample-size pancakes for about $1.00. Why not double the recipe to have plenty? A bit of fruit yogurt makes a fancy topping.

Allow as many children (with freshly washed hands) as possible to participate in the math of measuring ingredients, but keep them at a safe distance from the hot griddle. A volunteer adult assistant is important for this project. Send copies of the recipe to parents beforehand so that you can have small rice

---

*Adapted from Mimi Chenfeld, *Creative Experiences for Young Children* (2nd ed., p. 243). (1995) Fort Worth, TX: Harcourt, 1995.

Measuring mixes math with good eating.

cakes on hand for children with lactose or gluten intolerance, for vegans, or for those whose religious dietary restrictions might rule out any of these simple ingredients.

Field Trips

Public Health Clinic. If a public facility can be toured, try to have the visit serve the children in a nonthreatening way, such as having children measured and weighed. Be certain that the children are prepared for what to anticipate at the clinic.

A Visit from the Field. Your community emergency medical service squad may be willing to bring a field trip to your school. Children feel more at ease if a health professional visits them in a familiar setting. A careful look at the emergency vehicle can be fascinating and reassuring. The squad members evoke the awe of heroism, rather than the shadow of anxiety that may be aroused in some children when they meet healthcare professionals.

PROMOTING CONCEPT CONNECTIONS

Maintaining Concepts

Teachers who are committed to the principle of accepting responsibility for one's own health find it easy to use teachable moments to promote this goal. When a respected teacher joins the children in routine handwashing and toothbrushing, children emulate the patterns readily. When giving first aid to a scraped-knee victim, reassure the child that parts of the flowing blood are already beginning to make repairs so that new skin can grow over the scrape. Encourage children to discuss feelings about medical treatment when they have it, and express respect for the way they faced what had to be done to keep themselves healthy.

Undue "preaching" of health care messages to suggest home practices can become counterproductive. Young children are limited in their ability to change the habits or cultural patterns followed by their families. Therefore, pressing children to conform to healthful standards away from school may result in feelings of shame or resentment.

Improving School Grounds

Because North American children are suffering from lack of physical exercise, spruce up the asphalt playground with inviting exercise opportunities. Paint fresh graphics such as a curving snake, the segments of which invite hopping and number counting, or 100 squares for jumping among numbers, or colored concentric circles that allow games in which children follow directions such as "run into the yellow circle" or "throw the beanbag to the blue circle."

Connecting Concepts

1. When children are learning about their sense of sight, think about how light passing through curved glass makes things look larger (see Chapter 15, Light). "This is how glasses help some people see better."

2. When discussing hearing, mention the delicate part inside each ear that vibrates to let us hear sounds (see Chapter 14, Sound).

3. Identify the calcium that our bones and teeth get from milk and dark green vegetables as the same mineral that makes hard shells for some animals (see Chapter 5, Animals) and compresses or combines with other minerals to form certain rocks (see Chapter 10, Rocks and Minerals).

4. When children are learning about the muscles that keep the lungs expanding and contracting, remind them that all living things need air to stay alive.

Family and Community Support

Two goals of this chapter—valuing oneself and assuming responsibility early in life for one's own health—cannot be achieved without parental involvement. Although few parents intend to neglect their children's health, there has been a marked decrease in communicable disease immunization for young children. The large number of malnourished children in our affluent country is also discouraging. These problems are being addressed by the American Pediatrics Association campaign to urge prevention of illness through responsible self-care rather than through reliance on costly treatment to cure illness. Teachers and families together can encourage responsible attitudes in children.

Alert families to interactive anatomy exhibits in the nearest children's science museum and to local hospital preventive healthcare programs designed for children.

RESOURCES

BENBOW, ANN, & MABLY, COLIN. (2010). *Sensational human body science projects.* Berkeley Heights, NJ. Enslow. Good instructions for fingerprinting are included.

CHENFELD, MIMI. (1995). *Creative experiences for young children* (2nd ed.). Orlando, FL: Harcourt Brace. This book is a treasure chest of creative activities across the curriculum.

CLEMENTS, RHONDA, & SCHNEIDER, SHARON. (2006). *Movement-based learning: Academic concepts and physical activity for ages 3 through 8.* Reston, VA: American Alliance for Health, Physical Education, Recreation, and Dance.

COBB, VICKI. (2000). *Follow your nose.* Brookfield, CT: Millbrook Press. There's excellent information in this book for advanced students, but the easy experiments will fascinate all ages. Other books in this series include *Perk up your ears* (2001); *Your tongue can tell* (2000); *Feeling your way* (2001); and *Open your eyes* (2002).

CRACKNELL, JAMES. (2009). *Body science.* New York: Dorling Kindersley. This lively reference reveals the science beneath the awesome body you occupy.

OLIEN, REBECCA. (2006). *The respiratory system.* Mankato, MN: Capstone Press. Information about the anatomy and physiology of the lungs as part of the whole respiratory system is presented. The book has an excellent illlustration of the diaphragm muscle.

MACAULY, DAVID. (2008). *The way we work: Getting to know the amazing human body.* Boston: Houghton Mifflin. This award-winning illustrator/author offers incredibly detailed drawings of the intricacies of our anatomy, and does so with a humorous touch.

PARKER, STEVE. (2004). *Heart, blood, and lungs.* Milwaukee: Gareth Stevens. Key information, clear, eye-catching illustrations, and an "Instant Fact" feature make this a fascinating resource.

PARKER, STEVE. (2004). *The skeleton and muscles.* Chicago: Raintree. Accessible background is offered on the function and composition of bones and muscles.

PICA, RAE. (2003). *Your active child.* Chicago: Contemporary Books. A good resource for promoting age-appropriate fitness for children.

PICA, RAE. (2006). Physical fitness and the early childhood curriculum. *Young Children, 61*(3), 12–19.

ROMANEK, TRUDEE. (2004). *ACHOO! The most interesting book you'll ever read about germs.* Tonawanda, NY: Kids Can Press. Written for older readers, news-flash style information in this intriguing resource can be shared selectively with younger children. Also in her series, *Wow! The most interesting book you'll ever read about the five senses.*

SANDERS, STEPHEN S. (2002). *Active for life: Developmentally appropriate movement programs for young children.* Washington, DC: National Association for the Education of Young Children.

SIMON, SEYMOUR. (2003). *Eyes and ears.* New York: Harper Collins. Advanced information about the anatomy and physiology of the eyes and ears provides excellent background for teachers. NSTA* Outstanding Trade book.

TIERNO, PHILLIP. (2004). *The secret life of germs: What they are, why we need them, and how we can protect ourselves against them.* New York: Atria Books.

WOLFE, ALLAN, & CLARKE, GREG. *The blood hungry spleen and other poems about our parts.* (2003). Cambridge, MA: Candlewick Press.

*National Science Teachers Association.

YOUNGQUIST, JOAN. (2004). From medicine to microbes. *Young Children, 59*(2), 28–32. Here is an excellent long-term preschool investigation of healthcare and microbes.

ONLINE RESOURCES

Kids' Health: http://www.kidshealth.org/kid/stay_healthy

National Geographic. *Explore the Human Body: http://science.nationalgeographic.com/science/health-and-human-body/human-body*

Air

Take a moment to pull a slow, deep breath of air into your throat and lungs. Envision the oxygen traveling through your body, keeping you alive. This precious medium, the air in which we live, affects everything on Earth. Bring this wonder with you as you explore the fascinating properties of air with children.

Children become acquainted with hundreds of substances through sensory encounters. Air intrigues children because it is an invisible, ever-present substance that is not directly encountered by the senses until it affects something tangible. The activities in this chapter are designed to explore the following concepts:

- Air is almost everywhere.
- Air is real; it takes up space.
- Air presses on everything on all sides.
- Moving air pushes things.
- Fast-moving air keeps planes aloft.
- Air slows moving objects.
- Living things need air to survive.

In the experiences that follow, children will find air in empty containers and become aware of the air that they breathe. They will feel air enclosed in something, see how it occupies space, and note how it pushes on everything. Also, they will enjoy making things for moving air to push.

Introduce the topic of air to children by holding up your hands, cupped together, suggesting, "There is something important inside my hands. You may peek in, but you won't be able to see what it is. The important stuff is invisible! We'll be finding out more about it."

CONCEPT: **Air is almost everywhere.**

1. What comes out of an empty can?

LEARNING OBJECTIVE: To enjoy finding that invisible air is almost everywhere.

MATERIALS:

Empty metal can
Nail
Hammer
Dishpan
Water

SMALL-GROUP ACTIVITY:

1. Ask children to examine the can. Do they notice anything in it?
2. Use a hammer and nail to punch a hole in the bottom. Let a child do it, if possible.
3. Ask: "If there is something in the can, could we push it out through this hole? Let's see."
4. Invert the can; slowly push it into the water. Ask a child to hold a hand just above the nail hole. What does the child feel being pushed out of the hole? (A stream of air) "Could something real be in that empty can—something real that we can't see?"
5. Let the children experiment.

2. What can we find out about "empty" containers?

LEARNING OBJECTIVE: To confirm that invisible air is reliably almost everywhere.

MATERIALS:

Empty clear plastic shampoo bottles or tubes, uncapped
Downy feathers, milkweed fluff, or bits of tissue paper

SMALL-GROUP ACTIVITY:

1. Ask children to examine the bottles or tubes. Do they notice anything inside?
2. "Point the bottle top toward your chin and squeeze the bottle. Do you feel something? What? See if you can squeeze it out. Keep trying."
3. Offer a feather to each child. "If your bottle is really empty, nothing will come out to push the feather from your hand. See what happens if you point the bottle toward the feather." (This activity can be disorderly unless you set limits for a feather-blowing space.)

Math Skills: Observing air being pushed ahead, with measurable results.

3. How does air get inside us?

LEARNING OBJECTIVE: To be impressed by our constant need to breathe in air.

Group Activity: Suggest that all the children take a deep breath, shut their lips tightly, and pinch their nostrils shut as long as possible. "What happened? Why did you let go of your nose? What did your body seem to need so much that you had to let go? Let's try again.

"Our bodies need the part of air called *oxygen*. We need to breathe air into our bodies about every 6 seconds because the oxygen is used up so quickly inside of us." Guide the discussion to bring out the idea that *living things must have air to stay alive.* Discuss the danger of climbing into boxes with heavy lids or other enclosed spaces that cannot be opened from the inside. Give examples.

Give each child an unfolded tissue to hold near the nose and mouth. "Let's see what happens to the tissue when you bring air into your body and then when you push this air out. Try it with your lips closed; now with your lips opened a bit. Are there two ways for the air to come in and out? Let's see if we can tell where the air is going inside our bodies." Ask children to take turns lying on the floor or putting their heads on the table so that others can watch their chests go up and down as they breathe.

Read: Air Is Everywhere by Melissa Stewart.

CONCEPT: **Air is real; it takes up space.**

1. How can we feel the substance of air?

LEARNING OBJECTIVE: To delight in containing air as tangible stuff.

MATERIALS:
Plain plastic sandwich bags, twist closures (or small zip-top bag)
Drinking straws
Transparent tape

GETTING READY:
Prepare a blowing bag for each child participating by gathering the top of a bag to form a neck, inserting a straw in the neck, and securing the neck of the bag to the straw with tape.

SMALL-GROUP ACTIVITY:
1. Ask: "Is the table real? How can you tell? If your eyes were closed, could you still tell that the table is real? Is feeling something a good way to know that it is real?"
2. Let children blow into the prepared bags. "What are you blowing into the bag? Look in the bag. Feel it. Do you think something real is in there?"
3. Remove straw and tie with wire closure, or zip seal so the children can keep their bags full of air to feel.

Children should leave the plastic bags at school so that younger children at home will not pick up the idea of playing with plastic bags.

2. What can a glassful of air do?

LEARNING OBJECTIVE: To be surprised by the force of air.

MATERIALS:

Clear plastic bowl (corn popper dome is fine) or 5-in. (12-cm) deep glass mixer bowl, if it can be used safely

Pitcher of water

Cork

Clear plastic tumbler

Splash catcher, aprons

GETTING READY:

If indoors, inflate a wading pool. Put the bowl in the center.

SMALL-GROUP ACTIVITY:

1. Put cork in the bowl. "The cork is touching the bowl now. What will happen if we pour water into the bowl? Let's see."
2. Fill half the bowl with water. "Notice if the cork is touching the bottom of the bowl now."
3. Ask: "Can someone put the cork back on the bottom?" Let children try to do this. "Will it stay if you let go?"
4. "See if something in the tumbler will push water away so that the cork can stay on the bottom of the bowl." Invert the tumbler and push straight down to the bottom. "What could be inside the glass pushing the water away? Do you see anything?"
5. Let the children experiment.

Group Discussion: Ask the children to catch some air in their cupped hands. "Poke your nose into your hands. Can you smell the air? Peek in. Can you see it? Can you hear it? Try to taste it." (Children love to hang their tongues out for research purposes.) Ask those who have experimented how they know that air is real. Children are proud of their new information and are willing to repeat a discussion like this one. Next time, let a hand puppet be the skeptic who doesn't believe that invisible things can be real. The children will be happy to convince the puppet otherwise.

3. What can a bag of air do?

LEARNING OBJECTIVE: To take pride in using air as a force.

MATERIALS:

Large, sturdy paper bag, wire twist closure, or tape

Bicycle tire pump, bellows-type pump, or hand pump

Heavy book or block

GETTING READY:

Gather bag top into a neck, fasten with wire twist, or tape.

SMALL-GROUP ACTIVITY:

1. Demonstrate the pump if children don't know what it is or how it works. Look at the air intake hole where air comes in to be pushed out by the pump. (Remove the intake valve cap from the bellows pump.) Feel air being pushed out.
2. Ask: "Do you think a bag full of air could push that book over? How could we find out?"

FIGURE 7–1

Put bag on floor and stand book upright on it. Put pump near bag.

3. Insert the end of the pump hose into the bag (see Figure 7–1). Tighten the closure, or simply hold bag firmly while children take turns pumping air into it, pushing the book over. "Could air be doing that? Do you think air is real stuff, even though we can't see it?" Discuss car airbag purpose.

Math skills: Observing the force of air pushing.

CONCEPT: **Air presses on everything on all sides.**

1. What can push up water in a narrow tube?

LEARNING OBJECTIVE: To be amazed that air can press liquids in or out of narrow tubes.

MATERIALS:

Baster (kitchen tool)

Medicine droppers (plastic or thick glass tubes are safest)

Small containers of water for each child

Pint jar half full of water

Sponge, pan, and newspapers for cleanup

Drinking straws, cut in half

SMALL-GROUP ACTIVITY:

1. Let children examine the baster. Is the tube empty? Squeeze the bulb to feel what comes out.

2. Put the baster in the jar of water. Ask, "What do you see when I push air out of the baster? Watch the tube when I slowly let go of the rubber bulb on top. What is happening?"

3. Hold up the filled baster. Ask, "What's happening to the water now? What could

FIGURE 7–2

Suction cups (desirable)

be keeping the water in? Perhaps something invisible is in the baster with the water."

4. Squeeze the bulb to push out water. Release bulb to pull in air. "What's happening now? Try it."

5. "Now let's try the same thing with straws." Insert a straw in the water. Put your index fingers over the top and bottom of the straw and lift it from the water. Keep finger on top and remove finger from bottom. Most of the water will stay in the straw. Why? (Air pressure keeps it in.) See Figure 7–2.

6. "Nothing can get into the straw from the top with my finger on it. Watch as I let some air push into the straw." Remove finger from top. Water is pushed out of the straw. Let children experiment.

Note: Some children may believe that a dropper is filled with water if drops just cling to the outside. Help them hold the dropper tube in the water while releasing the bulb.

Listen for the squish of air forced out of the cup when you press a suction cup against a flat surface. Let children know that air pressing on the outside of the cup keeps it attached to the surface.

Learning to manipulate a tool of science.

CONCEPT: **Moving air pushes things.**

Introduction: Ask the children to wave their hands back and forth in front of their faces. "Can you feel something on your skin? When air is moving, you can feel it. You don't notice it when it isn't moving." Explain that we feel air moving against us in the same way whether we are moving when the air is still or whether air is moving by itself (as wind) when we are still.

1. ♣ *What can we feel pushing on us?*

LEARNING OBJECTIVE: To revel in the effect of air moving and pushing against us.

MATERIALS:

Sheets of newspaper
Crepe paper streamers
Pinwheels or kites

OUTDOOR ACTIVITY:

Give children sheets of paper outside. "As you stand still, will paper stick to the front of you if you don't hold it there? Now see what happens to it when you run as fast as you can. Do you have to hold the paper to press it to yourself? What could be holding it?" Let children enjoy running with pinwheels or paper streamers. Launch the kite running toward the wind. Try flying the kite on a calm day and on a windy day.

Math skills: Observing the force of air pushing.

Read: About a struggle to fly a kite in *Days with Frog and Toad* by Arnold Lobel.

Read: Simple kite-making instructions in *Air Is Everywhere* by Melissa Stewart.

2. ♣ *How can we make a glider drift on moving air?*

LEARNING OBJECTIVE: To be reassured that moving air can carry certain things.

MATERIALS:

A sheet of copier paper and a paper clip for each child

GETTING READY:

Draw a lengthwise line down the center of the paper. (A)

Draw parallel lines 1½ in. (4 cm) from the center line. (B)

Draw a line ¾ in. (2 cm) from the bottom across the paper.

SMALL-GROUP ACTIVITY:

1. Show the children how to fold up ¾ in. (2 cm) from the bottom of the paper. Continue to fold this amount four times, forming a cuff.
2. With the cuff side down, fold the paper and cuff lengthwise on the center line A. Form wings by folding back each side on B lines. Fasten the fold with a paper clip. (See Figure 7–3.)
3. Launch glider with cuff in front, holding the center. If the glider always nosedives, reduce the weight of the front end by removing the clip or unfolding one fold of the cuff. Push the glider ahead by keeping the hand and arm straight, not sweeping downward, when launching the glider.

Math skills: Observing the force of air holding a glider up.

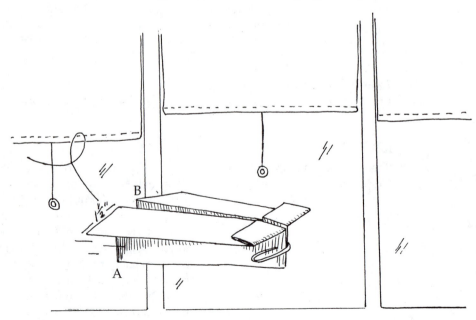

FIGURE 7–3

3. ♣ *Can we make a helicopter spin in moving air?*

LEARNING OBJECTIVE: To enjoy watching moving air twirl a helicopter.

MATERIALS:

Two duplicated templates of a helicopter for each child, plus extra scissors for each child

GETTING READY:

Enlarge and reproduce template from Figure 7–4.

Four templates will fit on a sheet of copier paper, using dimensions of 2½ in. (6 cm) × 8½ in. (21 cm).

SMALL-GROUP ACTIVITY:

1. Show children the template for the helicopter (Figure 7–4) and demonstrate cutting on the solid lines and folding on the dotted lines. Fold the longer vertical edges to form a single base piece. Fold one smaller blade section forward and one backward. (See Figure 7–4).
2. Stand on a chair or table, reaching up to add height, to drop the helicopter. It should twirl as it descends. Add that the air pushes on the helicopter as it falls. Each blade steers the air to the other one, causing the twirling.

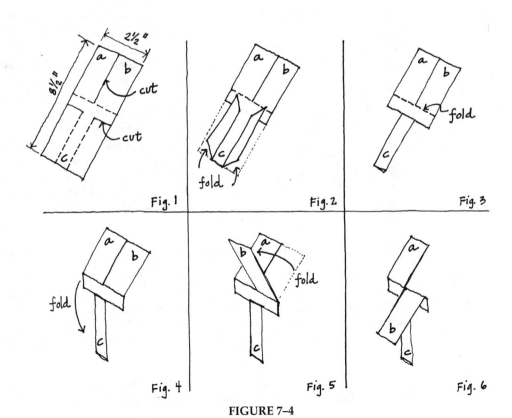

FIGURE 7–4

3. ♣ Let children experiment outdoors on playground equipment or an indoor stairwell.

? *Inquiry Activity:* Ask for predictions about what might happen when the helicopter is dropped upside down. Will it right itself? What might change when the blades are bent in the opposite direction? Will a different kind of paper change the twirling? Will helicopters of different sizes twirl differently? Can a really big one be made of a sheet of construction paper? How about a tiny one, tiny as a maple seed? Record changes and discuss results.

CONCEPT: Fast-moving air keeps planes aloft.

1. What can fast- and slow-moving air do?

LEARNING OBJECTIVE: To diminish the mystery of how heavy planes can stay up in the air.

MATERIALS:

Hair dryer (preferably with a cool setting)

Desk chair

Copier paper

Tissue paper

Transparent tape

GETTING READY:

Cut one 2-in. (5-cm) × 12-in. (30-cm) paper strip.

Cut a 1-in. (2.5-cm) × 6-in. (15-cm) tissue paper strip for each child.

LARGE-GROUP ACTIVITY:

1. Tape one end of a 2- × 12-in. (5 × 30-cm) strip of paper on back of chair, allowing the other end to droop forward.
2. Position hair dryer so that it blows air across the strip, starting at the chair back. Have children observe that the paper rises. What happens to the drooping end?*
3. Demonstrate holding one end of a strip of tissue paper between both hands, letting the other end droop forward. Bring the held end to your lips and blow over it, causing it to rise. What happens when you stop blowing? Let children experiment. *

Math skills: Observing the pressure of air pushing paper upward.

Discussion: Explain that heavy airplanes are *pushed ahead* by their powerful engines but are *lifted* into the sky by their wings. The wings lift the same way the paper strips lifted when faster air was moving over the top. Air moves faster over the top of the curved wings than it does beneath the wings. This makes the air pressure above the wing lighter. The flow of air beneath the wing is slower, mak-

---

*This demonstrates Bernoulli's principle that fast-moving air creates low-pressure zones into which paper—and airplane wings—can rise, pushed by the higher-pressure air below them.

ing the air pressure greater under the wings. This stronger pressure pushes the wings upward, lifting the plane and keeping it up in the air. Encourage children to simulate the effect with one hand lightly held out flat, representing lighter (low) air pressure and the other hand curled into a fist strongly pushing up beneath, representing greater (high) air pressure.

♣ To demonstrate how a curved wing creates fast air on the top and slow air on the bottom, chalk a large semicircle on the playground. One child can walk around the curved half-circle and another one can walk across the straight diameter. Who gets to the other side first? Now the circle child should try to get to the other side at the same time. What does the child have to do to get there? Run—just like the fast-moving air. All children can try this.

Explore another airborne phenomenon. Ask children to sit with their eyes and ears closed while you do something mysterious for them to identify. Then puff a bit of hypoallergenic air freshener into the air. How long does it take for them to notice the drifting fragrance molecules? Suggest that children make a smell survey of the room, just sniffing the air, not touching anything. Discuss the findings and record them on a class chart. If a stopwatch is available, find out and record how long it takes for moving air to carry the aroma molecules from a dish of vinegar all the way across the room. Compare with other scent-releasing things: peeling an orange or slicing an onion, for example.

Read: Let's Try It Out: In the Air by Seymour Simon.

CONCEPT: Air slows moving objects.

Group Discussion: Show the children two pieces of copier paper. Crunch one piece into a tight ball as the children watch. Ask: "If I hold these two things up as high as I can reach and then let go of them, what will happen to them?" (Wait for responses.) "Do you think that both things will fall in just the same way? Let's find out." Repeat the action as needed to allow the children to carefully observe and report. "Which one fell more slowly? Can you think of anything beneath the wide paper that might have pushed against it and slowed its fall?" Mention that everything that moves above ground or above water must push air aside as it moves. Big things push more air aside than do small things.

Read: Galileo's Leaning Tower Experiment by Wendy Macdonald.

CONCEPT: Living things need air to survive.

1. Do plants need air to live?
LEARNING OBJECTIVE: To be awed by evidence of plants' need for air to live.

? *Inquiry:* Open a class discussion about important things that invisible air does. Guide children's recollections about what the oxygen part of air does for people and animals. "It keeps all parts of our bodies working! Do you suppose that air could help plants live, too?" Record children's responses. "Let's find out."

Recall how the class found out that plants need light and water (see p. 63). "We experimented with plants to find out what happens when we kept light and water from them. Then we compared them with plants that had enough water and light to grow well. Could we also find a way to keep air from this plant? That's harder to investigate." Encourage and record suggestions from the class. (If the class is eager to keep things going later, try to use different experimental ideas as follow-up investigation. Or, if plenty of plants are available, have several experiments going at once.)

"It would be too hard for us to take air away from this whole plant, but there may be a way to keep air from just one leaf. It may take a while to find our answer."

Needed Materials: A sunny location; a healthy, *sturdy* potted plant, such as a geranium; vegetable oil cooking spray (or, if the plant's leaf has a smooth texture rather than the furry texture of a geranium leaf, spreadable margerine or petroleum jelly); paper towels; a small piece of yarn; a watering can; and a magnifying lens.

"Let's try keeping air from touching just one leaf." (Zealous handling can easily break stems, so the next step is an adult task.) Arrange paper towels under the plant. Spray both sides of the leaf generously three different times. Allow time between sprayings for excess spray to drip off. By the third spraying, the leaf should be well soaked to ensure good coverage. (A plant with a smooth leaf can simply be generously spread on both sides with margerine or petroleum jelly.) Tag the experimental leaf by loosely tying it with a bit of yarn.

"Should our sample leaf still get water and light, like the rest of the plant? . . . What will be kept from this leaf that the rest of the plant will have?"

"We can keep a daily record to compare any changes in the leaf from the rest of the plant. We can use the magnifying lens to compare the leaves without touching the leaves with our fingers and hurting the leaves."

Arrange to have the plant watered moderately, about every other day. (It can take a few weeks for observable changes to occur. Be patient.) When the leaf deteriorates, record the results.

Conclude the investigation by reinforcing that *all plants and animals (including people) need air to live!* Add the awesome facts that leaves need to *take in* the part of air (carbon dioxide) that people breathe *out*, and that plants *send out* the part of air (oxygen) that people must *breathe in* to live! *We could not live on Earth without the oxygen that plants give us.*

INTEGRATING ACTIVITIES

Math Experiences

Observing and measuring: Blow up a small balloon. Then let go of it to see how air escaping (pushing out) from it in one direction pushes the balloon in the opposite direction. Mark the distance the balloon traveled when it lands. (This is an illustration of Newton's Third Law of Motion: "For every action, there is an equal and opposite reaction.") Blow up a larger balloon to compare the distance traveled when more air was pushing out.

Music (Resources in Appendix A)

1. After children have finished clapping the rhythm of a song they enjoy singing, compare two styles of clapping. Listen to the sound made by clapping with palms open and flat, then to the sound made by clapping with slightly cupped hands. What is caught between the cupped hands to change the sound?

2. Sing this song to the chorus of the folksong "Goober Peas," sung by Burl Ives in *My Space Music*.

> *Air, air, air, air*
>
> *air is everywhere.*
>
> *We can't taste or see it,*
>
> *but we know it's there.*
>
> .   —*J.H.*

Use appropriate tasting and peering gestures to add fun.

3. Listen to Joyce Rouse sing "The Same Air" from *Around the World with Earth Mama*. (See Appendix A.)

Literature Links

BAYROCK, FIONA. (2009). *Bubble homes and fish farts*. Watertown, MA: Charlesbridge. Sixteen different fish and sea creatures cleverly use air bubbles to protect themselves.

BRANLEY, FRANKLYN. (2009) *Air is all around you*. New York: HarperCollins. Children bounce through these pages describing properties of air, proclaiming our need for air to live.

COBB, VICKI. (2003). *I face the wind*. New York: HarperCollins. The interactive weaving of a child's simple firsthand discoveries into the explanatory narrative makes concepts easy to absorb. The clever graphics and collages add fun. American Library Association Notable Book.

COOPER, SHARON. (2007). *Using air*. Chicago: Heinemann. Beginning readers are introduced to air as a natural resource. Plants' use of air is explained.

GAFFNEY, TIMOTHY. (2004). *Wee and the Wright Brothers*. New York: Holt. A venturesome mouse observer retells the story of how the Wright brothers developed and flew the first airplane.

GLASS, ANDREW. (2003). *The wondrous whirligig; The Wright brothers' first flying machine*. New York: Holiday House. Rollicking sketches remind us that this retelling of the Wright boys' early interest in flying machines is offered as a tall tale. The whirligig toy episode is based on fact.

MACDONALD, WENDY. (2009). *Galileo's leaning tower experiment*. Watertown, MA: Charlesbridge. This fictionalized tale of a Galileo discovery shows how air can slow a spread-out falling object. It points out the importance of wondering why and paying attention to how things really happen.

PILEGARD, VIRGINIA. (2004). *The warlord's kites*. Gretna, LA: Pelican. Ingenuity, air, and mastery of nonstandard measurements save the palace from an approaching army. Older children will appreciate this tale of ancient China. Simple kite-making instructions are included.

STEWART, MELISSA. (2004). *Air is everywhere*. Minneapolis: Compass Point. Clear directions in this book of hands-on experiments develop understanding of air properties.

STILLE, DARLENE. (2004) *Air outside, inside, and all around.* Minneapolis: Picture Window. Breezy, appealing illustrations match the fresh writing in this book. Each topic emerges from children's real-world experiences.

Classics

BRADLELY, KIMBERLY. (2001). *Pop! A book about bubbles.* New York: HarperCollins. Cheery photographs and a chatty text let children absorb air pressure and water cohesiveness information effortlessly. NSTA* Outstanding Trade Book.

LOBEL, ARNOLD. (1990). *Days with Frog and Toad.* New York: Harper. In spite of discouragement, Frog and Toad are finally able to fly their kite.

SIMON, SEYMOUR. (2003). *Let's try it out: In the air.* New York: Simon & Schuster. Preschoolers will enjoy this active, playful approach to discovering some basic air properties.

Poems (Resources in Appendix A)

The wind is a favorite topic in poems for children. The following are recommended.

In *Sing a Song of Popcorn,* compiled by de Regniers; Beatrice Shenk et al.:

> "Who Has Seen the Wind" by Christina Rossetti
> "Wind Song" by Lillian Moore
> In *Now We Are Six* by A. A. Milne:
> "Wind On the Hill"
> In *Poems to Grow On* by Jean Thompson:
> "The Kite" by Harry Behn

Fingerplays

Seeds with silky wings are scattered by moving air (see Chapter 4, Plants). Recall the milkweed blowing that children may have enjoyed in plant life experiences, or try to find a milkweed pod to open outdoors now if it is a new idea.

Baby Seeds

In a milkweed cradle	(Cup hands.)
Snug and warm	
Baby seeds are hiding	(Make yourself small.)
Safe from harm.	
Open wide the cradle	(Open hands.)
Hold it high.	
Come Mr. Wind	(Blow in the hands.)
Help them to fly.	

—AUTHOR UNKNOWN

---

*National Science Teachers Association.

Art Activities

Easel Painting. Cut newsprint into the shapes of things that move on the air, such as birds, balloons (tape a dangling string to the back), butterflies, and kites. Let the children choose shapes to paint with designs of their own creation.

Collage. Use airborne nature materials such as chicken feathers, milkweed fluff and seeds, and maple tree seeds. Cut some actual air bubbles from sheets of plastic packing material to glue on the collage.

Paper Fans. Make paper fans to move air. They may be accordion-pleated sheets of paper that the children decorate or small paper plates stapled to Popsicle sticks.

Gliders. Make simple gliders and decorate them with crayon designs.

Air Pressure Art. With medicine droppers, make use of air pressure as an art medium. Let children use the droppers to make designs by dropping diluted food coloring on absorbent paper. A fleeting, fascinating art form—snow painting— also makes use of droppers and food coloring. Gather a big bucket of snow. Store it on the windowsill. Quickly pack individual foam meat trays with snow, ready to receive the drops of color. Have another bucket ready for the sloshy end results.

Air Power Art. Let children use straws and air pressure to pick up tempera paint from jars and drop it on smooth-surfaced paper. The puddles of paint can then be changed in shape by blowing on them through the straws.

Play

Boat. Help the children create a block-and-plank boat, with two planks angled together to form a prow. Let them blow up a plastic ring for a life preserver.

Plane. Angled planks form the nose of the plane, hollow blocks form the tail and sides, and two more planks stretch out to form the wings. Children who have flown can contribute ideas about oxygen and air to the play.

Parachute Play. Children moving a group-size parachute up and down can see the lifting power of moving air. Children particularly enjoy one-at-a-time running across the circle under the billowing parachute before it falls. Taking turns holding and running cultivates cooperation. *Parachute Games* by T. Strong and D. LeFeure has many more ideas (see Resources).

Air and Soapy Water Play. Let children make soap bubbles, using straws in cups of water and detergent. For younger children, use baby shampoo, which won't irritate eyes, instead of detergent. Snip out a small notch above the middle of the straws to prevent sucking solution into mouths.

Air Cushion Play. Let children take turns pumping up a sturdy air mattress to use as a tumbling mat for somersaults.

Paper Dance Play. Cut a spiral from a sheet of paper to make one long, curving strip. Dangle it from the ceiling by attaching it to a long thread. Let children fan the air with a card to make the spiral twirl. Create a fantasy effect by dangling several spirals. Circulating air will keep them gently moving.

Creative Movement

1. Let children pretend to be balloons that are blown into large shapes. Suggest that they make themselves into flat, limp shapes on the floor. "Now I'm blowing, and blowing, and blowing some more. And you are getting bigger and bigger." When the shapes have been stretched as large as they can be, suggest that you will pretend to prick each imaginary balloon shape. Each shape is pushed about, then collapses into a limp piece of rubber on the floor as the air goes out of it.

2. Children can move like birds or butterflies soaring on moving air. They might enjoy holding a turkey wing feather in each hand to become a bird with outstretched-arm "wings."

Creative Thinking

Slowly guide a quiet imagery experience: "Close your eyes and take a very deep breath of air. Feel it fill your lungs. Let the air seep out slowly and imagine yourself getting lighter than air, so light that you can just float out the window and drift above our school. How does it look from above? Catch an air current to let yourself drift over to your favorite place to play. Enjoy watching people below flying kites. Change into that air current and give the kites a strong, gentle push. Don't the kites look fine, tugging at their strings? Now feel yourself getting smaller, until you're just a tiny handful of air—good. Now find some small spaces to fill. Slip under a mosquito's wing . . . creep into a key hole . . . swing on a spider's web . . . slide into a French horn, up and around in the tubing and out the horn on a blast of sound. Now ease yourself back into our classroom to open your eyes and share your air travels with us."

Food Experiences

If an electric mixer is available, whip up a treat. Explain that the beater is stirring many tiny air bubbles into the mixture. Watch it change and expand.

> Combine:
> ½ cup instant dry skim milk
> ½ cup ice cold water
> 1 level teaspoon sugar-free gelatin (berry flavors seem to work best)

Beat at highest speed 4 to 5 minutes until mixture forms stiff peaks. The mixture makes about 3 cups, enough to provide each child a dollop to enjoy. Save some of it to examine quickly with a hand lens to see air bubbles. Edible science is impressive. Children really remember that air was part of the tidbit they enjoyed eating.

Field Trips

Small Airport Visit. If this is possible, keep the science focus simple. There will be too many exciting things to see to make lengthy explanations of flight principles bearable for the children. Be sure that any adult who offers a guided tour of the facility understands this.

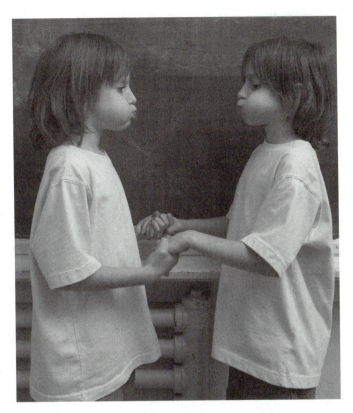

We're testing air. It wants to get out.

PROMOTING CONCEPT CONNECTIONS

Maintaining Concepts

1. Make casual comments or inquiries about the function or presence of air when suitable opportunities arise. When outdoors with a class, observe planes or birds flying overhead or leaves, seeds, or litter blowing past.

2. Suggest that children fill their mouths with a giant air bubble when the class needs to walk quietly through school corridors. Puff up your own cheeks to model this funny way to stay quiet. It's more positive than saying, "Be quiet!" Air takes up talking space.

3. Use medicine droppers to water tiny seedlings, to give moisture to insects in jars, and for art projects. If necessary, remind children to push the air out of the dropper while it is still in the liquid. Can they see the air bubbling into the liquid?

4. If you need to open a vacuum-sealed container, such as by using a punch-type opener with a can of juice, let the children listen closely for the hiss of air rushing into the can. When using the bellows-type step pump, show the

rubber cap on the air intake valve. Push the air out so that the bellows are flat. Remove the cap so that air rushes in with a hiss, and watch the bellows expand dramatically.

Improving School Grounds

If you are fortunate enough to have swings at your school, they are very useful for allowing children to experience the presence of air, especially on their faces as they rush through the air. (Swings are also excellent examples of pendulums. Try to maintain them if at all possible.)

Connecting Concepts

1. Relate water concepts to air when investigating evaporation. Water droplets, or vapor, become part of the air. Speak of fog and clouds as very wet air.
2. Relate plant propagation (seed scattering) to moving air.
3. Relate sound to air concepts. Sound travels through air; moving air causes some things to vibrate and make sounds; air vibrates when enclosed in a column like a flute or a whistle (see Chapter 14, Sound).
4. Point out the crucial role of air in ecological relationships. Air is one of the non-living substances that all living things depend on to stay alive. Air that is spoiled by pollution creates problems for all living things. There is no way to make new air. It is used over and over again, so people must find ways to keep air clean.

Family and Community Support

A newsletter to parents can suggest ways to support and add to the air experiences at school. When families are out together, they can watch for soaring birds, planes, and clouds being pushed along by moving air. They can point out how air is heated in their homes to keep people comfortable in winter and passed through coolers in summer.

Notify families about places in the area where gliders or small planes, windmills, fancy-kite flying, hot-air balloons, or parasailing can be seen.

RESOURCES

Lauw, Darlene, & Puay, Lim. (2003). *Science alive: Air.* New York: Crabtree. Here is good background information explaining more advanced air concepts. Activities include very clear kite-making instructions.

Parker, Steve. (2005). *The science of air: Projects and experiments with air and flight.* Chicago: Heinemann. There is interesting background information amid the busy pages of this projects and reference book for older children. There are directions for making a sturdier helicopter spinner than the one we describe.

Strong, Todd, & LeFeure, Dale. (1999). *Parachute games.* Urbana, IL: Human Kinetics Press. Enjoyable group activites for playing with air under a grounded parachute.

ONLINE RESOURCES

Dragonfly TV: Paper helicopter investigations featuring open-ended suggestions, such as changing the length, weight, and width of propeller arms at http://pbskids.org/dragonflytv/

San Francisco Exploratorium: Consider one aspect of air that gives airplanes lift, lifting a ball on an air stream, at http://www.exploratorium.edu/snacks/balancing_ball.html

The Private Eye Project. Order inexpensive jeweler's loupes from http://www.theprivtateeye.com

Water

The vastness of an ocean or the perfection of a single drop; a trickling stream or raging rapids; just thinking about beautiful water can revive a cascade of awesome memories. Let your gratitude for life-sustaining water give meaning to these learning experiences with children.

All living things need water to survive. Our planet could not exist without water. Young children delight in pouring, spraying, and splashing in water. Help them learn more about this fascinating substance to build lasting respect for a precious resource. The experiences in this chapter will explore the following concepts:

- Water has weight.
- Water's weight and upthrust help things float.
- Water goes into the air.
- Water can change forms reversibly.
- Water is a solvent for many materials.
- Water clings to itself.
- Water clings to other materials.
- Water moves into other materials.

It is hard for a child to imagine that sparkling, transparent water weighs something. When attention is focused on experiencing water's weight, children begin to understand how water can support objects. In the following activities, children experience the weight of water and explore buoyancy. Other activities deal with evaporation, condensation, freezing, and melting; water as a solvent; and water's cohesion, adhesion, and surface tension properties.

CONCEPT: **Water has weight.**

1. ♣ How can we feel water's weight?

LEARNING OBJECTIVE: To spark interest in the characteristics of water.

MATERIALS:

*As a warm-weather outdoor
   activity:*

Water source

Small wading pool

Large bucket

Large pitcher or milk cartons

For indoor use, add:

Rubber boots

Plastic smock

GETTING READY:

♣ If outdoors, have children remove shoes and socks and roll
   up pant legs.

If indoors, have children wear
   boots and smock.

SMALL-GROUP ACTIVITY:

1. Encourage children to dip fingers into
   water. "Think about this: Could water be
   heavy? Let's find out."
2. Let children take turns standing in the
   pool, holding the empty bucket.
3. Let others pour pitchers or cartons of water
   into the bucket until it becomes too heavy
   to hold. Conclusions about the weight of
   water are easily formed and communi-
   cated by this direct investigation.

Math skills: Experiencing and observing the weight of water.

CONCEPT: **Water's weight and upthrust help things float.**

1. Which things float? Which things sink?

LEARNING OBJECTIVE: To enjoy exploring water's upthrust effect.

MATERIALS:

Dishpans of water

Plastic aprons

Assorted objects such as rocks,
   twigs, corks, and washers

SMALL-GROUP ACTIVITY:

1. Let children gently place the palms of
   their hands against the water's surface
   to feel water pushing up against their
   hands (upthrust*). "Let's see if that push
   and water's weight will hold all these
   things up."

*Upthrust is the natural tendency of a body of water to push upward.

Pairs of objects of contrasting weight: ping-pong/golf ball, plastic/steel spoon, plastic/steel paper clip

Old kitchen scale, postage scale, or balance

Two trays

GETTING READY:

Tape a card marked FLOAT on one tray and another card marked SINK on the other.

2. "Try to make a floating thing stay on the bottom of the tub. What happens when you stop holding it down?" (Water's upthrust pushes it up.)

3. Suggest classifying objects on float/sink trays. "Why do you think some things sank?"

4. Let children weigh matching objects to confirm that the objects' weight influenced the outcome.* "Things sink if they weigh more than the water below them weighs."

Math skills: Observing that an object's weight related to water's weight causes sinking or floating.

2. How does shape help some things float?

LEARNING OBJECTIVE: To be reassured by discovering that shape affects buoyancy.

MATERIALS:

Dishpans of water

Plastic aprons

Modeling clay: one small baseball-size lump for each child

Rolling pin

Postage or kitchen scale (desirable)

Pennies

GETTING READY:

Prepare a four-column chart headed Weight, Shape, Float, Sink.

SMALL-GROUP ACTIVITY:

1. Recall observations from Activity 1. "Sometimes things that seem heavy float. Let's see if something else helped them float."

2. Have children form two small, equal-sized balls of clay, confirming their equal weight if a scale is available.

3. "Do both balls sink? What do you predict would happen if one ball was spread out? Find out." Have a rolling pin at hand as a shape-changing hint. Allow plenty of time for repeated trials.

4. Record observations for each condition: weight, shape and result. Which shape floated and which one sank?
   Conclude the exploration with the fact that there was more water under the flat clay. "All that water weighed more than the spread-out clay weighed. It held up the flat clay."

---

*Weight is an acceptable first explanation. Density of water and displacement are accurate, but more difficult, explanations.

5. Let children enjoy forming clay boat shapes, comparing them with flat or ball shapes.
6. "Can the boat hold pennies and still stay afloat? Drop in one penny at a time." Discuss children's experiences with floating and sinking at the swimming pool.

Math skills: Observing that floating relates to objects' shape and water's weight.

Read: Who Sank the Boat? by Pamela Allen and *The Wonders of Water* by Melissa Stewart.

CONCEPT: Water goes into the air.

1. How can we tell that air and moving air take up water?

LEARNING OBJECTIVE: To take pride in noticing and hastening evaporation.

MATERIALS:

Two trays

Pans of water

Paper towels

Blackboard or another dark, smooth surface

Cardboard or paper fans

Handheld hair dryer

Paper

GETTING READY:

Safety Precaution: Prevent tripping over the cord or inappropriate dryer use.

Let children make folded paper fans.

SMALL-GROUP ACTIVITY:

1. "What do you think will happen if we wet some towels and spread them out on these trays? Let's see." Put one tray in a sunny or warm place, the other in a cool, darker place. Check them in half an hour.
2. Meanwhile, show children the hair dryer; let them feel warm air coming from it. "What do you feel? This warm air can help us understand what is happening to the towels."
3. Let children dip a finger in water, then trace their names on the blackboard. "Blow warm air on your wet name. Watch closely to see what happens to the water. Where did it go? Only air touched it." The water has gone into the air in such tiny drops that they are invisible (vapor). When air takes up water, we say that the water *evaporates.*
4. "Write your name with water on the blackboard again. Fold a paper fan and wave it near your name to make a breeze. Where does the water go? Let's see what happened to the paper towels. What happened to the wetness?"

Playground puddles—where will they be tomorrow?

? *Inquiry Activity:* Elicit children's predictions about where water will evaporate fastest in the room. "Let's find out." Record all predictions. Provide children with numbered pieces of damp paper towel. Record on a group chart where the towels are placed in the room. Check progress frequently. Chart drying times for different locations. Record and compare observation data. How did the variables of temperature, moving air, sunshine, and proximity to a heat source affect evaporation times?

CONCEPT: Water can change forms reversibly.

1. How does changing air temperature make water change?

LEARNING OBJECTIVE: To feel assured by the regularity of water changing/reversing forms.

MATERIALS:

Water

Two identical shallow plastic bowls

(Do not use ice cube trays. In some parts of the country, children may believe that

SMALL-GROUP ACTIVITY:

1. Early in the morning, let children fill bowls almost to the top with water. Help them deliver one bowl to the freezer or to the below-freezing outdoor location. Leave the other bowl in the room (out of spilling range) for an hour or more.

ice is formed only in cube shapes.)

Access to a freezing compartment or, better yet, to below-freezing weather

2. Ask: "Do you think both bowls of water will stay the same or will one change? Let's check."

3. Bring ice back to the room when it is solid. Dump it out onto a pie pan for all to see and touch. "What's it like?" (hard, cold, smooth, slippery, shaped like the bowl). Use the term *solid*. Compare ice to water in a bowl–"what's it like?" (soft, warm, moving, no single shape, clear). Use the term *liquid*. Brainstorm examples of other liquids.

4. "What do you think will happen if we leave the ice here in this warm room? And what do you think will happen if we leave the bowl of water, the liquid water, in the cold place? Let's find out." Use the term *reversible*. Connect the term to what cars do, going into reverse gear, and to other every-day examples that children think of. Repeat the activity if the children request it.*

5. Bring snowballs or icicles indoors to melt in a pan when possible. Collect snow in a coffee can and measure its depth. Measure the depth of the water after the snow has melted completely. Is it as deep as the snow was?

Math skills: Informal air temperature measuring related to the state of water.

2. How does water change to vapor and vapor change to water?

LEARNING OBJECTIVE: To delight in demystifying the source of rain and fog.

MATERIALS:

Foil potpie pan

Clear plastic tumbler

Dark paper or folder

Water, ice cubes

Thermos of boiling water

Magnifying glass

SMALL-GROUP ACTIVITY:

1. Recall the earlier experience in which air temperature helped water change forms. "Let's watch what happens in this tumbler."

2. Let children examine the tumbler and pan to be sure that they are dry and free of holes. "The tumbler looks empty; do you think it is? Is it easy to see through the tumbler of air now?"

---

*Some children have enough experience with water and ice to predict reversibility of this change. The transformation from water to vapor and back to water is less familiar. Both forms of reversibility may need to be repeated several times for less experienced children to grasp cause-and-effect ideas.

GETTING READY:

Form a backdrop with dark paper to make the water vapor more visible.

Try to provide more than one setup to avoid crowding observers.

Repeat as needed.

3. Let children add ice to the pan and feel the air temperature just below it. Pour hot water into the tumbler to the depth of 2 in. (5 cm).
4. Let children feel the warm air temperature in the tumbler and the cold air temperature under the pan. "We'll watch for changes in the tumbler for a few minutes."
5. Immediately cover the tumbler with the pan of ice (Figure 8–1). "What's happening?" (Evaporation is occurring. Tiny bits of water are mixing with air to form water vapor.) "Is the water vapor moving up to the cool air? Let's lift the pan to see what's happening underneath. What does it look like?"
6. Look through the magnifier at the collected droplets. "How could those drops get on a dry pan?" There should be large drops falling before long. Help children recall water bits going into warm air; warm air rising up to the cold air; moist cooling air changing to larger and larger drops; and drops falling back down as water again.

Math skills: Informally measuring air and water temperatures; relating warm air to vapor and cold air to condensation.

Note: Children are likely to describe the collected condensation drops as rain. Using the same analogy, mention that the visible water vapor in the jar is like a fog or a small cloud. To be accurate, condensation occurs in clouds when droplets collect on dust particles to form raindrops. We should say that the drops in the tumbler formed almost the same way as rain is formed. Be certain that children know that air far from Earth is cold because it is far from Earth's warmth. Air close to Earth is warmed by reflected heat from Earth. (Be sure that children understand that there are no pans of ice in the sky.)

Group Experience: Ask the children to breathe slowly into their cupped hands. Does their breath feel warm or cold when it comes from their bodies? Pass out small mirrors or foil pans for children to exhale on. Are these surfaces cool? Ask for

FIGURE 8–1

predictions about the outcome of breathing on the cool mirror or metal. Find out what happens. Can the children see results? "How does the cloudy place feel? Is it wet or dry? Try it again. Feel the cloudy place, and then feel a place that wasn't breathed on. Why do we feel wetness?" Discuss common occurrences of condensation in homes: on bathroom mirrors after steamy showers, on kitchen windows when pots are boiling, and on eyeglasses when a dishwasher door is opened to let dishes air-dry.

CONCEPT: **Water is a solvent for many materials.**

1. Which things dissolve in water?

LEARNING OBJECTIVE: To enjoy discovering how water changes certain materials.

MATERIALS:

Muffin pans or plastic ice cube trays

Pitcher of water

Assorted dry materials: salt, sand, cornstarch, flour, fine gravel, seeds, cornmeal

Spoons for dry materials

Salad oil

Small screw-top bottle

Plastic aprons

Newspaper

Sponge

Sticks for stirring

Cleanup bucket

GETTING READY:

Spread newspapers on the work table.

Half-fill pans with water.

SMALL-GROUP ACTIVITY:

1. "See what happens when you put a little salt in one of your pans of water. Stir it. Can you see it? Feel it? Where is it?"
2. "Dip a finger in the pan. How does the water taste? The salt is still there, but it is in such tiny bits now that it can't be seen. It dissolved in the water."
3. "Try the other materials; put each in its own pan of water. Find out which ones dissolve."
4. Half-fill the bottle with water. Add some oil. Cap securely. Let the children shake it. "Does it seem to dissolve? Let it stand a while. Where is the oil now?"

Group Experience: Mix some sand, dirt, and gravel with water in a pint jar. Let it stand undisturbed for a day or more. Check the jar. Is the water still muddy-looking? Did the sand and dirt really dissolve? Which is on the bottom?

CONCEPT: Water clings to itself.

1. How do water drops behave?

LEARNING OBJECTIVE: To be delighted by clinging or stretching water drops.

MATERIALS:

Water

For each child: small container, such as film canisters or medicine vials

Plastic droppers

Baster

Waxed paper

Toothpicks, popsicle sticks, grass blades, or bits of straw

Sponge to absorb spills

Pennies

GETTING READY:

Cut 5-in. (17-cm) squares of waxed paper for each child.

Fill individual containers with water.

(Children like to help, using the baster.)

SMALL-GROUP INDOOR ACTIVITY:

1. Squeeze a single drop of water on each child's index fingertip. "What can you find out about your drop by looking at it?" Enjoy the perfection of water drops. "Carefully touch that drop with your thumb. Pull it gently. What happens?" (The drop stretches and re-forms as its tiniest bits— molecules—cling together.)

2. Give each child a square of waxed paper. "What will happen if you squeeze a drop of water on this paper? Find out. Is your drop flat or curved?"

3. Add that the edges of a drop pull together tightly to act like an invisible "skin." The tiniest possible bits of water (molecules) cling tightly to each other. "Make more drops on your paper. What happens when you pull drops together with a grass blade?" Let children see how many drops they can fit on a penny.

Group Experience: Review small-group findings. Read aloud the charming poems "At the Window" from *Now We Are Six* by A. A. Milne and "Ice Cycle" from *Once Upon Ice and Other Frozen Poems* by Mary Anne Hoberman. Read *A Drop of Water* by Walter Wick about how icicles form, one clinging drop at a time.

♣ *Outdoor Experience:* After the next rain, take magnifying glasses, a notebook, and a pen with you to the playground to record the places where children find raindrops clinging. Discuss the sightings with the group later.

2. How does the surface of water behave?

LEARNING OBJECTIVE: To be amazed by the strength of surface tension.*

*Tension describes the tight clinging of molecules on the surface of the water.

MATERIALS:

Clear plastic tumblers

Water

Syringe-type baster

Uncooked spaghetti bits, steel
paper clips, twigs

Sponge and newspapers to
absorb spills

SMALL-GROUP ACTIVITY:

1. Fill a tumbler to the top with water.
2. While children watch with heads close to
the table, use the dropper or baster to
slowly add drops of water to fill the tumbler. "What might happen if more drops
are added?" Find out, drop by drop. (A
curved dome stretches above the rim as
more drops are added until surface tension
weakens and breaks.)
3. "I wonder if those bits of water at the top
are clinging tightly enough to let something rest on them?" Hold a dry piece of
spaghetti horizontally; gently rest it on the
surface. "Let's see if an upright piece rests
on the surface." (No, it breaks through the
surface.) Let children try steel paper clips
and twigs.

Math skills: Counting the drops of water needed to break surface tension.

3. How does soap change water's surface tension?
LEARNING OBJECTIVE: To be surprised by changing surface tension effects.

MATERIALS:

Pitcher of water

Small foil pans

Shaker can of pepper or talcum
powder

Cotton-tipped swabs

Liquid soap or slivers of bar
soap

Liquid detergent

Small twigs, grass, and paper
clips

GETTING READY:

Pour 1 in. (2.5 cm) of water in
foil pans.

SMALL-GROUP ACTIVITY:

1. "We can't see the tiniest bits of water
pulling tightly across this water, but perhaps we can see what the tightness does to
other things."
2. Sprinkle pepper or powder on the
water. "What do you see happening?
Try it."
3. Dab the tip of a swab into detergent or
soap. "Let's see what happens when we
touch the surface with a bit of soap."
Be prepared to empty the pans often for
re-experimenting.
4. Let pairs of children join hands and tug
against one another like tightly clinging
bits of water. "If I pushed through your
grip, what would happen to you? That's
almost like soap breaking up the pull
between water bits."

CONCEPT: Water clings to other materials.

1. Where can we see water bits clinging?

LEARNING OBJECTIVE: To appreciate the beauty and strength of clinging water drops.

MATERIALS:

2-in. (5-cm)-diameter coffee mug

2 clear plastic deli container lids (unsmudged)

(Try to have a clean lid for each child as well.)

Tape

Magnifier

Water

4 more clear plastic lids

Grass blades, twigs

GETTING READY:

Out of children's reach, put a clear lid on a mug of hot water. Let steam condense on the lid until it is covered with visible tiny droplets. Join this lid to a dry lid with tape to make a sealed case. (See Figure 4–1 on p. 57.)

Collect condensation on single lids for children to observe and touch with blades of grass or twigs.*

Trim off the rims of four plastic lids.

SMALL-GROUP INDOOR ACTIVITY:

1. Recall the condensation experience. Pass around the droplets case and a magnifier. What is observed? "Let's see how long these beautiful droplets will cling to the plastic." Check at regular intervals.

2. "Do you think water can cling to something tightly enough for us to feel?" Sprinkle water on one rimless lid. Cover it with another. "Try getting these apart. What do you feel? Try getting two dry lids apart. How does that feel different?"

3. Let children dip their fingers in water and see how long it takes for water to drip off their fingertips.

4. ♣ Take a bucket of water and basters outdoors for children to see what water will stick to on the playground.

CONCEPT: Water moves into other materials.

1. Which things can water move into?

LEARNING OBJECTIVE: To be intrigued by water spreading or climbing into things.

---

*This is a simple, powerful way to help children appreciate the extraordinary laws of nature underlying ordinary, unnoticed events. Do it often.

Water studies absorb Brooke.

MATERIALS:

Water

Small medicine vial and plastic dropper for each child

Pressed foam meat trays

Small test materials such as bark, cotton, tissues, paper towels, smooth paper, stones, bits of fabric, and dry sponge cut into small cubes

Food coloring

Magnifiers

Plastic jar

Celery stalk

Clear straw or narrow pipette (desirable)

SMALL-GROUP ACTIVITY:

1. "What happens when you put drops of water on different things in your tray?" Discuss the results.

2. "Let's see if paper towels and smooth paper look the same under the magnifier. Which has tiny holes for water bits to move into?" (Water sticks to both, but there are more places for water to fill and cling to in the toweling.)

3. Offer fresh toweling, tinted water, and magnifiers so that water can be better observed as it crawls through the soft paper. Use the term *absorbs* when discussing how the materials let water travel through.

GETTING READY:

Fill vials with water.

Tint water in jar and one small
container with food coloring.

Arrange a tray of test materials
for each child.

Group Experience: Recall with children how water clung and crawled through some test materials. "Would you imagine that water might also cling inside and crawl *up* narrow tubes?" Listen to children's ideas. "Let's find out whether or not water can crawl up these tiny tubes in the celery stalk." (A small capillary effect can be seen immediately by inserting a clear drinking straw or pipette in a tumbler of tinted water.) Check the celery for several days until the colored water has traveled into the leaves. Cut slices from the stalk for children to examine with magnifiers. Talk about moisture in the soil traveling up roots and tubes in stalks to help trees and plants grow.

INTEGRATING ACTIVITIES

Math Experiences

1. Provide two or three sets of measuring cups for casual use by children playing with water. Ask how many small cups of water it takes to fill a cup of this size, and so on.

2. Let the children record the weight of different materials in dry and wet states. Weigh a dry sponge on a kitchen scale. Drop it in a bowl of water. Ask children for predictions about the weight of the wet sponge. Reweigh the sponge. Let the children decide what caused the weight difference. Squeeze the water out over a dry bowl. Weigh the sponge again. A discussion of the results could bring in more-than/less-than comparisons.

3. Measure water absorption with dried beans. Early in the day, begin to soak 1/4 cup of washed and sorted, dried beans in 1 cup of water in one container, and 1/4 cup of dried beans and 2 cups of water in another. Drain off, measure the cups, and return the water after 2 hours, 6 hours, and the next morning. How much water did the beans absorb? Several small groups can do this with different kinds of beans and different amounts of water. Results can be compared and charted, and the now softened beans can be sampled to compare with dry beans. The soft beans may also be cooked for a snack.

Music (Resources in Appendix A)

1. Sing "Row, Row, Row Your Boat," with children joining hands with a partner and touching feet to pull back and forth. Ask: "Does water hold boats up? Is water heavy to push?"

2. Sing "The Eency Weency Spider" after the evaporation experiences, making an adaptation in lyrics. Change "and dried up all the rain" to "and evaporated the rain." Look for rain spouts near the school for children to watch after a rain.

3. Sing this song, after experimenting with forms of water, to the tune of "Twinkle, Twinkle, Little Star":

Water, water from the stream

When it boils it turns to steam.

Water, water is so nice;

Freeze it cold, it turns to ice.

Cool the steam; warm the ice

It's water again, clear and nice.

Literature Links

BAILLEY, JACQUI. (2004). *A drop in the ocean.* Minneapolis: Picture Window Books. The big picture of the water cycle is cartooned and explained in clear prose.

COBB, VICKI. (2002). *I get wet.* New York: HarperCollins. Clever graphics delight as the carefully focused, simple text explores three water charateristics: its flow, its cohesiveness, and its adhesiveness. Interactive experiments for preschoolers are woven into the story line.

COOPER, SHARON. (2007). *Using water.* Chicago: Heinemann. Water as a natural resource and as the water cycle is presented to the emergent reader.

LEVINE, SHAR, & JOHNSTONE, LESLIE. (2003). *The ultimate bubble book!* New York: Sterling. Here is a neat blend of science and pure fun! Every aspect of bubble-making is covered: the physics of bubbles, recipes, success tips, troubleshooting, and levels of difficulty.

MORRISON, GORDON. (2006). *A drop of water;* Boston: Houghton Mifflin. Here is a gorgeous tracing of the course of water from a single drop of water on a child's fingertip through waterways and back, and the life it influences on the way.

PARKER, STEVE. (2005). *The science of water.* Chicago: Heinemann. This sparkling book offers more advanced water concepts and projects for children ready for a greater challenge.

ROSS, MICHAEL. (2004). *What's the matter in Mr. Whisker's room?* Cambridge, MA: Candlewick. Children are exploring forms of matter in Mr. Whiskers's easygoing but engaging classroom. Water's changeable forms, water as a solvent, and buoyancy are part of the project.

SCHUH, MARI. (2009). *Drinking water.* Mankato, MN: Capstone. Beginning readers will get this clear message about their bodily needs for water for good health.

STEWART, MELISSA. (2004). *The wonders of water.* Minneapolis: Compass Points. One of the experiments in this book describes stretching out to float on water compared to curling up.

STEWART, MELISSA. (2006). *Will it float or sink?* New York: Scholastic. Have plenty of experiences with water's weight before beginning readers open this simple concept book. Basic concepts are written for emergent readers.

TOCCI, SALVATORE. (2003). *Experiments with soap.* New York: Children's Press. Experiments investigate how soap works, surface tension, and soap bubble activities, plus a great soap bubble recipe and a list of bubble activity Web sites.

Classics

ALLEN, PAMELA. (1996). *Who sank the boat?* New York: Putnam & Grosset. Amusing illustrations clearly demonstrate that every substance has weight in this funny book.

BRADLEY, KIMBERLY. (2001). *Pop! A book about bubbles.* New York: HarperCollins. The fun of bubble-making is captured in great photographs. The science of bubbles slides in easily in the chatty text. NSTA* Outstanding Trade Book.

BRANLEY, FRANKLYN. (1997). *Down comes the rain.* New York: HarperCollins. Cheerful children join the discussion of evaporation and condensation as it occurs naturally. The size of a droplet of water vapor is approximated.

---

*National Science Teachers Association.

FLACK, MARJORIE. (1970). *The story about Ping* (Seafarer Edition). New York: Viking Press. In this classic story, a barrel full of air tied to his back keeps a houseboat boy afloat after he tumbles into the Yangtze River.

MILNE, A. A. (1961). *Winnie-the-Pooh.* (Chapter 9 "In Which Piglet Is Entirely Surrounded by Water.") New York: E. P. Dutton. Pooh and Christopher Robin use unorthodox means of floating through flood waters.

SIMON, SEYMOUR. (2001). *Let's try it out in the water.* New York: Simon & Schuster. Playful sinking and floating experiences for the youngest children are guided toward understanding.

WICK, WALTER. (1997). *A drop of water: A book of science and wonder.* New York: Scholastic Press. Striking, delicate photographs by the author let us marvel at the properties of water from dewdrops, to frost, to clouds of steam. NSTA* Outstanding Trade Book.

Poems (Resources in Appendix A)

From *Sing a Song of Poporh,* read "Dragon Smoke."
From *Now We Are Six* by A. A. Milne, read "Waiting at the Window."
From *Once Upon Ice: And Other Frozen Poems* by Mary Ann Hoberman, read "Ice Cycle."

The 34 poems in Constance Levy's book *Splash! Poems of Our Watery World* consider all aspects of water in nature and in ourselves—from teardrops to ocean waves—in fine, read-aloud rhythms.

Fingerplays

Here is a fingerplay about evaporation.

In soapy water	(Scrubbing motion.)
I wash my clothes,	
I hang them out to dry.	(Pantomime.)
The sun it shines,	(Hands form a circle.)
The wind it blows,	(Wave arms, sway.)
The wetness goes into the sky.	

—J. H.

Art Activities

Ice Cube Painting. Use finger paint and glossy paper, but do not wet the paper as you would to prepare for finger painting. Instead, offer the children ice cubes, frozen with a Popsicle stick "handle," with which to spread and dilute the paint while making designs.

Tempera Painting. Let children watch or help you mix dry tempera paint with water. When the finished paintings are hung to dry, use the term *evaporate* to explain how this drying occurs.

Cohesion/Adhesion Effects. Tint water in cups so that drops of different colors can be mixed together on children's papers. The cohesive action of different colors jumping together is exciting to watch. Add adhesion to the experience another time, comparing what happens with different papers, such as finger paint paper, paper towels, and coffee filters.

---

*National Science Teachers Association.

Play

Housekeeping Play. Wash doll clothes. If possible, hang some to dry in the sunshine, others in a shady location, and still others indoors. Compare drying times. Add a bowl of soapy water and one of plain water with an eggbeater for each. Encourage children to notice that much more air can be beaten into the soapy water. Ask for explanations.

Outdoor Water Play. Place two or three tubs of water in the water table. Provide plastic pitchers, funnels, small containers, and lengths of tubing. Let bare-footed children transfer water from buckets to the wading pool using plastic tubing and a small plastic squeeze pump from the automotive supply section of a variety store. Raise the bucket of water on a pile of hollow blocks next to the wading pool for further experimentation. Add a water play pump, available from school equipment sources, if possible.

Bubble-Making. Choose some of these ways to have fun with surface tension:

- ♣ Use commercial bubble solutions and ring-tipped wands to wave or blow bubbles. Replenish the solution with a concentrated mixture of 1/4 cup of liquid dishwashing detergent (Joy and Dawn are good) and 1 cup of water. Glycerin, from the drugstore, about 1 teaspoon for the above recipe, increases bubble strength. If available, try the commercial set of giant rings and multiple bubble template or try plastic berry baskets. Use these outdoors. (Bubbles last longer on cloudy days.)
- Provide straws and cans of detergent/water solution to blow bubbles into. This is easier for children who aren't able to blow bubbles into the air. **Safety Precaution:** Prepare individual plastic straws. Print children's names on the straws with a permanent felt pen. Flatten each straw, then cut a tiny notch 1 in. (2.5 cm) from the mouth end to prevent children from accidentally sucking up soapy water.
- Try using fat drinking straws as pipes for blowing detergent/water solution bubbles into the air. Show the children how to dip the end of the straw into the solution to let a film collect across the bottom of the straw. Suggest holding the straw slightly down to avoid dripping solution into the mouth.
- Try using soft plastic funnels to blow giant bubbles. (Have several ready, and be prepared to wash the mouthpieces before sharing them.) Put the funnel upside down in a bowl of detergent solution. Gently blow a few bubbles into the bowl to allow a film of solution to coat the inside of the funnel. Lift out the funnel and softly blow a bubble.
- Talk with the children about how the outside surface of the soap film pulled together, almost like a balloon around the air. The soap or detergent mixture makes a more flexible, stretchier "skin" than the water makes alone.

Creative Movement

Bubbles. Add a soap bubble movement stimulus to your collection of emergency ideas (i.e., ideas to use when you have a group of children ready to do something that isn't quite ready for them). Tell the children that you will blow imaginary bubbles to them to catch. "Here's a high one. Catch this one on your elbow . . . your shoulder . . . your chin. Don't let this one touch the ground. Catch this one on a fingertip and blow it back to me. Pretend that your hands are made of soap film. Blow into them until they can't stretch anymore and they pop."

Snowmen. Guide the children as they roll imaginary snowmen, rolling more and more slowly as the ball gets larger. "Let's make a smaller ball for a chest, now a smaller ball for a head. Lift them into place. Oh! There it goes! Snowballs this size are very heavy. Now, be the snowman yourself, all curvy and cold and tall. But wait, the sun is beginning to shine and warm the air. Oh! What's happening to your arms and your body?" Continue with your suggestions and the children's responses until the snowman is a puddle that will soon evaporate and vanish without a trace.

Cohesion. Use this activity to help children grasp the concept of water molecules being attracted to, and bonding to, one another. "Let's pretend to shrink into the tiniest bits of water possible, so tiny that we can't be seen without a microscope. Move around now and find ways to connect with other water bits to form droplets (linking elbows, arms, and feet inventively). Now let's find ways for everyone to connect into a single drop of water. Make as many connections as possible. Now let's see what happens when the water bits on the outside edges pull together tightly, linking elbows. Look, the outside edges are pulling us into a circle. Now, outside droplets disconnect those elbows. Reach out your arms and hold hands to stretch that drop of water. Good. We're still clinging together, but we've stretched into a bigger drop now."

Creative Thinking

Invent a story mixup that includes references to water concepts. Illustrate the story with mounted pictures cut from magazines or catalogs. When the concept is referred to, let it be in the form of an obvious misstatement for the children to catch and correct. Perhaps it could be a camping story where "the children could hardly wait to cool off by skating on the lake in the summer sunshine" or "John and Anne filled the boat with heavy rocks to help it float on the water" or "Dad put the teakettle in the icebox to boil the water for soup."

Food Experiences

Water is—or has been—part of everything we eat. Children put many water concepts to use when they cook, such as boiling water to dissolve gelatin, melting ice cubes to thicken it, and freezing fruit juice into popsicles. Cooking rice for lunch offers both water absorption and volume measurement experiences. Popping corn is an exciting, edible way to illustrate a property of water: High temperature changes water to steam. Children are surprised and pleased to learn that moisture inside the kernels of corn changes to steam so fast that it pops the kernel open. The steam is clearly evident in a plastic-domed corn popper.

PROMOTING CONCEPT CONNECTIONS

Maintaining Concepts

1. Discuss evaporation whenever clothes have to be dried at school—after play in the snow or a fall into a puddle. It's especially reassuring to a child who is worried about staying neat to know that an accidental stain can be washed out, the moisture will evaporate, and the garment will look fine again. When children come to school in raincoats and boots, look for drops of water still on the outside of the garments—evidence that these materials don't absorb water.

2. ♣ Examine puddles in the playground after a rain. Using stones, mark the outline of the puddle size when it is fullest. (Make a chalk outline if the puddle is on concrete or asphalt.) This will make it easier for the children to make comparisons from day to day as they watch for changes in the puddle. They will remind you if you happen to forget the puddle-checking ritual. Those in the northern latitudes might be able to see the puddle freeze and thaw as well as evaporate. Relate that cold air causes the water to freeze.

Improving School Grounds

To teach water conservation and to reduce rain runoff, install a rain barrel under a downspout of your building. The captured water can be used to irrigate the school gardens and lawn. Modern barrels have spigots near the bottom for attaching a hose and runoff valves at the top to prevent overflow in unwanted areas; they are covered to prevent insects, larger animals, and debris from getting in. Garden centers sell them; cooperative extension agents can provide advice, as can the Internet.

We collect the rain off our roof and water our plants with it.

Connecting Concepts

Some of the relationships between air and water can be observed in caring for classroom fish and plant life; some can effectively be demonstrated with simple experiments.

1. Children can see evidence of air in water when they watch a covered jar of water that has been allowed to stand in the room. Rows of tiny air bubbles will appear on the sides of the jar. Point out that fish must have air to live and that water takes in air. Fish have their own way of getting the air they need from the water. Point out the safety fact that children cannot get air from the water when they swim. They must learn how to breathe, how to let the water hold them up, and how to use their arms and legs to move along when they swim.

2. Plant dependence on water can be seen quite well in thin-leaved plants that have gone without water for a weekend. An avocado plant droops dramatically but recuperates within an hour or so after a good watering.

3. Air pressure (see Chapter 7, Air) can be used to empty an aquarium, to drain water from a large water play tub, or to provide outdoor water play. Make a siphon by completely filling approximately 1 yard (1 m) of tubing with water, pinching the ends together to keep air from entering the tube. Place one end of the tube in the water and the other in the bucket below. The water will drain into the bucket unless air entered the tube. Explain that air presses on the surface of the bucket of water, pushing water up the tube. Read about how liquids are moved from one place to another in *Messing Around with Water Pumps and Siphons* by Bernie Zubrowski (see Resources).

Family and Community Support

There are many opportunities for families to point out examples of water and water/air concepts at home: moisture condensing on mirrors and windows at bath time, steamy kitchen windows when dinner is cooking, and the "smoke" of moisture condensation emitted from clothes dryer vents in cold weather. All of these amplify the classroom experiences.

During family visits to the swimming pool or beach, children can stride through shallow water to test its weight and substance. With encouraging parents standing by, children can learn that the buoyancy principles work to support their own floating bodies.

Notify families if popular giant bubble performances and other bubble activities are offered at an area children's science center or as part of community summer programs.

RESOURCES

DAMONT, KATHLEEN. (2003). Sticking together. *Science and Children, 41*(3), 47–48. Surface tension experiments.
ZUBROWSKI, BERNIE. (1981). *Messing around with water pumps and siphons.* Boston: Little, Brown. This book will still be on children's library shelves; it hasn't been supplanted.

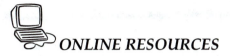 *ONLINE RESOURCES*

San Francisco Exploratorium: Activities from its popular water exhibits include a bubble tray (creating giant bubbles), soap bubbles, and a water sphere lens at *http://www.exploratorium.edu/snacks/snacksintro.html*

Wikipedia: The online encyclopedia offers good information on the water cycle at *http://en.wikipedia.org/wiki/water_cycle*

Weather

Powerful lightning splitting the night sky, spectacular rainbows in full glory, brilliant sunlight shafts breaking through storm clouds; your personal store of awesome weather memories can energize your explorations of weather with children.

"Who turns on the sun? Where does the wind come from?" Early in life, children wonder and worry about the weather. Exploring simple concepts about the sun, the water cycle, and moving air makes weather something interesting to observe rather than something to endure. Understanding something about the nature of lightning can soften fearfulness about storms. The following concepts are presented in this chapter:

- The sun warms Earth.
- Changing air temperatures make the wind.
- Evaporation and condensation cause precipitation.
- Raindrops can break up sunlight.
- Weather can be measured.
- Lightning is static electricity.
- Charged electrons make sparks when they jump.

In the activities that follow, children feel the sun's effects, observe the effect of warm-air movement, observe a small cloud in a cup, simulate a rainbow, record the weather, and imitate the movement of Earth around the sun.

CONCEPT: **The sun warms Earth.**

1. What feels warm on a sunny day?

LEARNING OBJECTIVE: To experience and appreciate the sun as a source of warmth.

? *Inquiry Activity:* Do this activity on a mild, sunny day. You will need sand, water, and two containers of equal size. For older children, provide two thermometers.

1. Encourage children to share ideas about the day's temperature. How did they decide what to wear? "What's happening to make the temperature pleasant today? Let's see if we can find out."

2. Let children spread a layer of sand in each container. Let younger children touch the sand to decide if both containers of sand feel about the same temperature. Have older children check sand temperatures with thermometers. ♣ Move outdoors with the containers. Place one container in heavy shade; place the other container in the sun. Plan to return to these places in an hour. "Do you think both pans of sand will feel the same when we come back?" Return to check the predictions. Which feels warmer? What might have caused the difference? Where do the children feel warmer, in the sunlight or in the shady place where a building or tree blocks the sunlight? (The sun warms Earth—the land, air, and everything the sunlight reaches.)

3. "What else can you find out about how the sun warms our world?" Move around the school area and have children touch the building, blacktop, and sidewalks on the sunniest side; then repeat on the shadiest side. Which side feels warmer? Feel a car parked in the sunlight, then one parked in the shade. Feel the top of a rock on the ground; turn the rock over to feel the underside. "Where are things warmest? What could cause the difference?" If it's possible to dig a hole on the school grounds, let children compare the temperatures on the surface of the ground and at the bottom of the hole. Continue with other surface temperatures children may suggest. Record findings.

Group Discussion: Summarize children's findings and conclusions about how the sun affects the temperature. Expand the topic to think about which feels warmer on bare feet: the sand or the water at the beach? The deck of a pool or the water? Help children decide whether some things take in (absorb) more warmth from the sun than others.

Math skills: Informally, and formally with thermometers, measure and compare the temperature in two outdoor locations.

CONCEPT: Changing air temperatures make the wind.

1. What makes air move as wind?

LEARNING OBJECTIVE: To experience the surprising effect of heat on air.

Introduction: The A. A. Milne poem "Wind on the Hill" makes a nice introduction to this activity. Encourage children to tell how they know that the wind is blowing, as wind is invisible. Summarize their ideas with a comment about knowing that wind is blowing because of what it does to things we can see.

MATERIALS:

Part 1

Unshaded table lamp (regular 60- or 75-watt bulb)

Strips of crisp tissue paper about 3/4 × 4 in. (2 × 10 cm)

SMALL-GROUP ACTIVITY:

Part 1

1. Children can find out something about how air moves as wind by experimenting with air that is heated.
2. Let children feel the air just above the unlighted light bulb. Give each child a strip of paper to hold steadily by one end just above the bulb. What happens to the other end of the paper? (A strip of crisp tissue paper will droop down.)
3. Repeat this action after the bulb has been turned on long enough to become hot. (Urge caution near the hot bulb.) How does the air above the bulb feel now? What happens to the paper in the warm air?
4. Recall that when air is moving, it pushes against things. We can tell which way the air is moving because of the direction in which it pushes things. Encourage children to observe in which direction the hot air pushes the tip of the paper strip. **Safety Precaution:** Be sure to tell children, *"We must never allow anything that could burn to touch a hot light bulb."*
5. Does the free end droop down or is it being pushed up so that it is straight or moving up somewhat? (Hot air rises.) Ask children if they have seen other evidence of hot air rising. Smoke (carbon particles mixed with heated air and gases) goes up chimneys; steam rises from a teakettle on the stove; balloonists heat the air in their balloons to make the balloon rise off the ground. Add, "When the sun heats the Earth, the air above the warm parts of the Earth heats up, too. *Warm air rises,* just as the air above the bulb moves up. The rising warm air is part of the reason for wind. Cold air rushes in beneath it; *that moving air is wind!"*

Math skills: Experience the air above a light bulb. Judge its temperature with the bulb turned off and on.

Part 2

Clear plastic tumbler
Chilled water
Steaming water
Small, clear medicine vials
Food coloring

GETTING READY:

If water is heated in the classroom, use a safely located
electric pot.

Safety Precaution: *Do not use
immersion water-heating coils
directly in a cup.* They are too
hazardous to use.

Part 2

1. "Another thing happens to air that causes
   it to move like wind. We can see something
   like it using water instead of air."
2. "Let's pretend that the cold water in this
   glass is cold air and the hot water I pour in
   is like hot air." Add 2 or 3 drops of food
   coloring to the vial of hot water to make it
   distinguishable. (Children can observe the
   effect better when they are at eye level with
   the tumbler.)
3. "How is the dyed hot water moving?"
   Watch for a few minutes without disturbing the tumbler. Repeat with the glass of
   cold water and a few drops of dyed cold
   water. What happens? Does the cold, dyed
   water move slowly upward and stay
   around the top in a layer, or does it mix
   with all the water right away?

Comment, "Both water and air get lighter when they are heated. Cold water
moves under heated water and pushes it upward. Cold air moves under heated
air and pushes it upward. We saw it happen with the colored water model, but we
can't see the same thing happening in the invisible air outdoors.

"Hot air is lighter than cold air, so cold air rushes under hot air and pushes it
up. When that happens, we feel the cold air rushing under the warm air. The air
moves fast. *This is wind! Air is always moving like this somewhere around the Earth.*
Warm air moves up and cooler air rushes in under it, pushing against leaves, flags,
people, *everything.*"

Encourage children to find out at home what happens when freezer
doors are opened in warm, steamy kitchens. Which way does that foggy air move?

Read: Gusts and Gales: A Book about Wind by Josepha Sherman.

For younger children read: *I Face the Wind* by Vicki Cobb.

CONCEPT: Evaporation and condensation cause precipitation.

1. How is rain formed?
LEARNING OBJECTIVE: To reassuringly affirm the continual evaporation/
                    condensation water cycle.

MATERIALS:

Zip-top plastic bag
Small, clear plastic vial such as a film canister or protective cap from a spray-top
   product

Tape
Cranberry juice, or water and food coloring

FIGURE 9–1

Group Experience: Ask children, "How do you think rain gets up in the air?" Responses will vary with age and experience with prior evaporation/condensation/precipitation activities (see Chapter 8, Water). Accept all responses tentatively. "Let's make a model to see what we can find out for ourselves."

Make a demonstration kit. Place a container half-filled with juice or tinted water inside the plastic bag and seal it shut. Tape the bag to a sunny window (see Figure 9–1). Ask for predictions about what might happen to the liquid and air in the bag after a few days. "Let's find out." Children can observe water vapor clinging to the inside of the bag, then forming into a few drops that eventually slide down to the bottom. Ask children to draw and report what they observe. Does the bag look different on a cloudy day, or early in the day compared to noon sunshine? Are the raindrops the same color as the juice?

Leave a small amount of juice out in the room in a shallow container for a day or so until all the moisture evaporates. Did air pick up the solid bits from the juice or just the water in the juice? Does air pick up salt water over the oceans to make salty rain? Evaporate a small amount of salted water for a few days to find the answer. Recall with the group that air picks up water as vapor. Sun-warmed air in the bag picked up just the water part of the juice.

Warm air can hold more vapor than can cool air. Did the water vapor in the bag look different on a cloudy day? Outdoors this happens all the time, all over Earth. The sun warms the air and speeds up the evaporation process. Air picks up bits of moisture everywhere. Vapor collects into clouds as it rises high into the sky. Droplets in the clouds collect into larger drops. Cool air temperatures high above Earth speed up this condensation process. Eventually, the drops fall to Earth as rain. Then the evaporation and condensation cycle happens again and again.

Read: Clouds by Anne Rockwell.

2. How do water drops change in freezing air?
LEARNING OBJECTIVE: To enjoy facilitating reversible water changes.

MATERIALS:

Medicine dropper (narrow tips
  make more spherical drops)
Cookie-baking pan

SMALL-GROUP ACTIVITY:

1. "We've seen water vapor in the bag get cold and change to drops of water. What do you think might happen to the drops if

Aluminum foil

Water

Freezer or below-freezing
   weather

they got freezing cold before they fell?
Let's find out."

2. Place foil on the baking pan. Carefully
   squeeze out a drop of water onto the foil
   for each child, spacing drops so they can't
   touch. Carry the pan to the freezer or, on a
   freezing day, to a sheltered spot outdoors.

3. Return to the freezer in 10 minutes. Show
   the frozen drops to the children. "Is this
   how they looked before? What happened?" Quickly spoon a frozen drop into
   the palm of each child's hand. "What's
   happening now?" Later, comment that
   large frozen raindrops become ice (sleet).
   Frozen water vapor becomes snowflakes.

Math skills: Observe how warm hands and cold freezers change the state of a
water drop and make judgments about temperature.

Read: The Secret Life of a Snowflake by Kenneth Libbrect.

A close look at snowflakes is awesome!

CONCEPT: Raindrops can break up sunlight.

1. What makes a rainbow?

LEARNING OBJECTIVE: To delight in creating exciting rainbow effects.

Note: This activity needs to be done in direct sunlight. Practice before doing it with children.

Introduction: Open a discussion about rainbows and the joy of being lucky enough to see one or even part of one. Comment that rainbows form when sunlight happens to shine just the right way through air that holds just the right amount of water vapor after a rain. Tiny water vapor drops are nature's prisms that spread out light and show its colors, just the way it can happen with soap bubbles or with a fine mist of water spraying upward from a hose on a sunny day when we see sunlight slanting through the drops. When the water vapor droplets evaporate, the rainbow disappears.

"We don't often see rainbows, but on a day when sunlight shines into our room, we can use a mirror to send back some sunlight through water and make a bit of a rainbow."

MATERIALS:

Shallow baking pan
White cardboard
Small pocket mirror
Small pitcher of water
A sunny location

SMALL-GROUP ACTIVITY:

1. Place the mirror at a 45-degree angle at one end of the baking pan. Let children take turns holding a piece of white cardboard near a sunny tabletop or windowsill while other children take turns trying to reflect a spot of sunlight from the mirror to the cardboard.
2. When the spot of light hits the cardboard, slowly pour water into the pan to cover about 2 in. (5 cm) of the mirror. Small adjustments to the angle may be needed until the white light is broken up into the spectrum ("like a bit of rainbow") on the cardboard.
3. Verify that it is light refracted through the water that caused the light to separate into the spectrum colors. To do this, hold a hand above the submerged portion of the mirror, blocking the reflection. What happens to the spectrum reflection?

CONCEPT: Weather can be measured.

1. How does a thermometer work?

LEARNING OBJECTIVE: To take pride in recalling how temperature changes affect liquids, making thermometers understandable.

MATERIALS:

Cooking thermometer
Hot water
Ice cubes
Small container
Outdoor thermometer

LARGE-GROUP ACTIVITY:

1. Recall the experience of feeling warm in the sunshine and cool in the shade. "How else can we find how warm air is?" Show outdoor thermometer. Record the level of the liquid column (the current indoor temperature). Ask for predictions about where the liquid column might move if the thermometer is taken outdoors for a while. Place the thermometer outside and compare the difference after a while.

2. Examine the cooking thermometer. Note that the numbers start with higher readings than those on the outdoor thermometer because food is cooked at hotter temperatures than the weather reaches. Put the thermometer into a container of hot water. "Is the liquid going up or down?" Record the final temperature. Ask for predictions of what will occur if ice cubes are added to the water. Let children add them. Check the results. Read the thermometers and record the new temperatures. Make a plan to check the outdoor thermometer daily. (The thermometer must be in the shade.) Keep a record of your readings and the daily weather forecast. Guide children through the thermometer creative movement on page 189.

What information does a weather station give us?

Math skills: Reading a thermometer and recording measurement.

2. How fast is the wind blowing?

LEARNING OBJECTIVE: To become engaged in discerning wind speed.

Group Activity: Move the group to the windows. Can children tell if the wind is blowing? How? What do they see? In a group discussion, introduce the idea that the wind, the heat of the sun, and water work together to make the weather. Winds move rain clouds and dry air.

Weather is more interesting to observe when we know many ways to describe and compare it. For generations, people have judged the wind's speed by observing its effect on things around them. The following chart is part of the Beaufort scale of wind velocity and provides visual guidelines for determining the wind's speed.

Beaufort Scale of Wind Velocity.

What to Look For	Description	Miles per Hours
Leaves don't move. Smoke rises straight up from chimneys.	Calm	Less than 1
Light flags blow; leaves and twigs move constantly.	Gentle breeze	8–12
Large branches sway. It's hard to hold an open umbrella.	Strong breeze	25–31
Whole, large trees move. It is hard to walk against the wind.	High wind	32–38
Whole trees uprooted.	Full gale	55–63

End the group discussion by talking about the measures we take to stay safe in storms. Assure children that weather forecasters collect information very carefully so that we can be warned about serious storms and find safety when necessary.

Plan to make a daily check at the windows to decide how fast the wind is moving. Record the children's description of the wind on a wind chart. Children can check the direction of the wind each day by observing the school flag or by holding up a wet finger to see which side is cooled by the wind. Wind is named for the direction it blows from. (A north wind pushes the flag south.)

Math skills: Observing outdoor objects to estimate wind speed.

Read: Wind (*Watching the Weather*) by Elizabeth Miles.

3. How much rain falls?

LEARNING OBJECTIVE: To arouse curiosity about weather measurements.

Group Activity: Elicit children's ideas about why rain is needed. Emphasize that every living thing needs water to survive, and also that lakes, rivers, reservoirs, and underground water stores are filled by rain. Explore the reasons *why* it is important to many people to know how much rain falls. (Farm children, those living in flood areas, or those living in cities dependent on reservoirs for their water supply may have information to share about rainfall amounts.)

Tell children, "Weather forecasters use special measuring equipment to find out how much rain has fallen. We can make something like it. We can put our rain gauge outside in a safe, open place. After each rain, we can check to see how much rain fell." (This will be a relative measurement. It will allow comparisons of the amount of rain collected in the jar from day to day.)

MATERIALS:

Widemouthed glass or clear plastic jar

Heavy rubber bands

Small plastic ruler

Use rubber bands to attach the ruler to the jar. Place the jar in a safe, open place where it will be undisturbed. Check the level of water in the jar as soon as possible after a rain. Empty the jar. Keep a record of the number of inches (centimeters) of rain that falls for several weeks during your rainy season.

Math skills: Using and interpreting a ruler on a jar of rainwater.

CONCEPT: Lightning is static electricity.

Introduction: Encourage children to share what they understand about lightning. Add, "Lightning is a powerful spark of static electricity. It develops when huge quantities of water droplets and tiny particles of ice in rain clouds rub together. Every one of those droplets and ice bits has something invisible that gets active this way: *electrons.* Electrons are part of everything. The activity caused by rubbing together is called *charging* the electrons. We can't see electrons, but we can see how they make things behave."

Show the children a 2-in. (5-cm) square of plastic wrap held between your thumb and forefinger. "What do you think might happen when I let go of this plastic?" Find out.

"Let's see if rubbing (friction) might make a difference in what happens to the plastic." Rub the plastic on a piece of wool or nylon fabric. Pick it up again and let go. "Look at this. I have let go, but the plastic hasn't let go this time. Friction did change some things in the plastic, things so tiny that they are invisible. They are *electrons.* Electrons are *even part of us.* Friction gets the energy of the electrons ready to move. That builds up an electric charge called *static electricity.*" Encourage children to share their ideas about static electricity. They may mention hair flying up when a sweater is pulled off or the crackle of static when TV screens or computer monitors go off. Allow children to apply static-cling window decals decorations if you use them.

Give children their own pieces of plastic to try. A sample of nylon carpeting or garments that children are wearing can be good synthetic fibers to rub the plastic against. "Electrons are part of everything, but we don't notice them until they are charged enough to move. You can have fun building an electric charge to make some little things jump."

1. How can we build up an electric charge to make things move?
LEARNING OBJECTIVE: To have fun creating static electricity.

MATERIALS:

Clear, flat plastic boxes
Tissue paper
Combs (plastic or nylon)
Small pieces of cotton thread
Scraps of wool, fur, silk, or nylon

SMALL-GROUP ACTIVITY:

1. Ask children to tear up tissue paper into rice-sized shreds. Put some shreds in the boxes.
2. "Let's rub a box top with a bit of fabric very fast to see what happens to the shreds of paper." (The shreds are attracted to the top. See Figure 9–2.)
3. Gradually add these ideas: "Rubbing two things together (friction) makes invisible bits, called *electrons,* in one thing (the fabric) leave it and jump to the other thing (the box top). The jumping is called a *static electricity charge.* The charge can pull or push other things. The charged box top pulled the paper shreds to it."

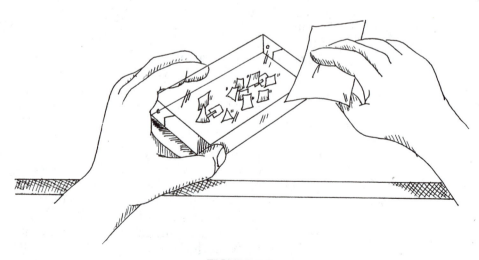

FIGURE 9–2

4. Suggest turning the boxes over to build a charge on the bottom of the box. What happens?
5. "Now try to build a charge on the comb with the fabric. Hold a thread near it. What happens? Did the static charge pull the thread to the comb?"
6. "Hold the charged comb near your hair. Does the static charge pull the hair toward the comb?"

CONCEPT: Charged electrons make sparks when they jump.

1. How can we make a tiny lightning flash? (This is a dry-weather activity.)
LEARNING OBJECTIVE: To ease fear of lightning by making and managing a spark of static electricity.

Introduction: "Join me in a special dark place to find out something interesting." Arrange yourself and the small group around the blanket-covered table, lying prone, with heads, arms, and shoulders slipped beneath the blanket-draped table.
"We saw how something charged with static electricity pulled other things to it. Now let's find out what we can see when jumping electrons make a static electricity charge. Perhaps we can see a spark in this dark place. The spark will be like a tiny flash of lightning. We'll pretend that balloons are storm clouds full of water and tiny ice crystals. The water droplets and crystals are blowing about and rubbing together in a storm cloud. The energy will be building up to make a huge spark: a big charge of electricity: a lightning flash!"

MATERIALS:

Small, long balloons
Small wool or nylon rug or carpet sample
Heavy blanket
Table

GETTING READY:

Drape table with the blanket to make a very dark place.
Place rug on the floor under the table.
Blow up balloons.

SMALL-GROUP ACTIVITY:

1. Show children how to stroke the balloons on the rug to build the electric charge. Count 20 strokes with them.
2. "Now pretend that my finger is another cloud or the Earth. I'll bring the charged balloon close to it. Watch! Listen! Did you see the spark jump to my finger? Now you try it."

Math skills: Counting charge strokes.

Group Discussion: "You can make a tiny lightning flash at home in a room that is almost dark. Scuffle your feet on a wool or nylon rug, then touch something metal. You can feel, hear, and see a small charge of electricity jump from yourself to the metal.

"A small spark like this is not dangerous, but lightning from storm clouds is very powerful when it strikes the Earth. That is why we take shelter in a building or car during an electrical storm."

Note: The experiences with electric charges will not be successful in a humid atmosphere. Save these experiences for dry weather.

Read: Nature's Fireworks: A Book About Lightning by Mark Seeley.

Note: In a follow-up discussion, mention that the movement of suddenly heated air and fast-moving cold air is also the cause of thunder. When lightning streaks through a cloud, it moves so fast that it heats the air around it very quickly. The cold air pushes under the hot air so fast that it makes the loud sound we call *thunder*. Let children listen to the very small popping noise they can make by drawing their lips over their front teeth, compressing their lips together, then pushing air out as they would to make the sound of a *b*. A small popping noise is made by fast-moving air from a small space. Thunder is made by huge amounts of fast-moving air.

INTEGRATING ACTIVITIES

Math Experiences

Weather Charting. For the remaining months of the school year, weather data gathering lends itself to chart-making.

For Younger Children. Mark off a calendar on a large sheet of newsprint. Make a yellow sun symbol in each square to remind children that the sun is shining whether we can see it or not. (Speak accurately when asking children about the day's weather: "Can we see the sun today?", not "Has the sun come out today?") Cut squares of white tissue paper to tape over the sun on foggy days and opaque white cloud shapes to cover the sun on rainy and snowy days, according to the children's decision about the day's weather.

For Older Children. Record the weather on the calendar by charting the temperature, the class estimate of the wind speed, and sky conditions (clear, cloudy, rainy, sunny). At the end of the month, summarize the total number of days of each condition. A bar graph makes comparisons of the month's weather easy, providing ready answers to questions such as "Which kind of weather did we have the most often?" and "How many more days were cloudy than sunny?" Go back to compare monthly or seasonal summaries. Children can learn to identify cloud types and graph the number of days each type was seen. They can watch the weather forecast at home or bring in the newspaper forecast and compare it with the data gathered by the class the next day, recording when the two agree.

Music (Resources in Appendix A)

1. Sing the songs that children have been singing about the weather for generations: "One Misty Moisty Morning," "Rain, Rain, Go Away," and "The North Wind Doth Blow."

2. Sing "The Eency Weency Spider," remembering to change "dried up all the rain" to "evaporated the rain." Check the rain spouts around your building after a rain.

3. Play "Air Cycle Swing" from the Banana Slug String Band cassette *Adventures on the Air Cycle.*

4. Hang a melodic wind chime near or in your classroom on a breezy day. Let the weather provide the music.

5. Listen to Rick Charette sing "The First Time I Saw a Rainbow" From *Popcorn and Other Songs.*

Literature Links

BANG, MOLLY. (2004). *My light.* New York: Scholastic. In simple prose and remarkable art, the author/artist conveys the crucial role of the sun's energy in creating weather and sustaining all life on our planet.

BAUER, MARION. (2004) *Wind.* New York: Aladdin. Beginning readers will enjoy discovering the ways of wind in simple, accurate sentences, one to a page. Also in this series: *Clouds.*

BAUER, MARION. (2005). *If frogs made the weather.* New York: Holiday House. A young boy considers ideal weather for different animals. Clever collages will fascinate readers and listeners.

BRANLEY, FRANKLYN. (2005). *Sunshine makes the seasons.* New York: HarperCollins. Step by step, with the aid of an orange, a pencil, a pin, and a flashlight, this book explains day and night, the rotation of Earth, and changing seasons.

COBB, VICKI. (2003). *I face the wind.* New York: HarperCollins. This fine interactive book begins with children's firsthand, intimate experiences with wind, leads to simple experiments with air, and ends with basic explanations of air as a substance.

CRUM, SHUTTA. (2009). *Thunder boomer.* New York: Clarion. There is family humor and reassurance when a sudden thunderstorm sweeps through a farmyard.

DEMAREST, CHRIS. (2006). *Hurricane hunters.* New York: Margaret McElderberry Books. Bold art and a succinct text by the author/artist capture the drama of an oncoming hurricane, and the urgency of the crew that measures the power of the storm and predicts its path. NSTA* Outstanding Trade Book.

KANNER, ETTA. (2006). *Who likes the wind?* Tanawanda, NY: Kids Can Press. Creative thinking will flow as questions of special interest to children are probed. NSTA* recommended.

KARAS, BRIAN. (2005). *On Earth.* New York: Putnam. With amazing simplicity and clarity, Karas tells the story of our spinning, rotating Earth as it journeys around the

---

*National Science Teachers Association.

sun. Charming, child-centered art adds to the accessibility of the concepts. NSTA*
recommended.

LIBBRECT, KENNETH. (2009). *The secret life of a snowflake*. Minneapolis: Voyageur. See awesome
photographs and read amazing information about snowflakes and their formation.

MCMILLAN, BRUCE. ((2007). *How the ladies stopped the wind*. Boston: Houghton Mifflin. This
charming picture book is recommended by NSTA.*

MILES, ELIZABETH. (2005). *Wind (watching the weather)*. Chicago: Heinemann-Raintree.

MORTENSEN, DENISE. (2006). *Ohio thunderstorm*. New York: Clarion. Crisp verse and powerful illustrations depict the drama of a powerful thunderstorm sweeping over a family
farm.

ROCKWELL, ANNE. (2008). *Clouds*. New York: HarperCollins. Delightful art connects children
with cloud types that predict the weather. Use it when keeping weather records.

SCHUH, MARI. (2010). *Hurricanes*. Mankato, MN: Capstone. Powerful photographs of dan-
gers, calming scenes of forecasting, and safety plans will interest emergent readers.

SEELEY, MARK. (2004). *Nature's fireworks: A book about lightning*. Minneapolis: Picture Window
Books. The basic information about lightning includes an experiment and safety tips.

SHERMAN, JOSEPHA. (2004). *Flakes and flurries*. Minneapolis: Picture Window Books. Here
is an intriguing close-up look at the crystal patterns that form snowflakes, with lively
illustrations and added weather facts. Also in this series: *Gusts and gales: A book about
wind*.

STEWARD, MELISSA. (2009). *Under the snow*. Atlanta: Peachtree. A reassuring response to
children concerned about animals surviving severe winters. Also: *When rain falls*. How
animals manage rain in different habitats.

STILLE, DARLENE. (2004). *Temperature: Heating up and cooling down*. Minneapolis: Picture
Window Books. Here is a cheerfully written resource for children who want deeper
answers about weather. Instructions for making a thermometer are included.

THOMAS, RICK. (2005). *Eye of the storm: A book about hurricanes*. Minneapolis: Picture Window
Books. Tension builds, page by page, in describing the gathering elements of a hurricane
in this dramatic narrative. End pages give survival rules and hurricane facts. NSTA*
recommended.

THOMAS, RICK. (2005). *Rumble, boom! A book about thunderstorms*. Minneapolis: Picture
Window Books. Wind-tossed illustrations and the sobering facts about the power of thunderstorms will attract and inform readers and listeners. Survival tips are given.

Classics

BRANLEY, FRANKLYN. (1997). *Down comes the rain*. New York: HarperCollins. How big is a
droplet? Find out in this book for young children, with its approachable presentation of
the water cycle.

BRANLEY, FRANKLYN. (1999). *Flash, crash, rumble and roll*. New York: Thomas Y. Crowell. Clear information in this book about thunderstorms helps reassure fearful young children.

MARTIN, JACQUELINE. (1998). *Snowflake Bentley*. Boston: Houghton Mifflin. Read about this
self-taught man who invented a way to photograph single snowflakes in order to share
their beauty with all of us. NSTA* Outstanding Trade Book. Caldecott Award winner.

Poems (Resources in Appendix A)

In A. A. Milne's *Now We Are Six*, "Wind on the Hill" reveals a child's problem-solving logic
about where the wind blows and raises the unanswered question of where the wind
comes from.

From Robert Louis Stevenson's book *A Child's Garden of Verses*, read "The Wind," in which
another child tries to understand the wind

From Arnold Lobel's book, *The Frogs and Toads All Sang*, get poetry-writing inspiration.

---

*National Science Teachers Association.

Lee Bennett Hopkins has compiled readable, likable poems in his book *Weather*.
Jane Yolen has compiled poems appealing to a wide range of tastes in *Weather Report*.
From *Sing a Song of Popcorn*, compiled by DeRegniers and colleagues, read "Dragon Smoke"
    and "Wind Song" by Lillian Moore.
"Snowflakes" by David McCord is in Lee Bennett Hopkins's poetry collection, *Spectacular
    Science*. (Read it before heading outdoors with magnifiers in hand during a gentle
    snowfall.)

Art Activities

Weather Mobile. Let children help you create weather symbols to hang in
your classroom. Cut out pairs of cloud shapes from newsprint. Staple them together over a wire coat hanger. Let children stuff them with shredded paper or
polyester fiber to create a soft sculpture appearance. Place ends of plastic silver
tinsel on strips of tape. Fold the tape lengthwise over the bottom of a white wire
coat hanger to simulate rain. Let children crayon spectrum colors on a cardboard
rainbow arch. Add a yellow construction paper sun to the mobile.

Fog Pictures. Let children draw outdoor scenes on light blue paper. Attach a
sheet of white tissue paper of matching size to the top edge to give the effect of
fog. The "fog" can be lifted by folding back the tissue paper.

Rain Painting. See what changes will be created by holding children's
finger paintings outdoors in a light rain for a few seconds.

Sidewalk Painting. Give children wide brushes and cans of water to
paint huge designs on the sidewalk on a cloudy day. Ask for predictions about
what will happen to the designs when the sun comes out or a warm wind blows
over them.

Creative Movement

Thermometers. "Find a space where you can stand without touching anyone.
Pretend that you are a special liquid that gets bigger when it is warm and smaller
when it is cool. Now you are going into a long, skinny tube with a round space at
the bottom. Are you standing straight up with stomachs pulled in tight so that you
fit into the thermometer tube? I'll tell you when the sun is warming the air around
you. When you get warm and grow bigger, you can only go up in your skinny tube.
When you shrink and get smaller in cold air, you can only sink straight down.

"Now the sun is shining in a clear blue sky. It is lunchtime. The air is getting
hotter and hotter. You have to get bigger and bigger because the air is so warm. Oh!
Your fingertips have reached all the way up to 40 degrees Centigrade on the number
marks. I'll pretend to carry you indoors, where it is cooler. The sun isn't shining inside. Ah, it feels cooler here. What will happen inside the tube when you are cooler?
There you go, shrinking down a bit. It must be about 25 degrees Centigrade in here.
Now I'll take you outdoors again. It's getting warmer. But wait, a big cloud comes
between me and the sun. I can't see the sun now. What happens to you? Do you get
bigger or smaller? I see some liquid columns starting to shrink down when the sunlight is blocked and the air feels a bit cooler. Now it is night; the sun isn't shining on

our part of Earth. You are shrinking down more and more because it's cooler than it was in the daytime sunlight. Let's see what happens when there is a snowstorm. Look, there are icicles and snowmen. Now I see liquids shrinking down. Let the liquid slide all the way down to the floor. Now become yourselves again."

Creative Thinking

Print as a story or tape-record children's responses to stimulus phrases such as "If I could drift on the wind like a bird, . . ." "If I were a raindrop, . . ." or "If I could sail away on a cloud." Read the completed story or play the finished tape for the whole class to enjoy. Make a booklet of the ideas evoked by the children, including illustrations by each idea's author.

Food Experiences

1. For centuries, warm air has been used to preserve fruits, vegetables, fish, meat, and herbs. Children enjoy preparing dried apple rings. Let them wash several apples. Then you core the apples and slice them crosswise into ¼-in. (0.6-cm) rings. Children then drop the apple rings into a bowl of water to which 2 tablespoons of lemon juice have been added. Pat the rings dry. String them on a long, clean dowel or on a heavy cord. Tie the cord or place the dowel across a warm corner of the classroom, away from direct sunlight, to dry for several days. Cover loosely with cheesecloth to discourage insects. Apples will be dry, to the touch, darker in color, and slightly rubbery. Rinse slices, dry, and eat. Read about apple and berry drying during pioneer days in *The Little House Cookbook* by Barbara Walker.

2. Try your hand at solar cooking. Directions for making a pizza box solar oven and some interesting recipes are in *Toad Cottages and Shooting Stars* by Sharon Lovejoy.

Field Trips

♣ After a rain stops, tour the school neighborhood to examine the effects of wind and rain on the environment. Where has water collected in a puddle? Why there? Is a wooden sandbox seat as wet as a blacktop area? Is the ground under the playground swings as dry as a graveled area? Have leaves (or small branches or large branches) been blown down? What might this indicate about the speed of the wind? Was there enough rain to flood the gutters or to wash earthworms out of their tunnels?

PROMOTING CONCEPT CONNECTIONS

Maintaining Concepts

1. Expand the weather chart with questions about adaptations children may have made to cope with the day's weather. It can become part of the day's routine to inquire about how the weather affected their lives positively or negatively.

2. If a small dehumidifier is available, examine it on a humid day with the children. See how this adaptation to change a room's climate uses the process of condensing water vapor to water. Unless your dehumidifier poses a special safety hazard, let the children feel the condenser coil before turning on the unit. Switch on the unit and let children hold a piece of paper next to the condenser, then in front of the blower screen, to discover which way air is being moved. Watch the changes gradually taking place on the condenser coils. Does the coil feel the same after the unit has run for a while as it did before? Let children help empty the water from the collection pan. Help them relate this process to the cloud in a jar and to clouds in the cold atmosphere.

Improving School Grounds

To show which way the wind is blowing, install a windsock. Windsocks are used by air traffic controllers, meteorologists, and NASA engineers when helping the space shuttle land. NASA's Web site provides directions for making windsocks as well as the names of various vendors. (See Online Resources.)

Connecting Concepts

1. A miniature water cycle can be observed in a classroom terrarium. At times, condensation will be visible inside the glass enclosure. At other times, the enclosure will appear to be dry. The plants survive without additional watering for many weeks. Why?
2. Recall the experiences with water-changing forms; with air taking up water; with the effects of moving air; with water pushing up objects that are less heavy than water; and with air supporting gliders.
3. Note that the water cycle (the evaporation/condensation process) is one of nature's ways of keeping our limited supply of water clean.
4. Make a connection with wellness practices and the need for protecting ourselves against overexposure to ultraviolet (UV) radiation, especially on sunny days. Check the UV Index on the Internet or newspaper weather reports. Consider participating in the EPA-sponsored SunWise Program (see Online Resources).

Family and Community Support

Encourage families to show children the cold, wet air that rolls down from an open freezer door on a humid day, or the direction hot steam takes when it escapes from pots of simmering food or from a teakettle. Suggest that families owning Swedish holiday candle chimes examine the before-and-after effects of heating the air below the figures with the small candle flames. Note how the blades of the candelabra are bent to catch the rush of hot air and begin to move. Tell families which nearby homes or businesses have visible solar energy panels on their rooftops. You could mention that the sun's energy can be used to heat water in those homes. Mention the location of local windmills used to generate electricity.

An urban TV meteorologist may be available to present a forecasting program for your classroom. Alert families to small weather stations in your area that might encourage visits.

RESOURCES

DAY, JOHN. (2003). *The book of clouds.* New York: Silver Lining Books. An abundance of awesome cloud photographs enrich this beautifully written introduction to cloud formation and weather prediction. A great resource for the classroom.

LOVEJOY, SHARON. (2009). *Toad cottages and shooting stars.* New York: Workman. This delightful book includes directions for making a simple solar oven and provides four good recipes to make in it.

ROBERTSON, WILLIAM. (2005). *Stop faking it! Finally understanding science so you can teach it: Air, water and weather.* Arlington, VA: NSTA Press. You'll teach more confidently after this book slows down and eases the process of understanding these topics. It does so with humor.

VEKTERIS, DONNA, & OUELLET, MARIE. (2004). *Scholastic atlas of weather.* New York: Scholastic. This handsome reference for older children is a good background resource for teachers. It can be read selectively to or by younger children. Weather experiments are provided, including one for collecting individual raindrops and one to demonstrate the need for wearing a hat in cold weather! NSTA* Outstanding Trade Book.

WALKER, BARBARA. (1979). *The little house cookbook.* New York: HarperCollins.

 ONLINE RESOURCES

For Kids Only: Earth Science Enterprise. Information on how NASA scientists study weather at *http://Kids.earth.nasa.gov*

National Severe Storms Laboratory Weather Room: Basic information on weather for children, parents, and teachers at *http://www.nssl.noaa.gov/edu*

U.S. Environmental Protection Agency: The *SunWise Program* teaches children to protect themselves from overexposure to the sun. Available at *http://www.epa.gov/sunwise*

---

*National Science Teachers Association.

Rocks and Minerals

Massive mountains, incredible crystals in a museum case, the special pebble on your shelf: all are parts of Earth's awesome rocky crust. Recapture recollections about fine encounters with rocks and minerals. Carry your meaningful memories of rocks and minerals into the classroom to kindle children's natural interest in rocks and make their investigations satisfying.

"Oooooh! This one has shiny speckles! Look! This one is all little rocks joined into one. These three are a family. This one has a stripe all around and around." Children relish sifting through piles of rocks to find favorites. They are awed to hear that our Earth is a giant ball of rock and that rocks can be millions of years old. Learning about the importance of rocks promotes a feeling of security in youngsters, just as the Rock of Gibraltar can symbolize trust and stability to adults. Activities in this chapter explore the following concepts:

- There are many kinds of rocks.
- Rocks slowly change by wearing away.
- Crumbled rocks and dead plants make soil.
- Old plants and animals left prints in rocks.
- Minerals form crystals.

An unstructured experience with washing and examining ordinary highway gravel is suggested as a beginning activity. This is followed by classifying and hardness testing. Basic information is given about rock formation. Other suggested experiences include grinding soft rocks, breaking rocks open to compare the fresh surfaces with the worn exteriors, pulverizing rock to compare it with complete soil, and forming crystals.

INTRODUCTION

Tuck a small rock into your hand, then comment quietly, "I have something quite small but very old in my hand. It is so old that it might have been here long before any people lived on Earth or even before the dinosaurs were alive. Can you guess what it could be?" Slowly open your hand to reveal the humble but now significant rock.

CONCEPT: **There are many kinds of rocks.**

1. How do rocks look when dry and wet?

LEARNING OBJECTIVE: To enjoy examining rocks.

MATERIALS:

Bucket of #67 washed gravel (from a builder's supply warehouse)*

Dishpans, water

Few drops of detergent

Old, small brushes

Magnifiers

Trays for clean rocks

Cleanup sponge

Smocks for children

GETTING READY:

Fill dishpans one-quarter full with water.

SMALL-GROUP ACTIVITY:

1. Let children wash and scrub some of the rocks to discover whether or not they look the same wet or dry.
2. Have children choose and get acquainted with the shape, texture, and color of a favorite rock.
3. After they have examined it carefully with the magnifier, have children write, draw, or dictate a description of their favorite rock.
4. Leave the gravel out for children's independent examination during center times.

Note: Children seem to be drawn to a material that is available in quantity for them to explore freely. A heaping dishpan of common rocks will have more appeal than a box of neatly labeled special rocks.

2. Can we find rocks that are alike in some ways?

LEARNING OBJECTIVE: To appreciate and organize rocks by characteristics.

? *Inquiry Activity:* Suggest sorting rocks that are alike in some way into the same container. Sorting decisions are easy for many children to make (by color, size, shape, or texture). If children can't get started on their own, offer a suggestion such as "The flat rocks could go here; rocks that aren't flat could go there. How would you like to group the ones that seem to be alike?" Record and discuss the categories that children devise.

MATERIALS:

Bucket of #67 washed gravel

---

*No. 67 washed gravel consists of varied rocks (from old riverbeds) that range from almond to egg size. For school use, some building suppliers might give you a bucketful without charge. It is usually sold by the ton.

Sorting containers (egg cartons, margarine tubs, divided plastic snack trays, old muffin tins)

3. Which rocks are hard? Which are soft?

LEARNING OBJECTIVE: To introduce a satisfying way to group rocks.

MATERIALS:

#67 washed gravel

Blackboard chalk (pressed gypsum)

Pumice (from the drugstore)

Pennies

3 trays or boxes

GETTING READY:

Make two labels: *Soft* and *Hard*.

Place trays or boxes next to each other.

Put the *Soft* and *Hard* labels in the first and third trays or boxes; leave the middle tray or box unlabeled.

SMALL-GROUP ACTIVITY:

1. "Some rocks are soft enough for a finger-nail to scratch them. Rocks just a bit harder can't be scratched that way, but a penny edge will scratch them."
2. Let children experiment with scratch tests. Suggest sorting rocks by degree of hardness: "Put rocks scratched by your fingernail into the tray (or box) marked *Soft;* put rocks scratched only by the penny into the unmarked tray (or box); put rocks that can't be scratched by a penny into the tray (or box) marked *Hard.*"

Hands-on, bodies-on learning about rocks.

Math skills: Testing hardness of rocks; sorting by degree of hardness.

If children find it hard to form three classes of rocks, simplify the experience to form two classifications of hardness: hard rocks, not scratched by a penny, and softer rocks, scratched by a penny. Make a separate activity to find soft rocks, scratched by a fingernail, and harder rocks, not scratched by a fingernail. Perhaps a teacher is wearing the hardest rock of all on her finger—a diamond (crystallized pure carbon).

ROCK FORMATION

As children engage in the suggested experiences, they can be given bits of simple information about the mineral content of rocks and about the way rocks were (and are) formed.

Mineral Content

When children question the specks and streaks of color they see as they sort rocks, tell them that most rocks are mixtures of many kinds of material. The materials are called *minerals.* There are about 2,000 different minerals, but only about 20 minerals are abundant. Different mixtures of minerals make different kinds of rocks. (You might want to recall baking experiences with children. Talk about how sometimes the same materials are put together in different ways to make different things to eat. Cornbread and cookies are almost alike in ingredients.) Sometimes the mineral mixtures are easy to see as specks, sparkles, and stripes. Rocks may contain many different combinations of minerals. Small amounts of minerals are also important for healthy growth of plants, animals, and humans.

Three Types of Rock Formation

Igneous. Millions of years ago, some rocks were mixtures that melted deep inside Earth. When they cooled, they formed very hard rocks. As worn-down pebbles, they are usually somewhat ball-shaped.

Sedimentary. Some rocks were formed in layers or parts, like a sandwich. Layers of sand, clay, and gravel were pressed together very hard at the bottom of old lakes, rivers, and oceans. Sometimes animal shells were mixed into the rock. It takes many thousands of years of very hard pressure to form rocks this way. Some sedimentary rocks have stripes of color or line marks in them. Some feel sandy. Some have tiny rocks stuck together. They were all made under pressure. Bits may break off in thin layers. As worn-down pebbles, they are shaped like flat discs.

Metamorphic. Sometimes rocks that were already formed by pressure or by the cooling of melted mixtures were changed again by more heat and pressure, changing the rocks into still different types. Bits break away as slabs. As worn-down pebbles, they also are flat, disklike shapes.

Try to find out something about the rocks in your area, both the visible outcroppings and the rocks beneath the soil. Were rocks heaved up into mountains and hills in your area millions of years ago? Did ancient rivers wear away rocks and carve out valleys? Mention this to the children when a suitable time arises.

CONCEPT: **Rocks slowly change by wearing away.**

1. ♣ How can we wear away bits of rock?

LEARNING OBJECTIVE: To enjoy the power to change rocks.

MATERIALS:

Pieces of soft, crumbly rock
  (shale, soft sandstone)

Coffee cans with lids

Wrapped hard candy (one for
  each child)

Hammer

Bowl of replenishable water

GETTING READY:

Crack each wrapped candy with
  a *light* hammer tap.

SMALL-GROUP ACTIVITY:

1. Put several soft rocks in each can. Ask children to feel the rocks. Cover the cans tightly. Let children hold them tightly and shake them as long and hard as they can. Open the cans. Ask, "Has anything changed? Is there dusty stuff at the bottom?"

2. If this must be an indoor activity, try briskly rubbing two crumbly rocks together over a piece of white paper.

3. Have children wash their hands. Let each child unwrap a cracked candy. "Pretend this is a broken rock." Keep one broken bit in the wrapper. Swish another bit in the bowl of water for several minutes. "What do you think will happen in the water?" Compare the edges of the water-tumbled bit with the edges of the dry bit. "It takes much, much longer for moving water to smooth the edges of real rocks." Eat the results.

Group Discussion: Talk about the results of the rock-shaking activity in terms of wearing away pieces of rock. Discuss how pieces of rock break from large rocks. Over hundreds of years, the surfaces of the rocks are worn down by wind or water. Encourage children who have visited natural beaches to recall whether they found smooth pebbles or jagged rocks on the sand. Discuss how waves or running streams tumble the rocks against each other and smooth them, and how bits are very slowly rubbed off. If there are nearby rock formations with which children are familiar, describe how they were slowly changed and worn by winds or running streams of water.

2. How can we draw with rocks?

LEARNING OBJECTIVE: To enjoy the results of rocks wearing away.

Group Activity: If there is a safe sidewalk area where this activity can be performed, give children assorted soft rocks to use for outdoor sidewalk art. Mention that cave dwellers made pictures on rock walls with soft rocks of different colors.

Later, show the children two other rocks we use for writing: pencil "lead" (graphite) and blackboard chalk (pressed gypsum). They make marks because they are so soft that worn-away bits are left as the drawing or writing we see.

Does your schoolroom have an old-fashioned slate blackboard to draw on? (Slate is a metamorphic rock.) Perhaps you can buy an inexpensive one at a variety store. Slabs of slate can sometimes be found in salvage stores after wrecking crews have taken off old slate roofs. (They are fine to use under flowerpots on the windowsill after the writing experience is over.)

Intricate sand painting is an ancient art still practiced in some parts of the world. Simone patiently rubbed bits of red sandstone together to make red pigment for her small sand design.

3. How can we tell that rocks have changed?

LEARNING OBJECTIVE: To be fascinated by and wonder at the differences between the inside and weathered outside of rocks.

MATERIALS:

Rocks (ball shapes are hard to crack; avoid them)

Hammer

Old jeans fabric (precaution against flying rock chips)

Safety goggles

Magnifiers

Sidewalk or hard surface

SMALL-GROUP ACTIVITY:

1. **Safety Precaution:** All children must wear safety goggles. Place a rock on the sidewalk. Cover it with two thicknesses of the fabric. Strike it hard with the hammer. (Children experienced with hammers can do this successfully. A two-handed grip may help.) Very hard, round (*igneous*) rocks may not split well. Other rocks will split with one hammer blow.
2. Examine the inside; compare it with the outside appearance.

Note: This is a very exciting activity that may lead to "rock fever." Children will be curious to discover what is inside a rock: the glint of mica flakes, a streak of mineral, a sleek surface, a glittering bit of quartz crystal. Engage children's imagination by stating that the worn outside surface of the rock was once the same color and texture as the inside. Ask: "What might have happened to change the outside of these rocks?"

If there is access to a rock-tumbling machine and school permission, the class can embark on an intriguing 6-week rock-polishing project. This will help them understand how slowly rocks change. Each stone will be transformed into a smooth, gleaming gem, perhaps one for each child. The machine can be placed in a covered, inexpensive foam picnic cooler to muffle the noise. Children can appreciate the changes in appearance every 2 weeks when the grit size is changed. (Rock-tumbling machines are readily available online or in hobby stores.)

CONCEPT: Crumbled rocks and dead plants make soil.

1. What happens when we pound soft rocks?

LEARNING OBJECTIVE: To take satisfaction in converting rocks to part of soil.

MATERIALS:

Pieces of crumbly rock (shale, soft sandstone, etc.)

Discardable jeans

Hammers

Newspapers

Sieve

Empty can

SMALL-GROUP ACTIVITY:

1. Put one jeans leg inside the other. Put a few rocks in the double jeans leg and place them on the sidewalk. Let children take turns pounding rocks, checking the results often.
2. Spread newspaper on the ground. Fit sieve over the can. Shake contents of bags into sieve, catching spills on newspaper.
3. Keep pulverizing until children are tired.
4. Examine the powdered rock in the can and save for the next experience.

2. What does soil look like?

LEARNING OBJECTIVE: To enjoy exploring what makes up fertile soil.

MATERIALS:

Trowel

Container

Newspapers

Topsoil

Sieve, sticks

Magnifying glasses

Container of pulverized rock from the previous experience

2 paper cups

Water

SMALL-GROUP ACTIVITY:

1. Let children scoop up a trowelful of soil from a permitted digging area to bring indoors.
2. Spread the soil on newspapers; examine with a magnifying glass. Compare with rock pulverized by children.
3. Put soil through sieve. Good topsoil contains bits of leaves, twigs, roots, and worms. Some of this matter will be left in the sieve.
4. Put some sifted soil and powdered rock in separate cups. Stir a bit of water into each cup. Compare.

Note: Clay is like moist powdered rock. It must have lots of old vegetable and animal matter (and perhaps sand) added to it to make good soil for growing things.

CONCEPT: Old plants and animals left prints in rocks.

Recall splitting rocks open to find unexpected color, sparkle, and texture inside. Add that prints of animals, shells, and plants that lived on Earth millions of years before people did can be found pressed between layers of rocks. These rocks are called *fossils*. (Perhaps there are some fossils in the bucket of highway gravel that the children have been using.)

Children can have fun making prints of their hands, shells, or leaves using the kind of powdered stone that became clay. They can make prints similar to fossils, though they won't be as old or as hard as fossils, of course.

1. How can we make a "fossil" print?

LEARNING OBJECTIVE: To take pride in leaving one's mark like a mold fossil.

Let children use small rolling pins to roll out moist clay slabs about ¼ in. (1 cm) thick. Show them how to press a leaf, a shell, or their hand firmly into the clay. It may take several tries to get a clear print. "Erase" unsatisfactory leaf prints by rubbing the clay with water and lightly rerolling. Cut the slab into a plaque shape by using an empty coffee can as a cutter. Poke a hole through the top of the slab for a hanging loop of string. Scratch the child's initials in the clay. Allow several drying days. Mention that fossils took *much* longer to form. Teacher may shellac the dried clay to preserve it, if desired.

Read: Fossil by Claire Ewart or *Stone Girl, Bone Girl* by Lawrence Anholt.

CONCEPT: **Minerals form crystals.**

1. How do mineral crystals form?

LEARNING OBJECTIVE: To be intrigued by crystal formation.

Introduction: (Do this after children understand evaporation.) Try to bring in a geode or other intriguing crystal formations, perhaps borrowed from a rock collector, to share with the children. Include rocks the class broke open to reveal glittering bits of mica, or tiny, sparkling quartz crystals, or gemstone jewelry. Tell the children that when minerals dissolve in water, which then evaporates, or when minerals melt and cool slowly, they form such *crystals.* Each type of mineral forms its own special crystal pattern. "Let's see what will happen if we dissolve some ordinary minerals in hot water and leave the solutions out to evaporate for a few days."

(Be sure to try the following activities at home to see whether adjustments will be needed for your climate and to determine the approximate length of time required for crystals to form.)

Point out that solutions need to be undisturbed for crystals to slowly form, so this needs to be a "hands-off" observation for several days.

MATERIALS:

Measuring cup and spoon ¼ cup (60 mL) *steaming* hot water (bring to class in a thermos jug)

1 tablespoon plain salt (not light salt)

8-in. (20-cm) aluminum foil piepan

LARGE-GROUP OBSERVATION:

Let children help measure salt and carefully stir it into *steaming* water until it dissolves. Pour solution into piepan. Place pan in a location where it will be undisturbed. Have children make *Hands Off! Science in Progress* signs to indicate a designated science zone. Check the next day for changes. Let children use the magnifier to examine the residue that formed as water *slowly* evaporated. Already, a few beautiful salt crystal cubes may have formed. More should continue to form for another day or so.

Math skills: Measuring with standard kitchen units.

2. Do all crystals look alike?

LEARNING OBJECTIVE: To be amazed by unique differences in crystal formations.

   Introduction. Ask children, "Do you think other minerals will form crystals just like the salt crystal cubes?" (This will be another "hands-off" experiment at first.) Explain that when scientists experiment and compare different samples in the laboratory, they must be careful to use separate equipment for each mixture so that the results will be accurate.

MATERIALS:

Small containers of
Epsom Salts*
Table salt
Borax†
Measuring spoons
3 plastic spoons
3 small cups
6 clear plastic deli container lids
Indelible marker
Clear tape
Tray or cookie sheet
Waxed paper
Strong magnifier; 40X
   microscope

GETTING READY:

Label one lid for each mineral.
Line tray with waxed paper.
Put marked lids on tray.

WHOLE GROUP ACTIVITY:

1. Put 2 tablespoons of *steaming* water in each of 3 cups.

2. To each cup, stir in one of these: ½ teaspoon salt; ½ teaspoon Epsom salts; ½ teaspoon Borax.

3. Carefully spoon each solution into the corresponding marked plastic lid.

4. Leave tray of solutions undisturbed for 2 days. When crystals have formed, cover them with clean lids. Tape edges together (see Figure 10–1).

5. Examine with a magnifier and, if possible, with a 40X microscope. Compare results. If possible, repeat this experience to confirm the unique shape of each mineral's crystals.

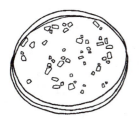

Math skills: Measuring with standard kitchen units.

3. How do stalagmites and stalactites form in caves?

LEARNING OBJECTIVE: To delight in watching a miniature crystal
                    pillar form.

FIGURE 10–1

---

*Available at drugstores.
†Available at supermarkets, shelved with laundry aids; also sold as "washing soda."
Warning: *Neither should be ingested.*

MATERIALS:

18 in. (45 cm) cotton or wool yarn or heavy string

2 small keys

Sheet of dark-colored paper

Paper towels

Tray or cookie sheet

2 pint jars

2 cups (500 mL) steaming hot water

¼ cup (60 mL) Epsom salts

Magnifier

WHOLE-GROUP OBSERVATION:

Learn what children may know about how icicles form from dripping, freezing water. If available, read aloud *Cave*, by Diane Siebert, or show reference illustrations of stalagmite/stalactite formations. Discuss how mineral solutions can drip into underground limestone caves for millions of years to form these crystal columns. "Perhaps we can watch something like this happening in a much faster way." Set up an observation as shown in Figure 10–2. Leave it undisturbed where it can be watched for several days by the children. Marvel at the results!

Math skills: Measuring with standard kitchen units.

GETTING READY:

Tie keys to either end of string.

Put colored paper over two layers of paper towels on a tray.

Pour 1 cup of steaming water into each jar.

Stir 2 tablespoons of Epsom salts into each jar, adding as much more as can be dissolved in the water.

Place jars on ends of colored paper.

Soak string in one jar briefly. Then put one key in each jar, letting string curve over the paper (see Figure 10–2).

Leave undisturbed in a draft-free place. Measure the dripping column daily to watch crystal buildup. It takes several days to form a solid column.

Read: "Plink by Plink" from Constance Levy's book *Splash! Poems of Our Watery World.*

FIGURE 10–2

FIGURE 10–3

Note: To explain how ancient trees, shells, and bones turned to stone (petrified), fill a jar with a cup of hot water and as much Borax as can be dissolved in it. Twist one end of a colored pipe cleaner into a tight spiral. Twist the other end around a pencil, adjusting the length so that the spiral doesn't touch the bottom of the jar when the pencil is suspended across the jar (see Figure 10–3). Allow crystals to build for several weeks. Remove and let the rock-hard spiral air dry. Tiny holes in dead trees and animal shells, as well as bones filled with mineral solutions, are turned into stone this same way.

INTEGRATING ACTIVITIES

Math Experiences

Counting. The Grab Bag Game may be played with stones. Place a container of stones in the center of a circle of children. Let them take turns reaching in to scoop out as many stones as they can hold in two hands. Then count the results. Keep score with an abacus or a handheld calculator.

Buried Treasure. If a sandbox is available, bury a specific number of stones (or stones and shells, if you wish to include classifying) for children to hunt. A large sandbox may be "staked out" with string to form separate territories for several children to use amicably.

Counting Cans. Mark numerals from 1 to 10 (or more) on the sides of low metal cans. Line up the cans in order on a table or shelf. Place a coffee can full of gravel beside them for independent counting of appropriate quantities of stones to put in numbered cans.

Ordering. Search through the bucket of gravel to find stones of conspicuously different sizes. Place them in a paper bag. One child at a time can reach into the bag to choose a stone to order by size. Allow time for much fingering and feeling in choosing. Ask for the smallest stone found. Next, ask children to compare their stones with the smallest one to find a stone just a bit larger to put next to it. Build up to the largest stone. Older children who have had experience measuring with rulers could use them for this activity. Suggest ordering rocks according to texture, from smoothest to roughest, and color, from lightest to darkest.

Weighing. Keep two coffee cans full of stones near the classroom balance for independent use by the children.

Music (Resources in Appendix A)

1. A familiar folk song can easily be adapted to help children remember that mountains are rock formations. Sing "The Bear Went Over the Mountain," substituting "But all that he could see was the rocky part of the mountain" for "But

all that he could see was the other part of the mountain." You could mention that some mountains are covered with soil and growing things, while other mountains are bare rock on top.

2. Listen to "I Love Mud" on Rick Charette's *Alligator in the Elevator.*

Literature Links

BRANLEY, FRANKLYN. (2005). *Earthquakes.* New York: HarperCollins. Household illustrations, geological background, and historical bits add reality to the earthquake experience. Safety tips prepare readers for survival.

EWART, CLAIRE. (2004). *Fossil.* New York: Walker. In this simple rhyming story, a child learns from her mother how a prehistoric animal bone became a stone.

FIRESTONE, MARY. (2005). *Clay.* Mankato, MN: Capstone. What is this common, but rarely discussed material? The answer is here, as well as a surprising recipe for making clay from mud.

McLARREN, ALICE. (2004). *Roxaboxen.* New York: HarperCollins. Children build a wonderful play village outlined by rocks.

McNULTY, FAITH. (2005). *If you decide to go to the moon.* New York: Scholastic. Igneous rock formation is included in this wonderful story about an imaginary trip to the moon.

MORGANELLI, ADRIANNA. (2004). *Minerals (rocks, minerals, and resources).* New York: Crabtree. An interesting array of topics and engaging photos make this a good browsing reference for independent readers.

OSTOPOWICH, MELANIE. (2005). *Rocks.* New York: Weigel. A bright text, intriguing rock facts, and excellent photos will hold independent readers' interest in rock fundamentals. NSTA* recommended.

ROSINSKY, NATALIE. (2003). *Rocks: Hard, soft, smooth and rough.* Minneapolis: Picture Window. Texture is featured as one way to classify rocks. NSTA* recommended.

ROSS, MICHAEL. (2004). *What's the matter in Mr. Whisker's room?* Cambridge, MA: Candlewick. Mr. Whisker's class has a good time exploring forms of matter. They compare rocks with magnifiers and a balance scale.

STEWART, MELISSA. *Down to earth.* (2004). Minneapolis: Compass Point. The wise author engages independent readers in sensory explorations of soil and rocks *before* providing explanations. A game, activities, and Web sites follow.

WALKER, SALLY. (2007). *Rocks.* Minneapolis: Lerner. Great photographs that reveal almost touchable rock textures will easily pull independent readers into learning how basic rock types are formed.

Classics

ANHOLT, LAWRENCE. (1999). *Stone girl, bone girl: The story of Mary Anning.* New York: Orchard. A determined young English girl unearths the rare fossil of a giant fish-lizard in the 1800s.

CHRISTIAN, PEGGY. (2000). *If you find a rock.* New York: Harcourt. Children are sure to connect with the personal meaning of special rocks charmingly photographed in this Zolotow Award–winning book

SIEBERT, DIANE. (2000). *Cave.* New York: HarperCollins. A poetic text accurately describes limestone cave formation, the special creatures that live within, and the "crystal world from weeping stones" (stalactites and stalagmites).

---

*National Science Teachers Association.

Poems (Resources in Appendix A)

Read "Plink by Plink," a poem about stalactite formation, by Constance Levy in *Splash! Poems of Our Watery World.*
Read the profound poem "Rocks" by Florence Parry Heide in *Spectacular Science: A Book of Poems.*
Read "Rock Tumbler" by Constance Levy in *A Tree Place: And Other Poems.*
Read the following poem with a box of your favorite rocks at hand.

> *My Rocks*
>
> *Here in this box*
>
> *I keep my rocks.*
>
> *They came from under the ground.*
>
> *Some are striped, some are plain,*
>
> *Some are tiny as a grain.*
>
> *My favorite is round.*
>
> —J. H.

Art Activities

Rock Sculpture. Let children create additive sculpture by joining rocks of assorted sizes using white glue. The resulting sculpture forms may be painted with tempera. Sculptures that have been coated with shellac (adult work) can be used as paperweights.

Sand Mosaics. For temporary pleasure, provide small, flat stones and small shells for children to create designs on dampened sand.

Zen Garden. Keep the connection with rocks alive during the rest of the school year by setting up a shallow tray of sand, one or two interesting rocks, and a toy rake or comb. Each day let a different child arrange satisfying sand patterns around the rock to create a peacefulness reminder.

Rock or Sand Collage. Small stones, painted if desired, can be glued in patterns to heavy cardboard. Color sand by shaking it in a tightly covered jar with dry tempera paint. Punch nail holes in the lids to make sand shakers. Let the children paint swirls of diluted white glue on construction paper using cotton swabs, then sprinkle colored sand over the glue patterns. Surplus sand can be tipped onto a small tray and reused.

Chalk Drawings. When children use chalk as an art medium, remind them that the chalk material was once a rock.

Sand Painting. Prepare four colors of sand as you did for the collages. Give each child a clear, screw-topped container. Let them spoon successive layers of sand into the container, being careful not to disturb the container. Probe gently along the inside of the container with a toothpick to produce interesting designs.

Complex traditional floor sand paintings are valued in many cultures. Six-year-old Simone made her own simple design on the floor of an Ohio cave, using pigment she gathered by rubbing together bits of red sandstone.

"Found-Clay" Making. Try to locate a natural source of clay: a stream bank, a ditch, or an eroded place are often good sources. (Ask a local potter for suggestions.) Dig out some clay together with the children, if possible. Notice the texture. Are there rocks in it? Do the children have ideas about how to make it as smooth as commercially available clay? One way is to soak the clay in a bucket of water for several days until it becomes liquid. Strain it, and allow it to settle into layers. This process takes several days, so be patient. When the clay dries somewhat, it can be worked and shaped.

Play

Introduce rocks as a play material in the indoor or outdoor sandbox. Rocks can be formed in lines to make the floor plan of a house. They can also be piled up to make furniture, and sticks or clothespins can become the people who live in the house. Lines of rocks can also outline highways for toy cars to travel through sand-table dunes and deserts. In addition, children find relaxed enjoyment using sifters to separate the rocks from the sand at cleanup time. *Roxaboxen* by Alice McLarren is the charming story of children who built a play town of rock outlines.

Creative Movement

Take a "rock walk." Children enjoy moving in a circle, interpreting movement suggestions, and following the rhythm of the teacher's drumbeats or clapping. Adult participation in the activity encourages the involvement of children. Suggest ways to move in a story form such as this: "Let's go for a rock walk. Let's pretend to be barefooted. We'll start on this gravel path. Oh! It's hard to put our feet down on the broken rocks. We'll have to move quickly and lightly to the end of the path. Step, step, step, step. There, that's better. We've come to a sandy place. Let's scuffle our feet in the sand. Scuffle, scuffle, push up little piles of sand with each step. Oh, look! We've come to a wet place where we have to walk on moss-covered rocks. They are so slippery to walk on; let's move very carefully with each step. Look at that huge rock. Let's try to climb it, bending way over to hold on with our hands. Climb slowly, slowly. Now we're at the top. Let's run down the other side to the beach ahead. Run, run, run to the sandy beach. But this sand is hot from the sunshine. We can't move slowly here. Let's move quickly down to the edge of the water to cool our feet. Now let's sit down to rest."

Creative Thinking

Encourage children to bring a favorite small rock to school or choose a special rock from the classroom supply. "Pick up your rock; feel its shape and texture. Now close your eyes and imagine that your rock has become 1,000 times larger than it is. It's huge! It's large enough to climb and explore. Is it a steep climb? How does it feel under your feet? Your hands? Are there crevices to explore? Can you find a flat place to sit on your rock?" Continue offering sensory ways to get acquainted with the rock; then let the rock resume its usual size so that the children can return from their rock climb to the classroom.

Food Experiences

Children are surprised to find that we eat small amounts of one kind of rock every day—salt. Show them some rock salt (available in grocery and hardware stores as *halite*). Mention that all the salt that is mined under the ground was once part of ancient oceans.

Another link between food and rocks is the use of grainy-surface rocks to grind seeds into meal and grain. Perhaps you can find a bag of stone-ground flour or cornmeal in a natural foods shop. (One teacher let fascinated children grind dried corn between two rocks as part of a study of Native Americans.)

The best pizzas are baked on special stones, and heated stones can be used in bun-warmer baskets. Primitive people cooked on stones heated in fire pits.

Bring in a cereal box and then read aloud the minerals listed on the nutrition facts label. Calcium, potassium, sodium, zinc, iron, and copper all play a part in keeping our bodies strong and healthy. They are found in small amounts in the nutritious foods we eat.

Field Trips

Walk around the school neighborhood to look for the following: rocks in their natural setting, rocks that have been cut for use in buildings, and products made from rocks and minerals. Look closely at the natural rock for signs of weathering, such as cracks or surfaces worn smooth by years of exposure to heat, cold, wind, and rain. Young children personalize familiar rocks according to the events they associate with them: our picnic rock, our sitting-on rock, our story-time rock, and our where-we-found-the-turtle rock. Use the special rock names when you can.

Look for old stone steps or stone curbings that have been worn down into sloping shapes by the thousands of feet treading on them. Look for monuments, stone walls, and stone windowsills in old brick buildings and flagstone or crushed limestone paths.

Manufactured materials containing rocks and minerals are everywhere. Concrete or blacktop playground surfaces contain coarse or fine gravel bonded together with concrete or asphalt, both derived from rocks. Cement blocks, bricks, tiles, terrazzo flooring, porcelain sinks, glass, iron railings, steel slides, and fences around school playgrounds are made with rock or mineral raw materials. No school is without structures of this sort to visit. Talking about these strong, solid parts of their environment seems to contribute to children's feeling of security.

Make an ecological scavenger hunt the focus of a field activity, as teacher Margaret Drysdale does. She takes her classes to an empty lot where they check the area for debris. They classify their collected materials into two piles: manufactured materials and natural materials. She explains that only the things from nature can be left on the ground, because they will decompose and eventually become part of the soil. The class carries the manufactured materials back to the school recycling/trash bin because those things won't decompose. She emphasizes that a discarded aluminum can or plastic item could still be littering the land when the children are old enough to be grandparents.

PROMOTING CONCEPT CONNECTIONS

Maintaining Concepts

Because rocks and minerals are so commonplace, the topic would become tedious if reference were made to them at every opportunity. Do mention rocks when something a bit different prompts a comment, such as "Is Lynn wearing a very special rock in her bracelet today? Tell us about it." Bring interesting rocks to share with the children whenever you come across one. Talk about its texture, color, or whatever appeals to you. The children will respond similarly with their favorites when they know about your appreciation of rocks.

Improving School Grounds

Think about developing the geologic features of the school grounds. A Boston school has a huge piece of native "puddingstone." At Coombes School, head Sue Humphries has trucked in rocks and boulders from every part of Great Britain. The local boulder sits by the school's front door for the children to pat and look at every day. A large throne-shaped rock from the area associated with King Arthur is at the edge of the school field, where children can climb and sit on it. A more modest project is at Washington School in Little Rock, Arkansas, where labeled basketball-sized rocks from across the state are placed on the path leading to a wildlife habitat. Such projects provide children with ongoing opportunities to learn about rocks.

Connecting Concepts

The inclusion of rocks as materials for experimentation is suggested for the topics of water and the effects of gravity. It could be pointed out in discussing the effects of magnetism that the original source of magnetic material is a rock called *lodestone* (magnetite). Magnetite is found in this country near Magnet Cove, Arkansas.

The tie between soil formation and growing things is an easy relationship to mention. Wet sand is sometimes used as a growing medium for rooting stems such as begonias or pineapple tops. The powdered rock made when children pounded soft rocks could be used in a seed-germinating experience. Compare the results with those of seeds growing in good topsoil containing humus and other rotted organic matter.

Discuss how thoroughly rotted natural materials improve the soil so that healthy, strong plants will grow. Ask: "Do people use some plants for food?" Talk about renewing the soil this way as one of the wonderful cycles of nature: from living plants to decomposition, from enriched soil to living plants and food, again and again. Talk about saving and improving the soil with compost as one way that people help to renew our planet.

If possible, in early fall, bury several nonbiodegradable materials such as a plastic spoon, a foam cup, or an aluminum can in a marked location on the school grounds. Also include a paper bag and a regular plastic bag. Dig them up in late spring to see if the biodegradable and nonbiodegradable materials were affected differently in the soil. Encourage the children to make the connection between what they observed and our need to reuse and recycle manufactured objects that do not decompose. Celebrate Earth Day, April 22.

Family and Community Support

Invite families to share special rocks or fossils with the class. Masking tape name labels are helpful for ensuring the safe return of borrowed rocks. Suggest that parents point out to their children areas of rock exposed by highway construction or special rocks that are landmarks in the area. Win the hearts of parents by forewarning them to check the pockets of their children's jackets and jeans for rocks before laundering them now that the children's interest in rocks has been whetted.

Many local museums have rock displays, some more engaging than others. A natural history museum in your area may have a dazzling display of crystals or mysterious phosphorescent rocks glowing in a darkened room. A nature center may have hands-on rock exploration tables. Local rock hobbyists may have an annual show.

RESOURCES

BOURGEOIS, PAULETTE. (2008*). The dirt on dirt.* Tonawanda, NY: Kids Can Press. This book for upper grades will add zest to your plans for soil investigations.

ESTIGARRIBIA, DIANA. (2005). *Learning about rocks, weathering, and erosion with graphic organizers.* New York: Power Kids Press. More advanced concepts of natural changes to rocks are easier to grasp when charted, diagrammed, and organized as this book suggests.

OGU, UCHENNA, & REYNARD-SCHMIDT, SUZIE. (2009). Investigating rocks and sand: Addressing multiple learning styles through an inquiry-based approach. *Young Children, 64*(2), 10–18.

PRESTWICH, DOROTHY, SUMRALL, JOSEPH, & CHESSIN, DEBBY. (2010). Science rocks! *Science and Children, 47*(7), 86–88. A rocks study is used as the medium for teaching reading and math to cognitively disabled children.

STEWART, MELISSA. (2002). *Crystals.* Chicago: Heinemann. This reference covers the nature, formation, and uses of crystals, gemstones, and a crystal-making activity.

STEWART, MELISSA. (2008). *Earthquakes and volcanoes.* New York: HarperCollins. Dramatic photographs, excellent background information, and tips for earthquake safety are provided.

SYMES, R. F. (2004). *Rocks and minerals.* New York: DK Publishing. A fascinating browsing book for classroom reference.

 ## *ONLINE RESOURCES*

Federal Emergency Management Agency offers a bibliography of books on disasters for kids and a variety of preparedness materials at *http://www.fema.gov/kids*

Mineralogy 4 Kids. Mineralogical Society of America: *http://www.minsocam.org/MSA/K12?K_12.html*

Mrs. Stewart's Bluing: The recipe for developing a salt crystal "garden," its scientific explanation, and information for ordering a Salt Crystal Garden Kit are available at *http://www.mrsstewart.com*

Smithsonian Gem and Mineral collection: *http://www.gimizu.de/sgmcol*

Walrus: U.S. Geological Services scientists provide e-mail answers for your questions about volcanoes, earthquakes, rocks, and mountains. *http://walrus.wr.usgs.gov/ask-a-geologist/*

Magnetism

Unseen, ever-present, constantly at work in our daily lives generating electricity and guiding electronic devices: that's the awesome force of magnetism! But it will be our childhood memories of the wonder and fun of magnets that will help us lead children to investigate magnetic effects they can feel and see in their own hands.

Magnets attract iron, steel, and the attention of young children. Although magnetic attraction cannot be seen or felt, its effects can. Children can accept the reality of this invisible force when they have experience putting that force to work. The following concepts underlie the experiences in this chapter:

- Magnets attract some things but not others.
- Magnets vary in strength.
- Magnets pull through some materials.
- One magnet can be used to make another magnet.
- Magnets are strongest at each end.
- Each end of a magnet acts differently.

In this chapter, children will experiment with familiar objects to see what magnets will pull and what they will pull through, make temporary magnets, and discover how opposite magnetic poles affect each other. For all magnet experiences, teachers are cautioned that computers, discs, peripherals, credit cards, and tapes rely on magnetic force to operate. Children experimenting with magnets near these objects can seriously disrupt them.

CONCEPT: **Magnets attract some things but not others.**

1. What will magnets attract?

LEARNING OBJECTIVE: To enjoy investigating and drawing conclusions about magnetic effects.

MATERIALS:

Magnets of assorted shapes and sizes

Small foam meat tray filled with test items for each pair of children (iron/steel suggestions: keys, key chains, bolts, screws, nails, paper clips; non-iron/steel items: pennies, brass fasteners, rubber bands, plastic, glass, wood, or aluminum objects)

2 large trays or box covers

GETTING READY:

Have only magnets on the table when children gather. Count them together. (Tiny magnets are easily misplaced.)

Prepare a mixed collection of objects for each pair of children.

Tape a *yes* label on one tray and a *no* label on the other.

SMALL-GROUP ACTIVITY:

1. Give each child a paper clip and a small magnet to try out. To see the effect well, slide the magnet toward the clip on the tabletop. To feel the effect, hold the clip in the palm of the hand.
2. "Do you think the magnet will pull everything to it? Find out with the things on the small trays."
3. After some exploration, suggest sorting objects pulled by the magnets from those that are not. Use the *yes/no* trays.
4. "Things on the *yes* tray do not look alike, but they are made of the same stuff." Children may note that all items are metal. You can use the specific terms *iron* or *steel*: "Magnets pull only on the iron or steel objects." (Magnets also attract cobalt and nickel, two minerals not commonly used alone in manufactured articles.)

♣ Take magnets outdoors for pairs of children to investigate which objects in the natural and built environments are attracted by magnets. One child in each pair can work with the magnet, and the other can take notes on a notepad. You may want to block off part of the school parking lot to allow children to investigate car bumpers, license plates, hubcaps, and tires. (Caution against investigating the rest of the car because magnets can scratch paint and make you unpopular in the school!) Include the school building in the investigation.

Note: Toy magnets are rarely strong enough for school use. School suppliers and scientific equipment suppliers sell sturdy magnets. A reusable magnet source is old sound system speakers. Scientific equipment outlet stores carry as many as 40 shapes (rings, cylinders, bars, horseshoes) and kinds (steel, ceramic, rubber) of magnets. (See Appendix A for catalogs.)

CONCEPT: Magnets vary in strength.

1. Which magnet is strongest? Which is weakest?

LEARNING OBJECTIVE: To take satisfaction in controlling variables and making accurate assessments.

? *Inquiry Activity:* Set up a center for pairs of children to compare the strength of several magnets of different sizes and shapes. Number the magnets with nail polish. Prepare a Magnet Strength Study chart with Pulling Power across and Magnet Number down. On a strip of paper, trace around a paper clip to indicate where investigators should put a paper clip. Mark a line a few inches away where the end of a magnet should be. Do this for each magnet. Investigators slowly slide the magnet toward the clip. When the clip is attracted to the magnet, investigators mark where the end of the magnet is; then they measure the distance between the two magnet marks with a ruler and record the results for each magnet on a class record sheet. The strongest magnet will pull the clip that is farthest away. The weaker magnets need to be closer to attract the clip. Encourage children to bring in name-marked magnets of all sorts from home to test. Compile the results when all investigators have completed their tests.

Math skill: Measuring how far a magnet can attract a paper clip.

CONCEPT: Magnets pull through some materials.

1. How well can magnets pull through things that are not attracted?

LEARNING OBJECTIVE: To enjoy investigating materials through which magnetic force can pass.

MATERIALS:

Magnets*

Steel wool pad

Iron and steel objects (nails, washers, bolts, clips)

Paper, cardboard, aluminum

Shoe box

Tumblers

SMALL-GROUP ACTIVITY:

1. "Do you know what this (steel wool) is made of? Could a magnet help you find the answer?"
2. Tear off bits of steel wool. Give some to each child. Find out if a magnet can pick up steel that is covered with a piece of paper. Try cardboard and aluminum. "Will

---

*The thickness of the noniron material and the strength of the magnet are factors in the success of this experiment. A strong, new magnet will attract a paper clip through one's fingertip or a magnetic earring through one's earlobe. A weak magnet will not attract a paper clip through cardboard. To keep magnets strong, always store two bar magnets together with opposite poles touching (north to south and south to north) when not in use.

Sand or dirt
Water

GETTING READY:

Put steel object in tumbler.

Put steel objects in box; cover with sand.

Put water in another tumbler; drop a washer in it.

magnetism pull through these things to pick up steel?"

3. Touch the magnet to the outside of a dry tumbler. Does it attract the steel object inside the tumbler? Try different magnets and different objects.

4. Suggest dipping the magnet into the sand-filled box and the tumbler of water. Can magnetism pass through materials that it does not attract? Later, if the classroom has an aquarium, use a magnetic scraper to clean off algae inside the tank.

Note: Children can help keep magnets strong by remembering to put a steel "keeper bar" across both ends of a horseshoe magnet. They can also keep magnets strong by not jarring them. A child may believe that a keeper bar is also a magnet—one that just doesn't happen to work right when it is separated from the magnet. Based on the child's experience, a plain bar of metal has no assigned function. Find a familiar iron or steel object to use as a temporary keeper bar. "Children's scissors are not magnets. Will a magnet attract them? If so, then we can leave this pair of scissors across the ends of the horseshoe magnet to keep it strong while you experiment with the other keeper bar." Experience may clarify a child's ideas about the keeper bar, while verbal persuasion by an adult may not.

CONCEPT: **One magnet can be used to make another magnet.**

1. How can we make a magnet?

LEARNING OBJECTIVE: To take pride in creating a temporary magnet.

MATERIALS:

2-in. (5-cm) blunt needles or straightened steel paper clips

Strong bar magnet

Steel wool

SMALL-GROUP ACTIVITY:

1. Let children use the magnet to determine if needles or clips are made of steel.

2. "Try to pick up steel wool bits with the needles or clips. Are they magnetic?" (They won't be, yet.)

3. Show children how to pull the needle across one end of the magnet in one direction. Count aloud about 25 strokes.

4. "Now try to attract steel wool with the needle. It should be magnetized. It has become a temporary magnet."

Note: This is a good time to demonstrate how jarring a magnet weakens it. Hit the magnetized needle against something hard a few times. Now try to pick up some light steel object. The pull will be very weak.

CONCEPT: Magnets are strongest at each end.

1. Which parts of a magnet are strongest?

LEARNING OBJECTIVE: To be fascinated by the location of power in magnets.

MATERIALS:

Bits of steel wool

Paper clips, steel key chain, or light switch pull chain about 3 in. (7.5 cm) long

Horseshoe and bar magnets

GETTING READY:

Cut the steel wool into fine bits. (Did some of the steel cling to the scissor edges? The scissors became a temporary magnet.)

Open the key chain full length.

SMALL-GROUP ACTIVITY:

1. Hold the curved end of the horseshoe magnet over steel wool. Notice if any steel is attracted to the middle of this magnet. "Now hold the ends of the magnet over the steel wool. Do the ends act differently from the middle?" Try using a bar magnet.
2. Touch the chain with both ends of a bar magnet. Notice whether the whole chain clings to the magnet or if the middle part dangles free. (The chain should be longer than the bar magnet.)
3. Dangle the key chain ¼ in. (1 cm) above the center of a bar magnet. (The pull of a strong magnet will visibly curve the end of the chain toward one end of the magnet.)

Math skill: Observing different parts of magnets to see where the effect is strongest.

CONCEPT: Each end of a magnet acts differently.

1. How do the ends of magnets act?

LEARNING OBJECTIVE: To see and feel the intriguing pulling power of unlike magnet ends and the push of like ends.

MATERIALS:

2 strong bar magnets

String

Nail polish or tape

Compass (desirable)

SMALL-GROUP ACTIVITY:

1. Tie the string to the center of a magnet, balancing it.
2. Let the magnet hang and swing freely. When it stops moving, one end of the bar

GETTING READY:

If using lightweight magnets, tape the string to a tabletop or chair seat.

Tie the string to any horizontal bar or chair back that will allow a heavy magnet to swing freely.

will be pointing north. Mark this end with tape or a dot of nail polish. Do the same for the second magnet. If a compass is available, place it on a level surface so that children can see the pointer swinging to the north.*

3. Let the children hold a magnet in each hand, then try to touch like ends (north to north, south to south). "What do you feel? Try to touch unlike ends. What happens?" Give children lots of time to explore the attraction and repulsion effects. With strong magnets, results are fascinating.

See where this magnet is strong?

*The magnetic compass pointer lines up the same way. When the compass is flat, the pointer swings freely and comes to rest with the tip pointing north. This happens because Earth is a gigantic magnet with a magnetic north pole and a magnetic south pole. Its force is pulling the north-seeking tip of the pointer that way. (The legendary Santa is at the geographic North Pole, not quite the same location.)

2. How strong are magnets of different shapes?

LEARNING OBJECTIVE: To be surprised that magnets, small or large, always have north and south ends.

MATERIALS:

Play dough
Table knife
3 ring magnets
Disc magnets
Horseshoe magnet

LARGE-GROUP ACTIVITY:

1. Show ring, disc, and horseshoe magnets. Learn what children think about the positive and negative ends of these magnets. (It can be confusing to perceive the sides of a flat disc as the ends of a magnet.)
2. Point to each end of a horseshoe magnet. "This magnet was bent, bringing the two ends close together to make the pulling power stronger. Let's find out how a disc magnet is made using a play-dough model." Roll a handful of dough into a long cylinder. "A long magnet is made first. The power is in each end. Where are the north and south ends?"
3. Cut the cylinder in half. "Now there are two magnets, each with north/south ends. The power collects at each end, whether the magnet is long or short." (See Figure 11–1.)
4. Cut a narrow slice from a cylinder. Find the north/south ends of the still vertical slice. "The power still collects at each end. Ring and disc magnets are slices of a longer magnet."

FIGURE 11–1

5. Stand several disc or ring magnets side by side, north/south poles together to form a cylinder. Then "float" three ring magnets by slipping them onto a vertically held pencil, with like ends facing to repel. "The power is always in the ends, no matter how they are turned." Let children explore the power of an assortment of disc and ring magnets to attract paper clips and other magnets.

INTEGRATING ACTIVITIES

Math Experiences

Magnet in the Grab Bag. Half-fill a large grocery bag with used steel bottle caps, common nails, paper clips, or other small steel objects. Use a string to tie a strong magnet to a stick, fishpole style. Let children take turns dipping the magnet into the bag and then counting aloud the number of objects they have pulled up. A numeral recognition version of this game can be played by cutting out colored paper fish, writing a numeral on each, and fastening a paper clip or safety pin to each fish.

Magnetic Numerals. Plastic numerals and counting shapes are made with magnets to use on steel-coated bulletin boards. Use them to form sets of objects, labeled with corresponding numerals. Make a game of this by letting children draw the numerals from a paper bag, choose the corresponding quantity of objects, and place them on the bulletin board. You may have an old tin-coated steel baking sheet in your kitchen that would substitute well for the commercial steel bulletin board.

Magnet Song

(To the tune of: "The Cat Came Back")

—J.H.

Music

Mention to children that we couldn't hear sounds from a stereo, VCR, radio, television set, or tape recorder without magnets. Recording tape is coated with magnetized powdered iron, and the other four devices have magnets in their mechanisms.

Sing the "Magnet Song."

Literature Links

HIRSCHMANN, KRIS. (2006). *Magnets.* Farmington Hills, MI: Thomson Gale. Good explanations of how the compass and magnetic toys work are given.
LEVINE, SHAR, & JOHNSTONE, LESLIE. (2006). *Magnet power.* New York: Sterling. Some fresh approaches to investigating magnetic force, each carefully explained.

MORGAN, BEN. (2003). *Magnetism.* Farmington Hills, MI: Blackbirch Press. Informative photographs, an uncluttered layout, and simple activities present concepts clearly and at a good level for independent readers.

ROSINSKY, NATALIE. (2003). *Magnets pulling together, pushing apart.* Minneapolis: Picture Window Books. Smoothly written information on the properties and uses of magnets.

SADLER, WENDY. (2006). *Magnets—sticking together.* Chicago: Raintree. There are few invitations to actively explore the concepts described in this book, but its coverage of applications of magnetic force will help readers appreciate the essential role of magnets in our everyday lives. Current ideas about how migrating animals are guided by Earth's magnetic field are included.

Classics

PFEFFER, WENDY. (1995). *Marta's magnets.* Parsippany, NJ: Silver Press. Marta shares her magnet collection with children in her new neighborhood and helps solve the problem of a down-the-drain-key. NSTA* Outstanding Trade Book.

PILEGARD, VIRGINIA. (2002). *The warlord's fish.* Gretna, LA: Pelican. A boy in ancient China saves his captors when a sandstorm wipes out their caravan trail. He makes a water compass to safely guide the band to an oasis in this exciting story.

ROYSTON, ANGELA. (2001). *Magnets.* Plymouth, NH: Heinemann. Written at a comfortable level for independent readers, this book describes and illustrates uses of magnets in familiar contexts. NSTA* recommended.

Poems (Resources in Appendix A)

Read "Magnet," by Valerie Worth in *Spectacular Science: A Book of Poems,* compiled by Lee Bennett Hopkins.

Storytelling with Magnets

Tell a story featuring practical uses of magnetic gadgets that could also be props for the telling. A small magnet could save the day when Father drops his keys down the register, when Sister's box of hair clips spills in her bubble bath, when someone upsets a box of pins, or when a glass jar of nails breaks on the garage floor. These and other calamities could be resolved with an upholsterer's tack hammer, a magnetic-holder flashlight, a paper clip or pin box with a magnetized top, or other magnetic equipment that may be available.

The effects of magnetism can be used throughout the school year as a storytelling device in the following three ways.

Magnetically Directed Puppets. Tape a paper clip to the bottoms of small wooden dollhouse dolls. Put an open shoe box on its side to make a platform for the puppets (Figure 11–2). Make the puppets move by holding magnets in each hand beneath the platform. (Puppets can be thread spools with button heads glued on, clothespin dolls with paper clip feet, or pipe cleaner dolls.) Children love using magnet puppets to retell familiar stories or to create their own plays.

---

*National Science Teachers Association.

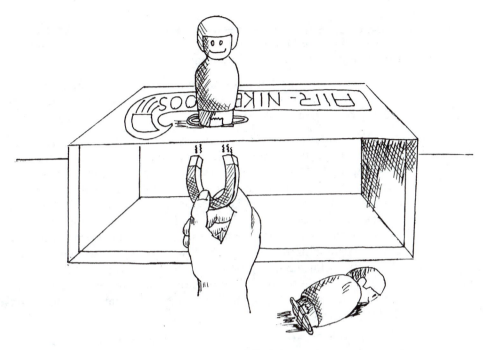

FIGURE 11–2

Paper Doll Stories. Cut out paper figures to illustrate a story. Tape paper clips or small safety pins to the backs. Invert a large grocery bag (plain or decorated) as a backdrop, and manipulate the paper figures with magnets held inside the bag.

Magnetic Bulletin Board Stories. Use fabric or paper figures as you would for a flannel board story. Hold them in place with a shirt-button-sized magnet. Try to fit one of the whimsical magnet insects into the story. Sheet steel bulletin boards with colorful magnet disks are sold in office supply stores. Use one for creating messages from magnetic poetry sets.

Art Activities

Make junk sculpture with iron or steel.

1. Prepare steel bottle caps by punching two nail holes into each one.

2. Prepare sculpture bases using mounds of damp clay, chunks of foam, or cardboard fruit trays.

3. Put out a tray full of iron and steel discards (paper clips, nails, steel bottle caps, hairpins, pipe cleaners, twist bag closures, washers, soft wire). Put out several magnets so that the children can test materials for magnetic attraction. Explain that the sculpture for today will be made only of iron or steel.

4. Show how wire can be threaded through the punched bottle caps, how paper clips can be opened, and how wire pipe cleaners can be coiled around a finger to make interesting shapes.

Play

Automobile Service. Tie a small magnet to a toy tow truck for children to use in hauling steel cars to the garage.

Block Play. Fasten disc magnets with rubber bands to the front of small plastic cars, some with north-seeking poles facing outward, others with south-seeking poles facing outward.

Fascinating Attractions. If magnetic marbles are available, prepare a dozen of them after school, making the poles evident. Choose six marbles of two different colors. Carefully separate the outside of the marbles at the seam, using a butter knife. Find the north pole of the small magnets inside. Then reconnect the marbles as two-tones, consistently using one color for the north pole and the other color for the south pole. Let children enjoy rolling marbles toward each other, sending them spinning, making chains and patterns, and holding one marble above the others to see what happens. Help them make the connection between the colors and the poles if they don't figure this out for themselves. (Confine this activity to a tray with sides. Also, announce the number of marbles that should always be on the tray, as pockets have a way of attracting these charming toys.)

Magnet Construction Box. Collect three or four small, strong magnets with keeper bars (or nails to serve that purpose). Find iron and steel discarded items similar to those suggested for the junk sculpture. Try to include steel key chains, notebook rings, old keys, and cocoa box lids. Children enjoy combining odd shapes that are held together by magnetic attraction. Try to find a tin cookie box for storing the game. The lid and the box can serve as bases for the constructions, since the tin is a coating for steel.

Commercial magnetic building sets are available through school equipment catalogs. Magnetic games and magnet sculpture sets are available in toy and specialty stores. The Magna Doodle toy uses a magnetic wand to make iron filing designs on a screen. A fine magnetic play set is available through HearthSong: Magnuts. These sturdy, flexible action figures wearing magnetic boots are ready to do acrobatics, climb steel cabinets, grasp cords, ride a cable car, and more.

Creative Thinking

I Am a Magnet. Collect a tray of assorted objects: key, steel bottle cap, spool, stick, rock, nail, bolt, paper clip. Sit with the children in a circle on the floor. Place the tray in the center. Start off as the leader when introducing the game. Ask the child next to you to choose one of the objects to pretend to be. Say, "I am a great, strong magnet. What are you, Maria?" If Maria replies that she is a bottle cap, say, "Then we'll cling together," and hold her hand. Encourage Maria to say to the child next to her, "Josh, I'm a magnetized bottle cap. What are you?" If Josh decides to be a rock, Maria goes on to the next child until she finds someone to cling to. End the game with "Now I am a teacher again, and my pulling strength is gone."

PROMOTING CONCEPT CONNECTIONS

Maintaining Concepts

Point out magnets in use around the school whenever they come to your attention: refrigerator door sealing strips, car seat belt clasps, fancy buckles on children's belts, cupboard door latches. For the last example, it is a good idea to suggest that children using those cupboards try to close them gently, without banging them, so that the magnets won't lose their strength. Show how the force of magnetism is used for banking, shopping, and other purposes by pointing out the magnetic strip on an ATM or credit card.

Make magnets a standard part of classroom cleanup equipment. Hang a magnet and a keeper bar on a low peg near the workbench if you have one. Let the children use it on the floor, in workbench drawers, or on the workbench to gather up stray nails. Use it to sort out tiny nails from wooden shapes after children have worked with hammer-on design kits. Use the magnet to locate small steel cars that have become buried in the sandbox.

Improving School Grounds

A compass showing the directions, N–S–E–W, can be painted on the asphalt. Upper elementary children can design and paint this graphic. Children can check pocket compasses against it.

Connecting Concepts

1. When discussing the effect of magnetism passing through materials, ask the children whether air is one of the substances that magnetism passes through. How can they tell? Recall with the children that even though we cannot see air or magnetism, we have discovered that both are real things.

2. Set up a water play game that depends on magnetic force passing through water. Let the children make barge-shaped boats from pressed foam, and fasten a paper clip to each boat with a rubber band. Stack three blocks under each end of a shallow cake pan. Fill the pan with water and launch the foam boats on it. Children can guide their boats through the water with magnets held beneath the pan.

3. Combine buoyancy and the principles of attraction and repulsion of like magnetic poles in a water play activity. Help the children magnetize 2-in. (5-cm) blunt needles, then place them on top of barge-shaped foam boats. Float the boats in a pan of water. Push the boats ahead by approaching the end of the needle with the like pole of a magnet; pull the boats back with the unlike pole of the magnet. If a needle rolls off a boat, the children can go fishing for it in the water with a magnet.

4. Make a simple marine compass model when studying explorers. Float a magnetized needle, which has been taped to a bit of foam tray, in a cereal bowl filled with water. Gently tilt the bowl back and forth, noting that the water level, and

therefore the needle compass, is constant. (Gravity pulls on all things, so both shallow and deep water in a container are pulled down to the same level.) Explorers had a reliable compass to guide them when the stars or sun weren't visible and storms rocked their ships. See *Science Through the Ages* by Janice VanCleave or *Reinvent the Wheel* by Ruth Kassinger.

Family and Community Support

Ask families to lend interesting souvenir or advertising magnets to a classroom steel cabinet or desk display. Label the collection with magnetic letters or put together a display slogan with words from a magnetic poetry set.

Notify families about the nearest children's museum or science museum that has interactive magnet exhibits. When families visit a public library with a magnetic scanning system at the exit, ask the librarian to explain how it works.

RESOURCES

KASSINGER, RUTH. (2001). *Reinvent the wheel.* New York: Wiley. Magnets have been used to guide sailors for about 2,000 years. Read the history of the marine compass and make a simple model. Columbus couldn't have sailed to the New World without one.

ROBERTSON, WILLIAM. (2004). *Stop faking it! Finally understanding science so you can teach it. Electricity and magnetism.* Arlington, VA: NSTA Press. You'll teach more confidently after this book slows down and eases the process of understanding magnetic force. It does so with a touch of humor.

VANCLEAVE, JANICE. (2002). *Science through the ages.* New York: Wiley. The history of compass development is offered in this book, together with directions for making simple wet and dry compasses.

WALKER, SALLY. (2006). *Magnetism.* Minneapolis: Lerner. Although the text seems to miss the target age for this children's book, the background information will be helpful for teachers. It offers a good translation of spinning electrons into children's kinesthetic understanding.

 **ONLINE RESOURCES**

Canada Science and Technology Museum: Find information for teachers about magnets at *http://www.sciencetech.technomuses.ca/english/schoolzone/Information_Magnetic.cfm*

HearthSong: Toy catalog at *http://www.hearthsong.com/-23K*

Wikipedia: Expand your background knowledge of magnetism with clear information at *http://en.wikipedia.org/wiki/Magnet*

The Effects of Gravity

Knowing about the force of gravity is a comforting revelation to children. Let your joy-ful memories of slipping down the highest slide, or flying skyward on the playground swings, or sledding down snowy slopes spark the activities that build children's awareness of gravity's presence in their lives.

Children who have felt the tug of invisible magnetic attraction with their own hands can move from this awareness to simple understanding about the effects of gravity. These children are ready to put credence in the far stronger invisible pull that holds people, houses, and schools on the ground—the force of gravity. The learning experiences in this chapter amplify one central concept:

Gravity pulls on everything.

Drawing children's attention to an ever-present effect that is rarely no-ticed or labeled calls for more preliminary description than we usually offer to action-loving children. The first suggested gravity experience is a story that provides basic information. The active experiences involve measuring and comparing gravity's pull on objects, exploring pendulums, and bringing things into balance.

INTRODUCTION

Lead into the gravity story by crushing a piece of paper into a ball and holding it between your fingers. Ask children, "What will happen to this ball of paper if I turn my hand over and open my fingers?" Find out if the children's predictions are correct. "Do you think the ball might do the same thing another time, or might it fall up instead? Did you ever stumble and fall up? Here is a story about the reason for this."

Use a flannel board and felt figures to illustrate your story. It could be stated somewhat as follows:

Once, a girl had a dream. Everything seemed very strange. The girl was floating in the air, looking for her house. She saw her friend floating close by with a ball in his arms. They wanted to play catch, but when the boy threw the ball, it drifted up out of reach. Then the girl saw her house bobbing up and down gently in the breeze. Her mom was very upset because somebody had spilled milk all over the ceiling. When the girl woke up, she was glad that her house was standing still.

"Something important was missing in that dream. Houses and balls and children don't float around. Milk doesn't spill up! There is a reason why those things don't happen. There is a very powerful force pulling down on everything in the world: the invisible force called *gravity*. We can't touch gravity or see it. We can just see what gravity does.

"Can you think of something else invisible that pulls some kinds of things? Gravity reminds us of the way magnets pull on iron and steel. But gravity is much, much stronger than magnetism. Gravity pulls from inside Earth. It pulls on everything all the time. We are so used to it that we don't even notice it happening."

Show a picture of an astronaut in his space suit. "The astronauts who walked on the moon had a strange experience. They had to wear very heavy boots to stand on the moon, because the moon's gravity pull is weaker than Earth's gravity pull.

"Let's see what we can find out about how much Earth's gravity is pulling on us."

CONCEPT: Gravity pulls on everything.

1. How can we become aware of gravity pulling on us?

LEARNING OBJECTIVE: To invite dawning awareness of the invisible force of gravity.

Invite a volunteer child to be the demonstration subject to introduce this activity. Have the child sit on a straight chair. Make sure that both of his or her feet are flat on the floor, the back is touching the chair back, and the hands are in the child's lap. Now ask the child to try to stand up without swaying his or her body forward and without moving any other muscles—not even a tiny bit. Encourage the child to try very hard to stand up and then report to the class what he or she is experiencing. Ask, "What will you have to do in order to stand up? Think about it."

Let the rest of the class take turns trying the experience in their small groups while others observe for motionlessness. Afterward, discuss what the children noticed. "What do you think held you to the chair when you didn't move a muscle? What did you need to do to stand up?"

Guide the discussion to the conclusion that it is gravity's force that holds us down in the chair. The force of gravity always pulls on everything. We have to use our energy to push ourselves out of the chair and stand up. It takes energy to move the muscles we use to stand up. It always takes energy to work against gravity's pull.

This child is feeling gravity's inexorable pull.

2. How does gravity's pull affect our body positioning?

LEARNING OBJECTIVE: To enjoy noticing how our bodies accommodate gravity's pull.

MATERIALS:

Bathroom scale

Kitchen scale

4 small, sturdy bags

Sand, pebbles

Market bag with handles

Containers, scoops

Long mirror, if possible

Low balance beam

GETTING READY:

Fill each small bag with 2 pounds of sand or stones.

SMALL-GROUP ACTIVITY:

1. "When we weigh ourselves on a scale, we find out how much gravity pulls on us."
2. Find out how much gravity pulls on each child. Record the weights.
3. Weigh the children again while they hold a sandbag in each hand. Compare with the first weight record. Which way does gravity pull more?
4. Put both sandbags in the market bag. Have children hold it in one hand so that the weight is on one side. Weigh each child again.
5. "Look in the mirror. Are you standing up straight now or leaning over? You lean away from the heavy side to keep your balance."

Math skills: Experiencing gravity's pull; comparing balance with weight location.

Let children discover how they use their arms as they walk, turn, and stand on one foot on a low balance beam.

Let children weigh objects on both scales. Containers of sand make good materials to weigh. Provide objects of varying weights and sizes. Let children discover that size does not always determine weight.

Group Discussion: Recall the earlier discussion about gravity holding everything down. Encourage children to share ideas about things that they see being pulled down from the sky by gravity (leaves, seeds, snowflakes, raindrops). Recall that, as long as it is moving, air can lift and keep gliders, kites, birds, and planes aloft for a while against gravity's pull. Can the children lift themselves all the way off the ground momentarily by using their energy to push against gravity?

3. How can we compare gravity's pull on objects?

LEARNING OBJECTIVE: To enjoy exploring how much gravity pulls on different materials by achieving equilibrium.

MATERIALS:

Scrap lumber: 2-ft (60-cm) piece of dowel or broomstick; 8-in. (20-cm) × 8-in. (20-cm) piece of shelving

Nails: 6d and 4d sizes

Yardstick (meterstick)

Pipe cleaners

2 or more small, reused yogurt cups, small holes poked near upper edge

Small objects to weigh: shells, washers, acorns, cotton balls, and the like

GETTING READY:

Drill holes or saw small notches 3 in. apart on a yardstick (8 cm apart on a meterstick).

Make a hole at 18 in. (50 cm) and mark with the 6d nail.

Make two holes on opposite sides of each cup.

SMALL-GROUP ACTIVITY:

1. To make base: Mark center of shelving square. Nail dowel perpendicular to center of base. (Let children do the hammering.)
2. Nail yardstick (meterstick) loosely near the top of the upright stick, driving a 4d nail through hole at the 18-in. (50-cm) mark. The yardstick (meterstick) should swing easily.
3. Insert pipe cleaners into yardstick (meterstick) holes. Hook them into cups. (Put one cup on either side. Let children add more cups as they wish.) If notches were made instead of drilled holes, make pipe cleaner handles for cups and hang them in notches.
4. Let children fill cups with small items to balance.
5. Provide materials as different in weight as cotton balls and shells. Do five cotton balls balance five shells? Is the balance arm lower on the shell side? What does this mean? (Gravity pulls more on shells; thus, we say that they weigh more than the cotton balls.)

Math skills: Experimenting with a balance beam scale; comparing gravity's pull on objects.

Set up a center with balances and containers of materials to weigh for independent investigations.

? *Inquiry Activity:* Show children a pebble and a palm-sized stone. Ask for, and record, their predictions and reasoning about whether or not the two objects would land on the floor at the same or different times if you dropped them simultaneously from the same height. With arms extended equally, as high as possible, drop the two objects. Without comment, ask children what they observed. (The effect is much clearer when objects are dropped from a great height.)

Take the class to the highest place accessible, outdoors or indoors, to conduct their own experiments. Provide two containers of indestructible objects to test: one container of small objects such as pebbles, marbles, acorns, sweetgum tree balls, cotton balls, or old keys, and one container of larger objects such as a baseball, rocks, a solid metal paperweight, or a #2 hand weight. Form small groups of experimenters, equipping groups with materials to record each person's comparison of two objects' weight, as well as the prediction of whether or not one object would fall faster than the other and the actual result. Discuss safety precautions; then let children experiment with items from each container, from the greatest height safely available.

Back in the classroom, compile the experiment results and draw conclusions.

Tell children that they have carried out a gravity experiment that astonished the scientific world about 400 years ago. Legend tells us that the famous scientist Galileo dropped balls of two sizes from the leaning tower of Pisa to show that the force of gravity pulls all falling objects down at the same speed, no matter how much they weigh. The real experiment didn't happen exactly this way, but Galileo's discovery is true.

Read: Galileo's Leaning Tower Experiment by Wendy Macdonald, which sets the legend in a boy's everyday life and helps children understand and remember this effect of gravity.

4. Can we keep objects in balance?
LEARNING OBJECTIVE: To discover satisfying strategies for balancing unequal weights.

MATERIALS:

12-in. (30-cm) ruler

Half-circle blocks

Small rocks

Tinkertoys

SMALL-GROUP ACTIVITY:

1. Gently place a ruler on a block, with the 6-in. (15-cm) mark resting on top of the curve. "Let's see if the ruler will tip or balance. Can you try this?"

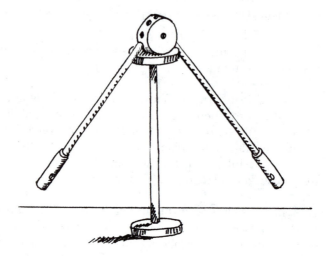

FIGURE 12–1

2. "Can we balance two rocks on the ruler?" Show how to slide a heavier rock toward the center (resting point) to balance a lighter rock at the other end of the ruler.
3. Make a platform of two Tinkertoy wheels and one long stick. Insert two sticks in a connector wheel and add small connectors to the stick ends. Rest the connector wheel on the platform edge, as shown in Figure 12–1.
4. Remove one stick, then the other, from the connector wheel. What happens? Is the connector wheel stable without the sticks? (The location and weight of the sticks change the way gravity pulls on the connector wheel.)

Math skills: Comparing the distance of objects from a fulcrum to achieve balance.

5. How do pendulums work?

LEARNING OBJECTIVE: To be reassured by the regularity of pendulum action.

Introduction: "People have been interested in telling time for hundreds of years, but there were no accurate clocks. About 400 years ago, the famous scientist named Galileo figured out a way to use pendulums to measure time. Others used his ideas to build better clocks. Let's see what we can find out about pendulums."

MATERIALS:

2 screw-eyes

Sturdy button-and-carpet thread or dental floss

3 flat steel washers*

Fine-tip marker

Meter stick/yardstick

Clock with second sweep

GETTING READY:[†]

Choose an open shelf, table, or horizontal bar from which to hang two pendulums. Allow a space about 1 yd. (1 m) in diameter for each.

Install two screw-eyes to the underside of the shelf or table edge.

For the first day: Firmly tie thread to the screw-eye. Mark thread exactly 12-in. (30 cm) from the screw-eye.

Holding the mark at the *top* edge of a washer, pull thread through the washer and tie it firmly at the exact 12-in. (30-cm) mark (see Figure 12–2).

Tape two washers together.

Repeat step 1 to make a second pendulum with the two taped washers. (You now have two pendulums of equal length but different weights.)

Prepare a recording chart:

Swings Count

Long	Long	Short
2 weights	1 weight	1 weight

PARTNER ACTIVITY:

1. Show how to *gently* pull up the pendulum weight about *halfway* (no higher) to the top of the cord and release it to begin swings. "What do you think pulls the weights back down?"

2. Have partners take turns timing 30 seconds with the second sweep clock, counting the number of complete back-and-forth swings, and recording swing numbers.

3. Allow explorations to take place all day, if possible. Discuss findings with the class. Compare the results. (The number of swings will be roughly the same for all observers for both weights.)

4. *Following day:* Untie and separate the two taped washers. Mark thread 6 in. (15 cm) from the screw-eye. Tie thread to *one* washer at the marked length. (You now have two pendulums of equal weight but different lengths.)

5. Repeat the investigation, now comparing pendulum swings with equal weights but two different lengths. Record and summarize findings. (If the thread lengths are accurate, the full swing of the long pendulum will take about 1 second; the full swing of short pendulum will take about half a second.)

Math skills: Using a second hand to count pendulum swings; comparing and recording the relationship between pendulum length, weight, and swing count.

---

*Low-cost hardware item, sold by hole size; ⁵⁄₁₆ in. is good.

[†]Hanging a pendulum takes patience. Do this after school!

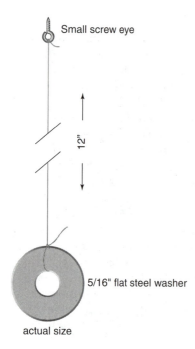

Small screw eye

12"

5/16" flat steel washer

actual size

FIGURE 12–2

Discussion: Consider what pulls the weight down for each swing. Why does it takes less time for the short-length pendulum to come back to the bottom of the swing? Hold two like objects, one above your head, one at knee height. Drop them at the same time. Which one hit the floor first? (The shorter distance to fall is similar to the shorter pendulum. That object came down first.) Compare this with the result of dropping two objects of different weights from the same height. Let children try the drops for themselves. Reaffirm that gravity influences the steady swing of the pendulums. Each swing takes the same length of time until the pendulum comes to a stop.

If possible, leave the pendulums in place permanently. Children can find continuing reassurance that pendulum swings are steady and reliable: a comfort for those whose private worlds are not reliable.

Read: About Time: A First Look at Time and Clocks by Bruce Koscielniak.

? *Inquiry Activity:* If your playground has swings, take the pendulum investigation outdoors to provide an opportunity to transfer observations to a different setting. ♣ Bring along a clipboard, paper, a pencil, and a watch with a second sweep. "Do you think that the swings we play on here will act like the pendulum we used indoors? What do you predict? Let's find out." Appoint a recorder and a minute minder. Ask for volunteers to sit on the swing as pendulum weights. "The rest of us will count swings out loud to find out how many swings happen in 1 minute. I will pull the swing back as high as my shoulders and let go exactly the same way for each swinger. The minder will tell me to let go when the second hand points to 12. Then we will count each swing until the minder tells us to stop counting at the end of 1 minute." Record several "child-pendulum" times.

If another adult can assist, start two child pendulums swinging simultaneously. What happens? Then, if possible, see what happens when one swing's chains are shortened. Discuss the results of the investigation to see if the predictions were accurate. Were there any surprises? Did children feel something moving against them as they were swinging—something besides gravity that slowed the swing (air resistance)?

INTEGRATING ACTIVITIES

Math Experiences

When they experiment with a pan balance and weights, children can strengthen their understanding of numerical equivalence. Make a pan balance available as a center for experimenting with equal and unequal quantities of cube blocks.

Provide sets of commercial standard weights for which size and weight are related. To devise substitute weights, fill screw-top plastic or metal containers with sand and gravel to equal 1-, 2-, and 4-oz. (25-, 50-, and 100-gr) weights as desired. Mark the corresponding numeral on each container.

Numeral balance equipment is made in several forms. One type uses weighted plastic numerals to make the mathematical equation balance as the weight balances. Keep a set of weights, along with boxes of materials to weigh, next to a pan balance for children to use when time permits.

Music

Listen to Michael Mish's "Gravity" song on his *I'm Blue* cassette.

When children are investigating the effects of gravity, they enjoy singing these nursery rhymes as though gravity were not operating. "Jack and Jill Went Up the Hill" might be sung ". . . Jack fell up, and broke his cup, and Jill bent over with laughter." "London Bridge" might be sung ". . . London Bridge is floating up." Here is a gravity song to sing.

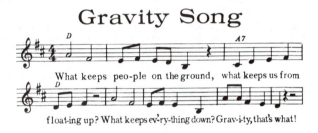

Gravity Song

What keeps peo-ple on the ground, what keeps us from

float-ing up? What keeps ev'-ry-thing down? Grav-i-ty, that's what!

—J.H.

Literature Links

CLYNE, MARGARET, & GRIFFITHS, RACHEL. (2004). *Time by the clock*. Washington, DC: National Geographic. Galileo's pendulum contribution is featured in this small, well-illustrated history of timekeeping.

COBB, VICKI. (2004). *I fall down*. New York: HarperCollins. Lively writing, appealing graphics, immediate examples, and convincing activities make the concept of gravity accessible to young children in a clear, interactive way. Don't miss it! NSTA* Outstanding Trade Book.

FLOCA, BRIAN. (2009). *Moonshot: The flight of Apollo II*. New York: Atheneum. The lyrical text begs to be read aloud. You will have to add facts about weightlessness away from Earth's gravity and the Moon's weak gravitational pull on the walking astronauts. NSTA* Outstanding Trade Book.

KOSCIELNIAK, BRUCE. (2004). *About time: A first look at time and clocks*. New York: Houghton Mifflin. Though Galileo's pendulum contribution isn't specified, the author's intricate illustrations of ancient time measurements are fascinating.

LILLY, MELINDA. (2004). *Gravity*. Vero Beach, FL: Rourke. Three carefully illustrated easy, intriguing experiments will make gravity facts memorable.

MACDONALD, WENDY. (2009). *Galileo's leaning tower experiment*. According to legend, Galileo used the leaning tower of Pisa to test his theory that objects of differing weight fall to Earth at the same speed. The legend is retold well here as a children's story.

*National Science Teachers Association.

McNULTY, FAITH. (2005). *If you decide to go to the moon.* New York: Scholastic. Fun, imagination, and information flow seamlessly in this fine story. Gorgeous paintings will inspire readers to start planning space voyages.

NELSON, ROBIN. (2004). *Gravity.* Minneapolis: Lerner. This single-concept book for independent readers ends with notes about Galileo and Newton.

WEAVER, JEANNE, & WEAVER, BRADLEY. (2004). *Lighter on the moon.* Washington, DC: National Geographic. This small book explains our weight as gravity's pull on us. It provides the math to calculate our weight on Earth compared to our weight on the Moon.

Classics

BRANLEY, FRANKLYN. (2000). *Gravity is a mystery.* New York: HarperCollins. Although this book doesn't explain what gravity is because no one has been able to explain it yet, it shares what is known in good, child-level style.

FALCONER, IAN. (2001). *Olivia saves the circus.* New York: Atheneum. Olivia steps in for sick circus performers. Balance is critical in tightrope acts, stilt walking, and unicycle riding. School Library Journal Best Book of 2001.

FARANDON, JOHN. (2003). *Time.* Tarrytown, NY: Benchmark. A good explanation of how pendulum clocks work is offered on page 13.

McCULLY, EMILY. (1992). *Mirette on the high wire.* New York: G. P. Putnam's Sons. A venturesome girl persists and learns to concentrate and balance as a highwire walker. She saves a performer. A Caldecott Award winner.

PIPE, JIM. (2002). *Why does it fall over?* Brookfield, CT: CopperBeech Books. Youngsters think about everyday balancing experiences and enjoy experimenting to find answers.

Poems (Resources in Appendix A)

Here are some poems about gravity.

From *The Llama Who Had No Pajama* by Mary Ann Hoberman, read "The Folks Who Live in Backward Town," where gravity doesn't seem to operate.

For beginning readers, see *Blast Off! Poems About Space,* selected by Lee Bennett Hopkins.

Art Activities

Nature Mobiles: Collect fallen sticks outdoors. Let children help if the school grounds have trees. Using tape and string, suspend each stick at a level that allows children to work on it. Provide two small objects from nature, such as cones and pods, to hang by a string from each stick. Children can experiment to achieve a balance by moving the objects' strings closer to or farther away from the center of the stick, or by winding one string around the stick to make it shorter than the other (Figure 12–3). Shapes cut from pressed foam plastic can also be used.

Pendulum Floor Painting: Make a sand pendulum so that the children can observe the beautiful patterns made by the pendulum arcs. Make a funnel by cutting off the bottom of an empty dish detergent bottle. Make three evenly spaced holes near the cut edge. Tie three strong strings to the holes; bundle the strings and tie them to a sturdy cord (Figure 12–4). Suspend the upended funnel by the

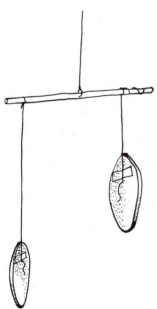

FIGURE 12–3

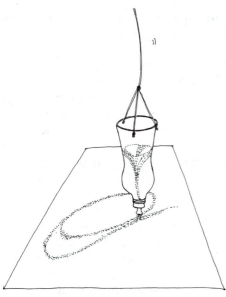

FIGURE 12–4

cord from a door frame or ceiling beam. The capped end of the funnel needs to be close to the floor, about ½ in. (1 cm) above, so that the sand doesn't bounce.

Spread a large plastic sheet under the pendulum. Fill the funnel halfway with two or more layers of sand mixed with dry tempera paint of different colors. Pull the cap open, give the funnel a push, and watch the sand flow into interesting arc patterns below. (To make the sand flow more smoothly, you may need to remove the bit of plastic that has been put there to slow down the flow of detergent.) Vary the way you start the pendulum arc to create different patterns. Let children experiment.

Play

Store. Put a pan balance or old kitchen scales, containers of materials like horse chestnuts, and artificial fruit and vegetables in the play store area.

Block Play. Help block builders think about why their structures collapse. Suggest making broad, sturdy bases for tall towers so that gravity will pull more on the bottom of the tower than on the top. When appropriate, ask if gravity is pulling equally on both sides of the weight-supporting blocks or whether an unbalanced load will tip over.

Add 1-yd (1-m) lengths of PVC roofing gutter material (purchased from a builder's supply store) to block an area for ramp building. Encourage children to experiment with varied block tower heights from which to launch small toy cars down the ramps. Which height allowed cars to travel the greatest distance? Which one let cars travel the fastest? Suggest continuing investigations by combining towers and gutter lengths as bridges to ramps to increase the distance from launch to stopping point. Compare the way a small ball travels down the ramps with the small cars. Investigators can draw pictures of their structures, indicating the results. This popular investigation can be conducted outdoors if classroom space limits the structure ideas.

Spaceship. Try to find a refrigerator shipping carton for the children to convert into a spaceship. Help them improvise space helmets by using small cartons and coils of telephone cable wire. Before setting up the spaceship play, supply play ideas by reading *If You Decide to Go to the Moon* by Faith McNulty.

Creative Movement

Help the children recognize, when they dance or exercise, the way their bodies involuntarily adjust to changes in body position to maintain their balance. When they lean in one direction, their bodies automatically compensate for gravity's pull by extending an arm or a leg in the opposite direction.

Let the children pretend that they are on a ship in a storm, rocking from side to side. They will stretch their legs into a wide-based stance or tip over. Suggest moving like ice skaters, swinging their arms and bending their bodies as they glide and stride on the ice. Now they are tightrope walkers sliding one foot in front of the other on a swaying rope, arms extended. Next, imagine that they are going to lift a heavy rock, working very hard with their muscles to force it up against gravity's pull, bit by bit. Now put the rock down carefully and push it ahead slowly. Then move like the astronauts on the moon, where gravity's pull is weak.

Whenever tension seems to be mounting in the classroom, or when excited children need help in shifting from physical activity to a learning situation that requires concentration, use this "antigravity relaxation fantasy." Guide it slowly and quietly, saying: "Let your eyelids slide down now to close . . . and let your hands be loose and comfortable in your lap. Let your arms be loose. . . . and limp . . . and light . . . so light that they seem to float, so light that it seems that gravity isn't pulling on them much at all. And now . . . notice how loose and light your neck and shoulders feel. There is just enough gravity pull to help them keep your head above them. . . . But your head might want to move all around slowly, until it finds a comfortable place to rest. There, it feels soooo comfortable now. . . . There is almost no heaviness in your body now. . . . Everything feels easy now. . . . Let your mind take you on a floating journey now. . . . You might want to have a cloud to rest on, feeling all that softness around you . . . or you might want to be an astronaut floating inside a space capsule, far, far, away from Earth's gravity pull. . . . It's your floating journey, so you can have it just the way you want it to be, because gravity doesn't pull on your thoughts—ever—so you can float as easily as you like in your imagination. . . . And then gradually, slowly, you begin to notice gravity's pull again. . . . You notice how well you are breathing now as you drift down closer, closer to Earth . . . feeling rested and fresh and relaxed now. . . . And you take three long, slow, deep breaths . . . and then your eyes open again, so that you can see what we will be doing next in school."

Creative Thinking

Use gravity pull as a topic to stimulate creative thinking. Ask, "What if there were no gravity pull from Earth? What would be different? What would it be like to play on the playground? What if we had to eat our meals as the astronauts do on space flights? Would we be sitting here in this room?"

Food Experiences

Take the class to the nearest food store where purchases are weighed on a balance beam scale. Buying and sharing a half pound of raisins or sunflower seeds with the children is a good investment learning about gravity.

If a science museum field trip is a possibility, be sure to purchase the astronaut ice cream, "Dip 'n Dots," to share a taste with the class. Packets of astronaut meals may also be available for purchase.

Field Trips

Knowing how much gravity pulls on objects is an important part of many businesses and services. Try to include a look at weighing devices during the field trips you plan to the post office, grocery store, feed store, or loading docks. It can be great fun for a whole class of children to be weighed together on loading dock scales.

PROMOTING CONCEPT CONNECTIONS

Maintaining Concepts

One child applied gravity concepts in a judgmental way when he picked himself up from a fall, complaining, "That ol' grabbity pulled me down!" Many of the large-muscle play activities provide opportunities to point out how gravity's pull makes some of our fun or work easier, such as balancing block towers; enjoying a slide, teeter-totter, or swing; or playing catch. Some activities are difficult to do because of gravity's pull. This is why children become tired when they put away blocks, climb the jungle gym, walk up the stairs, or trudge up a hill. Comment on how the force of gravity is affecting children's activities. When a tumbled block structure needs rebuilding, ask the builder where gravity's pull requires the heaviest blocks.

Improving School Grounds

Good playground equipment, especially slides and swings, provides lasting learning about the inexorable force of gravity. The child's body absorbs the knowledge that "What goes up must come down." A hill is a tremendous asset in a play space, demonstrating for a child the energy required to climb up against gravity and the "almost-flying" feeling of a running descent. Even a small, specially built hill is useful; cover it with sod.

Include some heavy branches or small logs for children to move around the play area.

Connecting Concepts

Gravity–Air Relationship. Balancing two air-filled balloons is a vivid way to demonstrate that gravity pulls on air. To make a long balance arm, insert one drinking straw partway into another straw. Insert a hanging loop in the center, as you did in making the mobile. Blow up two balloons to equal size; tie one to either end of the arm. Be sure that the balloons are the same color. Some children may believe that balloons of different colors also contain different amounts of air.

Hang up the arrangement and let the arm come to rest. To achieve balance, add bits of tape to the light side. It is hard to blow exactly the same amount of air into two balloons. Explain to the children that you are going to prick one balloon. "What will happen to that balloon?" Some children become scared when the balloon pops and forget to watch what happens to the balance. "Put your

We experience gravity when moving big objects.

hands over your ears if the noise might bother you." Pop the balloon. Ask, "Which side of the balance went down? Why did that happen? Gravity pulls on air, too!" (If the pricked balloon flies apart, gather the pieces and tape them onto the end of the balance stick so that a comparison of empty and air-filled balloons can still be made.)

Gravity–Water Relationship. Introduce the idea that gravity's pull plays a part in determining which objects sink and which float. Gravity pulls on water more than it pulls on corks, for instance. Recall that raindrops are pulled down to Earth when they become too heavy to float as droplets of vapor in clouds (see Chapter 9, Weather). Watch gravity's effect on raindrops clinging to classroom windows. Read A. A. Milne's poem "Waiting at the Window" from *Now We Are Six* (see Appendix A).

Gravity–Human Body Relationship. Galileo experimented with pendulums when he was studying to be a doctor 400 years ago. He wanted to find a way to measure pulse rates, but there were no clocks to check the number of beats against a length of time. His pendulum, with its steady, regular swings, became the measuring device. Children can take their pulse readings as Galileo did. Let one partner count 30 swings of the exactly 12-in. (30-cm) pendulum (30 seconds) while the other counts his or her own pulse beats. Multiply the pulse beats by 2 for the pulse rate per minute. Check it again this way after vigorous exercise.

Family and Community Support

Families often have opportunities to show their children things that go up and away from gravity's pull. Big motors help elevators and escalators lift people. Heavy motors are needed to lift loads of materials at building construction sites that families could visit together. Families can watch TV presentations of gymnastics, ballet, and figure skating, pointing out how the athletes and dancers use their arms and legs to maintain their balance.

Check with the closest children's science museum about its interactive gravity displays, such as spinning coins down a gravity well.

RESOURCES

FARNDON, JOHN. (2002). *Science experiments: Gravity.* Tarrytown, NY: Benchmark. Here is a good source of background information for teachers. NSTA* recommended.

HOPWOOD, JAMES (2008). *Cool gravity activities.* Edina, MN: ABDO Publishing. Some advanced activities in this book can be adapted for primary grades.

NEWTON, ROGER. (2005). *Galileo's pendulum: From the rhythm of time to the making of matter.* Cambridge, MA: Harvard University Press (Chap. 4). Sorts Galileo legend from fact about his development of the pendulum principle.

TAYLOR, BEVERLY, POTH, JAMES, & PORTMAN, DWIGHT. (1995). *Teaching physics with toys.* Middletown, OH: Terrific Science Press. The National Science Foundation supports this book. Clear directions for classroom activities with balance pans and making balance stick toys are included.

ONLINE RESOURCES

American Academy for the Advancement of Science (AAAS): Science Netlinks offers a lesson plan to explore the role of gravity in falling at *http://www.sciencenetlinks.com/lessons.php?BenchmarkID=4&DocID=158*

---

*National Science Teachers Association.

13

Simple Machines

Appreciate the wonderful gears that make it easier to cycle an uphill path and the sturdy pulleys that strengthen muscles at the gym. Mix in your childhood thrills with roller skates and ferris wheels for a positive spin on simple machines to share with young children.

Throbbing motors and turning wheels make little-noted daily background noises in the Western world. Children are proud to learn how to move and lift things with the help of simple machines. The knowledge invites interest in the complex machines they have previously taken for granted. Complex machines, like cars, incorporate several simple machines that work together. The learning experiences in this chapter explore the following concepts:

- Friction can heat, slow, and wear away objects.
- A lever helps lift objects.
- A ramp shares the work of lifting.
- A screw is a curved ramp.
- Simple machines help move things along.
- Some wheels turn alone; some turn together.
- Single wheels can turn other wheels.
- Single wheels can help us pull down to lift up.

Experiencing the advantages and disadvantages of friction is a useful preliminary to the experiments that follow. The simple machines experiments illustrate the lever, ramp, screw, wheel and axle, and pulley.

INTRODUCTION

"Rub the palms of your hands together as fast as you can. Keep going. Do you feel something happening to your hands? What we are doing makes heat. The reason for the heat is a force called *friction*."

CONCEPT: Friction can heat, slow, and wear away objects.

1. ♣ How does friction slow sliding objects?

LEARNING OBJECTIVE: To enjoy direct research on the slowing effect of friction.

MATERIALS:

Gum erasers

Small pieces of waxed paper

Magnifiers

Outdoor slide or smooth plank, propped against a table

Sheets of waxed paper

Rubber sink or tub mat

LARGE-GROUP ACTIVITY:

1. Pass around pieces of waxed paper. Tell children, "Try rubbing this on your arm. Does it slide fast? Try sliding the rubber eraser on your arm. Does it slide fast? Can you think of a reason for this?" (The rubber makes more friction.)

2. "Look at the paper and the eraser through a magnifier. Which is smooth? Which is fuzzy?"

3. ♣ Let children take turns on the slide outdoors, sitting first on waxed paper, then on the rubber mat. "Smooth paper doesn't make much friction, so you move fast."

Math skills: Observing quantitative changes (more/less) in friction per condition changes.

2. What can we feel and see friction do?

LEARNING OBJECTIVE: To spark immediate interest in the heat-producing, wearing-away effects of friction.

MATERIALS:

6-in. (15-cm) pieces of scrap lumber

Coarse sandpaper, cut into 3-in. (7-cm) squares

Hammer

Nails

Magnifiers

GETTING READY:

Hammer a few nails half of their length into a chunk of wood. (To use the hammer as a lever, catch a nail in the claw and roll the hammer back on the curve of the claw. Pull *down* on the handle to lift the nail *up* and out.)

SMALL-GROUP ACTIVITY:

1. Give each child sandpaper and scrap lumber. "Feel these. Are they smooth or rough? Do they look smooth or bumpy with the magnifier? Rub them together hard and long. See what happens."

2. "Are your fingers feeling warm? (Rough things rubbing together make lots of friction.) Are bits of wood wearing away? Look at your wood. Feel it. Is it getting smoother? Is the sandpaper changing? What does friction seem to do to things?"

3. "I'm going to pull a nail from this wood. Do you think that will make friction? Let's feel the nail quickly after it comes out. Is it warm or cool? Do you think the nail and wood rubbed together? How do you know?"

Math skills: Observing the quantitative changes (more/less) friction makes in interactions.

3. How can we cut down on friction?

LEARNING OBJECTIVE: To savor finding ways to reduce friction.

MATERIALS:

Coarse sandpaper

Petroleum jelly

Meat trays

Cream cheese or jelly

Soda or rice crackers

Waxed paper

Table knives

GETTING READY:

Cut sandpaper into 2-in. (5-cm) squares.

Put a spoonful of cream cheese or jelly on pieces of waxed paper for each child.

SMALL-GROUP ACTIVITY:

1. Give children two pieces of sandpaper. "Rub these together fast. What happens to the bits of sand?"

2. "Look at the sandpaper. Is it bumpy and rough? Do you think it would be smoother if something filled up the bumpy places? Try this petroleum jelly on it. See if the pieces of sandpaper slide past each other smoothly now."

3. Give each child two crackers on a tray. Repeat steps 1 and 2, offering cream cheese or jelly as a lubricant. Let the children eat this experiment.

Math skills: Observing quantitative changes (more/less) in friction per condition changes.

Group Discussion: Show the children a small can of household oil. Ask what they know about it and why it is used at home. Develop the idea that oil makes a smooth sliding surface on objects that rub together. It cuts down the friction that makes heat, wears bits away, makes things difficult to use, and makes things squeak.

Year-round programs can reduce friction and add cooling pleasure on the playground by hosing down the slide with water. As a safety tip, remind children that splashed water reduces friction, thus increasing slippery falls on tile surfaces near swimming pools.

4. How can friction be useful?

LEARNING OBJECTIVE: To find satisfaction in using friction to do work and stay safe.

MATERIALS:

Chalk

Dark-colored paper

Small pieces of waxed paper

Pencils

SMALL-GROUP ACTIVITY:

A

1. Give children paper and chalk. "What sound does the chalk make on the paper? Why do you think this happens?"

Petroleum jelly

Screw-top plastic containers, such as beverage bottles

2 pans of water

Soap

Towels

2. "Try dipping your chalk into the petroleum jelly. Now does it rub and scrape? What happened to the chalk mark? Do you need friction to draw?"

3. Let children try to draw on waxed paper with pencils. Explain that the wax coating is like a lubricant.

B

1. "Are your hands strong enough to un-screw this bottle cover? You can do it well."

2. "Try it again, but this time get your hands wet and soapy first. Why is it hard to do now? What is missing?"

3. "Try the doorknob with wet hands. Can you turn it?'

Math skills: Observing quantitative effects (more/less) of lubrication on friction.

Group Discussion: Ask the children to check each other's shoe soles. Are some of them smooth and slippery? Do some have rubber heels? Do others have one-piece rubber bottoms? Are sneakers good for stopping or do they skid? Are car tires smooth and slippery or more like the soles of sneakers? Why? Talk about slippery road conditions, slippery bathtubs, and wet bathroom floors. How can friction make these places safer?

CONCEPT: **A lever helps lift objects.**

1. What can a lever do?

LEARNING OBJECTIVE: To gratify the wish to be powerful, using a lever and a resting point.

Open a discussion about machines and the work they do. Elicit children's infor-mation. Add that all these mechanical inventions use one or more simple ma-chines to make work easier. Children are surprised to know that they, too, use sim-ple machines. "One day I watched Sophia on the playground pushing *down* to lift David *up* in the air. Then David pushed *down* to lift Sophia *up*. What were they doing? Did you notice how the seesaw worked? Did the board rest on something? Let's see what we can find out about making the work of lifting easier." And let's keep track of our experiments on these charts I made—'Easiest Lifting' and 'Lever Length.'

Make an "Easiest Lifting" chart with three columns—*Finger, Lever,* and *Same*—for the class to record the ease of book-lifting results.

Make a "Lever Length" chart with the columns *Short* and *Long* and the rows *Light* and *Heavy* to record experiment results.

MATERIALS:

Books

Sturdy 12-in. or 35-cm rulers

Pencils

String

6-ft (2-m) seesaw plank or balance beam board

Large block

Empty paint can

Short screwdriver

GETTING READY:

Make bundles of two or more books tied with string in a single bow. Place them in the science center with rulers, pencils, and "Easiest Lifting" and "Lever Length" charts.

? *Inquiry Activity:* Develop background information by identifying the lever* as one of the simple machines that makes work easier. Ask for predictions about whether or not it will be easier to lift a book bundle with one finger through the string loop than to press that finger on a ruler resting on a pencil to raise the books. Ask for ideas about how to make the ruler a lever, with a pencil resting point (*fulcrum* or *pivot*). If necessary, demonstrate sliding the ruler under the books, placing the pencil beneath it (Figure 13–1), pressing the end of the

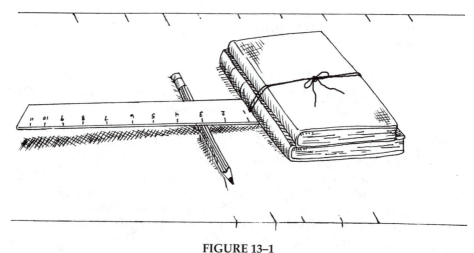

FIGURE 13–1

---

*There are three types (classes) of levers for different uses. The locations of the load, the fulcrum, and where the force is applied differ for various uses. This activity uses a first-class lever.

ruler. Let children experiment independently at the science center, comparing lifting the bundle by one finger slipped through the string loops with pressing that finger on a lever to lift the books at the other end. Encourage experimenting by placing the pencil under different measurement marks on the ruler, recording their findings on the "Easiest Lifting" chart. Discuss the results. Were the books raised higher if the pencil resting point was closer to the books or farther away?

♣ Later, place the plank and block on the floor or outdoors. Ask one volunteer to stand on one end of the board, and another to use the board to lift the child. Ask for predictions about success and for suggestions about finding a way to do this. (Use the block as a resting point [fulcrum] to make the plank a lever. Stand by to steady the child.) After a success, ask for predictions. "Can two volunteers be lifted exactly the same way?" Find out. "Why not? What is different?" (Their weight.) "What could be changed to make it work? Find out." After discovering that a change in the block's location makes lifting possible, point out the length of the lever on the pushing end from the resting point. Did that also change? Let small groups of children experiment and record their results on the "Lever Length" chart. Tally the results for the load weight and the length of the lever needed to lift it. At the end of the experiment, restate the principle: *The longer the lever, the easier the lifting. A load must be close to the resting point to make it easy to lift up.*

♣ On the playground seesaw, continue the inquiry about the weight of the load and the length of the lever by observing what happens when partners change their locations on the seesaw. Make a temporary seesaw, as shown in the photograph.

Group Discussion: At another group time, ask a volunteer to lift the lid off a small paint can or similar can. Have a small screwdriver nearby. Did the child push down to lift the lid up? Show that the resting point was the edge of the can. Many other things can be used as levers. Have the children seen other levers being used?

Math skills: Observing and recording the effects of load distances from the resting point.

Read: Levers to the Rescue by Sharon Thales.

CONCEPT: **A ramp shares the work of lifting.**

1. How can a ramp help us lift?
LEARNING OBJECTIVE: To take pride in raising a heavy load using a ramp.

MATERIALS:

Old, sturdy suitcase

Heavy objects to fill suitcase

SMALL-GROUP ACTIVITY:

1. "See if you can pick up this heavy case by the handle and lift it onto the table."

Changing where we stand changes how the lever works.

Plank, at least 4 ft (1.2 m) long
Table

GETTING READY:

Fill the suitcase with objects
   heavy enough to make it hard
   for a child to lift by the handle.

2. "See if this plank can make it easier to get
   the case up on the table." Lean the plank
   from the floor against the tabletop. Place
   the suitcase near the bottom on the plank.
   "We call this a *ramp*."
3. "A ramp holds some of the weight of the
   suitcase as you slide it along. Now you can
   get the suitcase up there."

♣ Take a fun variation of this activity to the playground if a slide is available. Tie
a rope the length of the slide to the suitcase handle. Let children take turns trying
to lift the suitcase as high as possible; then compare with climbing to the top step
of the slide and pulling the suitcase up the slide by the rope. Which method gets
the suitcase higher with less work?

   Keep a running record of ramps that the children observe in the community,
such as curb cuts and wheelchair ramps.

   Math skill: Experiencing quantitative differences in lifting an object up or
pushing it up a ramp.

CONCEPT: **A screw is a curved ramp.**

Introduction: Draw a thick crayon line diagonally from one corner of a sheet of 8½ × 11-in. paper to the other. Cut along the line, leaving a crayon-edged triangle. Bring the triangle, a pencil, a large screw, and a collection of nuts and bolts to a class discussion. "Does the line on this paper triangle look like a ramp? Let's see what we can do with it." Wind the triangle around the pencil so that the line looks like a screw thread. Trace the spiral path from the bottom of the ramp to the top. Compare it with a screw. Give children the bolts and nuts. "Can you make the nut go up the ramp that curves around the bolt? Try it."

1. How can screws help us?

LEARNING OBJECTIVE: To be surprised by the uses of screws to move things.

MATERIALS:

(Use as many as possible)
Screw-type cookie press
Tissue
C-clamps
Modeling clay
Empty lipstick tube
Screw-type nutcracker
Screw-top plastic jars
Plastic pipes and joints
Hand-turned food grinder
Old piano stool or office swivel
   chair

GETTING READY:

The bottom half of a lipstick
   tube is usually two pieces.
   Separate them to reveal
   the spiral ramp that the
   lipstick moves along as it
   is twisted up.
Set up an exploration center for
   taking apart and assembling
   the activity objects.

SMALL-GROUP ACTIVITY:

1. Remove the design plate from the cookie press. Stuff a tissue in the press. Let children see what happens when the screw knob is turned. "What lifted up the tissue?"
2. Put a small ball of clay on the end of the C-clamp, turning the screw. Hold the clamp upright; turn the screw until the clay rides up to be squashed by the top.
3. Show how two screws can be threaded together so that they can't be pulled apart. (Use jars with matching lids, or a hose and nozzle, or a large bolt and nut.)
4. Let children experience being lifted by a screw with a piano stool or office chair. Examine the emerging screw as it turns.

Read: Get to Know Screws by Paul Challen.

Drilling a hole in a maple tree to collect sap. A sweet use of a simple machine.

CONCEPT: Simple machines help move things along.

1. How do rollers move things?

LEARNING OBJECTIVE: To enjoy comparing ways to move: dragging, using rollers, and using wheels.

MATERIALS:

Grocery cartons

Jump ropes

4 cutoff broomsticks or cardboard cores from newsprint rolls to use as rollers

Platform dolly or board and 4 caster wheels

GETTING READY:

If the school custodian doesn't have a platform dolly for scrub buckets, make your own by screwing four swivel casters into a 1-in. (2.5-cm)-thick plank.

SMALL-GROUP ACTIVITY:

1. Loop jump ropes around cartons. Let children take turns pulling each other in boxes, using jump rope handles in each hand. (Cardboard boxes fall apart soon, so have many.) "Is pulling easy or hard?"
2. Place rollers side by side on the floor. Put box on top. Repeat Step 1. "See if rollers help move the box." (They don't stay under the box. Put them back for the next child's turn.)
3. "Which way made less friction?" Feel box bottoms after the dragging and after rolling.
4. "Now let's try rolling wheels that will stay under the box." Put the box on the platform dolly. "Which is the easier way to pull the box: dragging with rollers or with wheels?"

Math skills: Experiencing the quantitative difference in pushing a box with and without rollers; observing the amount of friction generated by each mode.

Group Discussion: Recall the rollers experiment. "Was the carton moved very far by four rollers? Would rollers be a good way to move cars and trucks? What if someone had to keep putting rollers in front of the car to keep it moving? Rollers are used that way when whole houses are moved a short distance. They give good support to the house. Rollers are also used to unload big trucks at the grocery store. Rollers are part of conveyor belts and escalators."

CONCEPT: Some wheels turn alone; some turn together.

1. How do single wheels and pairs of wheels work?

LEARNING OBJECTIVE: To enjoy comparing the ways single and paired wheels
work.

MATERIALS:

A light piece of furniture on four swivel wheels (office chair, typewriter stand, utility table, crate on casters, platform dolly)

Toy car with axles exposed

Small paper plates

Masking tape

Plastic drinking straws

Compass (circle-drawing type)

GETTING READY:

Find the exact centers of paper plates with a compass. Mark each center; with a pencil tip, push out a ¼-in. (1-cm) hole. Have one for each child.

Cut 1-in. (2.5-cm) pieces of tape; stick them lightly on a nearby table edge for children's use.

SMALL-GROUP ACTIVITY:

1. Divide children into two facing rows at least 5 ft (1.5 m) apart.
2. "Let's take turns pushing the chair to children across the room. Watch what happens. How does it move?"
3. "Now let's push these cars across. Do they move like the chair wheels?" Compare with the swivel again, watching the wheels very closely. Turn the swivel and the cars upside down to see if they look the same. Supply the word *axle* if a child doesn't offer it. Point out pairs of wheels that turn together on an axle.
4. Let children try to roll their plates across to another child. Offer straws and tape, suggesting that two children could join wheel plates to see if they will roll better as a pair with an axle.

Group Discussion: Talk about the advantages of single wheels and pairs of wheels. If your classroom has an old upright piano or a classroom storage chest on casters, have children push it. Tiny single wheels can make it easier to push something very heavy for a short distance in all directions. "Do you think wagons, cars, buses, and trucks have a single wheel on each corner?" Show some pictures of wheeled objects cut from catalogs. "Do these things use single wheels or pairs of wheels on axles?" Children are surprised to learn that doorknobs are pairs of wheels on an axle. Bring in an old doorknob or unscrew one at school. Try to bring in a conventional roller skate to compare with the single wheels of inline skates.

Read: Tires, Spokes and Sprockets: A Book about Wheels and Axles by Michael Dahl or *Wheels and Axles to the Rescue* by Sharon Thales.

Set up a center for inventing wheeled vehicles with Lego® bricks or K'nex® construction sets.

CONCEPT: Single wheels can turn other wheels.

1. How do gears work?

LEARNING OBJECTIVE: To delight in the details of meshing gears at work.

MATERIALS:

Eggbeater (hand operated)
  2 deep mixing bowls

Soup spoons

Water

Detergent

Gear toys, visible clockwork,
  visible music box works

Crayon

Newspapers

Sponge

GETTING READY:

Put ½ cup water and 1 teaspoon
  detergent in each bowl.

Spread papers on the floor.

Set up a center for exploring
  gear toys

SMALL-GROUP ACTIVITY:

1. Ask children, "Let's look very closely at a beater. How many wheels do you see? (Some wheels may look different.) Watch what happens to the little wheel when the big wheel is turned." Introduce the term *gear*, explaining that this is a wheel with teeth that mesh with teeth on the wheels next to it.

2. "Let's take turns using the beater to find out how the gears work. Let's compare beating bowls of soap suds with the beater and with a spoon to find out which works more easily."

3. Help children see that the big gear turns the little gears on the beater blades much faster.

Math skills: Observing and comparing gears of different sizes to the number of wheel turnings.

Group Discussion: Try to borrow a *single-speed* bicycle to examine with the group. Turn the bicycle upside down and look at the gears. Tell children, "Sometimes gears turn each other without touching each other (sprocket wheel). Instead, they fit into a chain that moves them. Is one gear large and one small, like the eggbeater? Let's turn the pedals and watch the chain make the small gear turn. Count how many times the back wheel turns while I turn the pedal one time." Count one turn when the air valve reaches the top. Compare, if possible, with mountain bike gears. "These gears make the work of bicycling easier."

Look at the tire tread. "Could friction help stop a bicycle? Why do you think the chain looks greasy? Would it need grease? What do you think is inside the tires?"

Read: Sally Jean, the Bicycle Queen by Cari Best.

CONCEPT: **Single wheels can help us pull down to lift up.**

1. How does a pulley help us lift things?

LEARNING OBJECTIVE: To take pride in finding that a pulley helps with heavy lifting.

MATERIALS:

Small pulley

Firm cord, double the length of floor-to-pulley distance

Bucket and blocks

Stopwatch

Screw hook

GETTING READY:

Install the screw hook in a ceiling beam or door frame (ask custodian).

Pass the cord over the pulley wheel; hang the pulley on the screw hook.

SMALL-GROUP ACTIVITY:

1. Show children the pulley. "Do you suppose this single wheel could make it easier to lift a bucketful of blocks?"
2. "First, let's see how long you can lift up and hold this bucket with one hand. Lift it as high as you can. I'll time you." Record the length of time each child can hold the bucket.
3. Tie cord firmly to bucket handle. "Now try pulling down on this cord to lift the load. I'll time you to see how long you can hold it up." (Demonstrate careful lowering of the bucket, but stand by in case someone lets it down too fast.) "Are you pulling down on the rope or lifting the rope to lift the bucket up? Does the pulley make the lifting job easier?"

Math skills: Experiencing quantitative differences in lifting a load with and without a pulley.

Group Discussion: (Try to find pictures of the following things to show.) "Pulleys help people load big ships, trains, and barns. Pulleys are used on steam shovels, on sailboats, on flagpoles, on scaffoldings, in draw-drapery rods, and inside the casings of windows. A pulley arrangement moves people up in large buildings on elevators. These single wheels help people and machines pull *down* to *lift up* or *pull across.*"

Read: Listen to the Wind by Greg Mortensen and Susan Roth.

INTEGRATING ACTIVITIES

Math Experiences

Screws, Bolts, and Nuts Grouping. Set up a sorting center with nuts, bolts, and screws of many sizes for children to match, seriate, and group. Many variations are possible. Children can explain their reasons for groupings.

Wheel Quantity Classification Game. Cut out and mount catalog pictures of wheeled objects. Ask children to sort them into groups according to the number of wheels each object has.

Music (Resources in Appendix A)

1. Sing this song about friction to the tune of "Here We Go Round the Mulberry Bush" while rubbing hands together.

Friction Song

This is the way we warm our hands, warm our hands, warm our hands.

This is the way we warm our hands, out in chilly weather.

Friction is what warms our hands, warms our hands, warms our hands.

Friction is what warms our hands, rubbing them together.

—J. H.

2. "Little Red Wagon" is a lively reminder of the usefulness of wheels and axles. One child created these three verses for his favorite song:

Both wheels are off and back end's dragging . . .

Four wheels are off and we're not even moving . . .

Now we're going to the repair shop . . .

3. Sing: "Move It! Work It! from *Move It! Work It! A Song about Simple Machines* by Laura Salas.

Literature Links

BEST, CARI. (2006). *Sally Jean, the bicycle queen.* New York: Farrar, Straus, Giroux. A plucky, passionate bicyclist earns money repairing bikes so that she can buy junkyard parts and eventually build a bike of her own.

BRADLEY, KIMBERLY. (2005). *Forces make things move.* New York: HarperCollins. The force of friction is given its due as part of this broad consideration of forces in general.

DAHL, MICHAEL. (2007). *Tires, spokes and sprockets: A book about wheels and axles.* Minneapolis: Picture Window. Dynamic prose and page layouts infuse this topic with lively momentum. Also in this NSTA* recommended series: *Roll, slope and slide* (Ramps) and *Scoops, seesaw and raise* (Levers).

FERN, TRACEY. (2009). *Pippo the fool.* Watertown, MA: Charlesbridge. Enjoy searching for simple machines in the fine illustrations for the story of the construction of a famous cathedral dome in 15th-century Florence.

GAFFNEY, TIMOTHY. (2004). *Wee and the Wright brothers.* New York: Henry Holt. Look closely at the charming illustrations for wheels, gears, pulleys, and printing press rollers in this retelling of the Wright brothers' first flight.

GEISERT, ARTHUR. (2005). *Lights out.* Boston: Houghton Mifflin. Four declarative sentences and 30 clever, meticulous line drawings full of wheels, gears, levers, and inclined planes will fascinate and delight young browsers.

GEISERT, ARTHUR. (2008). *Hogwash.* New York: Houghton Mifflin. Misbehaving piglets romp in mud. A contraption is created with simple machines to clean them. No text is required!

---

*National Science Teachers Association.

MORTENSEN, GREG, & ROTH, SUSAN. (2009). *Listen to the wind: The story of Dr. Greg and three cups of tea.* New York: Dial. A slender cable with a pulley is the only means of supplying school-building materials to a mountain village in this true story.

PRINCE, APRIL. (2006). *What do wheels do all day?* Boston: Houghton Mifflin. Vibrant art makes this simple book fun to share with groups of young children. Let them sort out single wheels from those that work in pairs.

SADLER, WENDY. (2005). *Using pulleys and gears.* Chicago: Raintree. Confident readers who have had hands-on experiences with simple machines will be intrigued by this reference. Excellent close-ups let readers peek inside common equipment to see the simple machine working parts. Also in the Machines Inside Machines series by this author are *Using levers, Using ramps and wedges, Using screws, Using wheels and axles,* and *Using springs.*

SCHONBERG, MARCIA. (2005). *I is for idea.* Chelsea, MI: Sleeping Bear Press. The author's charming, inventive illustrations will stimulate children's creative ideas as they browse this inventive alphabet book. Its format features a simple rhyming text for young readers and information sidebars for adults.

THALES, SHARON. (2007). *Wheels and axles to the rescue.* Mankato, MN: Capstone. Here is an enthusiastic approach to connecting the topic to children's real lives. Also in this series: *Inclined planes; Levers; Screws; Pulleys;* and *Wedges.* NSTA* Outstanding Trade Book.

Classics

ANHOLT, LAURENCE. (2000). *Leonardo and the flying boy.* London: Barrons. A true story of the unsuccessful flight in 1502 of Leonardo da Vinci's first flying machine. Pulleys and gears are visible in the illustrations.

FALCONER, IAN. (2001). *Olivia saves the circus.* New York: Atheneum. When the circus performers become sick, Olivia, the intrepid piglet, steps in to be the unicycle performer.

McPHERSON, JAN. (2001). *How does my bike work?* Washington DC: National Geographic. This close-up look at bicycle parts is almost as helpful as turning real pedals to understand how a bike works.

PIPE, JIM. (2002). *What does a wheel do?* Brookfield, CT: Millbrook. A question-answer format leads children to simple experiments for firsthand answers. An NSTA* Outstanding Trade Book.

WELLS, ROBERT. (1996). *How do you lift a lion?* Morton Grove, IL: Albert Whitman. In this fresh approach, the author/illustrator shows lively kids solving unusual lifting and moving problems with simple machines. A pleased lion, giggling baboons, and a jubilant panda will lock in wheel, pulley, and lever concepts. NSTA* recommended.

Poems (Resources in Appendix A)

To stimulate children to invent machines they may wish existed, read "Homework Machine," from *A Light in the Attic* by Shel Silverstein.

Fingerplays. The familiar fingerplay "The Wheels on the Bus" calls for arm rolling and active bouncing.

Art Activities

Collage. These collage materials are strongly suggestive of simple machines: macaroni wheels; pieces of thick string; bottle caps; popsicle sticks; and round, triangular, and rectangular construction paper shapes. (The macaroni wheels may become essential parts of pulleys and gears, or they may be quietly eaten by a child whose inspiration is not as strong as his or her curiosity about new tastes.)

---

*National Science Teachers Association.

Cutting and Pasting. Young children enjoy making their own books or contributing pages to a group book for classroom use. For individual books, staple a few sheets of folded paper together. For group books, use cardboard punched with holes at the top. Fasten with leather thongs or notebook rings. Provide scissors, glue, and pages cut from catalogs illustrating things with simple machine parts: clocks, eggbeaters, wheelbarrows, wheeled toys, mechanical toys, tools, carts, pepper mills, and so forth. If the supply of pictures is sufficient, they could be part of a math experience, making separate pages to show one-wheeled objects, two-wheeled objects, and so on.

Friction as an Art Medium. Sometimes when children are drawing with pencils and crayons or making chalk rubbings, remind them that friction is involved in making colors stay on the paper.

A Friction Project. This project requires at least 2 days. Let the children sand 3-in. × 5-in. (8- × 12-cm) pieces of scrap lumber to satin smoothness. Next, use markers to draw a design on paper to cut out and glue to the sanded wood. The teacher can coat the plaque and picture with clear varnish. Allow at least a day of drying time. Insert a small screw-eye in the top edge of the plaque for hanging. This makes an appreciated gift for parents.

Play

Packing Carton Vehicles. Young children usually need little more than grocery cartons, paper plate wheels, and paper fasteners to create play cars and trains. A real steering wheel from an auto salvage yard, an inner tube and tire pump, and some sets of discarded keys add fun to the play.

Elevator. A tall refrigerator packing carton can become an elevator with a door cut in one side and numerals marked above it to indicate floors. It can be part of block or housekeeping play as desired.

Pulley Fun. Make an elevator for a block skyscraper. Ask children to build a three-sided block tower directly below a pulley. Fasten a milk carton elevator to one end of the pulley cord. Cut a door in one side of the carton and fill it with toy passengers.

Attach two small pulleys to opposite sides of the block play area a few feet above the floor. Tie the handle of a small basket to the pulley cord and knot the cord into a continuous, taut loop running between the two pulleys. It can be an aerial tramway for toy passengers or a conveyor belt for block construction workers. Consider the feasibility of adding a working pulley to a play area.

Other Indoor Fun

Many commercial toys with visible working parts extend the simple machine concepts in play. Examples include construction sets, gear sets, clocks, music boxes, and locks with visible working parts. Add a toy sand or water wheel to a sandbox or water table.

PVC pipes and elbows screw together to create "inventions." Provide pieces of perforated hardboard and hardware odds and ends to attach to it: cupboard doorknobs and hinges, nuts, bolts, and washers. Short screwdrivers are easiest for children to control. Supply the workbench with bottle caps, metal ends from food container tubes, and discarded spools to inspire the construction of wheel-, gear-, and dial-encrusted inventions.

Creative Movement

Mechanical Toys. Children enjoy acting out the stiff, jerking movements of windup toys. Offer to wind up one child toy at a time so that other children can guess what kind of toy they are watching, or wind up all the toys at once so that they can all move to music. In addition, children can try to move like the Tin Man in *The Wizard of Oz*, both when he was too rusty to move and after friction was reduced by oil so that he could move. Encourage children to improvise other simple machine actions.

Creative Thinking

Read Shel Silverstein's poem "Homework Machine" in *A Light in the Attic*. Then ask children to imagine a new machine that would help them solve a problem. "What would it do? What it look like?" Read Marcia Schonberg's book, *I Is for Idea.* Encourage children to draw pictures and/or write a description of their inventions. Collect them in a class book of great inventions. Or let children write about a simple machine they like, or have used, and make a "What We Have Found Out About Simple Machines" class report.

What If? Collect pictures to illustrate a family picnic outing: getting food ready, climbing into the car, and gathering fishing poles and playthings. Ask, "What if there wasn't any friction anywhere one day? What would be different for this family on a picnic? The mother would have trouble opening the peanut butter jar to make the sandwiches, the children would skid and fall down trying to walk to the car, the baseball bat would slip out of the boy's hand when he hit the ball, and the fishing poles might slide out of their hands."

Food Experiences

Children feel very important when they turn a crank that contributes to good eating. Several simple machines can be used to prepare food in the classroom. Make molded cookies with a cookie press. Use a hand-cranked grinder to make graham cracker crumbs for unbaked cookies or to make toast crumbs for the birds. Use a rolling pin to make cutout cookies and a gear-driven eggbeater to mix instant pudding. Grind wheat berries in a hand-cranked coffee mill. Borrow an apple paring/slicing machine to prepare apples for a snack.

Field Trips

1. School kitchen: Field trips to see simple machines in action can be as close by as a walk to the school kitchen. A well-timed visit might allow the children to see a food order being unloaded on a hand truck from a delivery truck. Hand

trucks have one pair of wheels on an axle and use the lever principle to lift loads. The kitchen may have a swivel-wheeled utility cart and a large can opener that has a sharp wheel to cut metal, gears to turn the can, a crank that turns an axle, and a screw to clamp the opener to a counter.

2. Maintenance room: A patient repair worker in the building could show children an array of tools and equipment that apply simple machine principles.

3. Parking space: This could be the scene of an impressive sight if the teacher can demonstrate the screw or lever principle by jacking up her car. (Be sure to observe the safety precautions of blocking the wheels on the ground with a brick and keeping children a safe distance away.)

4. Fitness center: If a nearby fitness center has observation windows, children can see a fascinating array of pulleys, levers, and axles on weight training machines. Treadmill rollers are sometimes visible when the bed is lifted as an inclined plane.

5. Supermarket: Backstage operations include hanging meat from overhead rolling tracks, using sets of rollers enclosed in metal frames to slide cases of food from trucks to storerooms, and moving groceries on checkout counter conveyor belts.

Safety Precaution: Be sure to check for safety hazards when planning these field trips. Children should be well supervised.

PROMOTING CONCEPT CONNECTIONS

Maintaining Concepts

There are countless opportunities to bring simple machine principles to light during everyday school activities. When we want things to move or spin or slide easily, we can mention the need to reduce friction with a few drops of oil. There are times when too little friction poses safety hazards for young children: shoeless children moving fast on slippery floors or unwary children crossing streets on rainy or icy days.

For a vivid application of the lever and a pair of wheels, let children use a hand truck to help trundle heavy sandbags to the sandbox. Encourage them to try moving the sandbags without the hand truck so that they will realize how much the hand truck helps them.

Simple machine concepts are part of workbench use. Examples include the friction of sanding and sawing, the lever action of pulling out nails with the hammer, and the interlocking screw threads that hold wood tightly in a vice or clamp.

Relate levers to joints in our bodies. Where two bones meet as a joint, muscles can move those bones like levers to help us move and lift things.

Whenever possible, let children watch the repair and maintenance of classroom and playground equipment. Better still, enlist the help of a shy child or one who needs a chance to get attention and approval. One child who broke toys and mistreated other children to attract attention was able to give up these undesirable behaviors when he became our chief mechanic. He took such pride in using the oilcan and tightening tricycle bolts that he became a good steward of school property and a friend to other children.

Improving School Grounds

Provide some 6-ft planks for children to devise their own ramps and levers. Screw 2- × 2-in. pieces of wood under each end so that when a plank is on a climber crossbar, it will not slip. Establish safety rules about the height planks can rise to.

A slide and a balance beam are good additions. If you are making a walled garden area, give the wall a wide top for balancing walks.

Connecting Concepts

Simple machines help overcome the effect of gravity's pull. This can be brought out by speaking about the weight of the objects being lifted or moved in terms of gravity's pull. The effect of magnetism could be used to discover what a strong axle or wheel frame is composed of or to learn what kind of hinge rusts and needs oiling when it works hard and squeaks from too much friction.

Family and Community Support

Ask families if they would be willing to lend equipment or demonstrate skills that involve simple machines. Todd's mother loaned us a butter churn that her

Strong boys magnify their strength with levers known as *shovels*.

grandmother had used. Jenny's mother made bread with us, using her hand-cranked kneading bucket. Both children gained new status as a result of their parents' contributions.

Identify the interactive simple machine exhibits available at the nearest children's science museum. Using a giant lever to heave up a boulder, hoisting themselves up in a rope-and-pulleys display, and turning wheels to make big things happen are impressive hands-on learning activities for children.

RESOURCES

ASHBROOK, PEGGY. (2006). Roll with it. *Science and Children, 43*(8), 16–18. Simple activities are described for preschoolers to experience how rollers make work easier.

CHALLEN, PAUL. (2009). *Get to know screws.* New York: Crabtree. Almost life-size photographs, failure-proof activities, and a bit of Archimedes' history make this a fine resource.

KASSINGER, RUTH. (2001). *Reinvent the wheel.* New York: Wiley. Develop awareness for the historical importance of simple machines with the fascinating anecdotes and models in this book.

MACAULAY, DAVID. (1998). *The new way things work: A visual guide to the world of machines.* Boston: Houghton Mifflin. This book gives the teacher the same revelations of "so-that's-how-it-works" that children gain from their study of simple machines.

 *ONLINE RESOURCES*

Institute of Electrical and Electronic Engineers (IEEE) has background information and experiments for teachers at *http://ewh.ieee.org/r3/cnc/tisp/ed/TE/simpmach.pdf*

14

Sound

Something vibrates, and sound results: a cricket chirps, thunder crashes, engines throb. Sounds evoke feelings and stir us to action. We whistle in the dark for courage, we sing to praise, we shout for joy. Let meaningful sound memories energize the way you share these investigations with children.

The discovery that sound occurs when something vibrates can help children overcome fears about scary noises. Vibrations cause sound whether they originate in the distant clouds or in our own throats. The following concepts are explored in this chapter:

- Sounds are made when something vibrates.
- Sound travels through many things.
- Vibrating objects of different sizes make different sounds.

The experiences begin with a group activity to clarify the term *vibration* and to establish the idea that vibrations cause sounds. This is followed by experiencing vibrations, experimenting with media through which sound travels, and relating the pitch of sound to the size of vibrating objects.

INTRODUCTION

Help children understand what a vibration is by producing one. Say something like this: "Can you lift your arm and let your hand dangle from your wrist? Now, shake your hand as fast as you can. What do you call what is happening to your hand? *Shaking? Wiggling? Jiggling? Wobbling?* Those are good words. *Vibration* is another word that means moving back and forth very fast. Does your hand look different when it is vibrating? Some vibrating things move back and forth so fast that they look blurry. Another thing happens when something vibrates. You can find out if you listen very quietly. Hold your hand near your ear, then vibrate your fingers and hand very fast. What happens? Does someone hear a soft, whirring sound?

"Now put your fingers very lightly on the front of your throat, near the bottom. Very softly sing a sound like 'eeeeee.' Do you feel something with your fingertips? Try it again. Did something inside your throat vibrate? Yes, you made a sound in there. Whenever we hear a sound, it is being made by something vibrating. Try touching your lips while you say 'hummmmmm.' What's happening?"

Read: Whistle for Willie by Ezra Jack Keats.

CONCEPT: Sounds are made when something vibrates.

1. What's happening when we see things vibrate?

LEARNING OBJECTIVE: To make the surprising connection between sound and vibrating materials.

MATERIALS:

Binding strip from vinyl folder cover or flexible ruler

Coffee can with plastic lid or sturdy drum

Sand, rice, or foam packing chips

Quart milk carton

Rubber bands

GETTING READY:

Cut a window opening in one side of a milk carton.

Stretch a rubber band around the length of the milk carton.

SMALL-GROUP ACTIVITY:

1. "Watch and listen to this." Extend a folder strip from the edge of the table or chair, like a diving board. Bend the free end down, then release it. "What did you see and hear?"

2. Show the milk carton. "What will happen if you pluck the rubber band? Watch and listen. You try it."

3. "It was easy to see the plastic strip and the rubber band vibrate. Some vibrations are hard to see. Let's put light things on this can lid to find out if the lid vibrates." Put sand, rice, or chips on the lid. Tap the lid. "What happens? Now you try it."

2. What's happening when we feel things vibrate?

LEARNING OBJECTIVE: To enjoy memorable ways of associating sound with vibrations.

MATERIALS:

Windup alarm clock, windup toy music box, and ticking kitchen timer (not battery operated)

Combs

SMALL-GROUP ACTIVITY:

1. Pass the unwound clock, timer, and music box among the children. "Do you feel these things vibrating now? Are they making sounds?"

2. Wind the equipment and pass it again. "Now what do you feel and hear?"

Waxed paper (tissue paper disintegrates when damp)

GETTING READY:

Cut pieces of waxed paper to fold over teeth of combs.

3. "Try making some music with vibrating air and paper. Hold the paper at the bottom of the comb lightly between your lips. Now try to hum and blow a tune at the same time. The vibrations feel funny, but the sound is nice."
4. Tour the room and halls to feel vibrating electric motors (aquarium water pump, sound system speaker, water cooler, etc.).

CONCEPT: **Sound travels through many things.**

1. How can we tell that air carries sound?

LEARNING OBJECTIVE: To have fun confirming that air carries sound vibrations.

MATERIALS:

12-in. (30-cm) pieces of plastic garden hose

Clear PVC tubes

♣ If a full-length garden hose is available, use it to carry out the same experiment outdoors.

SMALL-GROUP ACTIVITY:

1. "What could be inside the pieces of hose? Put one end next to your mouth; put the other next to your ear. Whisper your name into the hose. Could you hear yourself? What could be vibrating inside the tube?"
2. "You can *feel* what is vibrating if you put your hand at the end of the hose. Try saying words like *toot* and *tut*. Can you feel something pushing on your hand each time you say a word?" (Air carried vibrations from their throats through the tubes.)
3. Let seated children enjoy speaking to each other through the PVC tubes.

Read: Goggles by Ezra Jack Keats.

♣ Take time for a seated, silent listening circle outdoors (see p. 293). How many sounds can be heard?

Group Discussion: "Peek into the ear of the child sitting next to you. Do you see anything inside the ear that is vibrating? Could something invisible be in there?"

Recall how the sand or foam chips bounced around when someone tapped the coffee can lid. One vibrating thing made the things next to it vibrate. "Air vibrates when something next to it vibrates. That is the way sound is carried by air. It is the way sounds usually come to our ears. The air inside our ears also vibrates, so we hear the sounds." Let children experiment with this idea by covering and uncovering their ears with their hands as they listen to some music. Could the air inside their ears vibrate very well when their hands were covering them?

Safety Precaution: "Our ears have an outside part that we can see and an inside part that we can't see. The inside part is so delicate that vibrating air can vibrate it. That is how we hear. We must be very careful with our ears to keep that delicate part working well. Listening to very loud music through earphones every day can damage a person's hearing forever. Can you think of some good safety rules for our ears?"

Read: *Before John Was a Jazz Giant* by Carole Weatherford.

2. How can we tell that water carries sound?

LEARNING OBJECTIVE: To make the surprising discovery that water can carry sound vibrations.

MATERIALS:

Two similar containers, such as plastic buckets

Pair of blunt scissors

Sponge, plastic sheet, or newspaper for spills

PVC tubes

GETTING READY:

Half-fill one container with water.

SMALL-GROUP ACTIVITY:

1. "Take turns pressing one ear to the side of the bucket to listen to the sound I'll make." Open and shut scissors to make a steady clicking noise while holding them inside the empty bucket.
2. "I'll make the same sound in the water in this bucket. Listen the same way here. Listen for clicks. Are they louder or softer in the water? Put the PVC tube in the water, then put your ear at the other end to listen. Is the sound louder coming through the air or through water?" Let the children make the scissors click for each other.

Math skills: Comparing the quality and volume of sounds moving through water.

Note: If children in your class have gone fishing, they will understand now why people try to be very quiet when they are fishing. Mention that whales can hear other whales miles away.

3. How can we tell that sound travels through solids?

LEARNING OBJECTIVE: To be amazed that solid objects can carry and intensify sounds.

MATERIALS:

Table

Bottle caps, sticks, small rock to tap on the table

SMALL-GROUP ACTIVITY:

1. "We're going to make sounds for each other. Some may be very soft, so we'll have to listen closely." Tap one fingernail on the tabletop. "Does this sound seem loud? Now, cover one ear with your hand and

Windup clock, timer, or musical toy (a uniform sound-maker that isn't quietly battery operated)

press the other ear on the tabletop while I do the same thing again."

2. "Which way was the sound louder, through the air or through the wooden table? Now put your ears to the table and close your eyes. Each one of you can take a turn tapping on the table with these things. We'll try to guess what made the sound."

3. Later, compare sounds made by the clock, motor, or musical toy when held in the hand, placed on the table while heads are up, and placed on the table while ears are pressed to the table. Which sounds are loudest? Finding out takes time. Keep the learning pace relaxed. Listen to the children's ideas.

Math skills: Comparing the quality and volume of sounds moving through solids.

Read: Apt.3 by Ezra Jack Keats.

? *Inquiry Activity:* Establish a center for ongoing investigations about how well various materials carry the sound of a small ticking object (or another uniform sound-maker). Investigators cover one ear with a hand and the other with a test material. A partner holds the ticker (sound-maker) next to the testing ear. Test materials could include a metal container lid, a quarter-cup measure (full of air, of course) to be cupped over the ear, a thick mitten, or ear muffs. Add other materials that children may want to test.

Record the "best" findings and comments on a class chart, listing test materials down and children's names across. Summarize the survey when most children have participated.

4. How does string carry sound?

LEARNING OBJECTIVE: To enjoy discovering that tight strings carry sounds well.

MATERIALS:

Light string

Metal spoons

Bar of soap

Empty soup cans, 2 for each telephone

1½-in. (4-cm) nail

Hammer

SMALL-GROUP ACTIVITY:

1. Dangle short string over a finger. "Do you think loose string will vibrate to make a sound if you pluck it? What if it is held tightly by both hands? Try it both ways with your string." (Loose string vibrates too slowly to produce audible sound.)

2. "Let's add heavy vibrating metal to the string ends and listen to find out if tight

GETTING READY:

Cut string into 2½-ft (75-cm) lengths for spoon chimes.

Make a hole in the center of each can bottom.

Cut string into 5-ft (1.5-m) lengths for metal can telephones. (String can be longer for use at home. Short lengths are best when many children will be using phones in the same room.)

string will carry sound." Tie a spoon to each end of string. Fold string in half; press the folded end to the ear. Lean over so that spoons dangle freely. Swing string to make spoons strike each other. Listen to the sounds traveling up the string.

3. Make soup can telephones along with children. To stiffen string ends, pull them across a soap bar or wrap them with clear tape. Put a string through the holes in two cans from the outside. Pull string into the can and tie it around a nail. Wedge the nail inside the can. "Keep the string straight and tight. You talk into one can and your friend listens through the other can."

Group Discussion: Give each child a rubber band to pluck when it is limp and when it is stretched. What did the spoon chime and metal-can telephone makers find out about how string vibrates to carry sound? How many things vibrated to carry the sound of their voices? (Air in cans, the cans, and the string.)

Vibration turns ordinary string and an ordinary spoon into sound.

CONCEPT: **Vibrating objects of different sizes make different sounds.**

1. How do different vibrating string lengths sound?

LEARNING OBJECTIVE: To take pleasure in discerning pitch differences and associating them with vibrating string lengths.

MATERIALS:

Three sizes of plastic boxes, such as 3 in., 4 in., 5 in. (8 cm, 10 cm, 13 cm)

Egg carton

Rubber bands large enough to stretch around the length of boxes and egg carton

Pencil

Autoharp or guitar (desirable)

GETTING READY:

Stretch a small rubber band over each opened plastic box, the smallest band on the smallest box, and so on. (The effect won't be the same if the same-size rubber band is used on all three boxes. Try to find out why.)

SMALL-GROUP ACTIVITY:

1. Pluck the rubber bands on the plastic boxes. "Do these all sound alike? Which one sounds highest? Lowest? Try it."

2. "Now try this." Stretch a long rubber band lengthwise over the egg carton. Slip the pencil under the band near the left end of the box. Pluck the length of the rubber band to the right of the pencil. Listen. Continue plucking and slide the pencil slowly toward the other end of the box. "Is it changing? Is it higher or lower? Does the whole rubber band length vibrate, or just the side being plucked? Is the part that vibrates getting shorter and higher?" Let children experiment, sliding the pencil and plucking. "Can you play the scale this way? Play a tune?"

Math skills: Comparing sounds of rubber bands of varying length and thickness.

Read: Moses Goes to a Concert by Isaac Millman.

Group Discussion: The autoharp clearly shows the relationship between string length and pitch. (A real harp and an upright piano with the front panel removed, or a grand piano with the top raised, will show the same thing.) If a guitar is used for this purpose, be sure to make clear which part of the string is vibrating so that the relationship between vibrating string length and pitch can be understood.

2. How do different vibrating air column lengths sound?

LEARNING OBJECTIVE: To enjoy associating differences in pitch with varying columns of vibrating air.

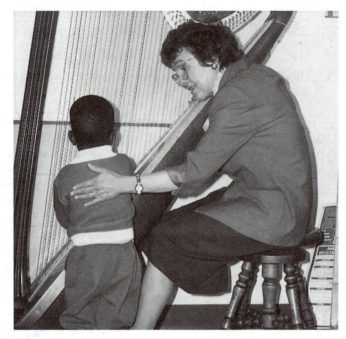

Vibrating strings, long and short, captivate Steven.

MATERIALS:

8 empty 16-oz (480-mL) bottles

Extra bottle to demonstrate
  blowing technique

Pitcher of water

Funnel

Masking tape

Sponge

Hand wipes (60% alcohol,
  non-triclosan)

GETTING READY:

Experiment at home with levels
  of water needed to produce

SMALL-GROUP ACTIVITY:

1. "What is inside these bottles? What will
   happen if the air inside the bottles
   vibrates? When air moves across the top
   of the bottle, the air inside vibrates."
   Demonstrate producing a tone.*

2. "We put some water in these bottles.
   Which bottle has space for more air? Let's
   see what happens when we make different
   amounts of air vibrate."

3. Arrange bottles in order, 1 through 8. Have
   eight children, one per bottle, blow across
   them in order, playing the scale. Can they
   play a tune? Wipe the tops with rubbing
   alcohol before others have turns.

---

*Demonstrate pressing your lower lip taut against your teeth, holding the bottle top to
your lower lip, and blowing "toooooo" *across, not into*, the bottle. Experiment at home.
Consult a flute player if you need help producing a tone.

tones of the octave. Internal shapes of bottles vary, but these are about right:

1. empty
2. 1¾ in. (4.5 cm)
3. 2½ in. (6.5 cm)
4. 4 in. (10 cm)
5. 4½ in. (11.5 cm)
6. 5¼ in. (13 cm)
7. 5½ in. (14 cm)
8. 6 in. (15 cm)

Place a band of tape around each bottle, with the upper edge of the tape at measurement level.

Let children pour water to marked levels of bottles, if possible.

Math skills: Comparing the relationship between pitch and vibrating air column lengths.

Note: Listen to a beautiful recording of Romanian pan flute music. Zamfir plays this ancient pan-pipes instrument. Many of the covers for his recordings illustrate the graduated-size pipes he blows across. (See Appendix A.)

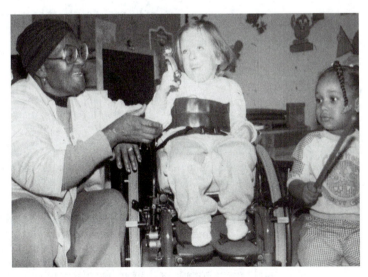

Sound-making is fun for everyone.

INTEGRATING ACTIVITIES

Math Experiences

Ordering by Pitch and Size. The mathematical relationship between the size of vibrating objects and the pitch they produce is fun to explore. Sets of bells and sets of detached metal chimes, available commercially, can be placed on a molded framework to form a xylophone. The bells and chimes can be arranged by children in one-step pitch order visually according to size (largest to smallest) or according to pitch (lowest to highest).

Music

Many familiar children's songs are easy extensions of the vibrations and pitch concepts, as they describe bell sounds and animal sounds. The concepts can be applied when rhythm instruments are used. "Charles, try holding your triangle by the string loop instead of with your hand. See if it vibrates more now." Prolong the life of school drums by suggesting that they will vibrate better when lightly tapped than when thumped very hard.

Children can make simple instruments to play. Directions are offered in *Making Music* by Ann Wiseman and John Langstaff.

The following song is about the cause of sounds:

Sounds

—J. H.

Literature Links

ALIKI. (2003). *Ah, music!* New York: HarperCollins. This joyful, rich account of music making shows its every form in many cultures, both historic and contemporary.

COMPENSTINE, YING. (2003). *The story of kites.* New York: Holiday House. The wind makes music when special kites carry bamboo flutes in this tale of kite invention in ancient China.

COX, JUDY. (2003). *My family plays music.* New York: Holiday House. Vibrating strings, skins, and air columns: Instruments of metal and wood tumble out of the pages of this book. Best of all, the joy of making music ripples throughout in vibrant pictures and text.

JOHNSON, ANGELA. (2004). *Violet's music.* New York: Dial. Perky Violet has two passions: making music and finding friends to share it. She makes musical sounds with zippers, toothbrushes, and spoons for starters.

LLEWELLYN, CLAIRE. (2005). *Sound and hearing.* North Mankato, MN: Cherrytree. Here is a nice interactive read-aloud book full of questions to start young children thinking about sound and trying simple explorations.

MCNULTY, FAITH. (2005). *If you decide to go to the moon.* New York: Scholastic. This charming story includes good information about the role of air in carrying sound.

ROSINSKY, NATALIE. (2003). *Sound: Loud, soft, high and low.* Minneapolis: Picture Window. Vibrant illustrations will attract confident readers to this book about sound concepts as they are experienced every day by children.

SADLER, WENDY. (2006). *Sound—listen up!* Chicago: Raintree. Confident readers will find good descriptions of bouncing sound waves, sound perception, and animal uses of sound in this reference.

WALKER, SALLY. (2006). *Sound.* Minneapolis: Lerner. The author engages children in active learning about the physics of sound first, then shows how to turn sound into music with straws, a ruler, cardboard, and tape. Well done!

WEATHERFORD, CAROLE. (2008). *Before John was a jazz giant.* New York: Henry Holt. Traces of sounds John Coltrane might have heard in childhood float across the pages of this simple story. What sounds do children in your class hear?

WISEMAN, ANN, & LANGSTAFF, JOHN. (2003). *Making music.* North Adams, MA: Storey Publishing. Cheerful drawings inspire making musical instruments from improbable objects!

Classics

COLE, JOANNA. (1999). *The magic schoolbus explores the senses.* New York: Scholastic. Travel the ear canal with Ms. Frizzle's class to discover how sound reaches the brain.

KEATS, EZRA JACK.* (1969) *Whistle for Willie.* New York: Viking. Peter discovers the thrill of learning to whistle.

KEATS, EZRA JACK.* (1971) *Goggles.* New York: Macmillan. Peter sends his voice through an empty drainpipe to confuse the big boys who are trying to catch him.

KEATS, EZRA JACK.* (1999). *Apt. 3.* New York: Viking. Varied sounds guide Sam to a sightless new friend who knows his neighbors by the sounds he associates with them.

MILLMAN, ISAAC. (2002). *Moses goes to a concert.* New York: Farrar, Strauss. Children from a school for the deaf watch and feel the concert by a deaf percussionist. Holding helium balloons in their laps helps them pick up vibrations. American Sign Language illustrations accompany this fine story.

PFEFFER, WENDY. (1999). *Sounds all around.* New York: HarperCollins. Young readers can feel vibrations as they speak, learning how sound guides bats in flight, how snakes feel sound, how whales and dolphins communicate, and how sound is measured. Simple sound activities are included. NSTA[†] Outstanding Trade Book.

Poems (Resources in Appendix A)

Many poems for children re-create sounds and extend the learning activities about sound.

> From *Poems to Grow On*, by Jean McKee Thompson, read "Kitchen Tunes" by Ida Pardue and "The Storm" by Dorothy Aldis.
>
> Paul Fleischman's *'Joyful Noise'* captures the sounds of familiar insects.

---

*Keats's simple books embody the emotional power of sounds in the life a boy whose playgrounds are drab city streets and vacant lots. They convey timeless meaning for children of many ages.

[†]National Science Teachers Association.

Fingerplays

Recall the soup can telephone fun with this fingerplay:

Soup Can Telephone

I called my friend on a soup can phone.	(Make cylinders with hands.)
Two soup cans were joined by a string.	(Extend little fingers to touch each other.)
I put it to my mouth,	(Put one cylinder up to mouth.)
I put it to my ear. I could hear my friend say everything!	(Put other cylinder up to ear.)

—J. H.

Art Activities

Drums. Use salt or oatmeal boxes, or cans with airtight plastic lids. Glue construction paper to the side of the drum, slipping rubber bands around the paper to hold it firmly while the glue dries. Children can decorate the drums with markers and fancy materials.

Horns. Let children wind and glue lengths of yarn around paper towel tubes or decorate them with markers. An adult can punch an air-vent hole near one end. Help children fasten a single piece of waxed paper over one end of the tube with a tight rubber band. A reedy sound is made by tooting tunes into the open end of the tube.

Play

1. A pair of soup can telephones can add interest to many dramatic play situations.
2. Medical play can include the experience of actually hearing each other's heartbeats. Use a real or improvised stethoscope to "gather" the sound so that it can be heard more clearly. Insert the tube ends of two soft plastic funnels into a short length of narrow-gauge plastic tubing. Place one funnel on a child's chest. Hold the other funnel close to the ear to hear the heartbeats.

Listening Activities

Match My Sound. Gather pairs of matching items that will produce sounds, such as metal spring "crickets," two squares of sandpaper to rub together, small brass bells, jingle bells, two bottle caps to tap together, blunt scissors to click, small pieces of corrugated paper to scrape with a fingertip, pocket combs and waxed paper to blow on, and two finger cymbals. Put one complete set of sound-making items in a teacher's bag. Distribute the matching items as evenly as possible into lunch-size paper bags. Fold down the tops and present a bag of secret sounds to each child at the table. While children keep their eyes tightly shut, the teacher reaches into his or her bag and makes a sound with one of the items. The children then search through their bags to see who can find things that produce a matching sound. Allow plenty of time for this activity.

Sound-Matching Tray. Use a divided cutlery tray and empty medicine vials or small opaque plastic bottles to adapt a Montessori sensory exercise. Loosely fill two matching containers with materials that make distinctive sounds when shaken, such as gravel, sand, pennies, rice, or puffed cereal. Mark matching pairs with matching numerals or letters on the container bottom as a self-correcting aid. Put one set of containers on one side of the tray; have children find the matching sound containers and place them next to their mates on the other side of the tray.

Creative Movement

Children can show their perceptions of high or low sounds by moving to the sounds of an instrument played by an adult. When the notes are low, the children move in a low position close to the floor; when they are high, the children move in a stretched-up position. They can also rise from a crouch to tiptoes in response to a slowly ascending scale and return to the crouch as the descending scale is played. Use a drumbeat to indicate varied movement tempos and rhythms as children move in the same direction around the room.

Creative Thinking

Pacing your comments softly and slowly, begin with something like this: "Close your eyes and let your imagination tune in to remembered sounds. Hear a loud bell ringing. Where are you when you hear that bell? What is it telling you? Now hear a softer bell ringing. What does its sound mean?" "Now listen for the blowing wind on a stormy day. Will you hear rain coming down soon?" "The crack of thunder?" "Will the wind blow through your window and make the blinds rattle?" "Now listen for sounds coming from the kitchen as someone fixes your breakfast. Do you hear the toaster popping up? What else do you hear?" Create other auditory images. Then let children report the sounds and their personal meanings.

Food Experience

Sound is a critical part of microwaving popcorn without burning it. If a microwave oven is accessible, let children time the pops.

Field Trips

Look around your school area for a place that will produce an echo. An empty gymnasium or a high, windowless wall that borders an empty lot might be good places. Tell children that when they shout their names toward the walls, the vibrations touch the walls and bounce back to them. Try it.

As you walk together for any special purpose, suggest walking very quietly so that you can listen for sounds to identify. An old church or auditorium with visible organ pipes, within walking distance of the school, is a good destination for this study.

Maya and Justin converse through the talk tube.

PROMOTING CONCEPT CONNECTIONS

Maintaining Concepts

Occasionally, two of the loudest and most frightening sounds occur while children are in school: thunder and sonic booms. When lightning moves through the air, that air suddenly gets warm and it swells so fast that it vibrates. Thunder is the way we hear the vibration from that fast-swelling air far up in the clouds.

Improving School Grounds

Hang a set of wind chimes in a quiet area of the yard. Children can construct chimes from shells or other recyclables. Install a talk tube, available from playground equipment suppliers, which is installed underground with vertical aboveground talking stations (see photos).

Connecting Concepts

1. Some of the suggested experiences relate to the children's existing concepts about the presence of air in empty-looking places and moving air pushing things (see Chapter 7, Air).

2. Friction is also involved in the production of some sounds, such as rubbing pieces of sandpaper or unlubricated metal parts together to produce squeaks from the vibrations (see Chapter 13, Simple Machines).

3. Nature-based musical instruments are traditionally made from plants, such as gourd horns, bamboo flutes and pan pipes, dried cactus rainsticks, and hollow log drums. Animal skins form drum heads, animal horns and conch shells are wind instruments, and animal bones are used as percussion instruments.

Family and Community Support

Any parent who is able to bring in and play a musical instrument can enrich the children's awareness of sound-making. Families could be encouraged to lend things like a bell collection or wind chimes for the children to enjoy. Suggest events of sound-making interest in the locality that parents might attend with their children, such as a bell-ringing choir or children's concerts.

Families will enjoy hands-on sound-making exhibits, such as whisper chambers and floor keyboards where children can hop out tunes, in the nearest children's museum.

RESOURCES

LAU, DARLENT, & LIM, CHENG. (2002). *Science alive! Sound.* New York: Crabtree. The experiments in this book are meant for older children. It offers easy directions for making panpipes from drinking straws that young children can follow and enjoy.

ROBERTSON, WILLIAM. (2004). *Stop faking it! Finally understanding science so you can teach it: Sound.* Arlington, VA: NSTA Press. You'll teach more confidently after this book slows down and eases the process of understanding sound. It does so with humor.

 ## ONLINE RESOURCES

Wikipedia: Look for mathematics of musical scales, and perception of sound at *http://en.wikipedia.org/wiki/Sound*

San Francisco Exploratorium: Contact the Science of Music at *http://www.exploratorium.edu/music/index.html*

Light

Light radiates, and we see! Awesome visual memories stay with us: brilliant stars shining through the curtain of night, a still pond mirroring shoreline trees, a harvest moon blooming on the horizon. Let such moments brighten children's explorations of light.

On the day of birth, infants are able to perceive light. Later, the playpen explorer may try to catch a sunbeam. The toddler may try to pounce on a shadow. Growing young children are fascinated by the sparkle of reflected light and the beauty of the color spectrum. The experiences that capture some children's closest attention, however, are those that help to allay their worries about darkness—the absence of light. The following concepts are suggested for investigation in this chapter:

- Nothing can be seen without light in everyday experience.
- Light appears to travel in a straight line.
- Shadows are made when light beams are blocked.
- Night is Earth's shadow.
- Everything we see reflects some light.
- Light contains many colors.
- Bending light beams make things look different.

Children can experiment by examining a box full of darkness, using a flashlight beam to note the straight path of light, creating shadows, and looking through filters. Other experiences explain night and day, reflection, and refraction.

INTRODUCTION

To lead into these experiences with light, read this story about the mastery of nighttime anxiety: *Switch on the Night* by Ray Bradbury.

CONCEPT: Nothing can be seen without light in everyday experience.

1. What can we see in a dark box?

LEARNING OBJECTIVE: To soften anxiety about the dark: It's dispelled by light to let us see.

MATERIALS:

Pen flashlight

Extra batteries

Shoe box with cover

Small picture

Old, heavy blanket

Low table

GETTING READY:

Cut a dime-size peephole in one end of the shoe box.

Cut a flap in top of box.

Paste picture to inside of box at end opposite the peephole.

Cover table with the blanket so it drapes to floor on all sides, making a dark place.

SMALL-GROUP ACTIVITY:

1. Tell children, "Let's stretch out on the floor and put just our heads into the dark place under the table."
2. "Here is a dark box. It has a hole in one end to look into. What do you see in there?" Pass the box to everyone.
3. "Now I am going to change something; then you can look into the box again." Turn on the flashlight and push it under the flap on the top of the box. "Can you see something in the box now? It was there before, but you couldn't see it. Let's try to find out why."
4. Remove the flashlight; pass the box again. "The picture is still in there. Can you see it? What happens when the light goes off? We always need light to see anything. *Nothing can be seen without light.*"

Be prepared to repeat this experience. Young children are impressed with, and reassured by, their ability to make the dark go away and come back at will.

Read: The Bird, the Frog, and the Light by Avi.

CONCEPT: Light appears to travel in a straight line.

1. How does a flashlight beam travel?

LEARNING OBJECTIVE: To confirm the intriguing way light seems to travel in a straight line.

MATERIALS:

Pen flashlight

Extra batteries

SMALL-GROUP ACTIVITY:

1. Tell children, "Let's find out how a beam of light travels. Lie down along the sides of

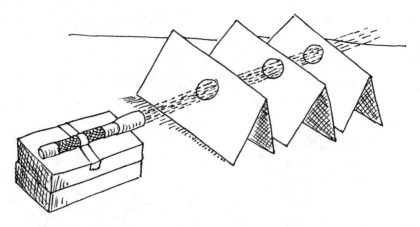

FIGURE 15–1

3 sheets of white paper
Heavy blanket and low table
2 blocks
Masking tape

GETTING READY:

To prepare three screens:

- Stack the two blocks and tape the flashlight to the top block. Turn the flashlight on.
- Fold paper as shown in Figure 15–1. Stand it in front of the light.
- Cut a small hole where the beam hits the center of the paper.
- Cut holes in the same location in the other screens.

Line up screens a few inches apart so that the light beam can pass through all the holes. Cover table with blanket.

the table. Put your heads under the blanket. I'll be at this end; no one will be at the other end."

2. Turn on the flashlight. "Notice the light shining on the blanket at the end of the table? It passes through each hole in the screens."

3. "Liz, will you put your hand in front of one hole, please? What happened? Did Liz's hand block the light or did it curve around the paper to shine through the next holes?"

4. "Take turns blocking the light beam as Liz did. Does the light curve around things or does light travel in a straight path?" Let children use the flashlight to check and recheck the path of light.

CONCEPT: **Shadows are made when light beams are blocked.**

1. Which things let light pass through?

LEARNING OBJECTIVE: To enjoy seeing how light passes through different materials and forms shadows when blocked.

Look, we're blocking the light!

MATERIALS:

Small flashlight

Blanket and low table

Waxed paper

Cardboard

Large shoe box

Clear glass jar

Water

Colored tissue paper

Clear acetate folder

GETTING READY:

Cut a large opening in shoe box bottom.

Cut a simple 3-in. (7.5-cm) cardboard doll figure.

Fill the jar with water.

Cover the table with the blanket.

SMALL-GROUP ACTIVITY:

1. "Let's find out what light will shine through. You stretch out along that side of the table and I'll be across from you."
2. Put the box on its side with the opening facing the children. Shine the light through the opening. "Let's see if light shines through air."
3. Put the water jar in the opening. "Let's see if light shines through water."
4. "Let's see if light will shine through waxed paper in the same way." Cover the opening with waxed paper. "Does the light shine in one spot or spread out?" Try using colored tissue paper and clear acetate at the opening.
5. "Let's see if light will shine through this cardboard doll." Remove the box; place the doll so that it makes a shadow on the blanket.
6. Tell children to notice that light shines on only one side of the doll. "There is a dark place where the doll blocked the light. It's a shadow."

Large-Group Activity: ♣ Move outdoors early on a sunny day. Use chalk to trace the outline of children's shadows on a paved area. As you trace, ask other children, "Is sunlight shining right through Nina, or does she block the light? I'm tracing the darkness that Nina's body makes where the sunlight can't shine through her." Return later to draw new outlines. Observe that the shadow has shifted and is not the same length.

Math Skills: Comparing shadow lengths at various times of day.

Read: "Recess" by Lillian Moore (see **Poems**)

CONCEPT: Night is Earth's shadow.

1. Why do we have day and night?

LEARNING OBJECTIVE: To be reassured that night's darkness is the turning Earth's shadow.

Large-Group Experience (You will need a globe or ball, projector or flashlight, chalk, and a darkened room.): "We had fun blocking the sunlight to make shadows. Did you know that the whole Earth does the same thing? That is the way day and night happen. Let's pretend that this light is the shining sun. This globe is a model of our huge Earth. I'll put a chalk mark here on the globe to show where our part of the world is. Watch the mark as I turn the globe the way the Earth always slowly turns. Is the mark in the light now? Does the light curve around the globe to keep shining on our part of the world? No, the light shines in a straight line. Our part of the world is in a shadow now—the shadow of the other side of the Earth."

Continue to turn the globe so that children can see the marked part of the globe alternately in the light and in the shadow. "What do we call the time when our part of the world is in Earth's shadow? When it is in the sunlight?" Let the children turn the globe.

When your class encounters mention of the sun's *rising* or *setting* in stories, poems, or songs, point out that such was the old, imaginary way of thinking about night and day. *We* know that it only *looks* like the sun is traveling around Earth. We have daylight when our part of the traveling Earth spins toward the sun. After a while, rely on the class to correct such misconceptions they may find.

Read: Faces of the Moon by Bob Crelin.

CONCEPT: Everything we see reflects some light.

Introduction: Put a lighted purse-size flashlight into your cupped hands. Open your hands to let the children see where the light is coming from. "Is the flashlight making this light?" Hold a pocket mirror in your hands. "Is the mirror making a light?" Now shine the flashlight beam on the mirror. Tilt the mirror so that the light is reflected onto the walls or ceiling. "Which thing made the light

Many reflections make many thoughts.

that is bouncing up there, the flashlight or the mirror?" Turn the flashlight off and on several times so that children can verify that the spot of light is reflected by the mirror to the ceiling only when the flashlight makes the light.

Note: A child may notice that a transparent glass window sometimes *reflects* light like a mirror. This occurs as a result of the way light strikes the surface of the glass. The surface of a still pond or a shallow swimming pool can also show a mirrorlike reflection. This happens when sunlight reflects back *up* from the bottom of the pond or pool.

1. Which things reflect light better than others?

LEARNING OBJECTIVE: To enjoy bouncing light beams and exploring differences in reflecting surfaces.

MATERIALS:

Strong sunlight or spotlight lamp

White paper

Easel

Cardboard pieces 3x5 in. (7x12cm)

Aluminum foil

Aluminum foil pan

Colored paper (include black)

Textured fabrics: velvet, satin,
   "fur," and the like

Balls (playground and/or tennis)

GETTING READY:

Fold smooth sheets of aluminum
   foil around pieces of cardboard.
   Tape securely. Repeat with well-
   crumpled foil to make two kinds
   of reflectors for children.

Whole-Group Activity: ♣ Take aluminum foil reflectors and balls outdoors to a paved area.

1. "Exactly what do you predict this ball will do if I hold it up and drop it straight down? Yes, it bounced straight back up. Do you think exactly the same thing will happen if I drop it over on the grass (or any rough surface, such as gravel or dirt)? Let's see." Give children balls to compare straight down and up bounces on the smooth pavement with the weaker, unpredictable return bounces on rough surfaces.

2. "Let's see if something like that happens with light bouncing on smooth and not-smooth surfaces." Hold up two different foil reflectors. "Which one bounces back the brightest light? Light is reflected back from everything we see, but in different ways for different things." Let children enjoy comparing the two foil reflector surfaces.

Math Skills: Comparing amounts of light reflected back by various surfaces.

❓ *Inquiry Activity:* Set up a way to reflect light by fastening the paper on the easel and placing it at a right angle to a sunny window or the spotlight lamp. Facing the window or lamp, hold an aluminum foil pan so that it reflects light onto the sheet of paper on the easel. "Do you think that different textures and different colors will reflect back as well as this pan?" Ask for predictions about bright or dull reflections.

Let small groups experiment with using other materials to reflect light back onto the white paper. Have them decide and record their comparisons of how well different materials (soft, rough, or smooth) and colors (light or dark) reflect light. Post and discuss the final results. Add that the soft or rough textures and dark colors also *absorb* more light than the smooth textures and light colors. "Does the sun just send out light? So, what colors might be good to wear in hot weather?"

CONCEPT: **Light contains many colors.**

1. Which things bend light to show its colors?

LEARNING OBJECTIVE: To be awed by light's hidden colors spreading out through a prism.

MATERIALS:

Magazine

Strong sunlight or a projector

Small piece of thick plate glass or plastic, edges taped*

Prisms or chandelier drops

Small, clear plastic boxes

Water

Soap bubble materials

Aquarium (desirable)

Diffraction grating cards, if available

Several free CDs

String

SMALL-GROUP ACTIVITY:

1. "There is a surprise in light beams. This magazine can help us find it." Hold the magazine with cut edges toward children and the bound edge toward you (Figure 15–2). "When pages are pressed together, does the edge look like one thick line? I'll bend it back toward me. Notice the line spread out to show many edges of paper. Try it."

2. Hold plate glass in front of the light source. "When light comes through this glass, it looks clear. Let's see how light looks when it is spread by glass that bends it."

3. Hold the prism edge in front of the light beam and rotate it until a spectrum can be seen in the room. "Now you see the secret! Light really has seven colors in it (the *spectrum*), but we only see them when light shines through something clear that is bent or curved." Let the children try it.

4. If possible, place an aquarium near sunny windows. Fill it with water. Help children stand where they can see the spectrum through the aquarium corners.

5. On a sunny day, let children experiment with water in small plastic boxes outdoors. Can they see the spectrum through the corners?

6. Try to make soap bubbles near a sunny window to see colors.

7. Let children examine diffraction grating cards and CDs to see the rainbow effects reflected by the patterns of lines.

8. Tie together pairs of free CDs, label sides facing each other. Hang from strings near windows to reflect light around the room. Some of them reflect spectrum colors as well.

*Do not use a magnifying glass.

FIGURE 15–2

Read: "Crystal Vision" by Lawrence Schimel, a poem about prisms, in Lee Bennett Hopkins's collection, *Spectacular Science* (Appendix A.).

CONCEPT: **Bending light beams make things look different.**

1. How do things look through a curved drop of water?
LEARNING OBJECTIVE: To wonder at how light bending into a curved path lets us see things differently.

MATERIALS:

Small bottles
Water
Medicine droppers
Waxed paper
Newspapers
Plastic card lens
2 strong magnifiers
Desirable: jeweler's loupes*

SMALL-GROUP ACTIVITY:

1. "What happens when you put *just one* drop of water on your piece of waxed paper? Look at the newspaper through the drop of water. What do you see? Is the water drop curved or flat?"
2. "Now add more water to the drop. Is it still curved, or is it a flat spot of water? Do the words beneath it still look bigger? Why not? What has changed?"

*Inexpensive jeweler's loupes and instructions for use can be ordered from The Private Eye Project (see Teaching Resources). When correctly used, they block off peripheral light, increasing both the focus and the viewer's concentration.

Toilet paper tube

Sponges

Small objects to examine

GETTING READY:

Fill bottles with water for each child.

Cut waxed paper and printed sections of newspaper into 3-in. (7.5-cm) squares.

Give each child a square of newspaper with waxed paper covering it.

3. "Absorb the water with a sponge and try again."

4. Show children the curved profile of a magnifying lens. "Hold up the curved water bottle. Look at your finger through the bottle and water. How does it look?" (The path of light bends when it passes through a clear, curved surface like glass or a curved drop of water. Things seen through them look different.) "Scientists call this *refraction*. We looked through curves that made things look bigger." Look at the rows of tiny curved surfaces in the plastic card lens magnifiers.

5. Explore the effect of holding the paper tube between two strong magnifiers (a simple microscope). Compare looking at newspaper type through a single magnifier, then through the two tube-joined magnifiers.

Math Skills: Observing that drops are curved and that objects' sizes appear different when viewed through curved surfaces.

Curved lenses bring things closer.

Children are intrigued by the upside-down reflections they see in the concave (inside) surface of a shiny spoon or the odd magnification made by the convex (outer) surface of the spoon. Light rays also bend when they pass from one transparent substance to another. Examine how a straw appears to bend when it rests on an angle in a glass of water. Continue to look for these instances of refraction that change the way things appear.

INTEGRATING ACTIVITIES

Math Experiences

Shadow Math. ♣ Early on a sunny morning, move outdoors and have children find a place to stand along a line with their backs to the sun. Let them trace one another's shadow outlines with chalk. Mark them with the owner's initials. Measure the length of each shadow with a meterstick and record the data indoors on a chart. At noon, return to the marked places and repeat the tracing and data collecting. Abstract explanations of Earth's spinning will not make much of an impression on most children, but this experience with changing shadows will contribute to eventual understanding.

Return to the marked places at the end of the school day. Where are the children's shadows? Measure the length of the afternoon shadows. Add to the chart. (As our part of Earth spins away from the sun, shadows change in direction as the day goes on. They change in size as the angle of sunlight reaching Earth changes.)

Make a Sundial. In late spring, older children will be intrigued by creating a primitive sundial on the school grounds that can be closed off for this purpose. Directions for making a sundial can be found in *Great Experiments with Light* by Phyllis and Noel Fiarotta.

Mirror Math. Explore easy symmetry experiences with mirrors. Give small rectangular mirrors to the children. Give them pictures cut from magazines to see if they can make the same pictures in the mirror. Provide objects like half circles to see if they can make whole circles in the mirror.

Further ideas for making these activities more challenging for older children are found in the Delta publication *Mirror Explorations* (see Appendix A).

Energy Conservation. (Adding 10s in a useful context.) Show children the wattage numbers on lightbulbs, explaining that the numbers mean different degrees of brightness. Using a small shadeless lamp, demonstrate the brightness of different wattages. Calculate with the children the total wattage used in the classroom so that they can understand the reason for turning off the lights when the classroom is empty. Mention that fluorescent bulbs use less watts.

Explore Angles. As a background experience for future geometry study, let children play with a flashlight and a plastic mirror to explore how the angle of light hitting the mirror is the same as the angle of light bouncing off the mirror.

Pose problems for them: "Can you use the mirror to make the light shine on the door? . . . On the ceiling? . . . On the big table?"

Music (Resources in Appendix A)

Mention that laser light beams are used instead of needles to play compact disc recordings. Sing this song after children have used prisms (to the tune of "Good Morning, Merry Sunshine"):

Prism Song

Good morning, merry sunshine,

Your light comes straight to me.

When glass or water bend your line,

Your colors I can see.

—J. H.

Literature Links

ARLON, PENELOPE. (2006). *Light.* London: Dorling Kindersley. A lively layout with flip pages and cutouts make crisply stated, basic light concepts easier to absorb.

BANG, MOLLY. (2004). *My light.* New York: Scholastic. In clear, pulsating prose and her remarkable illustrations, Molly Bang presents the *big picture* of how sunlight makes life on Earth possible. She shows the way energy can be transformed, harnessed, and misused. It is far more information than young children can absorb, but let them begin! NSTA* recommended.

BLEVENS, WILEY. (2003). *You can use a magnifying glass.* New York: Children's Press. Very simple information about handling a magnifier includes pictures of the correct way to ink and stamp fingerprints.

COBB, VICKI. (2002). *I see myself!* New York: HarperCollins. Text bounces across the pages of this excellent book as it explains reflections. Vicki Cobb tackles abstract concepts with amazing simplicity and clarity. Though it is meant for preschoolers, young readers may want to linger over it for further enlightenment. NSTA* Outstanding Trade Book.

CRELIN, BOB. (2009) *Faces of the moon.* Watertown, MA: Charlesbridge. A great poetic text, strong art, and die-cut pages add sensory input to help children understand how the shapes we see of the moon are caused by Earth's shadow.

LILLY, MELINDA. (2006). *Me and my shadow.* Vero Beach, FL: Rourke. Independent readers can explore shadow fun, art, and light source activities.

ROSINSKY, NATALIE. (2005). *Light, shadows, mirrors, and rainbows.* Minneapolis: Picture Window Books. Clear information about light and useful activities to demonstrate principles are provided.

SADLER, WENDY. (2006). *Light—look out!* Chicago: Raintree. Confident readers will find good descriptions of reflections, energy from light, and lasers in this reference.

STEWART, MELISSA. (2004). *Fun with the sun.* Minneapolis: Compasspoint. Directed to the confident reader, this book offers simple experiences with shadows, night and day, and the reason for seasons.

TRUMBAUER, LISA. (2004). *All about light.* New York: Scholastic. Good photographs and clearly stated light concepts are summarized in this small science reader.

*National Science Teachers Association.

WALKER, SALLY. (2006). *Light*. Minneapolis: Lerner. Here is a deeper look at the nature of traveling light rays, with activities to help understand the concepts of reflection, refraction, and color, as well as light waves as a heat source. NSTA* recommended.

WILLSON, SARAH. (2004). *Hocus focus*. New York: Kane. Many children will relate to this classroom-set story involving embarrassment about new glasses, a science field trip, and a bully. Facts about lenses and vision correction slip in naturally.

Classics

AVI. (1994). *The bird, the frog, and the light*. New York: Orchard Books. In this satisfying fable, an arrogant frog king can't see his dark underground kingdom. He asks a bird to bring a ray of sunshine into his tunnel, with disillusioning results.

BRADBURY, RAY. (2000). *Switch on the night*. New York: HarperCollins. A child learns to control his fear of darkness.

BRANLEY, FRANKLYN. (1998). *Day light, night light: Where light comes from*. New York: HarperCollins. Cozy illustrations and clear prose place difficult concepts into the context of ordinary events.

CHORAO, KAY. (2001). *Shadow night: A picture book with shadow play*. New York: Dutton. Essentially a hand-shadows story, this book makes a fine extended activity for light study.

DUSSLING, JENNIFER. (2002). *The rainbow mystery*. New York: Kane Press. Two children track down the source of unexplained spectrum colors on their walls. They investigate the mystery as scientists might.

LIONNI, LEO. (1959). *Little blue and little yellow*. Republished and widely available.

OTTO, CAROLYN. (1995). *Raccoon at Clear Creek Road*. Washington, DC: Smithsonian. This story connects nocturnal animal vision with aspects of light as a mother raccoon dodges light beams, hides in shadows, and is drawn to shiny foil reflections while she scavenges for food to sustain her young brood.

ROSENBERG, LIZ. (2001). *Eli's night light*. New York: Scholastic. When Eli's night light burns out, he notices other reassuring sources of reflected light in and around his darkened room. The youngest listeners and beginning readers will find comfort in this simple story

SAYRE, APRIL. (2002). *Shadows*. New York: Holt. In this pleasant story, two youngsters' playful search for shadows is interrupted when clouds "sponge shadows away."

Storytelling with Lights

Use a small high-intensity lamp and three-dimensional objects to animate and tell a simple shadow story. Do this on the floor of a darkened room with the children sitting in a circle around the story setting. Small dolls can be children playing shadow tag outdoors. A cardboard tree or a wall of blocks can form a shady place for the dolls to rest after the game. A cardboard cloud could pass between the dolls and the lamp to perplex the story children. They can't find their shadows for the tag game and think they've lost them. Walk the dolls over to the children watching the story to ask them for help finding the shadows.

Poems (Resources in Appendix A)

There are many poems about light.

From *A Light in the Attic* by Shel Silverstein, read "Shadow Race" and "Reflection."

---

*National Science Teachers Association.

From *Poems to Grow On*, compiled by Jean McKee Thompson, read "Shadow Dance" by Ivy O. Eastwick; "Kick a Little Stone" by Dorothy Aldis; "Mirrors" by Mary McB. Green; and "I Wonder" by Virginia Gibbons.

From *Sing a Song of Popcorn*, compiled by Beatrice deRegniers, read "8 A.M. Shadows" by Patricia Hubbell.

From *A Child's Garden of Verses* by Robert Louis Stevenson, read "My Shadow."

From *I Thought I'd Take My Rat to School*, compiled by Dorothy Kennedy, read Lillian Moore's "Recess," about children scribbling their shadows on the schoolyard.

From *Out and About* by Shirley Hughes, read "Squirting Rainbows."

From *Flicker Flash* by Joan Graham, read all 23 poems honoring forms of light familiar to children.

From *Spectacular Science*, compiled by Lee Bennett Hopkins, read "Crystal Vision" by Lawrence Schimel and "Under the Microscope" by Lee Bennett Hopkins.

Art Activities

A Reflecting Collage. Let children use pieces of foil gift wrap, aluminum foil, sequins, glitter, and gummed stars to make collages.

Reflector Hanging. Let children cut pairs of simple shapes from foil paper or aluminum foil. Help them place three or four shapes face down in a line. Put a few drops of white glue in the center of each shape. Place a 15-in. (38-cm) length of string on the glue spots and then let the children cover each shape with its mate. Tie a gold plastic thread spool to the bottom of the string. Tape to the ceiling or to a door frame.

"Stained Glass" Medallions. Cut apart separate rings of plastic "six-pack" holders from frozen juice or drink cans. Pierce a hole at the top of each ring with a heavy threaded needle. Tie a thread loop. Let children dot glue around the ring and press colored tissue paper and cellophane over it; then trim away excess paper. Hang the medallions in the windows. Ask, "Does light come through?"

Waxed Paper Translucents. Let children cut shapes from colored tissue paper and arrange them as they wish between two sheets of waxed paper. Children seal the papers together by placing them on a newspaper-covered food-warming tray and rubbing firmly across the waxed paper with a pizza roller.

Color Blending. After reading *Little Blue and Little Yellow* by Leo Lionni, children may be interested in blending paint colors. Younger children can try two primary colors at a time. Older children can try to create all the colors of the rainbow with three primary colors.

Play

♣ *Reflection Tag.* Take aluminum foil pans outdoors on a sunny day to tag players with reflected light. **Safety precaution:** Avoid directing reflected sunlight into anyone's eyes.

Shadow Fun. Draw the shades during active playtime on a rainy day and set up a projector at one end of the room. Turn on dance music and let the children enjoy creating shadows as they dance in a designated area. ♣ Play shadow tag outdoors with the children on a sunny day.

Reflection/Refraction Attraction. Follow up the reflection and refraction experiences by bringing in as many of these fascinating toys and practical items as you and your class can supply. Kaleidoscopes, octoscopes, and periscopes all depend on mirrors within them to create intriguing patterns and views. The Dragonfly Octoscope has 25 planes in its lens to imitate that insect's view of the world. Diffraction grating lenses and novelty items produce rainbow effects. These items are usually sold in nature stores and museum shops. Add old binoculars, varied plastic card magnifying lenses and other magnifying lenses, and a container of small things to examine. Have disinfectant wipes on hand to clean eyepieces between uses.

Creative Movement

Be My Mirror. Suggest to the children that they pretend to be your reflection in a mirror. They move silently as you move. You may be surprised at the number of movements you and the children can invent while you are seated, using your head, neck, shoulders, arms, hands, and fingers. This is a good activity to calm a restless group.

Creative Thinking

What If? Start a story for the class to complete. "What if you wake up one stormy night and find that the electricity isn't working? The moon isn't shining, and the stars are hidden by clouds. Your light won't click on. You don't have a flashlight. You don't feel sleepy. Feel around your room for your favorite book. Do you have the right book? Can you read it? Feel around for your box of crayons and some paper. Can you draw a picture? Which colors would you use? Can you see yourself in your mirror? How could someone in your house make some light for you? Does the light fill the room? Can you think of a way to make that light bigger? What else would seem different?"

Food Experiences

1. Make an edible jello lens following the directions on page 298 in *Exploratopia* by Pat Murphy et al. Make one or two of the largest curved lenses for the class to try out as magnifiers to read through. Then add a new comparison feature to the jello preparation you do at home. This will make it possible (and more sanitary) for children to eat the experiment afterward! Make a second batch of lemon jello in an 8 × 8-in. (20 × 20-cm) square baking pan. It will be a thin layer. Cut the jello into enough squares for each child to compare the light-bending possibilities of both flat and curved surfaces. "Which surface does light bend through? Investigate, then eat the square!"

2. Solar oven making and cooking fits here! Find oven-making directions and some neat recipes in *Toad Cottages and Shooting Stars* by Sharon Lovejoy.

PROMOTING CONCEPT CONNECTIONS

Maintaining Concepts

1. Point out reflections when you notice them in the classroom: in doorknobs, in a child's shiny brass button, in the spoons at lunchtime, or in the rain puddles on the playground.

2. Hang a prism in a classroom window that gets direct sunlight. Experiment with balance and location to produce a good spectrum.

3. Use the opportunities that arise to comment on the need for light to see well: when raising the shades after rest time, when looking closely at a scraped knee, and so on. Comment that we need light to see our wonderful world.

4. Store magnifying glasses in a place where children will have access to them when they want to examine something. If you have a classroom microscope, let the children know that you will get it out for them when they want to examine a specimen. Talk about reflecting more light onto the specimen with the adjustable mirror.

5. Keep track of the length of the shadow made by a special tree or building near the school playground. Use a chalk mark on a paved surface, or stones on a grassy area, to compare its length when you are outdoors in the morning, at noon, and in the afternoon. Assign this responsibility to specific children, who then demonstrate the change to the others.

6. When the subject of lasers is brought up by children in terms of the destructive weapons they see in television programs or in certain toy advertisements, balance these ideas by discussing the constructive uses of laser light. Tell them that this form of synthetic light is used by doctors to heal people. It is a powerful tool with many good uses. It is also used to "read" the bar codes on grocery packages at the supermarket checkout counter. A tiny laser beam shines on compact discs to produce sound.

Improving School Grounds

Make the school grounds more interesting and inviting by altering the light and shadow patterns. An arbor of vines creates both welcome shade on sunny days and shifting leafy patterns on the ground. In the fall or spring, plant the largest shade trees possible and make them places to play under by encircling them with decks that protect the root system and provide level, cool places for quiet activities. If you have a garden, cast-off CDs suspended from strings between stakes catch sunlight intriguingly and discourage hungry birds.

Connecting Concepts

Relate the bending of light beams to the surface tension experiences (see Chapter 8, Water). Recall that the pull on the outside of the water drop makes it curved. Light coming through this curve of water bends and changes the way in which we see through it. Surface tension keeps soap bubbles curved and lets us see rainbow colors of spread-out light beams. In caring for classroom plants, remind children that all plants need light to stay alive and grow. Animals and humans need light to live, too, because they need plants for food.

Read: *Raccoon at Clear Creek Road* by Carolyn Otto to connect aspects of light with nocturnal animal vision.

Family and Community Support

Encourage families to notice light coming through stained glass windows, the path of nighttime searchlights, car headlights on both clear and foggy nights, a lighthouse beacon, and the paths of stadium lights. Point out solar panels on roofs that capture the sun's energy for heating or electricity. Families may have pocket calculators that use photovoltaic material to convert light into electricity. At the supermarket, families can show children the electric-eye door openers and point out how the laser scanner units signal the price of groceries to the computer cash register.

If there is an observatory or planetarium in the community, find out if family programs are offered. Scout the nearest children's museum for interactive light and optics exhibits and notify families.

RESOURCES

Fiarotta, Noel, & Fiarotta, Phyllis. (1999). *Great experiments with light.* New York: Sterling.

Lovejoy, Sharon. (2009). *Toad cottages and shooting stars.* New York: Workman. Directions for making a pizza box solar oven are given, and four successful recipes are provided.

Magnusson, Shirley, & Palinscar, Annemarie. (2005). Teaching to promote the development of scientific knowledge and reasoning about light at the elementary school level. In M. S. Donovan & J. D. Bransford (Eds.), *How students learn history, mathematics, and science in the classroom* (pp. 421–426). Washington, DC: National Academies Press.

Murphy, Pat, McCaulay, Ellen, & Exploratorium. (2006). *Exploratopia.* New York: Little, Brown. This book for older children offers adaptable experiments. The jello lenses' directions are on page 298.

Parker, Steve. (2005). *The science of light: Projects and experiments with light and color.* Chicago: Heinemann. A good source of answers to your own questions.

Pettenati, Jeanne. (2006). *Galileo's journal: 1609–1610.* Watertown, MA: Charlesbridge. This imaginary journal captures Galileo's jubilant mood during the 9 months of intense work when he built his telescope and made his historic celestial discoveries. It reminds us that the father of modern science was human.

Robertson, William. (2005). *Stop faking it! Finally understanding science so you can teach it.* Arlington, VA: NSTA Press. You can teach about light more confidently after this book slows down and eases the process of understanding light principles. It does so with humor.

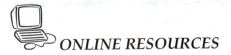

ONLINE RESOURCES

BANG, MOLLY. (2004). The author of *My Light* challenges adult readers to read more about the truly *big picture* on her Web site, *http://www.Mollybang.com/pages/mylight.html*

Teaching Resources

The Private Eye Project: Order inexpensive jeweler's loupes from this source at *http://www.theprivateeye.com*

Sunprint Kit. Create images using sunlight and light-sensitive paper. It can be ordered from Lawrence Hall of Science at *http:/lawrencehallofscience.stores.yahoo.net/sunprints.html*

Our Environment

Recapture moments in nature of breath-catching awe: encountering an incredible vista or discovering the peace of a quiet wood. Let these memories and feelings help you inspire young children to see and embrace their world. We are challenged to encourage them to take care of our beautiful planet home without becoming paralyzed by worry and fear about the future of the environment. Our job is to sustain the normal hopefulness of young children.

Sunlight, air, water, weather, rocks, plants, animals, and people are the primary natural elements of the environment that are accessible to children. Helping young children develop lasting affection for nature, by exploring and playing in it, is the necessary first step toward understanding the environment, the system in which each of us participates. As children mature, wanting to care for our world emerges from their happily remembered experiences in nature. The activities suggested for this chapter will help children make connections between other concepts offered in this book. To develop a beginning understanding of the environment, these concepts will be explored:

- We are interconnected with all the natural elements of the environment.
- There is an interconnectedness among things: plants, animals, air, water, weather, rocks, and ourselves.
- The environment is where we are. We can study it as well as live in it.
- We can work together to sustain the environment by reducing, rethinking, reusing, and recycling.

These concepts can be presented after plants, animals, air, water, weather, and rocks have been studied, or some of them can be used as an introduction to the year's science study, because they provide a framework for considering those primary elements. If the weather and school surroundings permit, most of the activities can be experienced outdoors. Because the broad topic of the environment is complex, it is better suited to second and third graders, though some of the activities can be successfully used with younger children. Teachers can best decide for their own classes when and how to use them.

CONCEPT: **We are interconnected with all the natural elements in the environment.**

1. What makes up the environment?

LEARNING OBJECTIVE: To expand children's ideas about their securely known world.

For Younger Children: Create and tape a banner, "All the World," to a wall. Have index cards, a marker, and tape on hand.

Introduction: Read aloud Elizabeth Scanlon's beautiful book, *All the World*, lingering over the illustrations and poetic text. Record children's comments about things they recognize in the world. Some will respond quickly. Almost four-year-old Josie offered "Trees, and *planets*, and clouds, and *peoples*." John's equally profound contribution, "Dirt," came the following morning. Respect all responses, and record each one on an index card. Tape the cards to the wall under the "All the World" banner. Explain that another way to say this is "Our Environment." Children could draw their ideas on the cards. Keep the idea cards in place for many days of discussion. Make a digital photograph of the children's initial thoughts, their collective knowledge, for your own records. Repeat the experience later after a number of nature experiences, recording the growth of ideas with another photograph to assess the group's progress.

For Older Children: Create a banner for a wall space: "Wonderful Things in Our Environment." Have large index cards, tape, and markers on hand.

Introduction: Open a group discussion presenting Robert Louis Stevenson, who wrote great books like *A Child's Garden of Verses*. He wrote this small poem:

HAPPY THOUGHT

The world is so full of a number of things,

I'm sure we should all be as happy as kings.

Share with the children some of the wonderful things in the environment, both small and grand, that delight you. "What are some wonderful things in the world that make you happy?" Conclude the discussion with the idea that *the part of the world where we are, and everything that surrounds us here, make up our environment.* Children can write or illustrate their responses to the poem on large index cards and tape them to the wall beneath the banner. Help group their idea cards according to the categories: *Natural Environment* and *People-made Environment*. Photograph the finished display of initial comments. Later in the school year, after many opportunities to explore and participate in nature, repeat the activity to assess the progress of your class.

CONCEPT: **There is an interconnectedness among things: plants, animals, air, water, weather, rocks, and ourselves.**

1. Who is connected to whom?

LEARNING OBJECTIVE: To feel security in being connected to others.

Group Activity: Gather a handful of snap-together or linking toy pieces, a ball of string or yarn, a marker, index cards, tape, and scissors. Cut some arm's-length pieces of string.

Introduction: Begin by letting children tell you what to do with the toy pieces. Explore what else children know about *connections* and whether they themselves can be connected to other people. "Here's one way to think about it." Hand one end of a length of string to a child while you hold the other end. "Now you and I are connected!"

Ask children to think of classmates or family members they are connected to. Use the connections they offer to begin shaping a web of connections. Write the offered names on the cards, tape them to a wall, and connect the cards with lengths of string. If Sarah says that she is connected to her mom, record both names on cards, tape them, and connect them. If Zach says that Sarah's mom walks him home from the bus, write and connect his name card to both Sarah's and Sarah's mom's cards. Continue as long as you can as other names are offered, shaping a web of cards and string. Answers will vary, but a web of connections should develop from the conversation. To ensure that each child has a connection of some kind firmly in mind, accept responses for all kinds of connections. Discuss things outdoors that children can think of as "connected." Leave the web in place for children to study. Leave extra string and cards nearby for children to add new ideas. Older children can add written explantions of the connections they make.

2. What is connected to what?

LEARNING OBJECTIVE: To enjoy exploring connections in the outdoor environment.

Note: The success of these explorations depends on having a natural, herbicide- and insecticide-free outdoor area available for study. Little may be found in chemically treated lawns. Commonsense precautions include previewing the area with custodians for possible hazards, such as nests of stinging insects and poison ivy. Always provide enough adult supervision.

Group Activity: Help children make simple "sit-upons," slipping folded newspaper into large slide-lock food storage bags. Carry them in a canvas shopping bag for any seated outdoor activity. Gather a pen, a pad of sticky notes, blank paper booklets, and pencils for each child and another bag for children's found nature treasures (see "Field Trips," p. 305).

"We're going out to find what's in our outdoor environment." Lead children to an approved spot in the school grounds. Ask them to stand in a circle, then turn around and sit down, *facing away from the center*. (This helps them focus on their surroundings rather than on their classmates. They're intrigued already!) "Take your time to look ahead, look up, and look down to see what you can see. Raise your hand and say softly when you find something. I'll make a note about it." Allow plenty of observation time for comments.

Whisper, "Now close your eyes and listen very carefully to what you can hear. Raise your hand when you want to whisper to me about what you hear." Allow listening and thinking time. Go on to what children can feel as they sit there and perhaps what they smell. Point out any features that may have been missed, such as air, sunlight, the sun's warmth, the earth. "All these things are interconnected in our environment." (Older children can do this independently in smaller groups with an elected note-taker.) Make observations often to notice changes.

Then let the children enjoy exploring on their own, perhaps collecting one small, found natural object to take back to school. Later, post the notes while you and the children discuss how the identified natural and people-made features interconnect. Some of the connections will be more direct than others.

Where do you think this little guy lives?

3. Who is living in the web of life?

LEARNING OBJECTIVE: To feel attached to elements of the environment and appreciate the sense of belonging.

With a large ball of string in hand, lead the children outdoors. "Come along to see what the web of life means!" The children form a circle, while you stand just inside. Ask someone to name a plant he or she found in the earlier observation. "Grass . . . a good answer. That will be your name for now!" Give that child the end of the string to hold. Ask, "What animal living around here eats grass?" Take the string to the child with a reasonable response. "Rabbit, fine. Now, you also hold onto the string. 'Rabbit,' you're connected to 'Grass,' because you depend on grass for your food. So, where does 'Rabbit' make a home?" Take the string to the 'Ground' responder. "'Rabbit' depends on the ground for a home," and so on. Leading questions could include "What else lives in the ground?" and "What would 'Ant' crawl on to get up high?" Include in your leading questions air, trees, clouds, rocks, water, sun, and all the familiar natural elements. Ask enough questions to link every child in the group. "Now we're like an interconnected web of life!"

Next, let children physically experience the importance of each part of that web by eliminating "elements," who then sit down. Say, "A wind storm knocked down the tree. Who felt the tug on the string or fell down with it?" and so on, until each child has felt that tug of inter dependences and has been affected by it. Sum up the experience: *"All parts of nature are inter-dependent."*

Read: A Place for Butterflies by Melissa Stewart.

CONCEPT: **The environment is where we are. We can study it as well as live in it.**

---

1. What lives just below our feet?

LEARNING OBJECTIVE: To enjoy exploring ground-level habitats.

Note: Commonsense precautions include previewing the area with custodians for possible hazards, such as nests of stinging insects and poison ivy. Always provide enough adult supervision. If the school landscape isn't suitable for such fieldwork, make a worm farm (see p. 87) or provide an ant farm to observe indoors.

For Younger Children: Take a 1 yard (1 m) piece of string for each child and a tote bag of magnifiers with you as you lead the children to a nearby grassy patch.

Introduction: "Do you know the story about Thumbelina? She was as tiny as your thumb. Can you imagine being so tiny? Can you feel your tiny legs walking through this grass? Would it seem tall to you? Let's see what it would be like to take a Thumbelina walk." Give each child a magnifier and a piece of string to stretch out on the grass. "Crawl along next to the string, pretending that you are Thumbelina." Supply ideas like these: "How tall is the grass? Is it higher than your head? Keep your head down low, and use your magnifying glass to see every detail. Do you see any other tiny creatures here? What are they doing? Is there a drop of water for them to drink or anything to eat? Is there any soft moss for a pillow?" Later, add that places where living things can get what they need to live are called *habitats*. Encourage children to draw their impressions afterward.

Read: Bob Barner's *Bug Safari,* or Robert Louis Stevenson's poem "The Little Land" from *A Child's Garden of Verses,* or Shirley Hughes's poem "The Grass House" from *Out and About.*

For Older Children: Cut 2-yard (about 2-m) lengths of cheap clothesline or heavy string for each group of four children. Fasten the ends with a clamp or clothespin to form a loop of string.

Take the loops, magnifiers, sit-upons and nature-journaling booklets outdoors for this activity:

1. Let groups of children choose a grassy spot or a weedy location to place their loops on the ground. "If you want to turn your loop into a square, just find four stones to hold down the corners. Take your time and use your magnifier to look carefully to see everything that you find: rocks, sticks, things that are growing and things that are moving inside your rope." Allow time for children to make journal notes and sketches on the spot. Compare group results to find out which observation spots had the most creatures and growing things in them.

2. Add a new feature for a second visit. Two weeks in advance, create some bug habitats in permitted areas by anchoring to the ground pieces of heavy material, such as carpet scraps. Dampen them if weather is dry. On the exploration day, let children turn the coverings over to observe the critters gathered there. Compare these findings with those in their observation loops. The children's nature journal notes may be more exciting this time!

Read: *Insect Detective* by Steve Voake or *Under One Rock* by Anthony Fredericks.

2. What lives or moves near our feet?

LEARNING OBJECTIVE: To enjoy exploring ground-level habitats.

Note: Before doing an aboveground exploration, investigate the area by yourself to locate spider webs. Look near walls and fences, inside corners, under steps, or next to any sturdy starting place for building a web. Then if no rabbit, chipmunk, squirrel, turtle, toad, bird, or other small wildlife can be observed, the spider webs will satisfy and interest the young explorers.

Staking out a grassy area for close study and collaboration.

Introduction: Surprise the class by playing field-recorded bird call tapes or CDs.* Or play individual bird calls using the electronic Birdsong Identiflyer.™ Either will set the mood for outdoor learning. Reassure anxious listeners that many animals living in the wild only come out at night to find food. "They stay hidden during the day." Talk about how to avoid disturbing any small creatures actually seen.

Head outside, carrying a spray bottle of water and a tote bag of magnifiers. Children carry their nature journal materials and sit-upons. Assign areas for small groups to explore in changing shifts. Allow time for quick sketches or note writing. Be an active participant yourself. Establish an "everyone gather" signal for a summary report. To be sure that some animal life is seen by all, lead the group to the spider webs you've identified. A light misting from the spray bottle will make the webs easier to see. Study the spiders' complex web engineering.

Later, post a list of the creatures, or evidence of their activity, observed by the class. Leave room for additional after-school sightings. Start the flow of children's contributions of safely contained small creatures with a few of your own (see p. 82). Explain safe capture techniques. Help children look online to learn about them. Release the visitors outdoors at the end of the day.

Read selectively from: How Do Spiders Make Webs? by Melissa Stewart.

---

*Nature stores, the Internet, and perhaps E-Bay are the most likely sources for environmental CDs and the electronic bird call device.

3. What lives in the ground and above our heads?

LEARNING OBJECTIVE: To develop affinity for a tree. The focus of this study is a mature tree with an accessible trunk.

Introduction: Share *Redwoods,* by Jason Chin, a fine book about a boy's imaginary journey through a redwood forest while he is actually riding home on a subway. Before you go outdoors, prepare a list of rotating positions, and possible things to observe in each, such as *the ground beneath the tree*: fallen twigs, leaves, cones, nuts, roots, small plants, shade or shadow pattern; *the trunk*: sensory observations of bark, texture rubbings, odors, mossy places, informal measurement of trunk size (hugs work here); and the *branches*: sketching leaf shapes, looking for animals' homes.

Lead the class outdoors with their sit-upons and nature journals, plus heavy paper and crayons for small bark rubbings. If only a single tree is available to study, divide the group into smaller ones with rotating activities and different observation posts.

Date the journal drawings, and return to the tree to draw seasonal changes. Talk about the amazing ways trees help our world. Emphasize that they keep our air healthy. *They give us oxygen, the part of air our bodies need to live. Humans and animals couldn't live without trees and other green plants.* "There's so much to love about trees. We're dependent on them!"

Read: One Small Place in a Tree by Barbara Brenner or *We Planted a Tree* by Diane Muldrow.

4. Can we make a little habitat for plants?

LEARNING OBJECTIVE: To enjoy creating and observing a small terrarium.

MATERIALS:

2-liter, empty soda bottle for each small group of children

Small plants dug from the grassy area, if permitted, or small plants started earlier as class activity (see p. 63)

Bits of moss

Pebbles or gravel, twigs, bits of bark, shells, small rocks

Potting soil, moistened.

Activated charcoal (from an aquarium supply store)

Old spoons

SMALL-GROUP ACTIVITY:

1. "Can you imagine making a tiny world where it rains by itself? Plants can live and grow there." Help children just cover the bottle base with a layer of pebbles for drainage, add a small amount of crushed charcoal, then spoon in a deeper layer of soil. Carefully make holes in the soil for each rooted plant. Then press soil down over roots. Decorate with bark or other natural objects. A shell could be a tiny pond.

2. Dampen plants with a few sprays of water. Replace the top half of the bottle, tucking the top into the base. Tape the top and base together. If the bottle cap is missing, tape over the cap opening as well (see

FIGURE 16–1

Newspaper, if working indoors
Spray bottle of water

GETTING READY:

Prepare bottles: Soak off labels
with warm water.

Cut the clean, dried bottles in
half crosswise. Keep the caps
on the top half.

Figure 16–1). Label it with group names.
Place it in a warm, light place, but not in
direct sunlight.

3. The next day, watch for evidence of water
evaporating and condensing inside as
drops of "rain" that return to the soil. If
children sprayed their plantings too generously, the domes will be covered heavily
with condensation. If you suspect the terrarium will start to mold due to excess
moisture, remove the cap for a few hours.
By contrast, if *no* moisture condenses
inside the dome, spray plants again.

These terraria should last for several weeks, allowing for much ongoing
observation and conversation. Talk about the self-sufficiency of this microworld.
"Do we have to water these plants? Why not? (See Figure 9–1.) Think about how
these plants get their water (see p. 65). Talk about the leaves as the plant's food
factories (see p. 65).

Read: Living Sunlight: How Plants Bring the Earth to Life by Molly Bang and
Penny Chisholm.

CONCEPT: **We can work together to sustain the environment by reducing, rethinking, reusing, and recycling.**

1. Can we reduce waste?

LEARNING OBJECTIVE: To feel proud and useful in helping the planet.

Introduction: Read poems from Douglas Florian's book *Poetrees.* Then show how his sidewise illustrations were originally painted on flattened, reused brown grocery bags! Talk about other ways to save paper: using cloth bags, cutting paper towels in half, using as few tissues as possible, and using both sides of paper for drawing and writing. These are ways children can help save trees and *reduce* the amount of trash buried in landfills. As a first step, make simple paper airplanes from completed schoolwork (see p. 142). Sail them outdoors, then tape them to varied lengths of thread to hang from a high place in the classroom as proud evidence that the class reuses paper. Keep a photographic record of the result!

Read: *Bag in the Wind* by Ted Kooser.

2. Can we use water more carefully?

LEARNING OBJECTIVE: To take pride in conserving precious water.

Do a quiet investigation at the corridor drinking fountain. Take two large plastic cups, a large bucket, and a watch with a second hand. "Clean drinking water is precious to all of us. Many people leave the water running while they brush their teeth for one minute. Let's see how much water goes down the drain during that time."

Assign one child to hold the fountain handle for one minute during the investigation. Assign two children to take turns catching the water in cups and pouring it in the bucket. Ask another child to demonstrate lifting the empty bucket as high as possible before putting it down near the fountain. "I'll keep track of one minute's toothbrushing time."

Start the experiment, pantomiming tooth brushing with the children for one minute. Then stop the water flow and the collecting. Ask the bucket holder, "Now can you hold the bucket as high as you did before? Why not?" Let every child lift the heavy bucket of collected water.

In the classroom, for younger children, represent graphically with stickers or sketches the amount of water the whole class might otherwise send down the drain in one minute. For older children, check the volume of water in the bucket with measuring cups. Calculate the total volume for the whole class. Talk about how we help planet Earth by turning off the water while brushing our teeth or soaping our hands. *"No way has been discovered to make new water, so we must use the world's supply carefully."*

Read: *Love Your World* by Dawn Sirett or *Let's Save Water* by Sara Nelson.

Math skills: Informal measuring of water volume.

3. Is water reused in nature?

LEARNING OBJECTIVE: To enjoy participating in shared problem solving.

? *Inquiry Activity:* Show children a jar of muddy water to introduce this activity. (Or mix dirt, mulch, and water to make your own.) "We know that all living things need water to live. Plants can use muddy water. A very thirsty animal might drink it. Would you?"

Recall the evaporation, condensation, and rain cycle observed in the terrarium dome. "Water is used over and over again in nature. When rainwater soaks deep into the ground, it goes through layers of soil and sand and rocks. Do you think the water gets cleaner or dirtier on the way? Write your prediction in your nature journal. Let's try to find out."

Prepare ahead (and reuse) by cutting off top 1/4 of a 2-liter soda bottle. Discard the cap. Turn the top half upside down, like a funnel, and slide it into the lower half. Line the funnel with two coffee filters. Let children help fill the funnel first with a layer of clean sand, then with fine gravel, bits of natural clay, and finally with pebbles. Pour in some of the muddy water. Save the rest. When the slow filtration is finished, compare the filtered water with the muddy water. Is it cleaner or dirtier? Children can draw or write the answer in their journals. Add that most water pumped up from deep in the ground still needs more work to make it healthy for people to drink. It's the most precious liquid in the world!

For older children, extend this experiment by letting them predict and test the effectiveness of other materials as filters—tissues, cotton balls, fabric, leaves, or other items they may bring from home as filter variables. More recycled funnels will be needed to compare results.

Read: Let's Save Water by Sara Nelson.

Math skills: Observing and comparing the amount of dirt in water.

4. Does recycling happen in nature? Can we help?

LEARNING OBJECTIVE: To enjoy participating in natural recycling.

Crisp fall weather, fallen deciduous tree leaves, and a few borrowed rakes offer children an irresistible invitation to help create and value a compost project. The school custodian's partnership is important as well. If your plans include a small garden, a flower border, or even a window-sill flower box, composting makes an important contribution to success. It also will demonstrate reassuringly to children how natural processes break down organic material and recycle excess leftover material into rich soil. Otherwise, the world would be overwhelmed by garbage! Use these guidelines:

1. Locate the compost pile in an unobtrusive place where it will be convenient to toss weeds, fruit and vegetable trimmings, and other plant waste.
2. Unless local ordinances require commercial compost bins, a simple structure of chicken wire and posts will suffice. The county extension agent will have advice for you.

3. Have rakes available for gathering leaves throughout the fall season. Occasionally, provide a trowel for digging up small amounts of soil, together with any resident worms, to add to the pile. Worms always improve the soil they live in.

4. Bury a few nonbiodegradable items (e.g., a yogurt container, a few plastic spoons, or an aluminum can) beneath the pile, or preferably in the ground nearby. When the bottom layer of material has finally decomposed into crumbly soil-enriching compost, scoop out the plastic and aluminum items to show why it's necessary to collect those things in recycling bins instead of leaving them on the ground (see p. 77).

Read: Compost Stew by Mary Siddols.

INTEGRATING ACTIVITIES

Math Experiences

1. Use found natural objects for ordering by size: twigs, stones, leaves, clean feathers. Interesting questions can arise with natural objects that commercial manipulatives do not present.

2. Use found objects to count big numbers. How many autumn leaves can you fit into a berry basket? How many does it take, stacked one on top of the other, to make a 1-in. (2.5-cm)-high stack?

3. Compare leaf areas. Give children sets of cardboard of various sizes and ask them to find leaves that approximately match each piece. Older children can work with graph paper to estimate how many square units each leaf covers.

4. Estimate measurements. Count out the steps it takes to walk around the perimeter of the schoolyard or blacktop area. Does everyone get the same measurement? Discuss the differences. How could those measurements be standardized?

5. Look for symmetry in nature. Are both sides of a leaf alike? Look at deciduous trees after the leaves have fallen. Are they symmetrical? Compare the shapes of freestanding trees with those in a more crowded area.

Music (Resources in Appendix A)

Tickle Tune Typhoon offers "A Place in the Choir" on their *Hug the Earth* cassette. "Oh Cedar Tree" is a Native American chant that even the youngest children could sing.

Ecology songs on Mary Miche's *Nature Nuts* cassette include "Bats Eat Bugs," "Recycle Blues," and "Garbage."

Raffi's cassette *Raffi on Broadway* includes "Big, Beautiful Planet," "May There Always Be Sunshine," and "One Light, One Sun."

The Banana Slug Band environmental songs include "Dirt Made My Lunch."

Literature Links: The Environment

Bang, Molly, & Chisholm, Renny. (2009). *Living sunlight: How plants bring the earth to life.* New York: Scholastic. Told in the voice of the sun, this clear, vibrantly illustrated story of photosynthesis makes the connection between the sun's energy, plants' use of it to make their food, and the subsequent release of oxygen vital to humans and animals. NSTA* Outstanding Trade Book.

Barner, Bob. (2006). *Bug safari.* New York: Holiday House. A boy in a hot jungle is surrounded by all sorts of insects. An adventure ensues.

Brenner, Barbara. (2004). *One small place in a tree.* New York: HarperCollins. This gentle story follows the evolving ecosystem in a single tree. NSTA* Outstanding Trade Book.

Brown, Peter. (2009). *The curious garden.* New York: Little, Brown. A boy tends the last wildflowers in his drab town. They thrive and ultimately transform the whole town in this acclaimed story. It echoes the real Manhattan Highline, a railroad track turned into a park.

Chin, Jason. (2009). *Redwoods.* New York: Roaringbrook. A subway-riding boy finds a book on his seat about redwood forests. He travels there in his imagination. His exploration is so skillfully told that ecosystem facts slip easily into the narrative. A multiple award winner!

Cooney, Barbara. (1982). *Miss Rumphius.* New York: Viking. This is the tale of how one person made her environment more beautiful by planting wildflowers in nearby meadows.

Fredericks, Anthony. (2001). *Under one rock: Bugs, slugs, and other ughs.* Nevada City, CA: Dawn. Here are rhyming facts about residents of an under-a-rock habitat.

Fredericks, Anthony. (2006). *On one flower: Butterflies, ticks, and a few more icks.* Nevada City, CA: Dawn Publications. A single blooming stalk of goldenrod is the habitat for seven different insects in this glowingly illustrated rhyme. NSTA* recommended.

Hughes, Shirley. (1992). *The big Alfie out of doors story book.* New York: Lothrop, Lee, & Shepard. Alfie and his family enjoy being outside: camping, playing store, walking in the country, cherishing a special rock, and playing on the beach.

Kooser, Ted. (2010). *Bag in the wind.* Somerville, MA: Candlewick. Who but a United States Poet Laureate could write a pleasant story about a much-reused plastic bag involving a landfill, homeless folk, and a child recycling for pin money?

McCully, Emily. (2004). *Squirrel and John Muir.* New York: Farrar, Straus, Giroux. The author's rich watercolors capture the splendor of the Yosemite Valley and the vitality of a mid-19th-century girl who makes it her playground. John Muir, the great naturalist, guides her to appreciate its glory as they roam the mountains together. It ends with an easily absorbed message of stewardship for our planet.

Morrison, Gordon. (2004). *Nature in the neighborhood.* Boston: Houghton Mifflin. Richly detailed sketches reveal the seasonal unfolding of the natural world in an unpromising urban landscape.

Morrison, Gordon. (2006). *A drop of water.* Boston: Houghton Mifflin. Here is a gorgeous tracing of water from a child's fingertip and back, and the life it influences along the way.

Muldrow, Diane. (2010). *We planted a tree.* New York: Golden Books. This appealing story introduces the very young to the key role trees play in the environment.

Pfeffer, Wendy. (2007). *A log's life.* New York: Aladdin. Focus shifts from animals inhabiting a strong oak early in its life cycle to the decomposers that eventually turn the fallen tree into rich soil for a new acorn to sprout and grow. NSTA* Outstanding Trade Book.

Posada, Mia. (2002). *Dandelions: Stars in the grass.* St. Paul, MN: Carolrhoda. The poetic story of the dandelion life cycle includes good activities. NSTA* Outstanding Trade Book.

Scanlon, Elizabeth. (2009). *All the world.* New York: Beach Lane. The lovely text follows a family through a day's outing, pointing out large and small important things around them. Caldecott Award, 2009; New York Times Best Picture Book, 2009.

Smith, Molly. (2008). *Helpful ladybugs.* New York: Bearport. Young readers will be pleased that such an appealing, fascinating beetle can be so important for organic gardens! Also in this series: *Roly-poly pillbugs.*

---

*National Science Teachers Association.

STEWART, MELISSA. (2006). *A place for butterflies.* Atlanta: Peachtree. Plant and butterfly interdependence, plus harmful and helpful human impacts on butterfly survival, are themes of this fine book. Gloriously detailed illustrations capture biodiversity.

STEWART, MELISSA. (2009). *How do spiders make webs?* Tarrytown, NY: Marshall Cavendish. Photographs and Web information can be shared selectively with younger children.

VOAKE, STEVE. (2010). *Insect detective.* Somerville, MA: Candlewick. This pleasant invitation to discover interesting insects includes lifting up a rock to see "what scuttles out."

WADE, MARY. (2010). *Amazing champion of the earth: Rachel Carson.* Berkeley Heights, NJ: Enslow. Competent readers will be impressed by the ability of one nature-loving woman to warn the world of damage caused by pesticides.

WINTER, JEANETTE. (2008). *Wangari's trees of peace: A true story from Africa.* New York: Harcourt. The 2004 Nobel Peace Prize was given to Wangari Maathe for standing up against deforestation and inspiring village women to plant 30 million trees in Kenya.

Literature Links: Children Helping the Environment

BETHEL, ELLIE. (2009). *Michael Recycle meets Litterbug Dug.* Santa Fe, NM: Worthwhile Press. Lively cartooning will capture children's attention. Added facts will keep the conversation going.

GREEN, JEN. (2004). *Precious earth: Waste and recycling,* North Mankato, MN: Chrysalis. Factual, straightforward description of recycling, with many types linked to home practices.

GREEN, JEN. (2005). *Why should I recycle?* Hauppauge, NY: Barrons. This cheerfully cartooned story explains recycling simply and fits it into children's everyday lives.

MORRIS, NEIL. (2008). *Green kids recycling.* Irvine, CA: QEB. Independent readers can be energized to reduce, reuse, and recycle by the positive spin emphasizing what *to do* rather than deploring the magnitude of environmental problems.

MURPHY, STUART. (2004). *Earth day, hooray!* New York: HarperCollins. The Save-the-Planet Club starts a can-recycling drive to earn money for planting flowers in the park.

NELSON, SARA. (2007). *Let's save water!* Mankato, MN: Pebble. Water-conserving toothbrushing is illustrated in this simple reader.

SIDDOLS, MARY. (2010). *Compost stew: An A to Z recipe for the earth.* Berkeley, CA: Triangle Press. Add a zany rhyming alphabet book to pages of clever collages to get an inspiring recipe for compost making! A closing chef's note advises about what *not* to include in the pile.

SIRETT, DAWN. (2009). *Love your world: How to take care of the plants, the animals, and the planet.* New York: DK. Preschoolers make a tiny garden in a pan, reuse paper, and turn off the water when they brush their teeth, guided by strong, simple messages.

WALSH, MELANIE. (2008). *10 things I can do to help my world.* Cambridge, MA: Candlewick. Clever art adds to this message about simple actions youngsters can take for sustainability.

Poems (Resources in Appendix A)

Here are some poems about the environment.

"The Little Land" and "Happy Thought" from *A Child's Garden of Verses* by Robert Louis Stevenson

"Trees" by Harry Behm in *Land, Sea, and Sky* by Catherine Paladino

Song of the Water Boatman and Other Pond Poems by Joyce Sidman

"Bark" in *Poetrees* by Douglas Florian

Art Activities

Brown Bag Art. Offer flattened, used paper grocery bags for children to paint their favorite tree or leaves. Display and photograph them as corridor art to demonstrate that *Our Class Reuses!*

Beeswax. Children soften pieces of beeswax by warming it with their hands until it is pliable. Then it can be modeled or stretched thin for translucency as desired. Beeswax melts under direct sunlight. It hardens when it cools, but it can be *reused* by softening it again.

Sand, Rocks, and "Found Clay." For art from the earth ideas, see page 226.

Sun Prints. Arrange leaves or other nature finds on dark-colored construction paper. Weight them down with rocks. Leave them for about an hour in bright sunlight. The paper shaded by the objects won't change color. The rest of the paper will be faded by the sunlight.

Leaf and Blossom Collages. For art with plant materials, see page 74. *Make It Wild: 101 Things to Make and Do Outdoors* by Fiona Danks and Jo Schofield offers inspired art activities to *do* outdoors (see Resources, p. 309).

Play

Shelter Building. Children enjoy setting up "houses" in natural areas. Branches, stumps, leaves, and stones are the ingredients for imaginative house play that encourage children to value natural objects. Try to trim bushes so that children can use them for refuge and privacy. Drooping forsythia branches work well for this. Inspire new play ideas by reading *The Big Alfie Out of Doors Story Book* by Shirley Hughes.

Fairy Houses. Many children spontaneously create tiny houses and imaginary worlds in settings where pods, cones, small sticks, pebbles, large leaves, and other natural toys are abundant. If your schoolyard is less fortunate, gather baskets of such materials from other areas so that children can build fairy houses (toad cottages, elf houses) in a quiet corner. *Toad Cottages and Shooting Stars* by Sharon Lovejoy will inspire you. Take photographs of children's fragile constructions to inspire others.

Creative Thinking

Lack of an available tree to study needn't stop your class from getting to know and appreciate a tree. Let them get acquainted with an imaginary tree! With a few small props for sensory examination, children can still enjoy learning about the trees they see in their minds. Why not imagine that the tree is near a brook? Listen to the sounds of a babbling brook environmental CD while children explore their imaginary tree. "Climb the tree, share its branches with animals, or build a tree house." Explore tree features described for the tree exploration on page 297.

Ask children to imagine what our world would be like if it never rained or if we had sunshine day and night. Encourage children to listen to one another and build on each other's ideas.

Food Experiences

Children love to gather fallen nuts and attractive berries. They do so indiscriminately, often sampling their treasures. **Safety precaution:** Get information about possible toxic seeds or berries on plants growing near the playground. (see In Resources, Robin Moore's *Plants for play* for a good list of common poisonous plant materials.) A reliable resource for learning more about foods in the wild is *Stalking the Wild Asparagus* by Euell Gibbons. Tell children that early Native Americans relied on wild fruits and plant foods to add to their food supplies because few groups cultivated crops. *They knew just what was safe to eat.*

Solar Cooking. Sharon Lovejoy gives clear directions for building a pizza box solar oven. In her book *Toad Cottages and Shooting Stars,* look at "The Sunshine Kitchen" for a handful of intriguing solar recipes.

Field Trips

The possibilities for learning outdoors are limited only by your time, weather, and location. Excellent help for planning field trips is available in the book *Hey Kids! Out the Door, Let's Explore!* by Rhoda Redleaf, as well as in the classic *Ten-Minute Field Trips* by Helen Russell.

Offer this hands-on message to children before your outdoor exploration. With children gathered in a circle, silently pass around a multipetaled flower (or a large leaf), telling each child to take one petal from the flower (or tear a piece off the leaf). When the last child receives the stripped flower or leaf, ask for thoughts about the flower or leaf and its missing parts. "Can we make it pretty again for someone else to enjoy? Let's try to put the petals back again." The message about the need to respect things growing in nature will emerge easily. Establish the rule of leaving growing things undisturbed for others to enjoy.

PROMOTING CONCEPT CONNECTIONS

1. Have children work in cooperative learning groups structured so that children are truly interdependent. Remind them that they are like the environment, where every part is connected and each part depends on other parts being there and functioning.

2. Assign different children each day to care for classroom pets and plants, maintaining the necessary microenvironments.

3. As children begin to appreciate trees as living things and understand that trees play a major part in the oxygen cycle, try to arrange to plant a tree seedling for the class. Plan for watering and maintaining the new trees. Our schools have done this for many years, so today's youngsters have shadier, screened-off playgrounds.

Improving School Grounds

Rehabilitating School Grounds for Children's Learning and Play. The most effective environmental teaching occurs in an outdoor environment rich in examples of ecological systems with which children can interact repeatedly. Although good outdoor environments used to be accessible to children, this is no longer true in many areas. Furthermore, many children today spend very little time outdoors, for a variety of reasons. Teachers who believe that children need outdoor experiences find that they must join with others in the school and community to create good outdoor environments at school. Administrators, the science coordinator, parent groups, the school board, community associations, and businesses all need to get involved in the major work of rehabilitating school grounds.

Many text and online resources have been generated. *Natural Learning* by Robin Moore and Herb Wong tells the story of an asphalt schoolyard transformed through school and community work into a "compact countryside," in one child's words. Many local and regional organizations are knowledgeable about fixing and using school grounds for teaching. Karen Mullin's *Toolkit for Schoolyard Habitat Program Development* is found usefully online.

Gardening. A good beginning project is beds for flowers, vegetables, and native plants. To ensure children's interest in and care for the garden, involve them from the beginning in deciding where and what to plant and how to maintain the garden. Here are some guidelines.

1. Locate beds where they won't be built over in the next year. Check this with school and school district buildings and grounds people. Consult with the maintenance staff to prevent the garden from being mowed down, sprayed with pesticides, used as a dump site, or allowed to appear unsightly to neighbors. Reviving the outdoors is a collaborative effort. Consultation is crucial.

2. Locate flower and vegetable beds where they will receive 6 hours of sunlight. If a sunny location isn't possible, shade gardens can be mossy, ferny havens for children, especially with rocks or logs to sit on.

3. Choose a spot close to a water source, preferably a faucet and hose; otherwise, only the most devoted gardener will help the beds through droughts and summer vacations.

4. If there is any chance of lead being in the soil, have it tested. To avoid contaminated soil, construct a raised bed with stones, bricks, recycled plastic-wood timbers, logs, or untreated wood timbers. Fill the bed with fresh soil. Wood pressure-treated with CCA (chromated copper arsenate) is no longer used around children because of the arsenic in it. The EPA banned it for home and school use in 2002. Another preserving compound, ACQ (alkaline copper quaternary ammonium) appears to be safer and equally effective in protecting wood. Used tires may be used for gardens, although there are safety concerns about old rubber for children's use.

5. Plan to use Integrated Pest Management (IPM), which minimizes the use of pesticides (herbicides, insecticides, rodenticides, and fungicides). There is growing concern over the widespread use of numerous toxins that, in killing pests, probably also harm children. The Children's Environmental Health Network maintains a very informative Web site (see Online Resources). Molly Smith's *Helpful Ladybugs* introduces children to this important idea.

A prairie restoration project shows the original habitat to Nebraska children.

Wildflower Meadows. Meadows abounded in this country before we fell in love with lawns. Restoring meadows of tall grass and wildflowers is both delighting and environmentally sound. Once the meadow is established, it provides children with plenty of flowers to pick. Native plant nurseries and county extension agents can help with seed selection.

Providing Water. A water feature is a more ambitious project that provides incredibly diverse learning opportunities. Children love to play in water, and wildlife requires it. Imaginative ponds and wetlands can be constructed in a school courtyard where access can be controlled.

Establishing Shrubs and Tree Areas. A longer-term project is planting a hedgerow of mixed shrubs in which birds can find shelter and nest. A hedgerow will also provide shade for seated children. Let children help research a variety of native species to plant.

The prospect of picking food off shrubs or trees is irresistible to most children, as well as educational. Pear trees and blueberry bushes are good choices. A school we know has its children plant a fruit tree every year. The trees then bear fruit for edible math lessons.

Trees are the big structures of the environmental yard. Because they provide valuable shade, wildlife habitat, and play materials like cones, pods, and leaves, start with the biggest affordable size. Plant them in the most carefully chosen places, and maintain them scrupulously throughout the entire first year. Native trees have evolved to survive in your climate, so they will require the least maintenance after getting established. Robin Moore's *Plants for Play* is useful for selecting plants that will do well and also provide play materials or structures for children.

Involving Everyone. Whatever you decide to undertake, involve the children and the community. Children will learn lessons about the environment and how to care for it that can last a lifetime. Parents can volunteer to adopt a garden during summer vacation weeks. In exchange for a week of care, parents take home the week's harvest. Community professionals can lend their expertise to landscape design and plant selection. The outdoor classroom is a profound link between the school building and the neighborhood, one that can enhance the lives of all children and their families (Humphries & Rowe, 2010).

Connecting Concepts

Generally speaking, the environment encompasses every element and every *thing* that exists in and around our planet. It would be easy to overwhelm youngsters by trying to pull together a multitude of possible connections in classroom discussions. For this reason, concept connections in this chapter have been limited to concepts found in Chapters 4 through 10. The topics of endangered species of animals, large-scale pollution, and depletion of nonrenewable resources have deliberately been avoided. It is our belief that issues of such scope needlessly burden and sadden young children who are helpless to remedy them. The concepts in this chapter focus on the positive connections in nature because children and adults are more likely to take care of what they truly appreciate.

Family and Community Support

Encourage families to model environmentally sensitive values. They can bring their own cloth bags to the grocery store instead of using plastic or paper bags. They can teach their children to help conserve energy by turning out unnecessary lights; to avoid letting faucets run needlessly; to use refillable containers for drinking water instead of plastic bottles; and to walk or bike instead of expecting to be driven short distances. Children can help with recycling by washing and flattening empty cans and stacking newspapers.

Newsletters to families can announce the dates and locations of community stream, roadway, or beach cleanup programs. National Walk to School Day occurs in October.

The *Leave No Child Inside* movement spreading through out the country promotes opportunities for urban families to participate in nature activities. City and state nature centers have expanded their family programming, and some are setting aside off-trail areas where children can dig, play, and explore at their own pace in natural settings. Botanical gardens, aquariums, children's science museums, and zoos offer nature programs for children. Older children can enjoy a planetarium visit where they can see evidence that our planet, big as it is to us, is a tiny part of a vast system. This is both provocative and reassuring: "We are part of a orderly universe and will be safe."

RESOURCES

BRODA, H. (2007). *Schoolyard enhanced learning: Using the outdoors as an instructional tool.* Portland, ME: Stenhouse.

CHAWLA, LOUISE, & CUSHING, D. (2007). *Benefits of nature for children's health. Fact Sheet #3.* Available at: http://www.cudenver.edu/cye.

DANKS, FIONA, & SCHOFIELD, JO. (2010). *Make it wild! 101 Things to make and do outdoors.* London: Frances Lincoln.

DANKS, FIONA, & SCHOFIELD, JO. (2007). *Nature's playground: Activities, crafts, and games to encourage children to get outdoors.* Chicago; Chicago Review Press.

GREENMAN, JIM. (2007). *Caring spaces, learning places: Children's environments that work (2nd ed).* Redmond, WA: Exchange Press.

HACHEY, A. C., & BUTLER, D. L. (2009). Seeds in the window, soil in the sensory table: Science education through gardening and nature-based play. *Young Children.* Also available at http://www.naeyc.org/yc/pastissues/2009/november.

HOOT, J., & SZENTE, J. (Eds.). (2010). *The Earth is our home: Children caring for the environment.* Olney, MD: Association for Childhood Education International.

HUMPHRIES, SUSAN, & ROWE, SUSAN. (2010). The school grounds: Learning and playing outdoors. In J. Hoot & J. Szente, (Eds.), *The Earth is our home: Children caring for the environment.* (pp. 111–129). Olney, MD: Association for Childhood Education International.

KEELER, RUSTY. (2008). *Natural playscapes: Creating outdoor play environments for the soul.* Redmond, WA: Exchange Press.

KELSEY, E. (2010). *Not your typical book about the environment.* Toronto, ON, Canada: Owlkid Books.

LOVEJOY, SHARON. (2009). *Toad cottages and shooting stars.* New York: Workman.

North American Association for Environmental Education. (2010). *Early Childhood Environmental Education Programs: Guidelines for Excellence* Washington, DC: Author.

PRANIS, E., & GIFFORD, A. (2003). *Schoolyard mosaics: Designing gardens and habitats.* South Burlington, VT: National Gardening Association.

PROJECT LEARNING TREE. (2010). *Environmental experiences for early childhood.* Washington, DC: American Forest Foundation. Available at http://www.plt.org

PROJECT WILD. (2009). *Growing up wild: Exploring nature with young children.* Washington, DC: Author. Available at http://www.projectwild.org/growingupwild.html

REDLEAF, RHODA. (2010). *Hey kids! Out the door, let's explore!* St. Paul, MN: Redleaf Press.

SHERWOOD, E., WILLIAMS, R., & ROCKWELL, R. (2008). *Science adventures: Nature activities for young children.* Beltsville, MD: Gryphon House.

STONE, M. (2010). *Smart by nature: Schooling for sustainability.* Berkeley, CA: Center for Ecoliteracy.

WARD, J. (2008). *I love dirt! 52 activities to help you and your kids discover the wonders of nature.* Boston: Trumpeter Press.

WILSON, RUTH. (2008). *Nature and young children: Fostering creative play and learning in natural environments.* London: Routledge.

WILSON, RUTH. (2010). Goodness of fit: Good for children and good for the Earth. In J. Hoot, & J. Szente (Eds.), *The Earth is our home: Children caring for the environment* (p. 17–35). Olney, MD: Association for Childhood Education International.

YOUNG, J., HAAS, E., & McGOWN, E. (2008). *Coyote's guide to connecting with nature: For kids of all ages and their mentors* (2nd ed.). Owlink Media.

CLASSIC RESOURCES

CORNELL, JOSEPH. (1979/1999). *Sharing nature with children.* Nevada City, CA: Dawn Publications. A classic in the field of connecting children to nature, especially through their feelings.

GIBBONS, EUELL. (1988). *Stalking the wild asparagus.* Brattleboro, VT: Allen Hood.

HORSFALL, J. (1997). *Play lightly on the Earth: Nature activities for children 3 to 9 years old.* Nevada City, CA: Dawn Publications.

MOORE, ROBIN. (1993). *Plants for play: A plant selection guide for children's outdoor environments.* Berkeley, CA: MIG Communications.

MOORE, ROBIN. & WONG, HERB. (1997). *Natural learning: The life history of an environmental schoolyard.* Berkeley, CA: MIG Communications.

RUSSELL, HELEN R. (1990). *Ten minute field trips* (2nd ed.). Washington, DC: National Science Teachers Association.

ONLINE RESOURCES

American Community Garden Association: *http://communitygarden.org*

American Horticultural Society: *http://ahs.org*

The Arbor Day Foundation and Dimensions Educational Research Foundation: *http://www.arborday.org/*

Center for Environmental Education: *http://www.ceeonline.org/*

The Children and Nature Network: *http://www.childrenandnature.org/*

Children's Environmental Health Network: *http:www.cehn.org*

Earth Partnership for Schools: *http://uwarboretum.org/eps/*

The Environmental Literacy Council: *http://www.enviroliteracy.org/*

The Farm to School Program: *http://www.farmtoschool.org/*

Green Hearts Institute for Nature in Childhood: *http://www.greenheartsinc.org/*

Green Teacher: *http://www.greenteacher.com/*

Mullin, Karen Kelly. *Toolkit for Schoolyard Habitat Program Development: http://www.fws.gov/chesapeakebay/school/PDF/SchoolyardProgramToolkit.pdf*

Natural Learning Initiative: *http://www.naturalearning.org/*

The National Audubon Society: *http://www.audubon.org/*

The National Wildlife Federation: *http://www.nwf.org/*

The North American Association for Environmental Education: *http://www.naaee.org/*

Project Learning Tree Green Schools! Program : *http://plt.org/*

U.S. Environmental Protection Agency: *http://www.epa.gov/pesticides/ipm*

The World Forum Foundation Nature Action Collaborative for Children: *http://www.worldforumfoundation.org/wf/nacc/*

A

Resources for Music, Recordings, Poetry, and Equipment Ordering

MUSIC

BANANA SLUG STRING BAND. *Adventures on the air cycle.* Music for Little People. "Air Cycle Swing," "Lizard," "No Bones Within," "Animals," and "Ecology."

BANANA SLUG STRING BAND. (1996). *Penguin parade.* Includes songs about raccoons, ants, otters, fish, and moose. American Library Association Notable Children's Recording Award.

BANANA SLUG STRING BAND. (2002). *Goin' wild in Yellowstone and the Tetons.* Includes songs about beavers, bears, and bisons. National Park Service Excellence Awards.

BERMAN, MARCIA. *Rabbits dance: Marcia Berman sings Malvina Reynolds.* B/B Records.

CHAPIN, TOM. (2003). *This pretty planet.* Sony Music Entertainment. Order at Sun-dance Music: http://www.chapinfo@aol.com

CHARETTE, RICK. *Bubble gum.* Educational Activities.

CHARETTE, RICK. *I love mud* and *Popcorn and other songs.* Pine Point Productions.

CHARETTE, RICK. (1994). *Alligator in the elevator.* Pine Point Records.

CHENILLE SISTERS. *1 2 3 kids.* Red House Records. Includes "The Kitchen Percussion Song": making music with things found in the kitchen.

CROW, DAN. *A friend, a laugh, a walk in the woods.* Sony Kids Music. Includes "Walking on My Wheels," in which a child uses a wheelchair to get around, "The Zucchini Song," "Blowing Up Balloons," and "The Shape of My Shadow."

JENKINS, ELLA. *Seasons for singing.* Smithsonian Folkways.

MICHE, MARY. *Nature nuts. Earthy tunes.* Star Trek.

MICHE, MICHAELO. *A kid's eye view of the environment.* Mishmash Music.

PALMER, HAP. *Easy does it,* "High Wire Artist." Educational Activities.

PALMER, HAP. *Walter the waltzing worm.* Educational Activities.

RAFFI. *Evergreen, everblue.* Shoreline/MCA.

RAFFI. *Raffi in concert.* Shoreline/MCA.

RAFFI. *Raffi on Broadway.* MCA Records.

ROUSE, JOYCE. (1997). *Around the world with Earth mama.* Rouse House.

SALAS, LAURA PURDIE. (2009). *Move it! Work it!: A song about simple machines.* Mankato, MN: Capstone. The song is sung to the tune of "Kookaburra."

SEEGER, PETE. *Animal folk songs for children.* Rounder Records.

SEEGER, PETE. *Birds, beasts, bugs, and little fishes.* Smithsonian Folkways.

SIDMAN, JOYCE. (2005). *Song of the water boatman and other pond poems.* New York: Houghton Mifflin.

Smithsonian Folkways. (1998). *Children's music collection.* Includes Woody Guthrie's "Riding in My Car" and Pete Seeger's "One Grain of Sand."

Tickle Tune Typhoon. *Hug the Earth.* Tickle Tune Typhoon.

Zamfir, Georghe. *Romance of the pan flute.* Cassette #32150. Polygram Classics.

MUSIC BOOKS

Levy, Michael. (2001). *La tierra el mar.* This Spanish/English songbook of compositions by the Banana Slug String Band includes "I'm a Tree," "Roots, Stems, Leaves," "Decomposition," and "Dirt Made My Lunch."

Mallett, David. (1995). *Inch by inch: The garden song.* New York: HarperCollins.

Raffi. (1987). *Singable songbook.* New York: Crown.

Raffi. (1989). *Everything grows.* New York: Crown.

Reader's Digest. (1985). *Oats, peas, beans.* Pleasantville, NY: Author.

Smithsonian Folkways. (1988). *Childrens' music collection.* Washington, DC: Author.

POETRY

Andrews, Julie. (2009). *Julie Andrews' collection of poems, songs, and lullabies.* New York: Little, Brown. Includes "Keep a Poem in Your Pocket" (p. 163).

Cyrus, Kurt. (2001). *Oddhoppers opera: A bug's garden of verses.* San Diego, CA: Harcourt Brace.

DeRegniers, Beatrice (Compiler). (1988). *Sing a song of popcorn: Every child's book of poems.* New York: Scholastic. A classic. Formerly titled *Poems Children Will Sit Still For.*

Facklam, Margery. (1999). *Bugs for lunch.* Watertown, MA: Charlesbridge.

Fleischman, Paul. (1988). *Joyful noise: Poems for two voices.* New York: Harper & Row. Awarded the Newberry Medal, this fine collection of poems captures the movement, sound, and essence of selected insects. Exquisite drawings by Eric Beddows reflect the imagery evoked by the poems.

Florian, Douglas. (1998). *Insectlopedia.* San Diego, CA: Harcourt, Brace.

Florian, Douglas. (2000). *Mammalabilia.* San Diego, CA: Harcourt Brace.

Florian, Douglas. (2001). *Lizards, frogs, and polliwogs.* San Diego, CA: Harcourt Brace.

Florian, Douglas. (2004). *Omnibeasts.* San Diego, CA: Harcourt Brace. A fun collection of animal poems to inspire children to play with words, as well as to remember animal characteristics.

Florian, Douglas. (2010). *Poetrees.* La Jolla, CA: Beach Lane Books.

Graham, Joan. (1999). *Flicker flash.* Boston: Houghton Mifflin.

Hoberman, Mary Ann. (1998). *The llama who had no pajama.* San Diego, CA: Harcourt Brace.

Hoberman, Mary Ann. (2003). "Ice Cycle." In Jane Yolen & Jason Stemple, eds., *Once Upon Ice: And Other Frozen Poems.* Honesdale, PA: Boyds Mill Press.

Hopkins, Lee Bennett (Compiler). (1994). *Weather.* New York: HarperCollins

Hopkins, Lee Bennett. (Compiler). (1995). *Blast off! Poems about space.* New York: HarperCollins.

Hopkins, Lee Bennett. (Compiler). (1999). *Spectacular science: A book of poems.* New York: Simon & Schuster.

Hopkins, Lee Bennett. (2000). *Yummy eating throughout the day.* New York: Simon & Schuster.

Hopkins, Lee Bennett (Compiler). (2002). *Spectacular science: A book of poems.* New York: Simon & Schuster. Includes "Rocks" by Florence Parry Heide.

Hughes, Shirley. (1988). *Out and about.* New York: Lothrop. It's worthwhile to hunt for this old book for the poem about a garden hose spray rainbow.

KENNEDY, DOROTHY M. (Ed.). (1993). *I thought I'd take my rat to school: Poems for September to June.* Boston: Little, Brown. Humorous poems about school realities include the topics of light, animals, plants, and nutrition.

KENNEDY, X. J. (1993). *Exploding gravy.* Boston: Little, Brown.

LEVY, CONSTANCE. (1994). *A tree place: And other poems.* Includes "Rock Tumbler."

LEVY, CONSTANCE. (1998). *A crack in the clouds.* New York: McElderry.

LEVY, CONSTANCE. (2002). *Splash! Poems of our watery world.* New York: Orchard.

LOBEL, ARNOLD. (2009). *The frogs and the toads all sang.* New York: HarperCollins.

MILNE, A. A. (1961). *Now we are six.* New York: E. P. Dutton.

MOSS, JEFF. (1997). *Bone poems.* New York: Workman.

PALADINO, CATHARINE. (1993). *Land, sea, and sky.* Boston: Little, Brown.

PHILLIP, NEIL. (2004). *Hot potato mealtime rhymes.* New York: Clarion. "Mix a pancake" is just right for making-pancakes-at-school day.

SILVERSTEIN, SHEL. (1996). *Falling up.* New York: HarperCollins.

SILVERSTEIN, SHEL. (2000). *Where the sidewalk ends.* New York: HarperCollins. Reissued.

SILVERSTEIN, SHEL. (2001). *A light in the attic.* New York: HarperCollins. Reissued.

SINGER, MARILYN. (1989). *Turtle in July.* Upper Saddle River, NJ: Prentice Hall.

STEVENSON, ROBERT LOUIS. (1999). *A child's garden of verses.* New York: Simon & Schuster.

THOMPSON, JEAN MCKEE. (1957). *Poems to grow on.* Boston: Beacon Press.

YOLEN, JANE. (1993). *Weather report.* Honesdale, PA: Boyds Mill Press.

EQUIPMENT SOURCES

Reasonably priced science equipment for classroom use is sold by:

American Science & Surplus: http://www.sciplus.com. Incredible stuff at unbelievable prices.

Delta Education, Inc.: http://www.delta-education.com

HearthSong: http://www.Hearthsong.com

The Nature Gift Store Company: http://www.thenaturestore.com

Exploring at-Home Activities*

PLANTS

Plants are important. Without them, nothing else could live on Earth. Encourage your child to talk with you about what she or he has enjoyed discovering about plants, how they grow, and how we use some of them. Watch for and talk about interesting plants when you are outdoors together. Then enjoy sharing some simple plant-growing activities with your child.

Family activities with seeds and plants have a big advantage over school activities. At home, your child can watch with you the beginning-to-end happenings. Together you can watch the whole life cycle of plants, from seed to plant to seed again. If you have use of a small, sunny piece of ground, plant a few dried beans. Let your child keep them watered. Watch for and talk about first sprouts, blossoms, and tiny beans. Eat some of the beans. Save some to dry. Then shell out the beans to plant next year. Bury the vines after they die down. Let them decay and renew the soil for next year's plants. Consider starting a compost bin for recycling yard wastes.

Bottle Botany

Suspend a fat, single clove of garlic in a small bottle of water, with the pointed tip out of the water. If the clove is too small to wedge firmly into the bottle top, poke three toothpicks into the clove to hang it across the top with the bottom half in the water. Keep the bottle filled with fresh water each day so that the clove stays in the water. Watch for fast, dramatic sprouting and root growth (Figure B–1).

---

*These suggestions may be copied and sent home to parents.

From Harlan & Rivkin, *Science Experiences for the Early Childhood Years* 10th ed. Copyright © 2012 by Pearson Education Inc. All rights reserved.

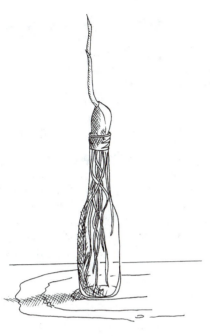

FIGURE B–1

Windowsill Gardening

Anytime you prepare fruits for meals, show your child the seeds you find. Soak some citrus seeds in water for a few days. Plant a few in potting soil in a small container. Put it on a sunny windowsill. Let your child give it a little water daily, and watch patiently. Plant a dried bean, a few lentils, or popcorn seeds in other containers. See which seeds grow faster and which plants live longer. Encourage thinking and talking about what happens.

ANIMALS

We share our planet with millions of animal species. All species of animals have some features in common. Encourage your child to talk about the small animals she or he has observed closely in school. Here are some ways you can help your child's interest in animals grow.

Watch and Wonder

Pause for a moment to watch the commonplace small animals you see when you are outdoors with your child. Ants, worms, pigeons, and squirrels exist nearly everywhere, even near city sidewalks. When you share that time together, you are teaching your child to respect our wild-animal neighbors. With some coaching, even a lively toddler can learn to be still and watch.

There are special adventures that school cannot provide your child. Only at home can children observe the insects, birds, and other small animals that come out at night. Some can be seen or heard in the city. Others can be seen or heard in the country or woods. A nature center near you might offer night hikes to observe signs of those animals. Good books on nature at night include *Nightprowlers* by Jerry Emory and *The Night Book* by Pamela Hickman.

Try attracting birds to your yard or windowsill with a simple feeding arrangement. To learn more about how to do this, check with your area U.S. Fish and Wildlife Service for these free booklets: *Attract Birds* and *Homes for Birds* (also obtainable through the U.S. Consumer Information Center, Pueblo, CO 81009).

Consider creating backyard habitats for birds and butterflies. To do so, include some native plants as they provide food for native creatures. Try to arrange for shelter, water, and places to rear young. The Backyard Habitat Program at the National Wildlife Federation has print and Web resources to guide you, or consult your county extension agent. The same habitat that attracts little creatures is also a very nice place for young children to play. Your child will enjoy working on this project with you.

HUMAN BODY

Your child has been gaining new knowledge about the marvelous, complex systems and structures in his or her body. Encourage your child to respect and care for these remarkable gifts. Enjoy sharing these simple but meaningful activities with your child.

Measuring Up

Your child is eager to grow. Children mainly grow taller as their long bones grow longer. Let your child gauge his or her growth against your full-grown size by comparing his or her leg bone length with yours. How much do his or her leg bones need to grow to match yours? Do the same for hands, fingers, and feet. Let your child try on your sweatshirt or jacket. Is there still growing to be done to reach your size? Talk about the milk your child needs to drink to help those bones grow longer. Mention that the bones grow fastest during sleep when our bodies aren't moving much. It's a good reason for getting enough rest!

Mark That Growth

Some parts of mature bodies continue to grow. Remind your child that even though you have stopped growing taller, your hair and nails are always growing and need cutting many times each year. Together, observe the slow growth of your fingernails. Place a dot of ballpoint ink next to the cuticle on one fingernail. Preserve the dot with a coat of clear nail polish if you have some. Find out how long it takes for the mark to move away from the cuticle. Compare your nail growth with your child's. Mention that skin can continue to grow throughout our lives.

Pancake Fun

Your child has been learning ways to stay strong and healthy. Have fun making these healthy, body-building, whole-grain pancakes with your child.

Oatmeal Pancakes

1 C + 2 T milk	½ C whole wheat flour
1 C oatmeal*	2 T brown sugar
2 T salad oil	1 t baking powder
2 medium eggs, beaten	¼ t salt

Mix milk and rolled oats in a bowl. Let the mixture stand for at least 5 minutes. Add oil and beaten eggs, mixing well. Combine the flour, sugar, baking powder, and salt; then add them to the oatmeal mixture, stirring until the dry ingredients are moistened. Bake on a preheated, lightly oiled griddle, using ¼ cup of batter

---

*Not instant oatmeal.

for each pancake. Turn them when the top is bubbly and the edges are slightly dry. Bake briefly to brown the underside. The recipe makes 10 to 12 four-inch pancakes.

(Children enjoy minipancakes, which use ⅛ cup of batter, the equivalent of 2 tablespoons, or a standard coffee grounds measuring spoon.)

AIR

Your child has been exploring some of the properties of air—that invisible, vital element essential to all life. Listen to what your child has discovered in science experiences. Then be a partner in doing a simple experiment in your kitchen.

Impressive Pressure!

Enjoy sharing this surprising air pressure experience with your child. You'll need a clean, lightweight plastic jar with a lid. (An empty peanut butter jar, ready for the recycling bin, will be just fine.) First, carefully punch a small hole about ½ in. above the bottom of the jar. (The hole should be about the diameter of a drinking straw.) At the sink, let your child fill the jar with water. Ask: "What happens?" (A small stream of water pours out of the hole.) Quickly screw the lid on the jar. Ask: "What changed?" (The flow of water stopped.) "What could be touching the sides of the jar and keeping the water from flowing out?" Give your child time to figure this out. (This is the same substance that helps to press down on the water, pushing the water out of the hole when the lid is off: air!) Let your child continue to play at the sink with the jar of water with the lid on and with the lid off. Talk about the experiment you shared later on—tomorrow, next week, next month. Air pressure will become a permanent part of your child's fund of information this way.

WATER

Water is the most common compound on Earth, covering almost three-quarters of the planet. This fascinating substance is critical to the survival of all living things. Listen to what your child has discovered about water. Then take a little time to have some water fun with your child.

Icy Shapes

You have better access to year-round freezing temperatures in your kitchen than we have at school. Enjoy discovering with your child that water freezes in the shape of its container. For this experience, freeze water in assorted plastic or metal containers of different sizes and shapes: thimble-size plastic tops for spray cleaner bottles or nesting measuring cups, for example. You could have fun devising a way to fill, fasten tightly with a rubber band, and freeze a plastic glove almost full of water. Find out together what happens to a damp mitten in the freezer. See what happens when you drape a wet paper towel over an inverted plastic bowl and freeze it. Then remove the stiff bowl-shaped paper towel. Enjoy the beautiful results when you carefully squeeze drops of water from a medicine dropper onto a piece of foil and freeze them. Do the same with a light coat of water droplets from a spray bottle.

Slippery Safety

(A winter lesson for children in northern climates) Fill a deep, clear container with water. Put it in the freezer or outdoors in below-freezing weather. See what's happening to it every few hours. When it has formed a layer of ice across the top, let your child look carefully to see that there is still water beneath the ice. The ice forms from the outside edges before it freezes in the center. The same is true when ponds or streams freeze outdoors. The ice might look safe enough to slide on near the edge, but it might not be thick and strong enough to hold a person near the center. Talk about your family rules about safe sliding and skating places.

Uplifting Discoveries

The next time you swim together, help your child feel the effect of water's upward push. Have your child stand in shoulder-deep water, with both arms a few inches away from his or her sides, not pressing tightly to the body. Ask if those arms will stay just where they are. What happens in a short while? (Water's natural upward push begins to move the arms upward. It takes some effort to push the arms back down.) Let your child predict what will happen if he or she curls into a tight ball in the water. Compare this with what happens when he or she stretches out on top of the water. Water's upward push helps us float.

WEATHER

The sun warms Earth. Air rises when it's heated by Earth and sinks when it cools, causing the movement we call *wind*. Together with the moisture it carries along, it makes all the conditions we call *weather*. Your child has been exploring some parts of the fascinating way that the sun, air, and water act together to make the weather. Share some weather-related investigations at home.

Ups and Downs of Air

Find out together if there is moving air in your house or apartment. Tape a small strip of thin paper to one end of a piece of thread. Tape the other end of the thread to a doorframe to let the paper dangle loosely. Quietly watch with your child as the paper drifts on the air current. Next, explore the ups and downs of air movement.

Carefully, let your child hold his or her hand just above a lighted 100-watt light-bulb to feel the warm air. Then hold a ½-in. strip of crisp tissue paper by one end horizontally above the bulb. Watch the free end of the paper strip flutter up as the warm air rising from the glowing bulb pushes the paper up. Next, let your child hold the strip of paper just below the freezer or refrigerator door as you open it a crack. The cold air pushes the paper end down. Talk with your child about how wind happens: All over the world some air is being warmed by the sun, and some air is cool. The cool air moves down under the warm air as the warm air rises. All that pushing and rushing air is what we call *wind*.

Dry Facts

Join your child in noticing and pointing out common, everyday ways that air picks up moisture: a withered carrot or apple from the back of the refrigerator; a piece of dried-out bread; once-damp mittens, now dry; air-dried dishes on the kitchen counter—all are examples of how air takes moisture from things it touches.

Getting It Together

Point out to your child how moisture from warmed air condenses into droplets when it meets a cooler surface: under the lid of a carry-out cup of hot beverage or on the bathroom mirror after someone's warm shower.

Freeze some water in a wide, deep plastic bowl. Check the freezing process every hour to notice how the water begins to freeze from the edges of the bowl long before the middle freezes. Mention that this also happens outdoors when ponds or streams freeze. This is important safety information for children living in cold climates. Ice may be thin and unsafe to walk on in the middle of a pond even when it is thick and safe to walk on near the shore.

ROCKS AND MINERALS

What are the oldest things your child can collect? Rocks! From the smallest grains of sand to the mammoth ball of rock we live on, rocks are an important part of our lives. Support your child's pleasure in collecting rocks. If you have a yard, let your child help you improve the soil.

Help a Rockhound

If your child is an avid rock collector, help him or her enjoy organizing and thinking about these wonderful finds. Ask your child to tell you about favorite rocks: what is special about their appearance and where they came from. Help your child identify favorite rocks by using a library book or buying an inexpensive paperback nature guidebook like *Rocks and Minerals* by Zim and Shaffer. Try to find a place to display as many rocks as possible. An egg carton makes a simple display box. Use the surplus rocks around the house in different ways: in the bottom of a soap dish to keep the soap dry; under potted plants; outdoors under a downspout.

Start a Soil Time Capsule

Dig a shallow hole, about 1 foot square, in a little-used spot of ground near your home. Put a layer of leaves or grass clippings on one side of the hole, a piece of aluminum foil on the other side. Cover these materials with soil. Mark the space with rocks so that you can find it and dig it up in 1 year. Circle the date on the calendar so that you won't forget to check the results. (You'll find that the natural materials have started to rot and perhaps get moldy. The foil will not have changed.) Let your child tell you as much as possible about what happened to the two kinds of material and why we need to recycle or reuse things that won't decompose in garbage landfill sites. Make this a family rule: "We don't waste and we don't litter. We save the Earth and make it better."

MAGNETISM

Your child has enjoyed discovering some ways magnets act. All magnets have two opposite poles: north and south (even that giant magnet, our Earth). Let your child share with you what he or she knows about magnets. Then have some magnet fun with your child.

A Scrap-Dance Box

Put together a magnet toy with your child. You'll need a small but strong magnet of any type, a shallow box, some plastic wrap, tape, and a steel wool pad. Shred very small bits of steel wool from the pad. Heavy kitchen shears work best for this job. Cut enough steel wool scraps to barely cover the bottom of the box. Stretch the plastic wrap over the top to make a cover and secure it to the box with tape. Together, enjoy making the scraps dance and creating patterns by pulling the magnet beneath the box.

A Hidden Magnet Hunt

Go on a hidden magnet hunt through your house with your child. Discover useful but unseen magnets in paper clip holders, cupboard door catches, flashlight holders, and message holders. Examine the magnetized plastic strip that holds the refrigerator door tightly shut. Talk about the invisible magnets that are important parts of car motors, electric motors, radios, speakers, computers, telephones, television sets, and tape recorders. Show your child the magnetized strip on the card that you slide into automatic bank teller machines to activate them or on the credit card you use at the gas pump or grocery checkout. Let your child know that we need magnets and use them every day!

GRAVITY

Your child has been investigating gravity—the force that pulls everything toward Earth's center. Encourage him or her to share these new ideas with you. Then have some fun with gravity.

FIGURE B–2

A Balky Balloon

Blow up two small balloons of the same size and color, if possible. Tie one; let the air out of the other. Using a small funnel, put a tablespoon of uncooked rice or a few small pebbles into the emptied balloon. Now blow it up again and tie it. Let your child try to blow the two balloons over the edge of a table. Which one rolls off? Which one tips but stays put on the edge of the table? Can your child figure out how gravity made the difference? Compare the weight of the balloons to find out.

A Balancing Act

You'll need a ball of play dough or a potato you are going to fix for dinner, and two metal forks to have a neat gravity experience. First, see if you or your child can balance the play dough or potato on the tip of one finger. Then insert the tines of the forks so that the forks angle downward on opposite sides of the dough ball or potato. They should be stuck in about one-third of the way from the bottom. Now try the balancing act. Most of the weight is below the finger now, so the potato or play dough stays balanced (see Figure B–2).

SIMPLE MACHINES

"What's inside?" "How does it work?" These are very familiar questions your child asks. We have been exploring simple machines in school. Simple machines are the basic designs for lifting and moving things. All the complex machines used around us are made up of one or more simple machine concepts. Now your child will enjoy discovering the devices you have in your house that are simple machines.

What and How?

Find out together about the simple machines you use:

A screwdriver becomes a lever when you pry open a paint can with it.
Inclined planes are easy to find: curb cutouts and other ramps for wheelchair users, parking garage ramps, playground slides, spiral charity coin-drops in malls, and fancy gumball machines with spiral chutes.
Traverse drapery rods or certain kinds of blinds have small pulleys inside the top rod.
A hand-operated eggbeater uses gears that are easy to see.

Gears are wheels that turn other wheels. Many can openers have small gears. Hand-wound clocks are full of gears. If you have one that's no longer being used, try to take it apart with your child, using the smallest screwdrivers you can find. (You should be the one to remove the flat, coiled spring. It may spring up suddenly, and its edges are sharp.)

Explore the workings of gears on bicycles. Encourage your child to compare how the chain and gears help a bicycle go faster with less effort than does a tricycle.

Watch for simple machines like gears, pulleys, and other wheels if you visit a science or historical museum with your child.

Easy Rollers

Check for small wheels that help you move things around the house. You may find them at the base of your refrigerator, vacuum cleaner, luggage or shopping cart, or outdoor grill. Take a close look at roller skates, roller blades, and skate boards. Make a game of counting all the wheels you see on the trucks you pass on the road.

SOUND

Your child has been making some discoveries about sound: the energy form that travels through air, water, and solids as vibrations. Listen to his or her new information about sound and then do some informal experimenting together at home.

Touch and Watch to Tell

Join your child in making some discoveries about the sounds of home. He or she already knows that sounds are made by vibrating things. First, do a *touch* test to find out if something is making a sound: Holding your ears shut with your fingers, touch a washer or dryer with your elbow when the appliance motor is on and then when it is turned off. Could you tell when it was making a sound, even with your ears shut? Let your child tell you about vibrating things causing sound.

Now put a small jar of water on top of the appliance. Close your ears again. *Watch* the water in the jar when the motor is on and when it is turned off. You can see the water vibrating in the glass—the effect of the motor's vibration and sound. Unstop your ears while you *hear* the sound of the motor and *see* the effect of the vibrating appliance.

Louder, Please!

Some things make sounds louder. Have fun with your child listening to yourselves whisper "Hello." Then close your ears with your fingers and whisper "Hello" again. The sound is louder when you hear it inside your head. The vibrating air inside your mouth and nose and the vibrating bony parts of your head amplify the sound. Enjoy listening to yourself!

Softer, Please!

We know now that permanent hearing loss can develop from prolonged listening to very loud music. Be sure that your child can still hear normal talk going on nearby when he or she is using headphones. Do not allow the use of ear-bud-style headphones. Both steps will help preserve precious hearing in later years.

LIGHT

Your child has been discovering some intriguing ideas about light: the energy form that makes plants grow and makes our world visible. Listen to what he or she has to say about how light behaves. Then have some informal fun together with shadows, the absence of light.

Sharing Shadows

One of the best places for your child to learn about shadows is at home with you after dark. Your child already knows that shadows form when light can't shine through something. So, find a strong flashlight or a spotlight-style lamp that you control, and join your child in a darkened room to try to share these explorations.

1. Shine the light on your child's back as he or she stands close to the light. Notice the shadow on the wall ahead. Notice how the shadow changes as your child slowly walks toward the wall.

2. Do the same thing, but this time with the light at floor level. Try it again with the light held high above the child's head. Enjoy noticing how each change makes a difference in the shadow's size or location.

3. Add a second light source, shining it from a different direction. How many shadows are there now? (Remember to point out the shadows of players if you go to a ball game under the night lights.)

4. Hold two layers of waxed paper in front of the light. Notice how your child's shadow changes when some of the light is blocked by the cloudy paper. Mention that shadows change like this when clouds block the sunlight from us.

5. Have fun making shadows of familiar objects: toys, forks, combs, and whatever else you think of. Make the shadow shapes you learned to make as a child.

6. Find out what happens to your child's shadow in a dark room.

7. When you and your child are outdoors together on a sunny day, you might want to protect your faces from too much sunlight by wearing a shadow maker: a visor or sun hat!

8. When you walk down a lighted street at night with your child, notice how your shadows are sometimes in front of you, sometimes in back, and some-

times in front, in back, and sideways. Figure out the directions light is coming from to make such different shadows. Your bodies are blocking the path of the lights. You can have more than one shadow when the lights come from several directions. Notice shadows in your home at different times of day. See if you and your child can figure out what blocks the light to make these shadows.

OUR ENVIRONMENT

Our class has been learning about some of the many ways children can help to improve their environment. They have a clearer understanding now that every person's cooperation is needed. Let your child put that learning about "restoring, rethinking, reusing, and recycling" into practice at home with you. Allow your child to help wash cans for recycling and stack old newspapers for bundling. Give your child responsibility for removing lids, caps, and rings from glass and plastic containers before recycling. Let your child remember to be in charge of taking your cloth or string bags to the grocery store when you go shopping (especially for healthy organic foods).

Gardening can be a wonderful family project to beautify the environment or to grow a healthy crop of vegetables. If you lack outdoor space, you could make a quick garden in a 40-lb plastic bag of potting soil to keep on a porch or balcony. Plop the bag down where there is at least partial sunshine. Cut several holes in the bag. Stick seeds or small plants into the soil through the holes and water as needed. The soil won't dry out fast, because it's so well covered with plastic. It won't have any weeds, either!

If you have space and energy, create a habitat for small wildlife in your backyard or neighborhood. The National Wildlife Foundation has a program to help you attract birds, butterflies, and other small creatures by creating special plantings and water arrangements. Consult www.nwf.org

Look for opportunities to have fun out in the world of nature with your child. It provides exercise for both of you, and it helps your child care about nature.

Index